Volume I:
From the Origins of Civilization
to the Age of Absolutism

Western
Civilization

Volume I:
From the Origins of Civilization
to the Age of Absolutism

Western
Civilization

Original and Secondary Source Readings

Benjamin C. Sax, professor of history,
University of Kansas, Book Editor

David L. Bender, Publisher
Bruno Leone, Executive Editor
Bonnie Szumski, Editorial Director
James C. Miller, Series Editor

Perspectives
P
on History

GREENHAVEN PRESS, INC., SAN DIEGO, CA

Every effort has been made to trace the owners of copyrighted material. The articles in this volume may have been edited for content, length, and/or reading level. Those interested in locating the original source will find the complete citation on the first page of each article.

Library of Congress Cataloging-in-Publication Data

Western civilization / Benjamin Sax, book editor.
        p.   cm. — (Perspectives on history)
    Includes bibliographical references and index.
    Contents: v. 1. From the Origins of Civilization to the Age of Absolutism
    ISBN 1-56510-988-0 (v. 1 : pbk. : alk. paper). — ISBN 1-56510-989-9
(v. 1 : lib. : alk. paper) — ISBN 1-56510-990-2 (v. 2 : pbk. bdg. : alk. paper) —
ISBN 1-56510-991-0 (v. 2 : lib. : alk. paper)
    1. Civilization, Western—History, I. Sax, Benjamin C., 1950–   II. Series.

CB245 .W475 2001
909'.09821—dc21   00-050339
                                                               CIP

Printed in the USA

CONTENTS

UNIT 2
The Medieval Heritage

UNIT 3
Early Modern Europe

INTRODUCTION

What is Western civilization? This is a difficult question to answer since it calls for a definition of what is a complex phenomenon consisting of disparate components. In the following two volumes of *Western Civilization: Perspectives on History*, no conclusive definition of the West will be offered. No simple identity will suffice to capture the variety of institutions, the multiplicity of political and social forms, and the diversity of values and beliefs we generally refer to as Western civilization. What will be offered are several ways of formulating possible answers to the question of the meaning of the West. There are, however, better and worse ways of doing so. In posing the question in this way, we seek an understanding of those features that make the West distinctive. To identify these distinctive features we need to proceed both internally and externally. Internally, we must strive to encompass the diversity and complexity of the West as we have come to know it in the present. Externally, we need to compare the West to other world civilizations. Only in the last two chapters of volume II will we be able to turn directly to this dual perspective. In the next-to-last chapter we will turn to the various challenges to the West, raised by a number of recent critics concerning the West's basic values and fundamental knowledge. In the final chapter, "The West Within the World," we will look at how Western civilization has come to be perceived by those outside the West. To define the term *Western Civilization* adequately, we also need to comprehend what constitutes a civilization and recognize what the West might share in common with other world civilizations.

The chapters of *Western Civilization* leading up to these final two will explore the long history of the civilization of the West. In them we will examine the various components that have formed the basis of and continue to shape the modern West. This history can be traced back to the origins of civilization itself, at least in the ways civilization arose in the first cities of the ancient Near East. There has not, however, been a simple unfolding of beliefs, values, and political and social forms from these origins. These early rituals, habits, customs, and institutions changed over time as they were interpreted and reinterpreted within changing situations. Equally important were the contributions from other civilizations. Ancient Greece and Rome contributed distinctive social and political forms and often alien values and beliefs. Christianity, especially as it evolved in late antiquity, combined and reinterpreted many strands inherited from these earlier civilizations. The Middle Ages continued to uphold several of these elements from the ancient world and added some of its own, creating a distinctive European phase to the civilization of the West. Finally, modern Europe developed new ways of understanding nature and refined the concepts of society, politics, and morals. These, in turn, would allow the West to develop forms of economic organization and instruments of technological control that were unknown to earlier phases of Western civilization as well as to the other civilizations of the world.

Even this brief sketch of the history of the West raises additional questions. How should we interpret the various components of this civilization and the complexities of its history? Is it sufficient for an understanding of a civilization merely to comprehend earlier and often alien political, social, or intellectual forms? Or should the historian reconstruct the various ways in which past individuals found meaning in their existence? Or should emphasis be placed only on what has come down today from the past, thereby downplaying what was historically specific to past societies and making only what interests us in the present the main criterion of historical significance and thus of historical study? Or does historical understanding involve not just a sense of the specific cultural forms of the past and the means through which they have been handed down by a tradition but also the various ways in which these forms and these traditions were formed, changed, and have continued—whether for good or bad, whether in acknowledged or unacknowledged ways—to define the present world?

As in every other great civilization, the West has no single line of continuity linking past and present. The history of the West lacks a single form of social organization, one type of political institution, one understanding of the nature of divinity, and a common set of shared values and attitudes about the world. In other words, none of these general areas of existence provides an uninterrupted line of continuity throughout history. Yet in studying this history we continually encounter a number of features that cut across the political, social, and ideational. Instead of simple continuity, we seem to have a continuum of multiple components, rearranged through the course of history into new, meaningful patterns. What has emerged as the modern form of Western civilization was actually a complex amalgam of differing institutions and values, social forms, and beliefs.

A distinctive historical dimension exists in the formation of this amalgam. Even if the theory of a progressive movement of history is entirely left aside, there is the sense that the West is the product of a long process of change and interchange, of formation and transformation. We should not conceive of the West as simply what has been handed down from earlier periods or built up through a steady series of increments from the past. Traditions are not constituted in such a fash-

ion, for much is lost and altered in the process of handing down. Those elements that can be inherited as a tradition, in other words, are not necessarily taken up in the forms and with the meanings established at their sites of origin. Traditions grow by repetition and constant use; they also progress by adding to and building on—that is, by transferring or transforming—what has been handed down within new situations. The original meanings given to various cultural forms can change as these forms are interpreted and incorporated in another epoch or by another people.

This process works in various ways. In accepting higher cultural forms, for example, less civilized peoples or epochs seem to degrade them. By adopting them to their needs, however, they also allow them to survive and thus provide possibilities of further development and even refinement in the future. Inheritance in this sense allows for the creation of new meanings, whether they are considered renaissances or entirely original forms. New patterns of civilization and new meanings are generated from these common components. The history of the West is not only long and complex, but also multilayered. Obvious changes on the political level and even on the level of social organization often reside on foundations of basic beliefs and interpretations about what constitutes reality. These foundations are not always clearly articulated or even recognized; yet they nevertheless continue to influence these other levels. And these foundations of the West themselves are neither simple nor uniform. They shift through time as weight is placed on the Hebraic rather than the Hellenic or the Christian rather then the classical side of the civilization.

What then is the meaning of Western civilization? If we need to understand the complex history of the West to answer this question, we also need to comprehend what is meant by the term *civilization*. Anthropologists would claim that *civilization* defines something distinctive of human existence. While civilization is obviously related to and interacts with biological processes and biological inheritances, it is perhaps best understood as all those aspects of human existence that escape biology. With this distinction established, we next confront the more vexing problem of the difference between *culture* and *civilization*. Although scholars do not agree on what distinguishes these two terms, or even that such a distinction exists, they concede that *culture* designates something generally human, in the sense that all humans have or are part of a culture, and that civilization seems to designate a "higher" or a "more complex" form of culture.

For historical reasons, the terms *civilization* and *culture* entered the Western vocabulary only as recently as the second half of the eighteenth century. *Civilization* clearly indicates the attitudes and intellectual qualities, or in Voltaire's usage, "good taste," that compose the "higher" forms of human existence and their intellectual and artistic expressions. *Culture*, on the other hand, was first employed by the German writer Johann Herder as a conscious reply to this notion of civilization. As Herder pointed out, no simple way exists to identify what are qualitatively higher or qualitatively lower forms of human life. A man or woman living within what we might consider a "primitive" culture could live a fuller and even a more humane existence—or as Herder would claim, even a more moral form of existence—than those who exist in supposedly "advanced" civilizations. This understanding led to a remarkable insight that only slowly emerged in the history of the West. Whereas Voltaire could only understand *civilization* in the singular, a single standard to measure the various human societies around the world and throughout history, Herder used the plural *cultures*, emphasizing that each culture contains its own values and its own "center" of existence. These values are incommensurate with those of any other.

Today, if we speak of "higher" cultures, it does not necessarily imply "better" but merely "more complex." The term *civilization*, in other words, does not express a value judgment; rather, it is used in a purely descriptive sense. Although we may agree that certain forms of human life are degrading and even less-than-human, we do not ascribe a hierarchy of human existence or forms of human society. However, a significant distinction exists between *culture* and *civilization*. Whereas the former term implies a generic quality of human existence, the latter indicates a higher, more com-

plex and perhaps a greater variety of the ways of being human. In this sense, we can still accept Voltaire's notion of civilization as expressing a higher form of life and combine it with Herder's emphasis on the great diversity of the forms of human existence.

Within the civilization of the West, questions immediately arise about the specific definitions and particular nature of these higher forms of life and how they should be understood. From the beginning, the term *human civilization* referred to many different civilizations. These civilizations arose independently in at least four major sites around the world: around the Tigris and Euphrates Rivers (ancient Mesopotamia—the land between the two rivers), in the Indus valley of India, along the Huang Ho (Yellow River) in China, and in Central America. Each developed distinctive forms of political and social organization, distinct notions of god and nature, and distinct sets of values and beliefs; yet, they all expressed definitive notions of what constituted the "civilized life."

Although the terms *culture* and *civilization* were coined during the eighteenth century as a result of the debates on the meaning and value of social existence, the notion of a civilized life, of course, did not first arise in this period. The ancient Romans, for instance, used the term *humanitas* to define a common human striving for the good life. The great Roman historian Tacitus drew an important distinction between a civilized and what only appeared to be a civilized form of life. He considered it barbaric and ignorant to think of civilization only in terms of fine buildings, material comforts, and technological power; civilization cannot be reduced to its material forms. And for Cicero, who developed this notion of *humanitas* to a high degree, civilization entailed a sense of dignity of one's own human existence, something that must be cared for and cultivated to the highest standards possible. Cicero does not, of course, mean this in a self-centered or egotistical way. Respect for oneself entails a recognition and respect for the worth of every other human being. In other words, *humanitas* implies self-restraint, compromise, consideration, and sympathy.

Western Civilization: Perspectives on History emphasizes those scholarly writings that have emphasized moral values, the relation of these values to the understanding of reality, and what earlier epochs have considered (for lack of a better term) "the good life." Again, in the history of the West, we find diversity and not uniformity. Is the good life a form of righteousness, following the commandments of the gods? This is how the early civilizations of the ancient Near East viewed the good life. Or is the good life a matter of individual striving for a type of human excellence that expresses itself in political leadership, the accumulation of material goods, in knowledge and control of the world? Such values were paramount among the ancient Greeks. Or is the good life understood as the type of spiritual equanimity and self-control favored by members of the ancient Roman elite? All these notions of the good life come into the modern West and indicate the richness and complexity of the Western heritage. Likewise. the modern West has developed its own ideas of the good life. The creation of a political and social community based on the freedom and equality of all—rich as well as poor, women as well as men—is part of our modern notion of the good life. With the technological and economic developments of the last two centuries, these ideals have been combined with the notion that a basic level of material security is also a necessary condition for the good life. These values provide a common background against which political actions, the establishment of institutions, and the reactions to social and economic forces are understood and evaluated.

Thus, what constitutes "the good life," varies with time and place, with various groups, and within various traditions. The notion of the good life is also connected to other ideas and beliefs. The fundamental ideals of a given people at a given time are intimately connected to what they consider the best way to be human. What is their understanding of truth, of nature, and of human beings' relation to nature? These questions have most often been related to conceptions of reality and the nature of divinity. Is the good life based on a belief in a transcendental god who created the world, directs its historical development, and provides an explicit notion of how human beings should lead their lives and organize their society? Or does the notion of divinity provide men and women with the freedom and responsibility to act on their own and to create their own political forms and social organizations, imploring the gods only for aid in achieving such ventures? Or, as has become characteristic of modern times, does an understanding of the workings of nature and of human nature provide a way of establishing universal notions of human rights and free association, which in turn legitimate governments and organize societies?

Questions of this nature also raise problems of how these truths are known and how they are interpreted. Is the knowledge of god revealed by him in sacred writings or through individuals called by him? Or are truths handed down by the ancestors, as with the ancient Romans, or discovered through the use of dialectical or logical reason, as with the ancient Greeks? The modern West is the heir of these competing and sometimes conflicting ways in which truth is known and the nature of reality defined. The ways in which nature has come to be defined, explained, and exploited in more recent times opened a new way of understanding truth and provided an insight into social organization and politics that have acted like catalysts for change.

Even within this limited range of the concerns, there is no consensus among modern scholars. In the following chapters, selections cover a wide range of interpretations by various historians, archaeologists, anthropologists, and mythologists who have attempted to address the questions of the meaning of the civilization of the West. Thus, this anthology brings together those scholars and philosophers who tend to think on the level of long-range trends and the meaning of civilizations, even when they are immediately addressing only limited questions dealing with specific events or historical periods.

In addition, the process of questioning the meaning of a civilization entails not only the verification of past facts—of historical dating or archaeological finds—but also the interpretation of these facts. And historical interpretation means not just interpreting within our own frame of references. Historical interpretation includes the various ways in which earlier ages interpreted themselves and gave meaning to their lives. These past interpretations must also be interpreted by the present-day historian. For this reason, a wide-ranging set of primary source materials, upon which these interpretations are based, have also been included. These historical documents are present because they illustrate the lives of past peoples and epochs (and in ways that secondary interpretations hardly ever can capture in their full richness) and because they provide the student with the opportunity of interpreting these sources themselves in relation to various scholarly interpretations.

Timeline:
From Ancient Times to Early Modern Europe

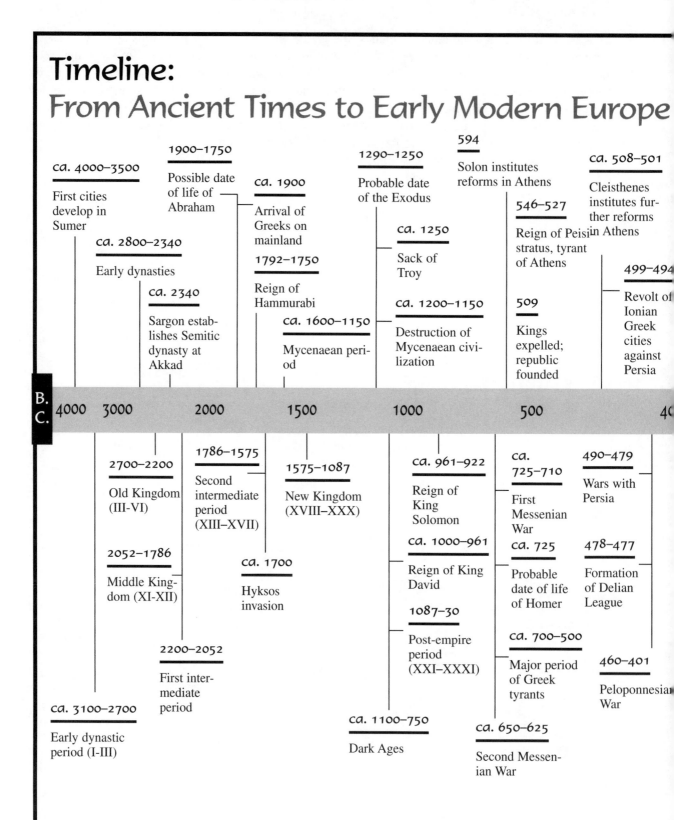

ca. 4000–3500
First cities develop in Sumer

1900–1750
Possible date of life of Abraham

ca. 2800–2340
Early dynasties

ca. 1900
Arrival of Greeks on mainland

1792–1750
Reign of Hammurabi

ca. 2340
Sargon establishes Semitic dynasty at Akkad

ca. 1600–1150
Mycenaean period

1290–1250
Probable date of the Exodus

ca. 1250
Sack of Troy

ca. 1200–1150
Destruction of Mycenaean civilization

594
Solon institutes reforms in Athens

546–527
Reign of Peisistratus, tyrant of Athens

509
Kings expelled; republic founded

ca. 508–501
Cleisthenes institutes further reforms in Athens

499–494
Revolt of Ionian Greek cities against Persia

B.C.   4000   3000   2000   1500   1000   500   4000

ca. 3100–2700
Early dynastic period (I-III)

2700–2200
Old Kingdom (III-VI)

2052–1786
Middle Kingdom (XI-XII)

1786–1575
Second intermediate period (XIII–XVII)

2200–2052
First intermediate period

ca. 1700
Hyksos invasion

1575–1087
New Kingdom (XVIII–XXX)

ca. 1100–750
Dark Ages

ca. 961–922
Reign of King Solomon

ca. 1000–961
Reign of King David

1087–30
Post-empire period (XXI–XXXI)

ca. 725–710
First Messenian War

ca. 725
Probable date of life of Homer

ca. 700–500
Major period of Greek tyrants

ca. 650–625
Second Messenian War

490–479
Wars with Persia

478–477
Formation of Delian League

460–401
Peloponnesian War

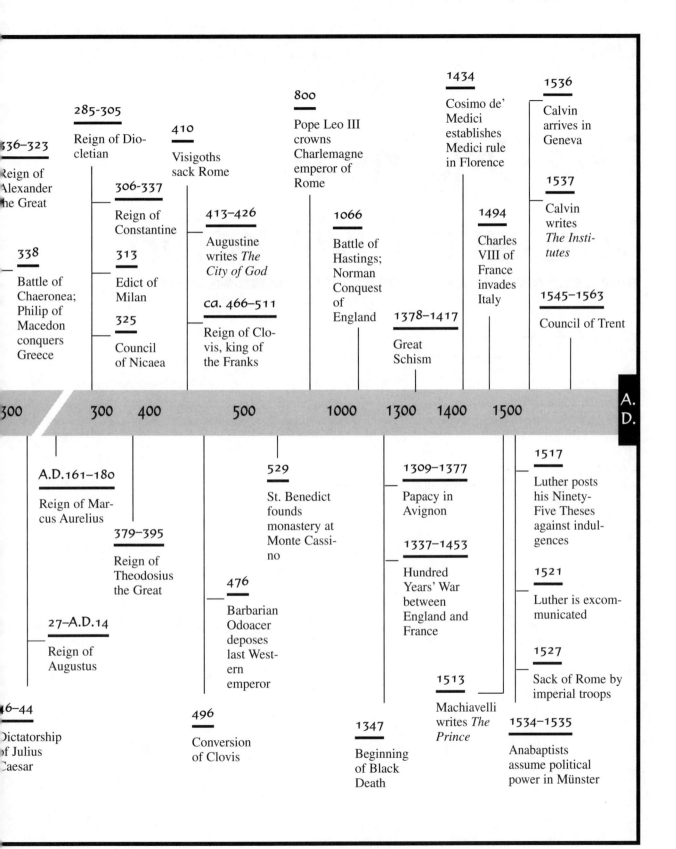

Above the timeline:

336–323 Reign of Alexander the Great

285-305 Reign of Diocletian

410 Visigoths sack Rome

800 Pope Leo III crowns Charlemagne emperor of Rome

1434 Cosimo de' Medici establishes Medici rule in Florence

1536 Calvin arrives in Geneva

306-337 Reign of Constantine

413–426 Augustine writes *The City of God*

1066 Battle of Hastings; Norman Conquest of England

1494 Charles VIII of France invades Italy

1537 Calvin writes *The Institutes*

338 Battle of Chaeronea; Philip of Macedon conquers Greece

313 Edict of Milan

325 Council of Nicaea

ca. 466–511 Reign of Clovis, king of the Franks

1378–1417 Great Schism

1545–1563 Council of Trent

Timeline axis: 300   300   400   500   1000   1300   1400   1500   A.D.

Below the timeline:

A.D.161–180 Reign of Marcus Aurelius

529 St. Benedict founds monastery at Monte Cassino

1309–1377 Papacy in Avignon

1517 Luther posts his Ninety-Five Theses against indulgences

379–395 Reign of Theodosius the Great

1337–1453 Hundred Years' War between England and France

1521 Luther is excommunicated

27–A.D.14 Reign of Augustus

476 Barbarian Odoacer deposes last Western emperor

1527 Sack of Rome by imperial troops

46–44 Dictatorship of Julius Caesar

496 Conversion of Clovis

1347 Beginning of Black Death

1513 Machiavelli writes *The Prince*

1534–1535 Anabaptists assume political power in Münster

UNIT 1

The Origins of Western Civilization

CONTENTS

Early Civilizations

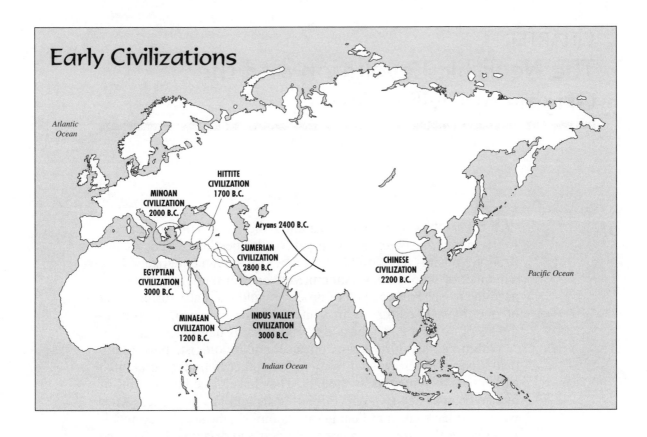

Atlantic Ocean

MINOAN CIVILIZATION 2000 B.C.

HITTITE CIVILIZATION 1700 B.C.

Aryans 2400 B.C.

SUMERIAN CIVILIZATION 2800 B.C.

EGYPTIAN CIVILIZATION 3000 B.C.

CHINESE CIVILIZATION 2200 B.C.

Pacific Ocean

MINAEAN CIVILIZATION 1200 B.C.

INDUS VALLEY CIVILIZATION 3000 B.C.

Indian Ocean

Ancient Greece and Rome

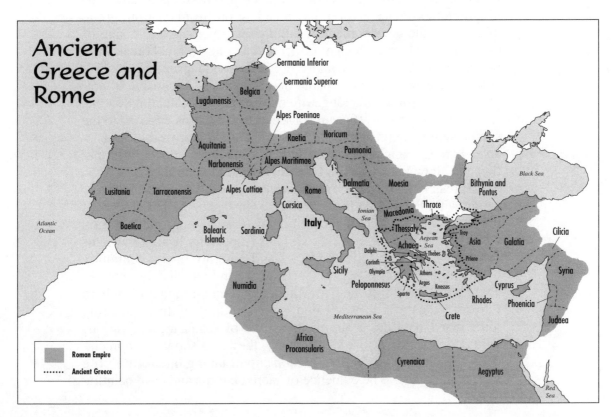

Germania Inferior

Germania Superior

Belgica

Lugdunensis

Alpes Poeninae

Aquitania

Raetia   Noricum

Pannonia

Narbonensis   Alpes Maritimae

Alpes Cottiae   Rome   Dalmatia   Moesia

Bithynia and Pontus

Black Sea

Lusitania   Tarraconensis

Corsica

Ionian Sea   Macedonia   Thrace

Atlantic Ocean

Baetica

Balearic Islands   Sardinia

Italy

Thessaly   Troy

Aegean Sea   Asia   Galatia   Cilicia

Delphi   Achaea   Thebes   Priene

Corinth

Sicily   Olympia   Athens

Peloponnesus   Argos   Knossos   Cyprus   Syria

Sparta   Phoenicia

Numidia   Rhodes

Judaea

Mediterranean Sea   Crete

Africa Proconsularis

Cyrenaica

Aegyptus

Red Sea

Roman Empire

Ancient Greece

CHAPTER 1
The Neolithic Revolution and the Origins of Civilization

What are the origins of civilization in the West? This question, as we have seen, involves asking the difficult questions: What is civilization? What is the West? But even before we can understand how a number of scholars have attempted to answer these questions, we need to envisage a larger set of processes and a slightly different set of questions. If culture is in some ways definitive of all human modes of existence, we must also ask: What is human?

Within the last thirty years, physical anthropologists have found that *Homo sapiens* evolved from various other hominids at a much earlier date than previously thought. They have placed the origins of human beings back to 5 or 7 million years ago in East Africa. After what must have taken millennia to accomplish, the species eventually spread itself across the major continents and developed some type of cultural existence. While the spreading out resulted from group migrations, the development of cultures was perhaps more significant since it indicated both a further and a nonbiological break from other hominids. *Homo sapiens* not only made primitive tools— something even apes are capable of—but were also capable of employing them for a wide range of enterprises and of handing on this technology to progeny. For this process, language (as opposed to the simple sign systems employed by some animals) proved indispensable. Through language human beings could both convey information and allow knowledge to be retained and increased.

Of greater significance, *Homo sapiens* were aware that they were acting within and upon their world. For instance, the burial sites of the Neanderthals, with their ceremonial arrangements and inclusion of what must have been sacred animals (especially bears), indicates consciousness of the life processes and possibly of the continuity between ongoing life and the death of the individual. The remarkable cave paintings of the Cro-Magnons found throughout southern Europe indicate a sophisticated understanding of the animating force that linked the group to its source of sustenance in various wild animal herds. More significantly, they also show an appreciation of the reciprocity in the relationship of taking one form of life to sustain another. The evidence of sacred burials and cave painting dates from thirty to forty thousand years ago. Therefore, within the grand scheme of the development of *Homo sapiens,* they are of relatively recent origin.

Anthropologists have seen another major break occurring around 10,000 B.C. This is generally known as the Neolithic Revolution. This revolution is marked by the change from the Old Stone Age (Paleolithic era)—the making of stone tools by chipping away at them—to the New Stone Age (Neolithic era)—the more refined process of grinding stone tools. But the transition from the Old to the New Stone Age was based on more than just a technological innovation. The development of agriculture was the central phenomenon of the Neolithic Revolution. Although we speak of it as a revolution, it was neither sudden nor dramatic. Rather, we speak of this change as a revolution because, though its causes were gradual and piecemeal, its consequences were overwhelming and far-reaching. From a life of hunting wild animals, catching fish, and gathering various fruits and vegetables, there slowly developed knowledge of planting and cultivating basic grains such as wheat and barley. From a life dependent on following large herds—a form of existence that lasted throughout the Paleolithic era from ca. 600,000 to ca. 10,000 B.C.—there gradually emerged permanent settlements alongside the cultivated crops. There seems to have been at least three distinct centers for the Neolithic Revolution. One occurred in Southeast Asia and became the source of Asian civilizations. A second took place in Central America, extending from Mexico to Peru and giving birth to the civilization of the Americas. Finally, the third wide-ranging site of the Neolithic Revolution, and perhaps the oldest, included the areas of southwestern Asia, Asia Minor (present-day Turkey), and southern Europe. This basic shift to agricultural production gave birth to all of the civilizations of the world and, in an extended sense, to the continuance of these civilizations today.

Other major breakthroughs followed the agricultural revolution. The Neolithic Revolution marked not only the cultivation of grains and the domestication of animals (in the first instance, of sheep and goats in some areas, cattle in others) but also the emergence of various crafts. Agriculture demanded the production of new agricultural tools, and pottery and basketmaking were invented to store various liquids and grains. Flax was cultivated and wool sheared from sheep for the making of clothing. In addition to these technological innovations, new forms of communal existence and new types of social organization developed. The agricultural village emerged with its greater differentiation of economic and social roles. The Neolithic Revolution also inaugurated an understanding of spiritual forces, which sustained agriculture and therefore the village and its existence.

Four to five thousand years ago, a second revolution, an urban one, was built on the Neolithic Revolution. The Urban Revolution saw the development of cities as opposed to villages. A city is not just a grand village; it has a distinct character. The city is not only larger in population than the village, but it also provides the possibilities for the development of new forms of manufacturing and commerce and demands new forms of social and political organization. Again, the notion of revolution in the phrase *Urban Revolution*, like that of a Neolithic Revolution, indicates less a single great moment than a gradual process that carried with it far-reaching consequences. Cities originated only after agriculture had developed to such a stage that large amounts of agricultural surplus were available. Unlike the origins of agriculture, which seem to have slowly emerged in upland valleys, areas of agricultural surplus were localized in a limited number of river valleys. These rivers provided sufficient water for irrigation. Such projects required a different type of social organization than existed in the Neolithic village. Irrigation projects necessitated the continual observation of the river's ebbs and flows and therefore demanded careful record keeping. In addition, the actual harnessing of the river called for the organization of human and animal labor and thus a more developed form of political authority. While great river civilizations arose in China, India, and the Americas, Mesopotamia—the land between the two rivers of the Tigris and the Euphrates—seems to be the site of the origin of the first cities of Erech, Lagash, Eridu, and Ur. By about 2500 B.C. these cities grew to populations of about twenty thousand inhabitants each.

Archaeologists and historians have pointed to the complex nature of this original process of urbanization. And this complexity is closely related to the development of civilization itself. In fact, the roots of the word *civilization* convey this relationship. Although *civilization*, in the sense we use it today, is of very recent coinage (dating only to the second half of the eighteenth century), the term is related to the Latin word for city—*civitas*—and has always been associated with the type of life that was only possible within cities. Whereas we can speak of *culture* in a more general sense and understand it as a distinctively human form of existence (be it in the Neolithic village or even within Paleolithic groups), *civilization* is reserved for the more complex kinds of political and social organization and with the more sophisticated forms of understanding the world.

To address the question "What is civilization?" then, entails understanding the complexities of urban existence. We need to comprehend both the various components of civilization—its social and political forms, its religious and artistic expressions—and the ways in which these components form or fail to form themselves into a totality we call a civilization. In analyzing these various components, historians have stressed that the development of writing was extremely important, though not absolutely necessary. They also show how urban life allows for division of labor, as various subgroups emerged from the less socially complex life of the village. We now find priests, kings, warriors, scribes, and merchants as well as farmers. Especially in the cities of the ancient Near East, family dynasties were founded within these various subgroups. The society of these new urban centers clearly defined a social hierarchy of warriors and priests, free men and merchants, peasants and slaves.

These two components—writing and specialization of labor—led to the creation of written laws. It was not only the increased number of individuals living within cities (although this is a factor) but also the increased divisions among types of individuals that necessitated a move beyond the customary laws and traditional ways of doing things that dominated village life. Setting these laws down in writing stabilized the law, making it a point of departure in the discussion of justice. The fact that they needed to be written down also indicates that laws had become too complex for anyone to remember them all and that the sense of belonging to a single community—of living justly within the community—could no longer be contained within the compass of traditional mores and group memory.

SELECTION 1:

The Origins of Cities

In the following selection, anthropologist Robert J. Wenke identifies a number of the earliest Neolithic sites.

Some of the earliest evidence for domesticated grain cultivation in the Levant comes from the lower levels of Jericho (c. 8350 to 7350 B.C.), next to the springs in the center of this oasis. At some time during this period domestic forms of wheat and barley were cultivated in quantity here. Neither wild wheat nor barley appears to have been native to the arid wastelands that surround the site, so these grains were probably brought down from the uplands of the Jordan Valley and grown at Jericho, perhaps as wild species initially. No domestic animals were used in this period, but wild gazelles, goats, cattle, and boars were intensively hunted. Two thousand or more

From *Patterns in Prehistory: Humankind's First Three Million Years*, 4th ed., by Robert J. Wenke. Copyright © 1990 by Oxford University Press, Inc. Used by permission of Oxford University Press, Inc.

people probably lived at Jericho at any time between 8350 and 7350 B.C., and although the earlier communities were apparently unwalled, around 7350 B.C. the inhabitants built a massive stone wall, 3 meters thick, 4 meters high [about 10 feet thick, 13 feet high], and perhaps 700 meters [about 2,297 feet] in circumference. Asphalt, sulphur, salt, and a little obsidian seem to have been traded, but in moderate quantities. The Biblical references to the collapse of Jericho's walls may have to do with the earthquakes that frequently in the past flattened the town.

At the same time that agricultural economies were evolving in Palestine, specialized nomadic economies were also probably developing. And people living on the flanks of the Zagros and Taurus mountains were making the transition to sedentary communities based on intensive plant collection. One of the earliest such communities was at Tell Mureybit, on the Euphrates River east of Aleppo, Syria. There, at about 8200 to 8000 B.C., people built circular stone huts, similar in almost every respect to the circular huts at Ain Mallaha. Charred wild einkorn seeds have been recovered from Tell Mureybit, as well as the remains of wild barley, lentils, bitter vetch, pistachios, toad rush, and possibly peas. Most of these plants can be found locally, but wild einkorn and barley are not native to this area and in fact can be found in natural stands no nearer than the Anatolian hills some 100 to 150 kilometers [approximately 62 to 93 miles] to the northwest. The impracticality of moving large amounts of grain this distance suggests that Tell Mureybit may be one of the earliest agricultural settlements in Southwest Asia, that here and in adjacent areas intensive collectors first tried to plant, cultivate, and harvest their own fields of grain. Tell Mureybit is a deep site, and its many levels of construction, first of circular compounds of crude huts, then larger rectangular villages, suggest the success of this experiment.

Soon after 8000 B.C., sedentary communities and domestic plants and animals had appeared at several places along the flanks of the Zagros. At Ali Kosh, situated on the arid steppe of western Iran, at about 7500 B.C. people hunted gazelles, onagers (wild asses), and pigs, fished in the Mehmeh River, collected shellfish, and snared wild fowl. They also collected vetch and other plants, and between 8000 and 6500 B.C. they began growing domestic, two-rowed, hulled barley and emmer wheat. These early farmers lived in crude clay huts furnished with reed mats, and had stone bowls and a few other small household goods, but this settlement was neither rich nor impressive. Possibly the people came here only in the winter, since summers are unearthly hot and the cooler mountains would have provided many plant and animal products. Wild wheat is not native to the Ali Kosh area, but wild barley is available within a few kilometers, and the people here may have been growing grains that had been domesticated elsewhere.

By 6000 B.C. there is evidence of domestic sheep and goats at sites all over Southwest Asia and even into Greece and southern Europe, and it appears that once domestication was well advanced, the spread of sheep and goat raising was very rapid. Most farming villages have hedgerows, patches of weeds and thorny plants, clippings, and stubble that are perfectly acceptable to the rather undiscriminating sheep and goats, and these animals, with their heavy fleece, are well protected against the sun and heat of the Middle East.

Domestic cattle were herded on the Anatolian Plateau (central Turkey) by about 5800 B.C. and were probably present in the Balkans by 6500 B.C. As with sheep and goats, cattle domestication seems to have been a widespread phenomenon, probably beginning sometime after 9000 B.C. and occurring in many areas from China to western Europe. Across this vast area, ancient farmers seem to have bred cattle for reduced size, increased docility and milk production, and increased tolerance of climatic conditions. An important step in the evolution of civilizations . . . was the process by which cattle were adapted to the hot lowlands of the river valleys. The cattle found there today are thin, small animals that seem woefully scrawny by comparison to European cattle, but these Mesopotamia varieties are extraordinarily hardy. The late Shah of Iran tried to "improve" the cattle in the hot lowlands of Iran by importing Dutch and Danish cows that were about four times the size of local varieties and produced vastly more milk and meat—until they strolled out into the hot plains (which we were surveying for archaeological remains), where most of them were felled by heat stroke. These European cattle had to be kept in air-conditioned barns to be productive, whereas the local varieties could do perfectly well on the hottest day, eating poor quality foods that would have killed the larger cattle.

Cattle were probably especially important to the first settlers on the southern Mesopotamian Alluvium. During the dry, hot summers in this region, few reliable protein sources are available to primitive agriculturalists, and cow meat and milk apparently provided a crucial nutritional component. Oxen (castrated bulls) may have been used to pull plows and carts. In many areas of Southwest Asia where rainfall is sufficient for cereal cultivation, plowing is essential because natural vegetation is thick. Later, the horse, donkey, and mule were also used as draught animals.

Another important domesticated animal was the pig, whose bones have been recovered from sites all over Southwest Asia. By 6000 B.C. and even as late as 2700 B.C., pig bones represented 20 to 30% of all mammal remains at many large sites. . . . However, sometime after about 2400 B.C., pork apparently was religiously proscribed in most Mesopotamian cities, as well as in Egypt and elsewhere in Southwest Asia.

By 6000 B.C. agricultural villages spread over much of Southwest Asia, most of them comprising just a few score mud huts, a few hundred people, and the same essential economic functions. From Greece to Afghanistan, these villages looked very much alike and, taken on the basis of their archaeological remains, they were not impressive in their material wealth. Even sites like Jericho and Çatal Hüyük, which were larger than most and had relatively impressive art and architecture, were self-sufficient communities without many economic, political, or social ties outside their region. And the vast majority of these villagers were simple farmers without great aesthetic, religious, or social diversions.

As unremarkable as these villages were, however, their inhabitants were the first to focus their lives on agricultural products and to live in the sedentary communities that even today are the basic component of Middle Eastern settlement patterns. And as early as 6000 B.C., the processes that were to transmute these villages into states and empires were already underway.

After reading this selection, consider these questions:

1. At what date did agricultural villages come into existence?
2. What grains and domesticated animals were important to the economy of these villages?
3. What were the names of some of the earliest cities and where were they located?

SELECTION 2:

The Dawn of Belief

In the Paleolithic era, human beings remained dependent on the annual migratory cycles of animal herds and understood their world in terms of this dependence. The spirit of the animal was taken in killing the beast and symbolically given back through various ritualistic activities. This reciprocity not only appeased the spirit of the individual animal but also of the larger force that united human beings to nature within an encompassing spirit of life. Failure to perform these rituals disrupted this natural relationship and threatened the success of future hunts. Thus, animism and shamanism were the foundational features of Paleolithic belief.

In the following selection, archaeologist D. Bruce Dickson reconstructs the belief system of the upper Paleolithic period of ca. 30,000 B.C., which Dickson believes was founded on the cycles of reproduction.

The sexual principle in human thought is closely and logically connected to the concept of fertility and regeneration. If Upper Paleolithic religious thought really did center on the sexual dichotomy, the associations between sexuality and regeneration might allow us to hypothesize that the Upper Paleolithic worldview was based on the doctrine of "eternalism.". . . Such religions "seek a regeneration, a cyclical recurrence or eternal return, of all creation: cosmic, biological, historical, human." Change is seen as illusory, and eternal repetition is viewed as the nature of the cosmos.

Such a doctrine contrasts markedly with the concept of time and reality found in most Western religious worldviews. Although there are elements of symbolic regeneration in both Judaism and Christianity, for example, such elements are not central to either faith. Instead, both these religions take . . . a "patristic" view of time. In them, time is seen as beginning with Creation and the Age of the Patriarchs and moving, not in a cyclical or endlessly regenerative trajectory, but along a unique, *linear* progression with a discrete beginning, middle, and end.

Granting for a moment that Upper Paleolithic period art and religion is based on a sexual dualism, what other evidence is consistent with the hypothesis that the people of this period held a regenerative and cyclical worldview? At least two strands of evidence point in that direction: [the] interpretation of some mobiliary marks as a notational system for recording the lunar cycle; and the apparent conjunction of the moon (and by implication, its cycle) with the human female (and by implication, the menstrual cycle and cycle of human birth, growth, and death).

Let me suggest that the Upper Paleolithic worldview probably represented a fusion of understanding of two separate, empirically knowable phenomena of the natural world: the passage of time and the nature of human—especially female—sexuality. Both of these natural phenomena are characterized by dramatic surficial or for-

From *The Dawn of Belief: Religion in the Upper Paleolithic of Southwestern Europe*, by D. Bruce Dickson. Copyright © 1990 The Arizona Board of Regents. Reprinted by permission of the University of Arizona Press.

mal changes that can be observed and predicted with great ease and precision by virtually anyone. The moon waxes, then wanes, then disappears, then waxes again; women are born, enter their menses, become pregnant, give birth, and die. The palpable nature and cyclicality of these two phenomena make them attractive and convenient models for thinking about nature in general. It is easy to see how they might become "grand analogies," useful in explaining the universe, in rationalizing it, and in investing it with meaning in terms readily and widely understood.

In such a worldview, the world is not random and inexplicable. Rather, it is based on the same principle of dynamic opposition and yet ultimate complementarity found in human sexuality. In such a worldview, reality is not all change and flux. Rather it is the experience of a grand cycle, like the smaller cycles observed in the menses of women, or in the changes of the seasons, or in the phases of the moon. An ethos that emphasizes the careful observation of these changes would fit conformably with such a worldview. Records of the moon's passage that time the changing of the seasons and allow the prediction of the behavior and movements of animals would serve to confirm the aptness of the cyclical world picture. . . .

The richness of the late Glacial environment of southwestern Europe must have enabled Upper Paleolithic hunting and gathering subsistence systems to support human populations in densities beyond those of recent pedestrian foragers and equal to or greater than those achieved in historic times by equestrian hunters on the Great Plains or fisher-forager-hunters on the Northwest Coast. Although forced to make scheduled moves in response to annual cycles of game and fish availability, Upper Paleolithic peoples probably lived in sedentary communities for extended periods of time during certain seasons in their annual round. The important rites of intensification and passage practiced by these peoples no doubt took place during these periods of extended sedentism and maximum social aggregation or group size. Male initiation rites were probably an important element in the religious cycle of these peoples and are likely to have been featured during the ceremonies held at times of maximum social aggregations. The larger cave

art sites in Franco-Cantabria were probably ceremonial centers which served as the focus of the
rites that occurred during these periodic aggregations. Like many historic and modern fisher-
forager-hunters of the subarctic, Upper Paleolithic
subsistence practices emphasized "delayed-return"
activities in the form of storage, surplus accumulation, funeral ceremonialism, and artistic display.
Because of their relatively high population densities and their annual periods of sedentary living,
the complexity of their political and social organization—at least during seasons of maximum social
aggregation—surpassed that of the "band."

The ethnographic record also suggests that the
religious life of Upper Paleolithic societies depended upon shamans, part-time practitioners
who vigorously and directly sought to confront
the spirit world in "ecstatic encounters." Given
the high value that historic and recent food collectors place on achieving these special or altered
states of consciousness, there no doubt was widespread group or communal participation in the religious life of the Upper Paleolithic period. In addition to its ecstatic and extraordinary elements,
the Upper Paleolithic religious ideology no doubt
sanctioned the rules governing interpersonal relations, sex roles, hunting procedures, the treatment
of game animals, and the distribution of meat.
But the reverse was also true: the complex social
and productive relations in the world of everyday
experience were, in turn, reflected in the rituals of
the Upper Paleolithic period as well as in the "sacred canon," the religious and symbolic model of
the social order that lay behind that ritual life.

In a related manner, the material patterns in
the archaeological record, together with the formal interpretations of those patterns, conforms
with the expectations of two hypotheses. First,
religion in Franco-Cantabria during the Upper
Paleolithic period was a) based upon a complex

intellectual and theological order and b) was ultimately experiential in inspiration. Second, two
profound natural phenomena—a) a perceived
cyclicality in the passage of time and b) the dialectic of human sexuality, especially the period-
icity and fecundity of women—were generalized
into universal principles or "grand analogies"
that formed the basis of speculation and thought
about nature, humankind, the universe, and reality. This model of social and material reality was
embodied and reflected in the great parietal art
caves of Franco-Cantabria.

Human life is fragile and transitory and its essential fact—the inevitability of death—can be
countered only by birth, by more life. Human existence is both obvious and mysterious: we know
it must end in death yet it is filled with signs and
portents suggesting otherwise. Fragility and mystery—fear and hope—provoke the yearnings for
fertility and immortality in humankind. To find
that we share these yearnings even with peoples
of as remote an age as the late Pleistocene is to
recognize our kinship with all humanity.

To the Classical Greeks, fear and hope were
the twin tyrants of humankind. No less than ourselves, the peoples of Ice Age Europe were tormented by these twin tyrants. Their reply to this
torment is frozen in the mighty art of the Upper
Paleolithic and has resonated down three hundred
centuries into our own time.

After reading this selection, consider these
questions:
1. What were the main features of
   Paleolithic religion?
2. How did Paleolithic cultures understand time?
3. What role did the shaman play in
   these societies?

SELECTION 3:

The Mother Goddess

In the Neolithic Revolution, with its development of village life, cultural emphasis on fertility increased. It is understandable since these early people relied heavily on the growth of crops and the reproduction of animals. Thus, men and women understood the sustaining spirit of life in terms of fertility. In her role as mother and nurturer, woman became the source and symbol of this great power of reproduction and of the transformation of the past into the future. Myths of birth, death, rebirth, and of the cycles of nature and human life developed, symbolized by images of change and renewal: the moon, with its constantly changing shapes; animals like the snake, which sheds its skin; and deer, which lose and then grow new horns.

A great multiplicity of myths attempt to explain what this fertility goddess represented and what she was called, but underlying this diversity is the notion of the fundamental powers of female fertility. This notion of divinity and of the human relation to it is captured in the notion of "the Great Mother" or "the Mother Goddess." Historian Elinor W. Gadon has made a study of both the origins and, though often submerged, the continuity of this goddess throughout history. As Gadon makes clear, the celebration of the Mother Goddess in the ancient cities of Sumer (today, southern Iraq) marked an important early manifestation. Her relation to the dominant male gods of the city established the legitimacy of their power.

The Goddess was continuously worshiped for thousands of years (ca. 3500–500 B.C.E.) in the ancient Near East "during the ascendance and decline of civilizations that flourished and were conquered." Her names were many: Ishtar, Astarte, Anahita, Ma, Asherah, but she was first known as Inanna, the beloved and revered deity of Sumer.

Despite hostile intrusions into her domain by the patriarchal sky gods, Inanna continued to be revered as the awesome Queen of Heaven and Earth. "Her womb was the vessel of Creation from which flowed grains, fruit, and legumes.

Hers was the nourishing breast of nature. Hers was the bountiful lap of nurturing mother earth. As the radiant Morning Star, she is birth, potential, all possibility; as Evening Star, she is completion and fulfillment." Inanna is the Goddess of Love, giving forth "desire that generates the energy of the universe.". . .

The *Hymn to Inanna* was sung at the sacred marriage rites between the Goddess and the Sumerian king to ensure the fertility of the land and to legitimize the king's rule. The sacred marriage (*hieros gamos*) was celebrated annually throughout the Near East. The role of the Goddess in the ritual sexual union was taken by her priestess, the hierodule, believed to be an embodiment of the Goddess herself. "Union with the goddess was of paramount importance for rule on earth." The cosmic powers of the Goddess had to be transferred to the king to ensure his powers of leadership and fertility. Their sexual union was necessary to activate the annual cycle of life.

The model for the sacred rite was the marriage of the Goddess Inanna to the Shepherd King Dumuzi. Every year Inanna, the Queen of Heaven and Earth, descended from heaven at the time of the autumn equinox to consummate her marriage to Dumuzi in her temple at Uruk. The sacred law of Sumer, which dictated the order and form of things, ordained that day as the beginning of the New Year when the earth awakened and the winter crop of barley from which they made their bread and beer was planted. . . .

In the Inanna narrative, the life force of the Goddess is still recognized as powerful and creative, but nature is no longer revered as sacred. The symbols of her authority as ruler of Sumer, her throne and her bed, rest on nature tamed. The world tree must be cut down, instincts curbed. The later proscriptions of Judeo-Christian religion that link the sacred with the moral order is a legacy of this emerging patriarchy that always seeks to control. The earlier morality of nature in which the ebb and flow of the life process is the highest good is of a different order.

Out of the wood of the world tree Inanna fashions her throne and her bed. "When [she] begins her rule, she will be sitting on the throne of the *huluppu*-tree, and her understanding of life and death, consciousness and lack of consciousness, will be increased accordingly. Likewise, when she holds a man in her arms, the bed will murmur to them both the secrets of life and death, light and darkness." The multivalent symbol of the tree retains the memory of a prehistoric time before patriarchal dualism split the wholeness of nature. "As Queen of Sumer, Inanna is responsible to and receives her power from the resources and fertility of the land." She puts on her crown, the *shugurra,* the crown of Sumer. . . .

As we have seen, the legendary "Dumuzi was wedded ritually to the Goddess Inanna in the city of Uruk. As one poet imagined it, it was Inanna herself who selected Dumuzi . . . for the Sacred Marriage. . . ." She cast her eyes over all the people and exalted him to the godship of the land. Subsequent Sumerian kings took Dumuzi's

place. The king was both human and the incarnation of the mythical Dumuzi, the Shepherd King. His identity was merged with the Vegetation God. His mother is the Lady of the Wild Cow, his father is Enki, the fertilizing waters upon which the harvest depends. Dumuzi is the god of the date palm, of the grain, and of the power of barley to produce beer. He is the vital spark of new life in nature, vegetable, and animal.

As king, Dumuzi is identified with the harvest of the land. But as the mortal husband of the Great Goddess, he must die in order for earth to renew itself. His sexual energy "is needed to claim the all-giving earth, Inanna's breast, and to plow the soil, Inanna's vulva, that she may be the fertility of the land."

In Sumer and the whole of the Near East, the symbolic mating of the Goddess with the king became an instrument of state policy, a way of legitimizing his rule: "kingship demanded a sacred foundation that could be provided only through the omnipotence of the Great Goddess." Through sacrifice, the ritual death of the God King, his sacred powers were renewed and his authority over the land reestablished.

The Goddess does not merely symbolize or represent well-being; she *is* well-being. She is both the fertile womb and fertile field. Over and over again the poets praise her overflow, abundance, and prosperity, bemoaning her absence in times of calamity. She is the "life-giving floodwaters and rain clouds, on fields and meadows covered with ripe grain, on the plants and herbs that are 'the delight of the steppes.'". . .

Under patriarchy, Ereshkigal, the former Grain Goddess, is banished to the underworld and becomes the symbol of dread death. Her message is that while life itself is ongoing, individual human life ends; there are limits. As death she is all destruction and chaos, monstrous to the patriarchal, heroic worldview with its emphasis on rational order and control.

Inanna, the embodiment of the earth's fertility, and Dumuzi, the wild bull, the symbol of male primordial energy, are yet another example of the ongoing theme of complementarity of female/ male we have been following. In the fullness of her passion, Inanna calls Dumuzi "the wild bull," and her heavenly spouse, the Sky God An, is "the fecund Breed-Bull, an apt personification of the overcast skies in spring whose thunder recalls the bellowing of a bull and whose rain engenders vegetation far and wide."

Yet, under patriarchy, the bull, symbol of the male life force in the Goddess culture, takes on a negative meaning—a "bull-like passion, raw desire and power, sadistic bull-dozing violence, demonic bullying." Gugalanna, the Great Bull of Heaven, the repressed side of the sky god Enlil, has been banished to the underworld for his violence.

Still creation continues to depend upon the stimulating force of the masculine fertilizing power, and when the Great Bull of Heaven is killed, Inanna offers her life to renew the cycle that has stopped. Death and decay are the basis of primordial fertility rites; through this process energy is transformed from one state to another. Inanna's death in the underworld plays out the female/male exchange of energy on one level; the sacred marriage ritual is the same dynamic on another.

After reading this selection, consider these questions:

1. What were the main characteristics of the worship of the Mother Goddess?
2. What is the meaning of the "sacred marriage" of the Mother Goddess?
3. How did this marriage set a pattern for other deities?

SELECTION 4:

The Epic of Enuma Elish

The development of cities in the ancient Near East brought forth a different understanding of divinity and the ways in which humans related to the gods. This new understanding was, however, not entirely new; the cities of the ancient Near East were still tied directly to agriculture and therefore to the Great Mother Goddess. But they developed and transformed the original myths and symbols of fertility into new and altered definitions of the gods and of the forces that these gods represented. These developments and displacement of the Mother Goddess are seen within the great Babylonian myth of creation, the Enuma Elish. Written in the twelfth century B.C. to celebrate the founding of the city of Babylon, the poem itself derives from older Sumerian stories of creation and clearly indicates the new mentality of urban existence as well as a continuity to the Neolithic Mother Goddess. According to this myth, orderly human life, or civilization, emerged from a violent struggle among the gods. The first two gods were the male Apsu ("the sweet, drinkable waters") and the female Tiamat ("the bitter water," perhaps the primal, abysmal watery chaos before creation). Mammu, the god of form, created the gods of the river banks and the gods of the horizon. These gods in turn generated the gods of the heavens.

The sky god Ea defeated the other gods and with his wife, Damkina, gave birth to Marduk, who would eventually become the chief god of Sumer. After defeating other gods, Marduk turned his vengeance against

*Tiamat, destroying her in a great battle. Marduk then created the land of
Mesopotamia from the blood of Tiamat's monsters and finally made human
beings so that they could serve and entertain the gods.*

When there was no heaven,
no earth, no height, no depth, no name,
when Apsu was alone,
the sweet water, the first begetter; and Tiamat
the bitter water, and that
return to the womb, her Mammu,
when there were no gods—

When sweet and bitter
mingled together, no reed was plaited, no rushes
muddied the water,
the gods were nameless, natureless, futureless,
   then
from Apsu and Tiamat
in the waters gods were created, in the waters
silt precipitated,

Lahmu and Lahamu,
were named; they were not yet old
not yet grown tall
when Anshar and Kishar overtook them both,
the lines of sky and earth
stretched where horizons meet to separate
cloud from silt.

Days on days, years
on years passed till Anu, the empty heaven,
heir and supplanter,
first-born of his father, in his own nature
begot Nudimmud-Ea,
intellect, wisdom, wider than heaven's horizon,
the strongest of all the kindred. . . .

When Tiamat heard him her wits scattered, she
was possessed and shrieked aloud, her legs shook
from the crotch down, she gabbled spells, mut-
tered maledictions, while the gods of war sharpened their weapons.
   Then they met: Marduk, that cleverest of gods,
and Tiamat grappled alone in singled fight.

The lord shot his net to entangle Tiamat, and
the pursuing tumid wind, Imhullu, came from
behind and beat in her face. When the mouth
gaped open to suck him down he drove Imhullu
in, so that the mouth would not shut but wind
raged through her belly; her carcass blown up,
tumescent. She gaped—and now he shot the
arrow that split the belly, that pierced the gut and
cut the womb.
   Now that the Lord had conquered Tiamat he
ended her life, he flung her down and straddled
the carcass; the leader was killed, Tiamat was
dead, her rout was shattered, her band dispersed.
   Those gods who had marched beside her now
quaked in terror, and to save their own lives, if
they could, they turned their backs on danger.
But they were surrounded, held in tight circle,
and there was no way out.
   He smashed their weapons and tossed them
into the net; they found themselves inside the
snare, they wept in holes and hid in corners suffering the wrath of god.
   When they resisted he put in chains the eleven
monsters, Tiamat's unholy brood, and all their
murderous armament. The demoniac band that has
marched in front of her he trampled in the ground;
   But Kingu the usurper, he chief of them, he
bound and made death's god. He took the Tables
of Fate, usurped without right, and sealed them
with his seal to wear on his own breast.
   When it was accomplished, the adversary vanquished, the haughty enemy humiliated; when
the triumph of Anshar was accomplished on the
enemy, and the will of Nudimmud was fulfilled,
then brave Marduk tightened the ropes of the
prisoners.
   He turned back to where Tiamat lay bound, he
straddled the legs and smashed her skull (for the
mace was merciless), he severed the arteries and
the blood streamed down the north wind to the
unknown ends of the world.
   When the gods saw all this they laughed out
loud, and they sent him presents. They sent him
their thankful tributes.

From "Enuma Elish," in *Poems of Heaven and Hell from Ancient
Mesopotamia*, translated by N.K. Sandars (Penguin Classics, 1971).
Copyright © N.K. Sandars, 1971. Reprinted with permission from
Penguin Books Ltd.

The lord rested; he gazed at the huge body, pondering how to use it, what to create from the dead carcass. He split it apart like a cockle-shell; with the upper half he constructed the arc of sky, he pulled down the bar and set a watch on the waters, so they should never escape.

He crossed the sky to survey the infinite distance; he stationed himself above Apsu, that Apsu built by Nudimmud over the old abyss which now he surveyed, measuring out and marking in.

He stretched the immensity of the firmament, he made Esharra, the Great Palace, to be its earthly image, and Anu and Enlil and Ea had each their right stations.

He projected positions for the Great Gods conspicuous in the sky, he gave them a starry aspect as constellations; he measured the year, gave it a beginning and an end, and to each month of the twelve three rising stars.

When he had marked the limits of the year, he gave them Nebiru, the pole of the universe, to hold their course, that never erring they should not stray through the sky. For the seasons of Ea and Enlil he drew the parallel.

Through her ribs he opened gates in the east and west, and gave them strong bolts on the right and left; and high in the belly of Tiamat he set the zenith.

He gave the moon the luster of a jewel, he gave him all the night, to mark off days, to watch by night each month the circle of a waxing waning light.

"New Moon, when you rise on the world, six days your horns are crescent, until half-circle on the seventh, waxing still phase follows phase, you will divide the month from full to full.

"Then wane, a gibbous light that fails, until low down on the horizon sun oversails you, drawing close his shadow lies across you, then dark of the moon—at thirty days the cycle's second starts again and follows through for ever and for ever.

"This is your emblem and the road you take, and when you close the sun, speak of both of you with you justice judgement uncorrupt. . . ."

When Marduk had sent out the moon, he took the sun and set him to complete the cycle from this one to the next New Year. . . . He gave him the Eastern Gate, and the ends of the night with the day, he gave to Shamash.

Then Marduk considered Tiamat. He skimmed spume from the bitter sea, heaped up the clouds, spindrift of wet and wind and cooling rain, the spittle of Tiamat.

With his own hands from the steaming mist he spread the clouds. He pressed hard down the head of water, heaping mountains over it, opening springs to flow: Euphrates and Tigris rose from her eyes, but he closed the nostrils and held back their springhead.

He piled huge mountains on her paps and through them drove water-holes to channel the deep sources; and high overhead he arched her tail, locked-in to the wheel of heaven; the pit was under his feet, between was the crotch, the sky's fulcrum. Now the earth had foundations and the sky its mantle.

When god's work was done, when he had fashioned it all and finished, then on earth he founded temples and made them over to Ea;

But the Temples of destiny taken from Kingu he returned as a first greeting to Anu; and those gods who hung up their weapons defeated, whom he had scattered, now fettered, he drove into his presence, the father of the gods.

With the weapons of war broken, he bound to his foot the eleven, Tiamat's monstrous creation. He made likenesses of them all and now they stand at the gate of the abyss, the Apsu Gate; he said,

"This is for recollection for Tiamat shall not be forgotten."

All the generations of the Great Gods when they saw him were full of joy, with Lahmu and Lahamu; their hearts bounded when they came over to meet him.

After reading this selection and the previous one, consider these questions:

1. According to the *Enuma Elish*, what were the origins of creation?
2. What is the meaning of Marduk's defeat of Tiamat?
3. What are the differences between the creation stories associated with the Goddess Inanna (selection 3) and that of the god Marduk?

SELECTION 5:
The Good Life in Mesopotamia

Archaeologists have often pointed to the irony that as human beings gained greater control over nature with the Neolithic and Urban Revolutions, they tended to find their gods more absolute in their power and more capricious. The success of these great river civilizations demanded a greater form of social and political unity. The king ensured this unity. Through his claimed descent from the gods, he reflected the divine order of the world. Historian Thorkild Jacobsen draws out the moral consequences of what could be generally called the Mesopotamian view of the gods. The myths clearly indicate that human life comprises violence and suffering, a basic condition that men and women must accept. Within the sense of life-as-struggle, there emerged also a notion of justice that emanated from the divine order. As Jacobsen shows, the notion of the good life for the men and women of Sumer and Babylon revolved around the notion of obedience.

In a civilization which sees the whole universe as a state, obedience must necessarily stand out as a prime virtue. For a state is built on obedience, on the unquestioned acceptance of authority. It can cause no wonder, therefore, to find that in Mesopotamia the "good life" was the "obedient life." The individual stood at the center of ever wider circles of authority which delimited his freedom of action. The nearest and smallest of these circles was constituted by authorities in his own family: father and mother, older brother and older sister. We possess a hymn which describes a coming golden age, and we find that age characterized as one of obedience, as

> Days when one man is not insolent to
>   another, when a son reveres his father,
> days when respect is shown in the land,
>   when the lowly honor the great,
> when the younger brother . . . respects (?)
>   his older brother,

From *The Intellectual Adventure of Ancient Man: An Essay on Speculative Thought in the Ancient Near East*, by H. and H.A. Frankfort, John A. Wilson, Thorkild Jacobsen, and William A. Irwin. Copyright © 1946 by The University of Chicago. Reprinted by permission of the University of Chicago Press.

> when the older child instructs the younger
>   child and he (i.e., the younger) abides
>   by his decisions.

The Mesopotamian is constantly admonished: "Pay heed to the word of thy mother as to the word of thy god"; "Revere thy older brother"; "Pay heed to the word of thy older brother as to the word of thy father"; "Anger not the heart of thy older sister."

But obedience to the older members of one's family is merely a beginning. Beyond the family lie other circles, other authorities: the state and society. There is the foreman where one works; there is the bailiff who oversees agricultural works in which one takes part; there is the king. All these can and must claim absolute obedience. The Mesopotamian looked with disapproval and pity, but also with fear, on the crowd which had no leader: "Soldiers without a king are sheep without their shepherd."

A crowd with no leader to organize and direct it is lost and bewildered, like a flock of sheep without a shepherd. It is also dangerous, however; it can be destructive, like waters which break the dams that hold them and submerge fields and gardens if the canal inspector is not there to keep the dams in repair: "Workmen without a foreman are waters without a canal inspector."

Finally, a leaderless, unorganized crowd is useless and unproductive, like a field which brings forth nothing if it is not plowed: "Peasants without a bailiff are a field without a plowman."

Hence an orderly world is unthinkable without a superior authority to impose his will. The Mesopotamian feels convinced that authorities are always right: "The command of the palace, like the command of Anu, cannot be altered. The king's word is right; his utterance, like that of a god, cannot be changed!" And, as there are circles of human authority in family, society, and state to circumscribe the freedom of the individual, so there are circles of divine authority which may not be trespassed upon. Here again we find more immediate and more remote ties of allegiance. For the ties of the individual to the great gods were—at least in the third millennium—of a somewhat remote character. He served them as a member of his community rather than as an individual; he worked their estates for them, with his neighbors and compatriots he obeyed their laws and decrees, and he took part in their yearly festivals as a spectator. But, just as the serf rarely has intimate personal relations with the lord of the manor, so the individual in Mesopotamia looked upon the great gods as remote forces to whom he could appeal only in some great crisis and then only through intermediaries. Close and personal relations—relations such as he had to the authorities in his family: father, mother, older brother and sister—the individual had only to one deity, to his personal god.

The personal god was usually some minor deity in the pantheon who took a special interest in a man's family or had taken a fancy to the man himself. In a sense, and probably this is the original aspect, the personal god appears as the personification of a man's luck and success. Success is interpreted as an outside power which infuses itself into a man's doings and makes them produce results. It is not man's own ability which brings results, for man is weak and has no power to influence the course of the universe to any appreciable degree. Only a god can do that; therefore, if things come out as man has hoped, or

even better, it must needs be that some god has taken an interest in him and his doings and brought him success. He has, to use the Mesopotamian expression for success, "acquired a god." This original aspect of the personal god as the power behind a man's success stands out quite clearly in such sayings as

Without a (personal) god man cannot make
    his living,
the young man cannot move his arm
    heroically in battle,

and in the way the personal god is linked with forethought and planning:

When thou dost plan ahead, thy god is
    thine;
when thou dost not plan ahead, thy god is
    not thine.

That is to say, only when you plan ahead do you have a chance to succeed; only then is your god with you.

Since the personal god is the power which makes a man's actions succeed, it is quite natural that he or she should also carry the moral responsibility for those actions. When Lugalzaggisi, the ruler of Umma, had attacked and partly destroyed the city of Lagash, the men of Lagash placed the blame unhesitantly on Lugalzaggisi's deity: "May his personal deity, the goddess Nidaba, bear this crime on her neck!" That is, may the proper divine authorities who rule the universe hold her responsible for what she has aided and abetted.

To this personal god, then, before any other, a man owed worship and obedience. In every house there was a small chapel for the personal god where the owner of the house worshiped and brought his daily offerings.

A man must truly proclaim the greatness
    of his god;
A young man must wholeheartedly obey
    the command of his god.

Now, if this monotonous theme of obedience—to family, to rulers, to gods—was the essence of the good, that is, the correct, life in ancient Mesopotamia, what, we may ask, did man stand to gain by leading the good life? The answer is best given in terms of the Mesopotamian world view, in terms of man's position in the cosmic state. Man, you will remember, was created to be the slave of the gods. He is their servant. Now, a diligent and obedient servant can call on his master for protection. A diligent and obedient servant, moreover, can expect to be promoted, to receive favors and rewards from his master. A slothful, disobedient servant, on the other hand, can hope for none of these things. Thus the way of obedience, of service and worship, is the way to achieve protection; and it is also the way to earthly success, to the highest values in Mesopotamian life: health and long life, honored standing in the community, many sons, wealth.

When we view the Mesopotamian universe from the aspect of what the individual can gain for himself, the personal god becomes a pivotal figure. He is the individual's link with the universe and its forces; he is the Archimedean point from which it may be moved. For the personal god is not remote and awesome like the great gods; he is near and familiar; and he cares. One can talk to him, plead with him, work on his pity—in short, use all the means which a child uses to get his way with his parents. The character of the relationship may be exemplified by a letter from a man to his god, for the Mesopotamians frequently wrote letters to their gods. Perhaps they thought that one could not always be certain to find the god at home when one called, whereas the god would be sure to look at his correspondence. Again, it may often have been because the writer was too ill to come in person and therefore had recourse to a letter. In the case of the letter which we shall quote, it would appear that the writer refrains from coming in person because he is sulking. His feelings are hurt because he thinks his god neglects him. He hints that such neglect is very unwise on the part of the god, for faithful worshipers are hard to get and difficult to replace. But if the god will only comply with his wishes, then he will be there right away and adore him. Finally, he works on the god's pity: the god must consider that there is not only himself but that he has a family and poor little children who also suffer with him. The letter reads:

To the god my father speak; thus says
    Apiladad, thy servant:
"Why have you neglected me (so)?
Who is going to give you one who can
    take my place?
Write to the god Marduk, who is fond of
    you,
that he may break my bondage;
then I shall see your face and kiss your
    feet!
Consider also my family, grownups and
    little ones;
have mercy on me for their sake, and let
    your help reach me!"

The bondage of which the letter speaks is some illness. Illness of any kind was seen as an evil demon who had seized the victim and held him captive. Such a case actually goes beyond the powers of the personal god. The personal god can help a man in his undertakings, can give him standing and respect in his community; but he is not strong enough to tear him from the clutches of an evil, lawless demon. However—and this is the most wonderful thing about having connections with those in high places—the personal god has influential friends. He moves in the circles of the great gods, knows them well. So now, when his ward has been seized by an evil demon, it is time to use whatever influence he has to set the cumbersome machinery of divine justice in motion: "Write to the god Marduk, who is fond of you," says our letter.

Now we who live in a modern state take for granted that the machinery of justice—courts, judges, police—is at the disposal of any man who considers himself wronged. But that is a very modern notion. We need go back only to medieval England to find a state in which it could be very difficult to get the king's court to take up one's case. And the early Mesopotamian state, upon which the cosmic state was patterned, was of far more primitive cast than medieval England. In this primitive state there was as yet no developed executive machinery to carry out the verdict of the court. Execution was left to the winning party; and for that reason a court would not touch a case unless it was certain that the plaintiff had power behind him, a powerful protector who would guarantee that the judgment would be executed. Accordingly, the first step for the personal god was to find such a protector among the great gods. Usually Ea, the god of the sweet waters, was willing to undertake the protectorship. But Ea was so august and remote that the personal god would not approach him directly. He would go to Ea's son, Marduk, and Marduk would then urge his father to act. If Ea agreed to act, he would send his messenger—a human incantation priest—to go with the personal god to the court of the gods, where the messenger would appeal on Ea's behalf that the sun-god (the divine judge) accept this particular case for judgment. This appeal was directed to the rising sun in an impressive ceremony in the temple. After praising the sun as judge, as able to give legal relief against all kinds of demons and to heal the afflicted, the priest continued:

> Sun-god, to relieve them is in thy power;
> thou dost set straight conflicting
>   testimonies as (were they but) one
>   statement.
> I am the messenger of Ea;
> for the relief of the plagued man he has
>   sent me hither,
> (and) the message which Ea gave I have
>   repeated to thee.
> (As for) the man, the son of his god, judge
>   his case, pronounce sentence for him,
> drive off the evil illness from his body.

Through the decision of the sun-god, guaranteed by the mighty Ea, the evil demon was thus constrained to release its hold.

The cases in which the personal god was asked to use his influence to procure divine justice are among those most typical of his usefulness, but naturally he was asked to use it for general well-being and advancement also. He is to say a good word for his ward whenever he can; the ruler Entemena, for example, prays that his personal god be allowed to stand forever before the great god Ningirsu, petitioning for health and long life for Entemena.

If we sum up, then, what our texts tell us about the rewards for the "good life," we find life to be a pretty arbitrary affair. Through obedience and service man may win the good will of his personal god. The personal god may use his influence with the higher gods to obtain favors for his protégé from them. But even justice is such a favor; it cannot be claimed, but it is obtained through personal connections, personal pressure, through favoritism. Even the most perfect "good life" held out but a promise, not a certainty, of tangible rewards.

After reading this selection, consider these questions:

1. What role did the personal gods play in the life of the Mesopotamian?
2. What was the most important moral value to the Mesopotamian?
3. What was the relationship between the individual and the cosmos in Mesopotamian mythology?

SELECTION 6:

Hammurabi's Code of Laws

The earliest evidence of written legal codes comes from ancient Sumer. The best-known example of these Near Eastern codes, which clearly built on these earlier Sumerian models, is the famous Code of Hammurabi. Hammurabi was king of Babylon from ca. 1792 to ca. 1750 B.C. The code is an extended document, remarkable in the detailed ways in which it dealt with the complexities confronting early urban life. The following excerpt can only give an indication of the nature of the social and economic relationships that comprised life in the crowded cities of the ancient Near East.

1. If a man weave a spell and bring a charge of murder against another man and has not justified himself, the accuser shall be put to death.

2. If a man has put a spell upon another man, and has not justified himself, the one who is charged with sorcery shall go to the holy river, he shall plunge into the holy river, and if the holy river overcomes him, his accuser shall take his estate. If the holy river shows that man to be innocent and has saved him, he who charged him with sorcery shall be put to death and the man who plunged into the river shall take the estate of him who brought the charge against him. . . .

21. If a man has broken into a house, he shall be killed before the breach and walled in it.

22. If a man has robbed and has been captured, that man shall be put to death.

23. If the robber has not been caught, the man who has been despoiled shall recount before the god what he has lost, and the city and governor in whose territory the robbery took place shall make good to him his loss. . . .

128. If a man has married a wife and has not drawn up a contract, that woman is no wife.

129. If the wife of a man has been caught lying with another man, they shall bind them and throw them into the waters. If the owner of the wife would save his wife then in turn the king could save his servant.

130. If a man has forced the wife of a man, who has had no intercourse with a male and is dwelling in her father's house, and has lain in her bosom, and he has been caught, that man shall be killed, the woman will go free.

131. If a wife has been accused by her husband and she has not been caught lying with another male, she shall swear by god and shall return to her house.

132. If a wife has the finger pointed at her on account of another male but has not been caught lying with another male, for the sake of her husband she shall throw herself into the holy river.

133. If a man has been taken captive and in his house there is maintenance, if his wife has gone out from her house and entered into the house of another, because that woman has not guarded her body and has entered the house of another, they shall prove it against that woman and throw her into the waters.

134. If a man has been taken captive and in his house there is no maintenance, and his wife has entered into the house of another, that woman has no blame.

135. If a man has been taken captive and in his house there is no maintenance, if his wife has entered the house of another and has borne children and afterwards her husband returns and regains his city, that woman shall return to her first husband, the children shall go after their father. . . .

137. If a man has decided to put away his concubine who has borne him children or his wife who has granted him children, to that woman he shall return her marriage portion and shall give her half of the field, orchard and goods, and she shall bring up her children. From the time that her children are grown up, from whatever is given to her children they shall give her a share like that of one son, and she shall marry the husband of her choice.

138. If a man has put away his bride who has not borne him children, he shall return her dowry and pay her the marriage portion which she brought from her father's house, and shall put her away.

139. If there was no dowry, he shall give her one mina of silver for a divorce.

140. If he is a poor man, he shall give her one third of a mina of silver.

141. If the wife of a man who is living in the house of her husband has made up her mind to leave the house to engage in business and has acted the fool, neglecting the house and humiliating the husband, it shall be proved against her;

From *The Oldest Code of Laws in the World*, translated by C.H.W. Johns (Edinburgh: T&T Clark, 1903).

and if her husband has said "I put her away," he shall put her away and she shall go her way, and he shall not give her anything for her divorce.

142. If a woman hates her husband and has said "You shall not possess me," they shall inquire into her record and if she has been economical and has no vice and her husband has gone out and greatly belittled her, that woman has no blame, she will take her marriage portion and go off to her father's house.

143. If she has not been economical, a gadabout, has neglected her house and humiliated her husband, that woman they shall throw into the waters. . . .

153. If a man's wife has caused her husband to be killed on account of another man, they shall impale that woman on a stake.

154. If a man has known his daughter, that man shall be expelled from the city. . . .

195. If a man has struck his father, his hand shall be cut off.

196. If a man has caused the loss of a gentleman's eye, they shall cause him to lose one eye.

197. If he has shattered a gentleman's limb, they shall shatter his limb.

198. If he has caused a commoner to lose his eye or shattered a commoner's limb, he shall pay one mina of silver.

199. If he has caused the loss of an eye of a gentleman's servant or has shattered his limb, he shall pay half his price.

200. If a man has made the tooth of a man that is his equal fall out, they shall make his tooth fall out.

201. If he has made the tooth of a commoner fall out, he shall pay one third of a mina of silver.

202. If a man has struck the cheek of his superior, he shall be struck in the assembly with 60 strokes of a cowhide whip.

203. If a man of gentle birth has struck a man of gentle birth who is his equal, he shall pay one mina of silver.

204. If a poor man has struck a poor man, he shall pay ten shekels of silver.

205. If a slave has struck a free man, they shall cut off his ear. . . .

215. If a doctor has treated a gentleman for a severe wound, with a bronze lancet and has cured him, or has opened an abscess of the eye for a gentleman with the bronze lancet and has cured the eye of the gentleman, he shall take ten shekels of silver. . . .

218. If the doctor has treated a gentleman for a severe wound with a lancet of bronze and has caused the gentleman to die or has opened an abscess of the eye of a gentleman with the bronze lancet and has caused the loss of the gentleman's eye, they shall cut off his hands.

219. If the doctor has treated the severe wound of a commoner's slave and has caused his death, he shall render slave for slave. . . .

229. If a builder has built a house and not made his work strong and the house he built has fallen and so has caused the death of the owner of the house, that builder shall be put to death.

230. If he has caused the son of the owner of the house to die, they shall put to death the son of the builder.

231. If he has caused the slave of the owner of the house to die, he shall give slave for slave to the owner of the house.

232. If he has caused the loss of goods, he shall restore whatever losses he has caused, and because he did not make strong the house he built and it fell, he shall rebuild the house that fell at his own cost.

After reading this selection, consider these questions:

1. What were some of the areas regulated by Hammurabi's code?
2. What was the basis of justice in the code?
3. How is this sense of justice related to the Mesopotamian sense of divinity?

CHAPTER 2
Ancient Egypt: The Value of Civilized Life

The advanced culture that emerged along the Nile valley was, like that of Mesopotamia, another great river civilization. It appears to be a somewhat younger civilization than Sumer's and to have been influenced by it. By the fourth millennium, however, Egypt developed a highly distinctive civilization of its own. Indeed, this civilization was extremely long-lived, lasting from approximately 4000 B.C. to its absorption into the Roman Empire in the first century B.C. There were low points and even breaks within these four millennia of continuity—the internal breakdown of the Old Kingdom in what is called the first intermediate period, the invasion of the Hyksos around 2000 B.C., and the invasions of the Persians and the Greeks in the fourth century B.C.—but through all this there survived a distinctly Egyptian conception of the gods, notion of the just society, and fundamental idea of the good life. Following these breaks, ancient Egyptian history is usually divided into three main periods: the Old Kingdom (2686–2181 B.C.), the Middle Kingdom (2050–1786 B.C.), and the New Kingdom (1567–1085 B.C.).

The remarkable continuum of ancient Egyptian civilization is only partly explained by the Egyptian conception of the world. It also seems to have resulted from a happy consequence of geography. Mesopotamia is open on all sides. Wide plains surround it, and the two major rivers of the area flow by the major settlements. Geography provides no natural defenses, and only man-made city walls protected its early urban areas from invaders. The history of Mesopotamia thus offers a confusing array of rising and falling cities and empires. The original Sumerian civilization was followed by an Akkadian civilization, and then a Babylonian, Assyrian, neo-Babylonian, Hittite, and Persian civilization. This broad outline can only provide a schematic overview of the confusing array of peoples and forms of domination that washed over this area in the Bronze and early Iron Ages (ca. 3500–1200 B.C.). The historically significant thing about Mesopotamia is that, through this confusion, there appears less of a sense of civilizations coming to an end and of permanent historical loss than a sense of transformation, adaptation, and continuity of certain basic images, ideas, belief systems, and styles of life. Because of this multilevel process of continuity, most scholars feel confident when speaking of a generic Mesopotamian civilization.

By contrast, the civilization that developed along the Nile appeared to be blessed with natural defenses. Surrounded on two sides by impenetrable (or at least easily defensible) deserts, by a sea in the north, and by a set of cataracts that made the Nile unnavigable in the south, Egypt was protected from waves of migrating peoples and expanding empires. The elongated Nile River valley also provided Egypt with an annual flood, that with its rich silt from the African interior replenished the soil of the narrow strips of alluvial lands on either side of the river. This yearly cycle called for collective irrigation projects and necessitated social and political forms capable of organizing such large-scale projects. Isolation, along with these annual floods, gave the Nile valley the foundation of a civilization of great stability.

This stability should not be confused with an overarching unity or an overwhelming monotony to Egyptian civilization. In fact, the earliest records indicate a wide variety of gods and even ritualistic practices as well as a large number of borrowings—both material and spiritual—from the civilizations of Mesopotamia. Yet, with the unification of Upper (southern) and Lower (northern) Egypt—traditionally the starting point of Egyptian history with the beginning of the dynasties—there appeared to be a general agreement about the nature of man, the position of the major deities, and the power and meaning of pharaonic rule.

SELECTION 1:

The Gods of Egypt

Local rituals and cults persisted throughout the long history of ancient Egypt, but the larger framing features of Egyptian civilization were there from the period of unification. The most important features have been identified as the Egyptian conceptions of the unity and rhythms of the universe. Within this unity, the Egyptians recognized numerous major and minor gods. The acceptance of so many deities, and even the apparent conflicting ideas and beliefs that they represented, make it difficult for us today to understand Egyptian religion. This diversity offered no such problem to the Egyptians, however. The eminent Egyptologist Henri Frankfort explains this polytheistic understanding of divinity.

We find . . . in Egyptian religion a number of doctrines which strike us as contradictory; but it is sheer presumption to accuse the ancients of muddleheadedness on this score. . . . The ancients did not attempt to solve the ultimate problems confronting man by a single and coherent theory; that has been the method of approach since the time of the Greeks. Ancient thought—mythopoeic, "myth-making" thought—admitted side by side certain *limited* insights, which were held to be *simultaneously* valid, each in its own proper context, each corresponding to a definite avenue of approach. I have called this "multiplicity of approaches," and we shall find many examples of it as we proceed. At the moment I want to point out that this habit of thought agrees with the basic experience of polytheism.

Polytheism is sustained by man's experience of a universe alive from end to end. Powers confront man wherever he moves, and in the immediacy of these confrontations the question of their ultimate unity does not arise. There are many gods—one cannot know how many; a small handbook of Egyptian religion enumerates more than eighty. . . .

There is one generic term which is most difficult to avoid when we discuss Egyptian religion. That is the word "animal-gods." It should not be used, as we shall show in a moment. But we must admit—and the Greek, Roman, and early Christian writers too were struck by the fact—that animals play an altogether unusual role in Egyptian religion. We . . . shall never know how certain gods came to be associated with certain animals. There are too many gods showing such an association and their cult is too widespread for us to pretend to understand Egyptian religion without at least a tentative explanation of this its most baffling, most persistent, and to us most alien feature.

It is wrong to say that the worship of animals is a survival from a primitive stratum of Egyptian religion. This view is often encountered and is supported by some plausible arguments. It is said

that these cults are often of purely local significance; that they sometimes center on quite insignificant creatures like the centipede or the toad; and that we must therefore place the sacred animals on a par with certain sacred objects, like the crossed arrows of the goddess Neith, and consider all these symbols as mere emblems of—and means of promoting—tribal unity. Some scholars have even interpreted them as totems. But the characteristic features of totemism, such as the claim of descent from the totem, its sacrifice for a ceremonial feast of the clan, and exogamy, can not be found in Egyptian sources. Moreover, any treatment of the sacred animals which stresses their local or political significance at the expense of their religious importance flies in the face of the evidence. It is undeniable that there is something altogether peculiar about the meaning which animals possessed for the Egyptians. Elsewhere, in Africa or North America, for example, it seems that either the terror of animal strength, or the strong bond, the mutual dependence of man and beast (in the case of cattle cults, for instance), explains animal worship. But in Egypt *the animal as such,* irrespective of its specific nature, seems to possess religious significance; and the significance was so great that even the mature speculation of later times rarely dispensed with animal forms in plastic or literary images referring to the gods.

But there was nothing metaphorical in the connection between god and animal in Egypt. It is not as if certain divine qualities were made articulate by the creature, in the way the eagle elucidates the character of Zeus. We observe, on the contrary, a strange link between divinity and actual beast, so that in times of decadence animal worship may gain a horrible concreteness. Then one finds mummified cats, dogs, falcons, bulls, crocodiles, and so forth, buried by the hundreds in vast cemeteries which fill the Egyptologist with painful embarrassment—for this, we must admit, is polytheism with a vengeance. Nevertheless, these are grotesque but significant symptoms of a characteristic trait in Egyptian religion. . . .

Our rapid survey of the various relationships between gods and animals in Egypt does not clarify the role of the latter. But the very absence of a general rule and the variety of the creatures involved suggests, it seems to me, that what in these relationships became articulate was an underlying religious awe felt before all animal life; in other words, it would seem that *animals as such* possessed religious significance for the Egyptians. Their attitude might well have arisen from a religious interpretation of the animals' *otherness*. A recognition of *otherness* is implied in all specifically religious feeling. . . . We assume, then, that the Egyptian interpreted the non-human as superhuman, in particular when he saw it in animals—in their inarticulate wisdom, their certainty, their unhesitating achievement, and above all in their static reality. . . . The animals never change, and in this respect especially they would appear to share—in a degree unknown to man—the fundamental nature of creation. . . . The Egyptians viewed their living universe as a rhythmic movement contained within an unchanging whole. Even their social order reflected this view; in fact, it determined their outlook to such an extent that it can only be understood as an intu-

itive—and therefore binding—interpretation of the world order. Now humanity would not appear to exist in this manner; in human beings individual characteristics outbalance generic resemblances. But the animals exist in their unchanging species, following their predestined modes of life, irrespective of the replacement of individuals. Thus animal life would appear superhuman to the Egyptian in that it shared directly, patently, in the static life of the universe. For that reason recognition of the animals' *otherness* would be, for the Egyptian, recognition of the divine.

After reading this selection, consider these questions:

1. To what factors does Frankfort attribute the large number of Egyptian gods?
2. In what images and forms did these gods appear to the Egyptians?
3. What was the meaning of the Egyptian animal gods?

SELECTION 2:
The Myth of Osiris

Even with this great diversity, the ancient Egyptian civilization had one unifying myth. This was the story of Osiris, the ruler of the underworld, and of his queen, Isis, who saved him from eternal death. Their son, Horus, was incarnated as the reigning pharaoh. The myth of Isis and Osiris is perhaps yet another transference of an original Mother Goddess mythology. It clearly represents the continuance of a female in the natural cycle of birth, death, and rebirth, and the dominance of a male god as ruler of the universe. In this, of course, Egyptian civilization paralleled that of Mesopotamia. What made Egypt unique, however, was the greater importance that the Egyptians gave to the notion of the afterlife. Today, this may seem to be a dreary preoccupation with death. But as the following selection makes clear, this concern with death only reinforced a celebration of life.

"Homage to thee, Osiris, Lord of eternity, King of the Gods, whose names are manifold, whose forms are holy, thou being of hidden form in the temples, whose Ka is holy. Thou art the governor of Tattu (Busiris), and also the mighty one in Sekhem (Letopolis). Thou art the Lord to whom praises are ascribed in the name of Ati, thou art the Prince of divine food in Anu. Thou art the Lord who is commemorated in Maati, the Hidden Soul, the Lord of Qerrt (Elephantine), the Ruler supreme in White Wall (Memphis). Thou art the Soul of Ra, his own body, and hast thy place of rest in Henensu (Herakleopolis). Thou art the beneficent one, and art praised in Nart. Thou makest thy soul to be raised up. Thou art the Lord of the Great House in Khemenu (Hermopolis). Thou art the mighty one of victories in Shas-hetep, the Lord of eternity, the Governor of Abydos. The path of his throne is in Ta-tcheser (a part of Abydos). Thy name is established in the mouths of men. Thou art the substance of Two Lands (Egypt). Thou art Tem, the feeder of Kau (Doubles), the Governor of the Companies of the gods. Thou art the beneficent Spirit among the spirits. The god of the Celestial Ocean (Nu) draweth from thee his waters. Thou sendest forth the north wind at eventide, and breath from thy nostrils to the satisfaction of thy heart. Thy heart reneweth its youth. . . . The stars in the celestial heights are obedient unto thee, and the great doors of the sky open themselves before thee. . . . Thou art he to whom praises are ascribed in the southern heaven, and thanks are given for thee in the northern heaven. The imperishable stars are under thy supervision, and the stars which never set are thy thrones. Offerings appear before thee at the decree of Keb. The Companies of the Gods praise thee, and the gods of the Tuat (Other World) smell the earth in paying homage to thee. The uttermost parts of the earth bow before thee, and the limits of the skies entreat thee with supplications when they see thee. The holy ones are overcome before thee, and all Egypt offereth

From *The Book of the Dead*, translated by E. Wallis Budge (London: Paul, 1898).

thanksgiving unto thee when it meeteth Thy Majesty. Thou art a shining Spirit-Body, the governor of Spirit-Bodies; permanent is thy rank, established is thy rule. Thou art the well-doing Sekhem (Power) of the Company of the Gods, gracious is thy face, and beloved by him that seeth it. Thy fear is set in all the lands by reason of thy perfect love, and they cry out to thy name making it the first of names, and all people make offerings to thee. Thou art the lord who art commemorated in heaven and upon earth. Many are the cries which are made to thee at the Uak festival, and with one heart and voice Egypt raiseth cries of joy to thee.

Thou art the Great Chief, the first among thy brethren, the Prince of the Company of the Gods, the stablisher of Right and Truth throughout the World, the Son who was set on the great throne of his father Keb. Thou art the beloved of thy mother Nut, the mighty one of valour, who overthrew the Sebau-fiend. Thou didst stand up and smite thine enemy, and set thy fear in thine adversary. Thou dost bring the boundaries of the mountains. Thy heart is fixed, thy legs are set firm. Thou art the heir of Keb and of the sovereignty of the Two Lands (Egypt). He (Keb) hath seen his splendours, he hath decreed for him the guidance of the world by thy hand as long as times endure. Thou hast made this earth with thy hand, and the waters, and the winds, and the vegetation, and all the cattle, and all the feathered fowl, and all the fish, and all the creeping things, and all the wild animals thereof. The desert is the lawful possession of the son of Nut. The Two Lands (Egypt) are content to crown thee upon the throne of thy father, like Ra.

Thou rollest up into the horizon, thou hast set light over the darkness, thou sendest forth air from thy plumes, and thou floodest the Two Lands like the Disk at daybreak. Thy crown penetrateth the height of heaven, thou art the companion of the stars, and the guide of every god. Thou art beneficent in decree and speech, the favoured one of the Great Company of the Gods, and the beloved of the Little Company of the Gods.

His sister [Isis] hath protected him, and hath repulsed the fiends, and turned aside calamities (of evil). She uttered the spell with the magical power of her mouth. Her tongue was perfect, and it never halted at a word. Beneficent in command and word was Isis, the woman of magical spells, the advocate of her brother. She sought him untiringly, she wandered round and round about this earth in sorrow, and she alighted not without finding him. She made light with her feathers, she created air with her wings, and she uttered the death wail for her brother. She raised up the inactive member of whose heart was still, she drew from him his essence, she made an heir, she reared the child in loneliness, and the place where he was not known, and he grew in strength

and stature, and his hand was mighty in the House of Keb. The Company of the Gods rejoiced, rejoiced, at the coming of Horus, the son of Osiris, whose heart was firm, the triumphant, the son of Isis, the heir of Osiris.

After reading this selection, consider these questions:
1. What was the myth of Osiris?
2. Who was Isis?
3. What was the meaning of the myth of Osiris?

SELECTION 3:

The Good Life in Ancient Egypt

What seems to be a preoccupation with death did not lessen the experience and even the joyful experience of life that many Egyptians felt and sought. For long periods of Egyptian history, a good life for many was achieved, within the relatively restricted and hierarchically organized social structure available to ancient civilizations. This belief in death and rebirth was also connected with—and indeed implied—a definite moral stance toward life. Documents indicating this relation have generally been labeled "wisdom literature." They contain various wise maxims and proverbial truths. There exist comparable collections of sayings from Mesopotamia, leading some scholars to see a general flow of influences, either from east to west or from west to east. It seems safer, however, to assume that there was a common store of maxims and even stories circulating throughout the ancient Near East. Confirmation of such an international source is furthered by other evidence as well. Scholars have also identified parallels with many of the stories and proverbial sections of the Hebrew Bible. Across the boundaries of geography and even of styles of civilization, as well as across what we often improperly conceive of as "religious" differences or ethnic divisions, there appears to have been a commonality and even a shared sense within the entire ancient Near East of what was right and just in everyday life.

Some of the closest of these parallels can be seen in The Teachings of Amenemope *(excerpts of which follow) and the book of Proverbs in the Hebrew Bible.* The Teachings *clearly dates from the New Kingdom, but within this long time span it is rather difficult to specify its original date of composition. Some scholars date it as recent as 600 B.C. but most would place it either at the beginning of the first millennium B.C. or as early as 1300 B.C. during the expansionist period of the Nineteenth Dynasty. What-ever its date of composition,* The Teachings *is clearly a work of the New Kingdom. Unlike earlier forms of wisdom literature, it rejects the empha-sis on material success derived from obedience to the gods and continual ritualistic practices. Instead, Amenemope stresses the necessity of piety and the need to follow a strict moral code. Piety and morals are necessary to lead a good life in this world and to guarantee life in the afterworld. Yet what we would consider—perhaps anachronistically—as the significance of the inner dedication to moral values rather than a mere external con-formity should not hide the fact that these teachings still emphasized the importance of obedience to the gods, which characterizes both earlier forms of Egyptian religion and, as we have seen, Mesopotamian notions of conformity to the ways of the gods. Amenemope's ideal was the life of silent obedience and acceptance of one's lot in life. He teaches that piety and benevolence, rather than discontent, hot-headedness, viciousness, or ambition, results in a tranquil and fulfilled human existence.*

The Teachings of Amenemope *is divided into thirty chapters, of which only six plus the preface are reproduced here.*

PREFACE

The beginning of instruction on how to live,
Guidance for well-being;
Every direction for consorting with elders,
Rules for a courtier;
Ability to refute him who uttereth an accusation,
And to bring back a report to one who hath sent
 him.
To direct him to the path of life,
To make him prosper upon the earth;
To let his heart go into its shrine,
Steering him clear of evil;
To save him from the mouth of strangers,
Praised in the mouth of men.

HE SAYS: FIRST CHAPTER

Give thine ears, hear what is said,
Give thy mind to interpret them.
To put them in thy heart is beneficial;
It is detrimental for him who neglecteth them.
Let them rest in the casket of thy belly,
That they may be a *pnat* in thy heart.
Even when there is a whirlwind of words,
They shall be a mooring-stake for thy tongue.

From *Documents from Old Testament Times*, translated by D. Win-ton Thomas (London: Thomas Nelson, 1958). Copyright © 1958 by Thomas Nelson and Sons Ltd. Reprinted by permission of the publisher.

If thou spendest thy lifetime while this is in thy
 heart,
Thou wilt find it a success,
Thou wilt find my words a treasury of life;
Thy body will prosper upon earth. . . .

SIXTH CHAPTER

Remove not the landmark at the boundaries of
 the arable land,
Nor disturb the position of the measuring-cord;
Covet not a cubit of land,
Nor throw down the boundaries of a widow . . .
Beware of throwing down the boundaries of the
 fields,
Lest a terror carry thee off. . . .
Better is poverty in the hand of the god
Than riches in a storehouse;
Better is bread, when the heart is happy,
Than riches with vexation.

SEVENTH CHAPTER

Cast not thy heart after riches;
There is no ignoring Shay and Renent.
Place not thy heart upon externals;
Every man belongeth to his hour.
Labour not to seek for increase;
Thy needs are safe for thee.
If riches are brought to thee by robbery,

They will not spend the night with thee;
At daybreak they are not in thy house:
Their places may be seen, but they are not.
The ground has opened its mouth—'Let him
    enter that it may swallow',
They sink into the underworld.
They have made for themselves a great breach
    suitable to their size
And are sunken down in the storehouse.
They have made themselves wings like geese
And are flown away to heaven.
Rejoice not thyself (over) riches (gained) by
    robbery,
Nor groan because of poverty. . . .

ELEVENTH CHAPTER

Covet not the property of an inferior person,
Nor hunger for his bread.
As for the property of an inferior person, it is an
    obstruction to the throat,
It maketh a vomiting in the gullet.
By false oaths he hath produced it,
His heart being perverted in his body. . . .

THIRTEENTH CHAPTER

Injure not a man, [with] pen upon papyrus—
O abomination of the god!
Bear not witness with lying words,
Nor seek another's reverse with thy tongue.
Make not a reckoning with him who hath noth-
    ing,
Nor falsify thy pen.
If thou hast found a large debt against a poor man,

Make it into three parts,
Forgive two, and let one remain,
In order that thou shalt find thereby the ways of
    life.
Thou wilt lie down—the night hasteneth
    away— (lo!) thou art in the morning;
Thou hast found it like good news.
Better is praise for one who loves men
Than riches in a storehouse;
Better is bread, when the heart is happy,
Than riches with contention. . . .

TWENTY-FIRST CHAPTER

Empty not thine inmost self to everybody,
And so damage thine influence.
Spread not thine utterances to the common
    people,
Nor associate with thyself the over-
    communicative.
Better is a man who concealeth his report in his
    inmost self
Than he who speaketh it out injuriously.

After reading this selection, consider these questions:

1. What are the central values expressed in *The Teachings of Amenemope?*
2. What importance is given to material possessions in this text?
3. What are the correct ways to relate to other human beings, according to *The Teachings?*

SELECTION 4:

Aton, the One God

*The parallels between the sacred literature of Egypt and that of the an-
cient Hebrews have been pointed to by generations of scholars. In what is
called the Amarna period, the pharaoh Akhenaton introduced the worship
of a single deity, the sun god Aton. Whether this was a genuine form of
monotheism or something less original (a recognition of a general form of*

divinity in the universe) is debated. Nor have scholars settled the question of whether this innovative form of Egyptian religion was the origin of the Hebrew god or just a rearrangement of the hierarchy of Egyptian gods. Modern scholars do not go so far as a number of earlier Egyptologists, who argued that the god of Moses was essentially a form of the beliefs developed by the heretical pharaoh Akhenaton. While stressing the belief in one major unifying god symbolized in the disk of the sun, the pharaoh and his followers neither denied the existence of the other gods of Egypt nor understood Aton as a jealous god, demanding total and exclusive devotion. Nonetheless, there are remarkable parallels between the hymns to the great god Aton and certain psalms in the Bible that point to a common understanding of a single divine creation. The following is the majestic "Hymn to Aton."

Thou appearest beautifully on the horizon of heaven,
Thou living Aton, the beginning of life!
When thou art risen on the eastern horizon,
Thou hast filled every land with thy beauty.
Thou art gracious, great, glistening, and high over every land;
Thy rays encompass the lands to the limit of all that thou hast made:
As thou art Re, thou reachest to the end of everything;
Thou subduest them for thy beloved son [Akhenaton].
Though thou art far away, thy rays are on earth;
Though thou art in their faces, no one knows thy going.

When thou settest in the western horizon,
The land is in darkness, in the manner of death.
They sleep in a room, with their heads wrapped up,
Nor sees one eye the other.
All their goods which are under their heads might be stolen,
But they would not perceive it.
Every lion is come forth from his den;
All creeping things, they sting.

Darkness is a shroud, and the earth is in stillness,
For he who made them rests in his horizon.

At daybreak, when thou arisest on the horizon,
When thou shinest as the Aton by day,
Thou drivest away the darkness and givest thy rays.
The Two Lands are in festivity every day,
Awake and standing upon their feet,
For thou hast raised them up.
Washing their bodies, taking their clothing,
Their arms are raised in praise at thy appearance.
All the world, they do their work.

All beasts are content with their pasturage;
Trees and plants are flourishing.
The birds which fly from their nests,
Their wings are stretched out in praise to thy *ka*.
All beasts spring upon their feet.
Whatever flies and alights,
They live when thou hast risen for them.
The ships are sailing north and south as well,
For every way is open at thy appearance.
The fish in the river dart before thy face;
Thy rays are in the midst of the great green sea.

Creator of seed in women,
Thou who makest fluid into man,
Who maintainest the son in the womb of his mother,
Who soothest him with that which stills his weeping,

From the "Hymn to Aton," translated by John A. Wilson, in *Ancient Near Eastern Texts Relating to the Old Testament*, edited by James B. Pritchard, 3rd ed. Copyright © 1969 by Princeton University Press. Reprinted by permission of Princeton University Press.

Thou nurse even in the womb,
Who givest breath to sustain all that he has made!
When he descends from the womb to breathe
On the day when he is born,
Thou openest his mouth completely,
Thou suppliest his necessities.
When the chick in the egg speaks within the
    shell,
Thou givest him breath within it to maintain him.
When thou hast made him his fulfillment within
    the egg, to break it,
He comes forth from the egg to speak at his
    completed time;
He walks upon his legs when he comes forth
    from it.

How manifold it is, what thou hast made!
They are hidden from the face of man.
O sole god, like whom there is no other!
Thou didst create the world according to thy
    desire,

Whilst thou wert alone:
All men, cattle and wild beasts,
Whatever is on earth, going upon its feet,
And what is on high, flying with its wings.
The countries of Syria and Nubia, the land of
    Egypt,
Thou settest every man in his place,
Thou suppliest their necessities:
Everyone has his food, and his time of life is
    reckoned.
Their tongues are separate in speech,
And their natures as well;
Their skins are distinguished,
As thou distinguishest the foreign peoples.

After reading this selection, consider these
questions:
1. Who was Aton?
2. What did Aton create?
3. How did Aton differ from other Egyptian deities?

SELECTION 5:

Psalm 104

A *comparison of the "Hymn to Aton" to the Bible's Psalm 104 is remarkable and probably indicates a shared source of myths and religious
literature throughout the ancient Near East.*

Bless the LORD, O My Soul!
O LORD my God, thou art
    very great!
Thou art clothed with honor and
        majesty,
    who coverest thyself with light as
        with a garment,
who hast stretched out the heavens

    like a tent,
    who hast laid the beams of thy
        chambers on the waters,
who makest the clouds thy chariot,
    who ridest on the wings of the
        wind,
who makest the winds thy
        messengers,
    fire and flame thy ministers.

Thou didst set the earth on its
        foundations,
    so that it should never be shaken.

Psalm 104 from *The New Oxford Annotated Bible*, edited by Herbert G. May and Bruce M. Metzger (Oxford: Oxford University
Press, 1962). Copyright © 1962, 1973 Oxford University Press, Inc.

Thou didst cover it with the deep
    as with a garment;
    the waters stood above the
    mountains.
At thy rebuke they fled;
    at the sound of thy thunder they
    took to flight.
The mountains rose, the valleys
    sank down
    to the place which thou didst
    appoint for them.
Thou didst set a bound which they
    should not pass,
    so that they might not again cover
    the earth.

Thou makest springs gush forth in
    the valleys;
    they flow between the hills,
they give drink to every beast of the
    field;
    the wild asses quench their thirst.
By them the birds of the air have
    their habitation;
    they sing among the branches.
From thy lofty abode thou waterest
    the mountains;
    the earth is satisfied with the fruit
    of thy work.

Thou dost cause the grass to grow
    for the cattle,
    and plants for man to cultivate,
that he may bring forth food from
    the earth,
    and wine to gladden the heart of
    man,
oil to make his face shine,
    and bread to strengthen man's
    heart.
The trees of the LORD are watered
    abundantly,
    the cedars of Lebanon which he
    planted.
In them the birds build their nests;
    the stork has her home in the fir
    trees.
The high mountains are for the wild
    goats;
    the rocks are a refuge for the
    badgers.
Thou hast made the moon to mark
    the seasons;
    the sun knows its time for setting.
Thou makest darkness, and it is
    night,
    when all the beasts of the forest
    creep forth.
The young lions roar for their prey,
    seeking their food from God.
When the sun rises, they get them
    away
    and lie down in their dens.
Man goes forth to his work
    and to his labor until the evening.

O LORD, how manifold are thy
    works!
    In wisdom hast thou made them
    all;
    the earth is full of thy creatures.
Yonder is the sea, great and wide,
    which teems with things
    innumerable,
    living things both small and great.
There go the ships,
    and Leviathan which thou didst
    form to sport in it.

These all look to thee,
    to give them their food in due
    season.
When thou givest to them,
    they gather it up;
    when thou openest thy hand, they
    are filled with good things.
When thou hidest thy face, they
    are dismayed;
    when thou takest away their
    breath, they die
    and return to their dust.
When thou sendest forth thy spirit,
    they are created;
    and thou renewest the face of the
    ground.

May the glory of the LORD endure
   for ever,
  may the LORD rejoice in his
    works,
who looks on the earth and it
   trembles,
  who touches the mountains,
    they smoke!
I will sing to the LORD as long as I
   live;

I will sing praise to my God
   while I have being.
May my meditation be pleasing to
   him,
  for I rejoice in the LORD.
Let sinners be consumed from the
   earth,
  and let the wicked be no more!
Bless the LORD, O My Soul!
Praise the LORD!

SELECTION 6:

Moses the Egyptian

Contemporary Egyptologist Jan Assmann contrasts and compares the Egyptian and Hebrew religions. In his recent work Moses the Egyptian, *Assmann identifies the foundational roots of Western civilization.*

The distinction I am concerned with . . . is the distinction between true and false in religion that underlies more specific distinctions such as Jews and Gentiles, Christians and pagans, Muslims and unbelievers. Once the distinction is drawn, there is no end of reentries or subdistinctions. We start with Christians and pagans and end up with Catholics and Protestants, Calvinists and Lutherans, Socinians and Latitudinarians, and a thousand more similar denominations and subdenominations. Cultural or intellectual distinctions such as these construct a universe that is not only full of meaning, identity, and orientation, but also full of conflict, intolerance, and violence. Therefore, there have always been attempts to overcome the conflict by reexamining the distinction, albeit at the risk of losing cultural meaning.

Let us call the distinction between true and false in religion the "Mosaic distinction" because

tradition ascribes it to Moses. We cannot be sure that Moses ever lived because there are no traces of his earthly existence outside the tradition. But we can be sure that he was not the first to draw the distinction. There was a precursor in the person of an Egyptian king who called himself Akhenaten and instituted a monotheistic religion in the fourteenth century B.C.E. His religion, however, spawned no tradition but was forgotten immediately after his death. Moses is a figure of memory but not of history, while Akhenaten is a figure of history but not of memory. Since memory is all that counts in the sphere of cultural distinctions and constructions, we are justified in speaking not of Akhenaten's distinction, but of the Mosaic distinction. The space severed or cloven by this distinction is the space of Western monotheism. It is this constructed mental or cultural space that has been inhabited by Europeans for nearly two millennia.

It is an error to believe that this distinction is as old as religion itself, though at first sight nothing might seem more plausible. Does not every religion quite automatically put everything outside itself in the position of error and falsehood and look down on other religions as "paganism"? Is this not quite simply the religious expression of ethnocentricity? Does not the distinction between true and false in reality amount to nothing other than the distinction between "us" and "them"? Does not every construction of identity by the very same process generate alterity? Does not every religion produce "pagans" in the same way that every civilization generates "barbarians"?

However plausible this may seem, it is not the case. Cultures not only generate otherness by constructing identity, but also develop techniques of translation. We have to distinguish here between the "real other," who is always there beyond the individual and independent of the individual's constructions of selfhood and otherhood, and the "constructed other," who is the shadow of the individual's identity. Moreover, we have to realize that in most cases we are dealing not with the "real other," but with our constructions and projections of the other. "Paganism" and "idolatry" belong to such constructions of the other. It is this inevitable construction of cultural otherness that is to a certain degree compensated by techniques of translation. Translation in this sense is not to be confused with the colonializing appropriation of the "real" other. It is simply an attempt to make more transparent the borders that were erected by cultural distinctions.

Ancient polytheisms functioned as such a technique of translation. They belong within the emergence of the "Ancient World" as a coherent ecumene of interconnected nations. The polytheistic religions overcame the primitive ethnocentrism of tribal religions by distinguishing several deities by name, shape, and function. The names are, of course, different in different cultures, because the languages are different. The shapes of the gods and the forms of worship may also differ significantly. But the functions are strikingly similar, especially in the case of cosmic deities; and most deities had a cosmic function. The sun god of one religion is easily equated to the sun god of another religion, and so forth. Because of their functional equivalence, deities of different religions can be equated. In Mesopotamia, the practice of translating divine names goes back to

the third millennium B.C.E. In the second millennium, this practice was extended to many different languages and civilizations of the Near East. The cultures, languages, and customs may have been as different as ever: the religions always had a common ground. Thus they functioned as a means of intercultural translatability. The gods were international because they were cosmic. The different peoples worshipped different gods, but nobody contested the reality of foreign gods and the legitimacy of foreign forms of worship. The distinction I am speaking of simply did not exist in the world of polytheistic religions.

The Mosaic distinction was therefore a radically new distinction which considerably changed the world in which it was drawn. The space which was "severed or cloven" by this distinction was not simply the space of religion in general, but that of a very specific kind of religion. We may call this new type of religion "counter-religion" because it rejects and repudiates everything that went before and what is outside itself as "paganism." It no longer functioned as a means of intercultural translation; on the contrary, it functioned as a means of intercultural estrangement. Whereas polytheism, or rather "cosmotheism," rendered different cultures mutually transparent and compatible, the new counter-religion blocked intercultural translatability. False gods cannot be translated.

All cultural distinctions need to be remembered in order to render permanent the space which they construct. Usually, this function of remembering the fundamental distinctions assumes the form of a "Grand Narrative," a master story that underlies and informs innumerable concrete tellings and retellings of the past. The Mosaic distinction between true and false in religion finds its expression in the story of Exodus. This means that it is symbolized by the constellation or opposition of Israel and Egypt. Books 2 through 5 of the Pentateuch unfold the distinction in a narrative and in a normative form. Narratively, the distinction is represented by the story of Israel's Exodus out of Egypt. Egypt thereby came to symbolize the rejected, the religiously wrong, the "pagan." As a consequence, Egypt's most conspicuous practice, the worship of images, came to be regarded as the greatest sin. Normatively, the distinction is expressed in a law code which conforms with the narrative in giving the prohibition of "idolatry" first priority. In the space that is constructed by the Mosaic distinction, the worship of images came to be regarded as the absolute horror, falsehood, and apostasy. Polytheism and idolatry were seen as the same form of religious error. The second commandment is a commentary on the first:

1. Thou shalt have no other gods before me.

2. Thou shalt not make unto thee any graven image.

Images are automatically "other gods," because the true god is invisible and cannot be iconically represented.

Both the story and the law code are symbolically expressive of the Mosaic distinction. The story is more than simply an account of historical events, and the Law is more than merely a basis for social order and religious purity. In addition to what they overtly tell and establish, they symbolize the distinction. Exodus is a symbolical story, the Law is a symbolical legislation, and Moses is a symbolical figure. The whole constellation of Israel and Egypt is symbolical and comes to symbolize all kinds of oppositions. But the leading one is the distinction between true religion and idolatry.

Both the concept of idolatry and the repudiation of it grew stronger and stronger in the course of Jewish history. The later the texts, the more elaborate the scorn and abomination which they heap on the idolators. . . .

This hatred was mutual and the "idolators" did not fail to retaliate. Understandably enough, most of them were Egyptians. For example, the Egyptian priest Manetho, who wrote an Egyptian history under Ptolemy II, represented Moses as a rebellious Egyptian priest who made himself the leader of a colony of lepers. Whereas the Jews depicted idolatry as a kind of mental aberration, of madness, the Egyptians associated iconoclasm with the idea of a highly contagious and bodily disfiguring epidemic. . . .

It is important to realize that we are dealing here with a strong mutual loathing that is rooted not in idiosyncratic aversions of Jews and Egyp-

tians but in the Mosaic distinction as such, which was originally Akhenaten's distinction. . . .

Monotheistic religions structure the relationship between the old and the new in terms not of evolution but of revolution, and reject all older and other religions as "paganism" or "idolatry." Monotheism always appears as a counter-religion. There is no natural or evolutionary way leading from the error of idolatry to the truth of monotheism. This truth can come only from outside, by way of revelation. The narrative of the Exodus emphasizes the temporal meaning of the religious antagonism between monotheism and idolatry. "Egypt" stands not only for "idolatry" but also for a past that is rejected. The Exodus is a story of emigration and conversion, of transformation and renovation, of stagnation and progress, and of past and future. Egypt represents the old, while Israel represents the new. The geographical border between the two countries assumes a temporal meaning and comes to symbolize two epochs in the history of humankind. The same figure reproduces itself on another level with the opposition between the "Old" and the "New" Testaments. Conversion presupposes and constructs an opposition between "old" and "new" in religion.

Remembering Egypt could fulfill two radically different functions. First, it could support the distinction between true religion and idolatry. We may call this function of memory the "memory of conversion." In the context of Jewish and Christian ritual memory, the memory of the Exodus forms and supports an identity of conversion. Conversion defines itself as the result of an overcoming and a liberation from one's own past which is no longer one's own. Remembering their disowned past is obligatory for converts in order not to relapse. "Those who cannot remember the past are condemned to repeat it" (George Santayana [an American philosopher]). Remembering is an act of constant disowning. Egypt must be remembered in order to know what lies in the past, and what must not be allowed to come back. The theme of remembering is therefore central to the Exodus myth and to the constellation of Egypt and Israel. This is not only a myth to be remembered but a myth about remembering, a myth about past and future. It remembers the past in order to win future. Idolatry means forgetting and regression; monotheism means remembering and progression.

Second, and inversely, remembering Egypt is important for an attempt to reexamine the Mosaic distinction. We may call this function of memory the "deconstructive memory." If the space of religious truth is constructed by the distinction between "Israel in truth" and "Egypt in error," any discoveries of Egyptian truths will necessarily invalidate the Mosaic distinction and deconstruct the space separated by this distinction.

After reading this selection, consider these questions:

1. What does Assmann argue concerning the nature of "otherness" in religion?
2. What were the distinctions between the religion of ancient Egypt and that of ancient Israel?
3. According to Assmann, what were the historical consequences of "the Mosaic distinction"?

CHAPTER 3
Ancient Israel and the Origins of Monotheism

It should now be clear that the various cultures of the ancient Near East developed into very distinctive civilizations. Yet, paradoxically, they also shared many common features and common sets of symbols of their divinities, common stories, and even common moral attitudes. This play of similarities and differences, of identity and difference, indicates one aspect of perhaps all higher civilizations, including the civilization that will eventually be identified as specifically Western. Major civilizations are not totally original; neither do they develop simply out of themselves alone. Even the relatively isolated existence of ancient Egypt indicates something of a back-and-forth movement of cultural influences.

These problems arise again when we turn our attention to the civilization of ancient Israel. With its powerful and apparently all-pervasive notion of a single and absolute God, the people of ancient Israel seem to have stood out from all the other people of the ancient Near East. Sumer and Babylon and all the successive kingdoms that dominated Mesopotamia believed in a great number of gods. More importantly, they comprehended the nature of reality as well as of divinity in terms of the forces, especially the fructifying forces, that pervade nature, bringing forth crops and generating humans and animals. Even when these basic forces identified with the Mother Goddess were suppressed by other, male deities, the female deities were neither fully destroyed nor totally forgotten. As we have seen in the myths of Marduk and of Osiris, female goddesses were only displaced—subdued, propitiated, or married—but never entirely eliminated.

The ancient Hebrew belief in Jehovah—Yahweh (YHVH), or the Lord (Elohim)—appears to mark a radical break and a new departure from other Near Eastern systems of belief. Until recently scholars supported this commonly held assumption. More recent historical scholarship and archaeological research points, as we have seen in the "Hymn to Aton," to a whole range of parallels and even common sources for many of the texts of the Hebrew Bible. Earlier notions of the uniqueness of Hebrew conceptions of divinity and of the moral code that followed from it may have been influenced by our modern sense of God and ethics and of the clear continuity between Hebrew civilization and our own. But it would be a mistake to think of this more recent scholarship as overthrowing older lines of interpretation. The question should be focused less on the question of the uniqueness of the Hebrew experience of divinity and more on how ancient Israel's common understanding of the nature of mankind and of the world developed into a very different comprehension of God, nature, and the moral life. Again, through an understanding of the similarities and differences, we can understand both the commonalities of the civilizations of the ancient Near East and the features that made them unique.

SELECTION 1:

The Uniqueness of the Hebrew Religion

Historian Stewart C. Easton emphasizes the particular qualities of the Hebrew religion and discusses the implications that the belief in one God had for the understanding of Hebrew ethics. He then contrasts the moral stance of the Babylonians with that of the Israelites.

The Hebrews are, of course, credited above all with the formulation of monotheism, the worship of one God; and this monotheism has been transmitted both to Christianity and to Islam, so that it is the fundamental religious belief of the West. But it is not always recognized that they are also responsible for the precise definition of the nature of sin; and their thought upon the question of sin and punishment has permeated Western thought as deeply as has the concept of monotheism itself. . . .

The supreme consequence of the Hebrew concept is in the field of human morality. Because God is a person, he can take part in human affairs, guiding them, rewarding and punishing his children, thus upholding the moral order. This monotheism is clearly an advance on Mesopotamian thought, since the many gods of the Babylonians were conceived of as so many arbitrary but powerful beings competing for man's worship. Each man had a personal god who was expected to use his influence with the higher gods on behalf of his protégé, as human beings use political influence to ensure personal favors. And among the higher gods it was impossible for a man to choose which to petition. He could not tell which one he had offended, nor did he know what was demanded of him.

Polytheism cannot escape the dilemma that the different gods may issue contradictory demands; unless these gods may be said to have agreed among themselves on what to demand from man, their different commands will necessarily at some time conflict with each other. The separate gods can only reward and punish in accordance with their limited power, and thus cannot command obedience from man and insist upon it on pain of punishment. Shamash, the Babylonian god of the sun and of justice, might give Hammurabi a code of laws, but it was only by virtue of his function as lawgiver among the numerous Babylonian gods. The Babylonian did not regard him as the enforcer of the laws, nor did he pray to Shamash to mitigate his severity. This was the task of the personal god of the Babylonian, who used his influence among his superiors in the pantheon.

But the Hebrew God, being one, not a force of nature but a transcendent being, separate from the world yet immanent in it, could act as ruler and governor, first of his chosen people and then of the whole world. He could issue a law which instructed the people as to exactly what he expected of them, could define disobedience to the law as sin, and could take steps to see that he was obeyed. The law thus removed any doubt in the sinner's mind as to what he was expected to do, and what was forbidden him, and held out the hope that if he fulfilled these duties toward God he would be prosperous and happy. . . . The following quotations from Babylonian and Hebrew documents will serve to point the contrast between the two attitudes, and reveal at the same time how greatly the Hebrew felt he had been privileged when God gave him his Law.

The Babylonian: "What is good in one's sight is evil for a god, what is bad in one's own mind is good for his god. Who can understand the counsel of the gods in the midst of heaven? Where has befuddled mankind ever learned what a god's conduct is?" Again: "Man is dumb; he knows nothing. Mankind, everyone that exists—what does he know? Whether he is committing sin or doing good he does not even know."

The Hebrew: "I have stored thy message in my heart that I may not sin against thee. . . . With my lips I recount all the ordinances of thy mouth. In the way of thy decrees I delight, as much as in all wealth. I meditate upon thy precepts, and I observe thy paths. I find joy in thy statutes, I will not forget thy word. . . . At midnight I rise up to give thee thanks because of thy righteous ordinances . . . the law of thy mouth is worth more to me than thousands in gold and silver."

Hebrew monotheism, then, with its consequent belief that God rewarded and punished men in accordance with their deeds, has been of incalculable importance in the religious and psychological history of mankind.

After reading this selection, consider these questions:
1. What, according to Easton, are the chief differences between monotheism and polytheism?
2. What was the relationship between God and the law in ancient Babylonia and ancient Israel?
3. What was the historical significance of the Hebrew understanding of God?

SELECTION 2:

The Hebrew Creation Story

The Hebrew understanding of divinity entails a different way of comprehending how to relate to God and how to act. As Stewart C. Easton points out in the previous selection, moral action for the Hebrews entailed a type of inner commitment by the individual, not just a search for specific, and most often material, rewards from the gods. For the Hebrews, the good life is the righteous life. One lives piously, attempting to follow as best one can the law that God has given to "the Children of Israel." Through a life thus lived, one grows in the ways of God, one "walks uprightly in the way of the Lord." Even the patriarchs—Abraham, Isaac, and Jacob—although beloved of God did not begin as righteous individuals; they developed into wise men.

Who was this God of the Hebrews? Singularity, jealousy, and exclusiveness were his distinctive traits as well as absoluteness and (at least eventually) universality. The gods of Mesopotamia and of Egypt shared none of these characteristics. One main reason why the civilizations of the ancient Near East survived for so long was that older and often more local gods could be associated and even identified with new and more general gods. In Egypt this took place with the merging of the various villages into an upper and lower kingdom and then into one unified state with one encompassing state religion. In Mesopotamia, with its more marked changes as various cities and empires came to dominance, this process was even more dramatic: Alien gods took on the characteristics and sometimes the names of the earlier deities. Historians of religion call this process syncretism, and it is a quality that most of the religions of the world share, including the forms of belief of ancient Greece and Rome.

The Hebrew God was different. In the time of Moses, the Hebrew religion was not the entire belief system it would become later. It was probably not even monotheistic (recognizing a single deity) but rather monolatristic (worshiping a single god while recognizing the existence of others). But once monotheism was fully developed, around the year 1000 B.C., God could not be identified with other deities. He was jealous of other gods and makes this point clear. Likewise, he did not contend with other or even lesser deities; he alone was the origin and end of creation, the meaning of being, and the only guide for the moral conduct of men and women. There was also no ultimate common reality behind God, as seemed to be the underlying assumption behind a syncretist understanding of divinity—each individual god or name of the god was only a vague sense of the power behind it. The Hebrew God was exclusive, and not just in the sense that he demanded full and unchallenged devotion but that he did not recognize the power of these other deities. They were all false *deities; they were devils. If syncretism helps explain the continuum of the major ancient Near Eastern civilizations, this does not mean that exclusivity results in its opposite. In fact, the reverse seems to be the case. The jealousy of the God of the Hebrews not only resulted in the persistence of the Jewish people and of the Hebrew religion (the celebration of the Passover commemorating the exodus from Egypt is the oldest known continuous religious festival) but also in the rise of two other world religions, Christianity and Islam.*

The distinctive nature of the Hebrew experience of God and of the moral consequences of such a belief can be increased, and several of the following readings will point to a number of them. Before we look at them, however, let us read the opening passages of the Hebrew Bible. Compare this creation account to the one presented in the Babylonian creation myth.

In the beginning God created the heavens and the earth. The earth was without form and void, and darkness was upon the face of the deep; and the Spirit of God was moving over the face of the waters.

And God said, "Let there be light"; and there was light. And God saw that the light was good; and God separated the light from the darkness. God called the light Day, and the darkness he called Night. And there was evening and there was morning, one day.

And God said, "Let there be a firmament in the midst of the waters, and let it separate the waters from the waters." And God made the firmament and separated the waters which were under the firmament from the waters which were above the firmament. And it was so. And God called the firmament Heaven. And there was evening and there was morning, a second day.

And God said, "Let the waters under the heavens be gathered together into one place, and let the dry land appear." And it was so. God called the dry land Earth, and the waters that were gathered together he called Seas. And God saw that it was good. And God said, "Let the earth put forth vegetation, plants yielding seed, and fruit trees bearing fruit in which is their seed, each according to its kind, upon the earth." And it was so. The earth brought forth vegetation, plants yielding seed according to their own kinds, and trees bearing fruit in which is their seed, each according to its kind. And God saw that it was good. And there was evening and there was morning, a third day.

And God said, "Let there be lights in the firmament of the heavens to separate the day from the night; and let them be for signs and for seasons and for days and years, and let them be lights in the firmament of the heavens to give light upon the earth." And it was so. And God made the two great lights, the greater light to rule the day, and the lesser light to rule the night; he made the stars also. And God set them in the firmament of the heavens to give light upon the earth, to rule over the day and over the night, and to separate the light from the darkness. And God saw that it was good. And there was evening and there was morning, a fourth day.

And God said, "Let the waters bring forth swarms of living creatures, and let birds fly above the earth across the firmament of the heavens." So God created the great sea monsters and every living creature that moves, with which the waters swarm, according to their kinds, and every winged bird according to its kind. And God saw that it was good. And God blessed them, saying, "Be fruitful and multiply and fill the waters in the seas, and let birds multiply on the earth." And there was evening and there was morning, a fifth day.

And God said, "Let the earth bring forth living creatures according to their kinds: cattle and creeping things and beasts of the earth according to their kinds." And it was so.

And God made the beasts of the earth according to their kinds and the cattle according to their kinds, and everything that creeps upon the ground according to its kind. And God saw that it was good.

Then God said, "Let us make man in our image, after our likeness; and let them have dominion over the fish of the sea, and over the birds of the air, and over the cattle, and over all the earth, and over every creeping thing that creeps upon the earth." So God created man in his own image, in the image of God he created him; male and female he created them. And God blessed them, and God said to them, "Be fruitful and multiply, and fill the earth and subdue it; and have dominion over the fish of the sea and over the birds of the air and over every living thing that moves upon the earth." And God said, "Behold, I have given you every plant yielding seed which is upon the face of all the earth, and every tree with seed in its fruit; you shall have them for food.

And to every beast of the earth, and to every bird of the air, and to everything that creeps on the earth, everything that has the breath of life, I have given every green plant for food." And it was so. And God saw everything that he had made, and behold, it was very good. And there was evening and there was morning, a sixth day.

Genesis 1:1–31, from *The New Oxford Annotated Bible*, edited by Herbert G. May and Bruce M. Metzger (Oxford: Oxford University Press, 1962). Copyright © 1962, 1973 Oxford University Press, Inc.

SELECTION 3:

The Common Roots of Religion in the Ancient Near East

On first reading, the contrasts between the Hebrew and the Babylonian creation stories seems marked. Aside from overall notions of gods creating out of an abyss or nothingness, there seems little point of comparison. Egyptologist John Romer, however, finds a number of significant parallels in the two accounts. He even sees a derivation, or better yet a transformation, of the Babylonian and ultimately Sumerian myth of creation in the biblical account. Romer begins the following selection from his book Testament: The Bible and History *with an examination of the Hebrew creation story.*

God's grand division of light and darkness marks out all the later events of his Creation: God has made himself a clock and with it he will measure out the making of his world in seven units; seven days.

'Man may mock at Moses and Sabbaths', a seventeenth-century New England puritan pithily observed, 'but neither doctors nor infidels can make a typhoid fever turn except upon the seventh day'. The preacher had seen that the entire Bible was haunted by sevens: the pull of the number runs through the Old and New Testaments. The world, created in seven days, was revived, he knew, by the Seven Last Words of Jesus on the cross; it will be undone with the Seven Seals of the Book of Revelations and returned to the keeping of Almighty God, at its ending, at the blast of seven trumpets. Nor was Jehovah the first Creator to base his universe upon a system of sevens. The *Enuma Elish*, the story of the creation of Mesopotamia and man, which was recited in the temples of Ur and Haran as in every Mesopotamian temple every year for some 4000 years and more,

also ordered its story in seven units, in seven generations of a family of gods.

And the convergence runs far beyond this magic number. Just as in the first three days of Genesis' Creation, Jehovah makes the elements of the world, so, in the *Enuma Elish*, the first three generations of gods are the gods of water, silt, and sky, the elements of the Mesopotamian world. And just as in the fourth, fifth and sixth days of Genesis' Creation, God makes the animate world, so, in the *Enuma Elish*, the fourth, fifth and sixth generation of gods are gods of moving things. Jehovah makes the sun, moon and stars of the calendar on the fourth day; so the male deity of the fourth generation of *Enuma Elish* is Anu, the god of heaven. Just as Jehovah rests after these six days and then makes man, so the god Marduk too of the sixth generation of *Enuma Elish*, creates man so that the Mesopotamian gods might rest. The two stories, the two universes are built of the same bricks. And both of them build the same environment: not Iceland, nor New England nor even ancient Israel, but a south Mesopotamian landscape where the sweet waters of the Tigris and Euphrates empty into the salt waters of the Persian Gulf, where there are cloudless dawns with no horizon to be seen in the morning haze. And slowly, the dark rivers drop their silty islands in the delta, and the sun, rising, burns through the cloud and then, in the blue-hazed sky, the earth and heavens both suddenly appear. At different times, in many different cities, the gods of *Enuma Elish* have changed their names, as does the hero of the flood story. But nonetheless, it is always the same Mesopotamian landscapes that these gods make, the same story that they act out. And their great saga clearly holds priority over Genesis. For the god Jehovah of the hardy tribes of hilly Israel orders a Mesopotamian creation, a distant memory of that wide, well-watered plain.

Like Adam's world outside Eden, Mesopotamia gave its people a hard uncertain life. Eden, indeed, was typical of thousands of walled gardens that sheltered kitchen crops and orchards from the sweeping rains, violent storms and the driven sand that constantly encroached from the deserts of the west to smother the ancient fields. Not only was Mesopotamia erratically devastated by this harsh climate but it was also raided and sacked periodically by nomads sweeping down from the surrounding mountains. And this violence, this continual tragedy, is movingly reflected in the cuneiform literature of the ancient cities, in tragic myths that alone survived their empires and their mud cities now dissolved away. How strange it is to watch as Genesis' scribes re-cast the violent saga of *Enuma Elish* to hold the solitary majesty of Jehovah, this ancient poem that the priests of the ancient cities chanted from the doorways of their temples each New Year's Day.

Enuma Elish la nabu shamanu, they began, 'When, on high, the heavens were not yet named', then, the story tells, there were only the gods Tiamat and Apsu, the deities of the sweet rivers and the salt seas. And the mixing of these waters with Mammu, the god of form, made the gods of the silt banks, Lahmu and Lahamu. In their turn they generated the gods of the horizons, Kinshar and Anshar, and they engendered the god of heaven, Anu, whose son was Ea, the god of the earth. Ea is the fifth generation; his son Marduk will make man and Mesopotamia itself.

Just as in the story of Abraham and Sarah, the story of *Enuma Elish* also grapples with the contradiction of ancestral purity and unlawful incest.

The entire saga is a serpentine and claustrophobic tale of seven generations of family passions. It begins with Apsu, the great patriarch resolving to kill all his descendants for making so much noise. But Ea, his great-grandson, kills him first, rousing Tiamat, Apsu's wife, to fury. Leading a host of demons, she and a new husband declare war upon the rest of the family, and so paralysed with fear are they all, that even crafty Ea cannot think of a ruse to save them. Then Marduk, the youngest of them all, offers to be their champion if they will accept him as their king, and this they gladly do. So Marduk goes off to war, routs the demon army and, catching Tiamat in a net, drives a tempest into her open mouth;

> the fierce wind filled her belly,
> her inside conjested and retching
> she opened wide her mouth.
> He let fly an arrow, it split her belly,
> cut through her inward parts
> and gashed her heart.
> He held her fast, extinguished her life.

Then Marduk smashes Tiamat's skull and orders the wind to return her spilled blood which blows in across the Mesopotamian plain like the rains of a storm. Marduk then splits her carcass in half to make heaven and earth and, from the arch of her legs, a vault to support the sky. Tiamat's head he buries under a mountain, piercing her eyes so that the Tigris and Euphrates can flow from them. Marduk has made Mesopotamia his royal estate. And he has set the stage for man. Kingu, Tiamat's second husband, is brought before the other gods and slaughtered. 'Arteries' says Marduk 'I will knot . . . I will create *lullu* and man will be his name . . .' The slave is put to work to finish a ziggurat which the gods were labouring to build for King Marduk; and which, the saga states, is the Tower of Babel at Babylon.

At first glance it seems highly improbable that such unholy mayhem could underpin the magisterial Creation of Jehovah in the Book of Genesis. Yet it does. Not only are the six building blocks of these two worlds the same, but the problems of emotion and intellect that are dealt with in Genesis and in *Enuma Elish* are also very similar. The differences are largely those of structure: Genesis separates the intense dramas of *Enuma Elish* into two halves. In the first, the abstract creation of Jehovah is played out alone; all the forces that drive *Enuma Elish,* jealousy, rage, all the underlying conflicts of incest and purity, are quite absent. In Genesis they will appear in the stories of the first generations of man. An essential difference, however, is that *Enuma Elish* not only describes the creation of the human race, but gives the ancestry of its creator too. And that Genesis cannot do, for Jehovah alone is the fount of all things.

With this solitary universal Creation, all the passions that the Mesopotamians thought were omnipresent, as natural as the winds, must be carefully invented and introduced inside the Book of Genesis. So Adam is first made innocent and unknowing, a blank slate. Then the subtle serpent faces Eve with two choices; sin and wisdom or the lack of them. After their liberative bite of the apple, Jehovah expels his first two people, now properly human, from their timeless Eden into the hard Mesopotamian plain. Unlike Abraham, Adam and Eve are not nomads, but farmers. (One ancient rabbi commented that the angels must have helped Adam in his first year away from Paradise'so that he did not fall behind with his ploughing'.) The subsequent founding of the race (Genesis 4:1) is part of the consequence of their fall, the knowledge of the Tree of Good and Evil. So the conundrum of incest that must always accompany stories of the first family is resolved, as it is again with Abraham and his family, by showing it as the lesser of two evils when faced with the necessity of procreation.

Enuma Elish takes another route in its resolution of incest. It separates Marduk, man's creator, from his partner, Tiamat, by several generations and then obscures their passion in the smoke of battle. Marduk tears into his partner with the ferocity of a psychopath, his arrows pierce her womb; Tiamat is a defeated enemy, not a lover. She is butchered to make Mesopotamia; her second husband, dispatched with all the resentment of an abandoned child, is also butchered; 'blood is massed and bones are caused to be'. And man is made mechanically.

Cultured Mesopotamians saw their civilization

as descending from a wild natural force that was changed into a sacred, civilizing order by the mediation of Marduk. When he goes off to do battle with Tiamat, Marduk's grandfather, the god of heaven, gives him the four winds that will later stop up Tiamat's mouth and, in exchange, he gives his grandfather a quiver full of arrows: works of civilization borne on the natural winds. Gross and terrifying as he is, though he raids the corpses of his family to make Mesopotamia and man, it is Marduk that mediates between wild nature and the culture of mankind.

This subtle dialectic of natural force and civilization appears in Genesis in the stories of Adam's family. Eve's two children are the founders of pastoral and urban society; Abel, the herdsman and hunter, lives in the West; Cain, the farmer, to the East of Eden with the sunrise and renewal. And both of them live in the Mesopotamian landscape of Tiamat. Cain, the first man to live apart from God, has his offerings rejected by Jehovah. But it is Cain who builds the first city and, when he murders his blameless brother, Jehovah does not punish him but marks him so that all will see that he is divinely protected. Cain's killing of Abel is a sacrifice that Jehovah accepts. Cain the murderer, the founder of cities, is the founder of civilization.

In separating the moods of man from the manufacture of the universe in this way, the opening chapter of Genesis has put the ancient gods on trial. In Genesis, man in all his wisdom takes responsibility. Just as Genesis' first people generate sin and anger and separation from God, so they also generate freedom. In the Book of Genesis, mankind is not God's slave—'let him be burdened with the toil of the gods' Marduk says— nor does emotion run as free, as natural as the winds; it is all accounted for in the world of man. And Jehovah, without beginning or end, the creator of everything, has become a lonely figure replacing an entire pantheon. But still the grand story is conducted inside the Mesopotamian order of the universe and on the Mesopotamian plain. And the tensions and pressures of that ancient fratricidal family of gods, bound and repelled inside relationships of love and hatred, have, through the Bible, given us a universe filled with the sense of a dynamic system of relationships. A model that scientists still use. And this whole process began when the sagas of Mesopotamia were carefully re-examined by the authors of Genesis and the thoughts and structures of that most ancient story were turned to the purposes of Israel and their most singular and solitary God.

After reading this selection and the previous one, consider these questions:

1. What are the parallels between the Hebrew and the Mesopotamian myths of creation?
2. What are the major differences between the two myths?
3. What does Romer mean when he says that the opening chapter of Genesis puts the Mesopotamian gods on trial?

SELECTION 4:

The Name of God

John Romer's point in the previous selection is not to deny the uniqueness of the Hebrew experience of God or of the distinctive quality of the Hebrew Bible. What should claim our attention is the fact that from a common set of stories and myths, of wise sayings and moral precepts, the Hebrews created something very different, if not entirely new. As Romer indicates, the Hebrew reworking of the story of Marduk transforms the basic meaning of creation and the nature of the divine spirit that informed this creation, and transvalues its basic conception of the good life and the meaning of human existence. We must understand this transformation—as well as realize that, even in this indirect manner, our own view of the world is connected to the development of the earliest cities and even the Neolithic Revolution—in order to comprehend the civilization of the West.

The great twentieth-century Jewish philosopher Martin Buber studied the Hebrew experience of divinity. He was concerned less with uncovering the common Near Eastern sources of this experience or of the sources of the Hebrew Bible than with comprehending in its full depth and power the nature of the experience of the great creator God. For our purposes Buber does not so much challenge or contradict the more recent account of scholars like Romer, but rather speaks to a different concern and develops another dimension of the same notion of divinity.

The selection from Buber's The Revelation and the Covenant *concentrates on God's name and the power in the revelation of his name. He turns specifically to the famous passage in which Moses, exiled in the desert of the Sinai, confronted God for the first time. Before turning to Buber, let us look at the passage in Genesis.*

Moses was minding the flock of his father-in-law Jethro, priest of Midian. He led the flock along the side of the wilderness and came to Horeb, the mountain of God. There the angel of the LORD appeared to him in the flame of a burning bush. Moses noticed that, although the bush was on fire, it was not being burnt up; so he said to himself, 'I must go across to see this wonderful sight. Why does not the bush burn away?' When the LORD saw that Moses had turned aside to look, He called to him out of the bush, 'Moses, Moses.' And Moses answered, 'Yes, I am here.' God said, 'Come no nearer; take off your sandals; the place where you are standing is holy ground.' Then he said, 'I am the God of your forefathers, the God of Abraham, the God of Isaac, the God of Jacob.' Moses covered his face, for he was afraid to gaze on God.

The LORD said, 'I have indeed seen the misery of my people in Egypt. I have heard their outcry against their slave-masters. I have taken heed of their sufferings, and have come down to rescue them from the power of Egypt, and to bring them up out of that country into a fine, broad land; it is a land flowing with milk and honey, the home of Canaanites, Hittites, Amorites, Perizzites, Hivites, and Jebusites. The outcry of the Israelites has now reached me; yes, I have seen the brutality of the Egyptians towards them. Come now; I will send you to Pharaoh and you shall bring my people Israel out of Egypt.' 'But who am I', Moses said to God, 'that I should go to Pharaoh, and that I should bring the Israelites out of Egypt?' God answered, 'I am with you. This shall be the proof that it is I who have sent you: when you have brought the people out of Egypt, you shall all worship God here on this mountain.'

Then Moses said to God, 'If I go to the Israelites and tell them that the God of their forefathers has sent me to them, and they ask me His name, what shall I say?' God answered, 'I AM; that is who I am. Tell them that I AM has sent you to them.' And God said further, 'You must tell the Israelites this, that it is JEHOVAH the God of their forefathers, the God of Abraham, the God of Isaac, the God of Jacob, who has sent you to them. This is my name for ever; this is my title in every generation. Go and assemble the elders of Israel and tell them that JEHOVAH the God of their forefathers, the God of Abraham, Isaac and Jacob, has appeared to you and has said, "I have indeed turned my eyes towards you; I have marked all that has been done to you in Egypt, and I am resolved to bring you up out of your misery in Egypt, into the country of the Canaanites, Hittites, Amorites, Perizzites, Hivites, and Jebusites, a land flowing with milk and honey." They will listen to you, and then you and the elders of Israel must go to the king of Egypt. Tell him, "It has happened that the LORD the God of the Hebrews met us. So now give us leave to go a three days' journey into the wilderness to offer sacrifice to the LORD our God." I know well that the king of Egypt will not give you leave unless he is compelled. I shall then stretch out my hand and assail the Egyptians with all the miracles I shall work among them. After that he will send you away. Further, I will bring this people into such favour with the Egyptians that, when you go, you will not go empty-handed. Every woman shall ask her neighbour or any woman who lives in her house for jewellery of silver and gold and for clothing. Load your sons and daughters with them, and plunder Egypt.'

SELECTION 5:

The Revelation

Before explicating this passage, Martin Buber challenges our all-too-easy notions of monotheism (and by extension, polytheism) in understanding not just ancient Hebrew religion but also modern forms of belief in a single deity.

It is a fundamental error to register the faith with which I deal as simple "Monotheism." Here may be applied what was written half a century ago by Paul Yorck von Wartenberg to the philosopher Wilhelm Dilthey, his friend and my master: "I should consider it desirable for an attempt to be made to disregard all these categories, Pantheism, Monotheism, Theism, Panentheism. In themselves they have no religious value whatsoever, being only formal and of quantitative character. They reflect views of the world and not views of God, and constitute only the outline of an intellectual attitude; and only a formal projection even for this." It is not so decisive whether the existence of a Unity exalted over all is assumed in one's consideration, but the way in which this Unity is viewed and experienced, and whether one stands to it in an exclusive relationship which shapes all other relations and thereby the whole order of life. Within the so-called Monotheism the concrete difference of the images of God and the vital relations with God made incisions which are sometimes far more important than the boundaries between a particular "Monotheism" and a particular "Polytheism." The universal sun-god of the imperialist "Monotheism" of Amenhotep IV [Akhenaton] is incomparably more close to the national sun-god of the ancient Egyptian Pantheon than to the God of early Israel, which some have endeavoured to derive from him.

From *Moses: The Revelation and the Covenant*, by Martin Buber (New York: Harper & Row, 1958). Reprinted by permission of the Balkin Agency as agent for the Estate of Martin Buber.

What is important for us about this God of Moses is the association of qualities and activities which is peculiar to Him. He is the One who brings His own out, He is their leader and advance guard; prince of the people, legislator and the sender of a great message. He acts at the level of history on the peoples and between the peoples. What He aims at and cares for is a people. He makes His demand that the people shall be entirely "His" people, a "holy" people; that means, a people whose entire life is hallowed by justice and loyalty, a people for God and for the world. And He is and does all this as a manifesting, addressing and revealing God. He is invisible and "lets Himself be seen," whatever may be the natural phenomena or historical process in which He may desire to let Himself be seen on any given occasion. He makes His word known to the men He summons, in such a fashion that it bursts forth in them and they become His "mouth." He lets His spirit possess the one whom He has chosen, and in this and through this lets him mature the work divine. That Moses experiences Him in this fashion and serves Him accordingly is what has set that man apart as a living and effective force at all times. . . .

Is he an alien god whom Moses meets, and through Moses, Israel, and who is made the national god of Israel by Moses? Or is he a "God of the fathers" [Abraham, Isaac, and Jacob]?

The Bible permits us to ascertain this. All we have to do is to compare the peculiarities of the God of Moses with those of the God of the Fathers. More precisely, it is our concern to reveal the peculiar divine likeness, first in the constituents of our tale which, beyond all question, lead back to early tradition, and then in the corresponding elements of the other, a likeness, that is to say, which it is impossible simply to classify by some type or other of the pre-Mosaic religious history of the Ancient East, for despite all its relationships with one or another of these types, it shows a character differing from them all. Thereafter we must compare the two divine likenesses with one another.

If the material in the Bible is subjected to such an examination, the two likenesses will be found to differ in a special manner; namely, just as a clan god in non-historical situations might be expected to differ from a national god in an historical situation. Yet at the same time it can be observed that both depict the identical god. To begin with the former, the clan god [of Abraham, Isaac, and Jacob]: we immediately observe two main characteristics which are both demonstrated in his relation to the men chosen by him. One is that he approaches these men, addresses them, manifests himself to them, demands and charges them and accepts them in his covenant; and the second, closely connected with the first, that he does not remain satisfied with withdrawing them from their surrounding world and sending them on new paths, but wanders with them himself and guides them along those new paths; meanwhile, however, remaining invisible insofar as he does not "make himself seen" by them. Taken both together, these cannot be compared with the attributes of any other divinity in the history of religion, despite certain analogies of detail. The prerequisite assumption for both is that this god is not bound to any place, and that the seats of his manifestations do not restrict him; above them open the gates of heaven (Gen. xxviii, 17), through which he descends and returns to his inaccessible realm.

We find all this once more in the second likeness, in the national god [of Moses]; but here it has the vivid colour of a historical driving force. The new and supplementary characteristics, striking as they may appear, nevertheless seem peripheral to us when compared with the central power of the common element. Once again the God makes his great demands of his men, commanding and promising, establishing a covenant with them. But now he no longer turns to single persons but to a people, and that people too he leads forth and himself conducts along the new way. Once again the invisible one becomes manifest from time to time. Once again heaven and earth are joined, and the God utters his words from heaven unto earth (Ex. xx, 22). . . .

Under such conditions an hour might well come when the people would ask this question of a man bringing them a message from the God of their fathers: "How about his name?" That means: "What is this God really like? We cannot find out from his name!" For as far as primitive human beings are concerned, the name of a person indicates his character. . . .

The "true" name of a person, like that of any other object, is far more than a mere denotative designation for men who think in categories of magic; it is the essence of the person, distilled from his real being, so that he is present in it once again. What is more, he is present in it in such a form that anybody who knows the true name and knows how to pronounce it in the correct way can gain control of him. The person himself is unapproachable, he offers resistance; but through the name he becomes approachable, the speaker has power over him. The true name may be entirely different from the generally familiar one which covers it; it may also, however, differ from the latter only in the "correct" pronunciation, which would also include the correct rhythm and the correct attitude of the body while engaged in the act of pronouncing it; all things which can only be taught and transmitted personally. And since the true name phoneticises the character of the object, the essential thing in the last resort is that the speaker shall recognize this essential being in the name, and direct his full attention upon it. Where that happens, where the magical work requires an aiming of the soul at the being meant, that is, when the "person" aimed at is a god or a demon, the fuel is provided into which the lightning of a religious experience can fall. Then the magical compulsion becomes the intimacy of prayer, the bundle of utilisable forces bearing a personal name becomes a Thou, and a demagisation of existence takes place.

As reply to his question about the name Moses is told: *Ehyeh asher ehyeh.* This is usually understood to mean "I am that I am" in the sense that YHVH describes himself as the Being One or even the Everlasting One, the one unalterably persisting in his being. But that would be abstraction of a kind which does not usually come about in periods of increasing religious vitality; while in addition the verb in the Biblical language does not carry this particular shade of meaning of pure existence. It means: happening, coming into being, being there, being present, being thus and thus; but not being in an abstract sense. "I am that I am" could only be understood as an avoiding of the question, as a "statement which withholds any information." Should we, however, really assume that in the view of the narrator the God who came to inform his people of their liberation wishes, at that hour of all hours, merely to secure his distance, and not to grant and warrant proximity as well? This concept is certainly discouraged by that twofold *ehyeh*, "I shall be present" (Ex. iii, 12; iv, 12), which precedes and follows the statement with unmistakable intention, and in which God promises to be present with those chosen by him, to remain present with them, to assist them. This promise is given unconditional validity in the first part of the statement: "I shall be present," not merely, as previously and subsequently, "with you, with your mouth," but absolutely, "I shall be present." Placed as the phrase is between two utterances of so concrete a kind that clearly means: I am and remain present. Behind it stands the implied reply to those influenced by the magical practices of Egypt, those infected by technical magic: it is superfluous for you to wish to invoke me; in accordance with my character I again and again stand by those whom I befriend; and I would have you know indeed that I befriend you.

This is followed in the second part by: "That I shall be present," or "As which I shall be present" [*asher ehyeh*]. In this way the sentence is reminiscent of the later statement of the God to Moses (Ex. xxxiii, 19): "I shall be merciful to him to whom I shall be merciful." But in it the future character is more strongly stressed. YHVH indeed states that he will always be present, but at any given moment as the one as whom he then, in

that given moment, will be present. He who promises his steady presence, his steady assistance, refuses to restrict himself to definite forms of manifestation; how could the people even venture to conjure and limit him! If the first part of the statement states: "I do not need to be conjured for I am always with you," the second adds: "but it is impossible to conjure me."

It is necessary to remember Egypt as the background of such a revelation: Egypt where the magician went so far as to threaten the gods that if they would not do his will he would not merely betray their names to the demons, but would also tear the hair from their heads as lotus blossoms are pulled out of the pond. Here religion was in practice little more than regulated magic. In the revelation at the Burning Bush religion is demagicized.

At the same time, however, the meaning and character of the Divine Name itself changes; that is, from the viewpoint of the narrator as well as from that of the tradition given shape by him, it is unfolded in its true sense. By means of the introduction of an inconsiderable change in vocalization, a change to which the consciousness of sound would not be too sensitive, a wildly ecstatic outcry, half interjection half pronoun, is replaced by a grammatically precise verbal form which, in the third person (*havah* is the same as *hayah*—to be—but belongs to an older stratum of language) means the same as is communicated by the *ehyeh*: YHVH is "He who will be present" or "He who is here," he who is present here; not merely some time and some where but in every now and in every here. Now the name expresses his character and assures the faithful of the richly protective presence of their Lord.

And it is the God Himself who unfolds his name after this fashion. The exclamation was its hidden form; the verb is its revelation. And in order to make it clear beyond all possibility of misapprehension that the direct word *ehyeh* explains the indirect name, Moses is first instructed, by an exceptionally daring linguistic device, to tell the people "*Ehyeh*, I shall be present, or I am present, sends me to you," and immediately afterwards: "YHVH the God of your fathers sends me to you." That *Ehyeh* is not a name; the God can never be named so; only on this one occasion, in this sole moment of transmitting his work, is Moses allowed and ordered to take the God's self-comprehension in his mouth as a name. . . .

Again and again, when God says in the narrative: "Then will the Egyptians recognize that I am YHVH," or "you will recognize that I am YHVH," it is clearly not the name as a sound, but the meaning revealed in it, which is meant. The Egyptians shall come to know that I (unlike their gods) am the really present One in the midst of the human world, the standing and acting One; you will know that I am He who is present with you, going with you and directing your cause. And until the very close of the Babylonian Exile, and later, saying such as "I am YHVH, that is my name" (Is. xlii, 8), or even more clearly, "Therefore let my people know my name, therefore on that day, that I am he who says 'Here I am'" (Is. lii, 6), cannot be otherwise understood. . . .

A speech like this *ehyeh asher ehyeh* does not belong to literature but to the sphere attained by the founders of religion. If it is theology, it is that archaic theology which, in the form of a historical narrative, stands at the threshold of every genuine historical religion. No matter who related that speech or when, he derived it from a tradition which, in the last resort, cannot go back to anybody other than the founder. What the latter revealed of his religious experience to his disciples we cannot know; that he informed them of what

had happened to him we must assume; in any case, the origin of such a tradition cannot be sought anywhere else.

At his relatively late period Moses did not establish the religious relationship between the Bnei Israel and YHVH. He was not the first to utter that "primal sound" in enthusiastic astonishment. That may have been done by somebody long before who, driven by an irresistible force along a new road, now felt himself to be preceded along that road by "him," the invisible one who permitted himself to be seen. But it was Moses who, on this religious relationship, established a covenant between the God and "his people." Nothing of such a kind can be imagined except on the assumption that a relation which had come down from ancient times has been melted in the fire of some new personal experience. The foundation takes place before the assembled host; the experience is undergone in solitude.

After reading this selection and the previous one, consider these questions:
1. How does Buber challenge the notion of monotheism?
2. What was the meaning of the divine name?
3. What was the historical significance of Moses' first experience on Mount Sinai?

SELECTION 6:

The Covenant

The experience of divinity to which Martin Buber points entails both a set of moral obligations and a special relationship between God and his people. The God of Abraham, Isaac, and Jacob spoke only to these patriarchs and their followers. Through the experience of slavery in Egypt and more importantly of the Exodus from Egypt and the subsequent giving of the law by God to Moses (again on Sinai), a people was formed (ca. 1200 B.C.). God was now the God of the children of Israel, children of the one, true God—with whom they had a special relationship and to whom they had a special set of obligations. Among these, and even central to these, was the moral code God gave to Moses on Mount Sinai, this time accompanied by the children of Israel. But the relationship between God and his people was not just a demand of absolute obedience (and, in fact, the Hebrew God often loved those who contended with him, such as Jacob and David, best of all), he also made promises to them for following his laws. This is the Covenant, the relation between God and his people. The Covenant is central to the development of a uniquely Hebrew understanding of God. Although unique, this understanding was not limited to ancient Israel. The exclusivity of the relationship and the distinctive nature of the moral code that follows it remain foundational features to Christianity and through Christianity to the entire Western tradition. There are several different formulations of it in the Hebrew Bible, but the following one from Exodus 34 provides a clear formulation of this relationship.

The LORD said to Moses, "Cut two tables of stone like the first; and I will write upon the tables the words that were on the first tables, which you broke. Be ready in the morning, and come up in the morning to Mount Sinai, and present yourself there to me on the top of the mountain. No man shall come up with you, and let no man be seen throughout all the mountain; let no flocks or herds feed before that mountain." So Moses cut two tables of stone like the first; and he rose early in the morning and went up on Mount Sinai, as the LORD had commanded him, and took in his hand two tables of stone. And the LORD descended in the cloud and stood with him there, and proclaimed the name of the LORD. The LORD passed before him, and proclaimed, "The LORD, the LORD, a God merciful and gracious, slow to anger, and abounding in steadfast love and faithfulness, keeping steadfast love for thousands, forgiving iniquity and transgression and sin, but who will by no means clear the guilty, visiting the iniquity of the fathers upon the children and the children's children, to the third and the fourth generation."

And Moses made haste to bow his head toward the earth, and worshiped.

And he said, "If now I have found favor in thy sight, O Lord, let the Lord, I pray thee, go in the

midst of us, although it is a stiff-necked people; and pardon our iniquity and our sin, and take us for thy inheritance."

And he said, "Behold, I make a covenant. Before all your people I will do marvels, such as have not been wrought in all the earth or in any nation; and all the people among whom you are shall see the work of the LORD; for it is a terrible thing that I will do with you.

"Observe what I command you this day. Behold, I will drive out before you the Amorites, the Canaanites, the Hittites, the Per'izzites, the Hivites, and the Jeb'usites. Take heed to yourself, lest you make a covenant with the inhabitants of the land whither you go, lest it become a snare in the midst of you. You shall tear down their altars, and break their pillars, and cut down their Ashe'rim [sacred poles] (for you shall worship no other god, for the LORD, whose name is Jealous, is a jealous God), lest you make a covenant with the inhabitants of the land, and when they play the harlot after their gods and sacrifice to their gods and one invites you, you eat of his sacrifice, and you take of their daughters for your sons, and their daughters play the harlot after their gods and make your sons play the harlot after their gods.

"You shall make for yourself no molten gods.

"The feast of unleavened bread you shall keep. Seven days you shall eat unleavened bread, as I commanded you, at the time appointed in the month Abib; for in the month Abib you came out from Egypt. All that opens the womb is mine, all

Exodus 34:1–28, from *The New Oxford Annotated Bible with the Apocrypha*, edited by Herbert G. May and Bruce M. Metzger (New York: Oxford University Press, 1977). Copyright 1973, 1977 by Oxford University Press, Inc.

ANCIENT ISRAEL AND THE ORIGINS OF MONOTHEISM 67

your male cattle, the firstlings of cow and sheep. The firstling of an ass you shall redeem with a lamb, or if you will not redeem it you shall break its neck. All the first-born of your sons you shall redeem. And none shall appear before me empty.

"Six days you shall work, but on the seventh day you shall rest; in plowing time and in harvest you shall rest.

"And you shall observe the feast of weeks, the first fruits of wheat harvest, and the feast of ingathering at the year's end. Three times in the year shall all your males appear before the LORD God, the God of Israel.

"For I will cast out nations before you, and enlarge your borders; neither shall any man desire your land, when you go up to appear before the LORD your God three times in the year.

"You shall not offer the blood of my sacrifice with leaven; neither shall the sacrifice of the feast of the passover be left until the morning. The first of the first fruits of your ground you shall bring to the house of the LORD your God. You shall not boil a kid in its mother's milk."

And the LORD said to Moses, "Write these words; in accordance with these words I have made a covenant with you and with Israel." And he was there with the LORD forty days and forty nights; he neither ate bread nor drank water. And he wrote upon the tables the words of the covenant, the ten commandments!

After reading this selection and the previous one, consider these questions:
1. What was the Hebrew definition of the Covenant?
2. What were the terms of the Covenant?
3. How did the Covenant relationship distinguish the Hebrew religion from the other religions of the ancient Near East?

CHAPTER 4
Ancient Greece: The Pursuit of Excellence

The ancient civilization of Greece, from the ninth to the fourth centuries B.C., provides one of the strongest and, on one level, the easiest identifiable contribution to the civilization of the West. This contribution is so easy for us to identify because it is so clearly still with us. Although modified in transmission through its adoption in later Hellenistic, Roman, and European forms, Greek culture nonetheless continues to define the classical style in literature and the plastic arts, the central tradition of rational thought (which has shaped all types of Western thought and philosophy), and the definition and methodologies of almost all of the Western sciences. Especially in its Athenian form, this civilization provides us with the ideal of a democratic political system in particular and with the meaning and the vocabulary of political life in general. This does not imply that there has been a continuous political tradition since the fourth century—for this has not been the case. Rather, it means that the fundamental way in which we understand and justify political power—and, more importantly, the ways in which we understand what constitutes a just society—derives in large measure from the Greeks and the Greek experience of the world.

The archaic period (750–500 B.C.) saw a number of major changes that greatly impacted subsequent Greek history. Probably the most significant is the development of the polis. Along the ample coastline of Asia Minor and the Greek mainland—but more often for protective purposes against raiding seafarers within several miles from the sea—arose a new form of political, social, and cultural formation. Originally a union of the smaller households (*oicoi*) of the surrounding areas into some type of central and well-protected site (the high city or acropolis), the various city-states (poleis) of ancient Greece remained independent, though often allied with one another, until their conquest by Philip of Macedon, their subordination into the kingdoms of the Hellenistic period, and their eventual submission to Rome. But at the time of its origins in the eighth century, this form of political organization of the polis was very new. In theory the polis called upon the active citizenship of all free adult male inhabitants, who participated in the internal rule and external defense of the city-state, upon an equal basis and not dependent upon wealth or social status.

In practice, of course, most poleis were ruled by much smaller groups than that of all male citizens. Oligarchies (rule by a small group) and rule by individuals who seized control by unconstitutional means—the tyrants—were very often the case. The earliest form of government within the polis was kingship and probably marked a continuation of the type of rule characteristic of the Homeric period. In the course of the seventh and sixth centuries, however, most of these kingships were transformed into various forms of oligarchic governments in which small groups of the most powerful (and invariably within these largely agricultural communities) the wealthiest members unquestionably controlled politics. Although all citizens possessed legal rights, such as access to the courts, protection against enslavement, and participation in the city's religious and cultural life, political decisions were limited to the wealthiest.

In the course of the archaic period many city-states enlarged the number of decision makers. Athens is the obvious example of emerging democracy. What caused the change in governmental forms? The phenomenon was too widespread to be the result of either accident or some "natural" process of political evolution. Some modern scholars emphasize the obvious consequences that resulted from the transformation of an economy based more on raiding and piracy to one based on settled agricultural communities. Others point to the rise of the tyrants, who called on a wider group of citizens to guarantee their rule. These explanations account for some of the changes in political and social organization, but they do not explain everything. Changing forms of military tactics and basic military organization also must have played an important part. Gradually, in the sixth and fifth centuries, a small number of these city-states moved to a more open and democratic form of government. Athens is the outstanding example. A relatively small and insignificant polis in the Homeric and archaic periods, Athens emerged to be not only the most powerful but also the most economically advanced city in Greece. By the late fifth century, Athens reached the height of its economic and military power. This power was largely based on its economic and commercial expansion and the creation of a union of city-states (the Delian League), which in reality, if not in name, was an Athenian empire. The late fifth century was also the great age of Athenian culture in which it set the standard in art and architecture, drama, and philosophy not only for Greece but also in a sense for the entire civilization of the West.

Despite all of its military strength and cultural achievements, democratic Athens lost its contest with Sparta (the Peloponnesian War) in 404 B.C. Although Athens recovered, it never again attained its position of military and political dominance in Greece. Greece itself, after periods of Spartan and then Theban hegemony, finally succumbed to the invasions of the northern "barbarians" of Macedon. Philip II of Macedon and then his son, Alexander, dominated the city-states of Greece. Alexander then united the Greeks for a war against their traditional foe, the Persians, whom he defeated in 340 B.C. Alexander did not stop there. Moving through the older empires of Mesopotamia, he eventually reached the northwest frontier of India. Before his death in 323 Alexander had established an empire that spread from Greece and Egypt to India.

Within this vast empire, even when divided into a number of large kingdoms under the successors of Alexander, a new civilization arose. Classical Greek lifestyles, values, and art forms generally prevailed, but they were further developed or were blended with the lifestyles and art forms indigenous to the East. Historians have labeled this civilization *Hellenistic* in order to distinguish it from the *Hellenic* civilization of earlier centuries. Political life within these various Hellenistic kingdoms no longer called for the intense political and military commitment of the ancient polis. Men and women became more concerned with what were considered private rather than public matters. Chief among these concerns was amassing wealth. Commercial enterprises only increased once the eastern Mediterranean was, for all intents and purposes, united politically and economically.

Building on Hellenic foundations, Hellenistic artists, architects, philosophers, and scholars flourished. The Hellenistic kings promoted vast building projects and promoted the cultural lives and scholarly pursuits of their subjects. In many ways, the various schools of ancient philosophy were either established during this period or fully came into their own as places of teaching and writing. Athens revived as the center of such philosophical training. Plato's Academy and Aristotle's Lyceum continued to thrive, and schools of Stoicism and Epicureanism were also founded. Alexandria on the Mediterranean coast of Egypt—the cosmopolitan city founded by Alexander the Great—became a meeting place for Greeks, Hebrews, and native Egyptians. The Ptolemaic rulers of Egypt established the world's first research institution, the Museum, where scholars produced encyclopedias of knowledge and the world's first major library (which took as its task the collection of all the written materials in the world). It also was a center of scholarly activities, especially in the literary arts and in scientific research. The poet and historian Callimachus and the poet Theocritus resided in Alexandria. In Alexandria, mathematics, physics, and astronomy emerged as distinct sciences for the first time. Euclid the mathematician, Ctesibius the engineer, Herophilus the physician, Eratosthenes the geographer, and Aristarchus the astronomer are only some of the names associated with Alexandrian sciences. The ways in which the West has come to understand science, philosophy, scholarship, and criticism all took on their original, decisive forms in the Hellenistic period.

The immensity and uniqueness of this Greek contribution has lead a number of scholars over the centuries to conceive of the modern West as constituted by the interconnection of two ancient civilizations. The civilizations of the ancient Israelites and the ancient Greeks, the Hebrews and the Hellenes, have provided the West with the foundations that can clearly be defined as our own—as opposed to the more indirect contributions of Mesopotamia and Egypt on the one hand, or the less powerful ones of the ancient Germans and the ancient Celts on the other.

Even if we accept these two civilizations as the foundations for the modern West, we still must understand that, in basic values and attitudes, ancient Israel was very different from ancient Greece. The resulting combination of these two civilizations is not always an easy one. Like oil and water, the mix tends to separate and form new relations when shaken up. At certain moments in their history of the West, the stabilization of the two sides of the tradition have been attempted, as in the philosophy and theology of the High Middle Ages or certain cultural trends of the eighteenth and nineteenth centuries. But for the most part these mixtures tend to separate, bringing out the dominance of one over the other. The instability itself might suggest a reason why the West, as opposed to the great civilizations of China and India for instance, seems constantly to change and even evolve. While we speak of the "classical" civilization of Greece and Rome and of the continuance of the classical tradition within the West, this notion of the classical and its origins cannot imply a single, founding moment. Nor can it define the history of the West as a series of moves toward or away from some original, defining moment. The West is too complex, too deeply permeated by *competing* traditions, to be comprehended in this way.

SELECTION 1:

Hebrews and Hellenes

Modern historian Crane Brinton directly confronts this difficult problem of defining the West. He attempts to identify the specific contributions of the Hebrews and the Greeks (or Hellenes, as they called themselves) in the formation of our civilization. By contrasting their various contributions, he also further defines the uniqueness of each. Brinton begins with the Hebrews and their historical experience, which resulted in a specific understanding of God and moral values. He then turns to the ancient Greeks. Their moral world was radically different. Although the two peoples both occupied lands on the far eastern side of the Mediterranean Sea, they seem to have been entirely unaware of each others existence until the time of Alexander the Great (the fourth century B.C.). Yet on a general level they shared a basic attitude about divinity that is often overlooked in playing out the contrasting points in the two cultural traditions. Like the nomadic Hebrews, the early Greeks were also a wandering group (or groups) of warrior peoples, and their notions of divinity were related to this lifestyle. The God of the Hebrews and the chief, ruling gods of the Greeks were male warrior gods, emphasizing warrior virtues. They were different then from the Mother Goddess of the Neolithic village. Rather, they were closer to the male gods of the cities of Mesopotamia to whom the female goddesses were subordinated.

Even with this general shared characteristic, what interests Brinton and most scholars is the remarkable dissimilarities between the fundamental values of the Hebrews and those of the Greeks. In his own account, Brinton discusses the common point of departure of the two peoples. Like the people of the ancient Near East in general, the Greeks understood human life as an experience of suffering through which, nonetheless, a sense of justice prevailed. But from this point, the two civilizations diverged.

The Greeks, too, were a people of the Book. Their Bible was Homer. . . .

We may find it difficult to realize that the poems of Homer, and, more especially, the *Iliad*, which to us are "literature," certainly better, greater, than *Hiawatha*, but like that poem, "literature," were as much "religion" to the Greeks as was the Bible to the Jews. But the educated Greek of the great ages, and right on to the triumph of Christianity in the West, was brought up on Homer. Plato himself, not, for reasons of principle, an admirer of poets, though he was, of course, one himself, called Homer the "educator of Greece." It is true that the poems were composed to amuse and elevate, and certainly to hold the attention of audiences of nobles, squires, and retainers who were presumably in no mood to be preached at, let alone indoctrinated with a theology. The priestly touch unmistakable even in the most straightforwardly historical books of the Old Testament, bloody and warlike though they are, is not in these poems. . . .

There is, incongruous though the notion may seem, a good deal of the didactic in Homer;

From *A History of Western Morals*, by Crane Brinton (New York: Harcourt, Brace, 1959). Copyright © 1959 by Crane Brinton. Reprinted by permission.

Homer knew well how a gentleman ought to behave, and he keeps reminding his audience of what they, too, well knew. . . . Yet it is equally clear that Homer was no more making a purely literary use of the Olympian gods than were the authors and amenders of the Pentateuch so using Jehovah. Perhaps that last is not put sharply enough. Homer *believed in* Zeus and Athena and the rest.

Of these Greek gods of Olympus, it is often said that, especially in Homeric times, but to a degree right down through to the end of Greco-Roman paganism, they were just like human beings, only more powerful, that the world of Olympus was simply a mirror image of this world, even a kind of huge realistic folk novel, in which the gods conducted themselves as human beings do in our realistic fiction—that is to say, rather worse than in real life. This is largely true, but it must not be interpreted as meaning that the Greek Olympian religion "taught" its believers that men could and should imitate the ways of the gods. The early Christian apologists were very fond of using the argument that the pagans could hardly help lying, cheating, whoring, and the like, because the gods did so. . . .

There is, indeed, in the relations between mortals and gods the element of contract: *do ut des*. But there is more. Odysseus is a favorite, a protégé, of Athena, who intrigues for him at court, struggles with Poseidon, whom Odysseus has offended, exults in his successes, mourns his misfortunes. Athena is the patron saint of Odysseus; but Odysseus has to deserve her support, not just by ritual acts, but by being the kind of man Athena approves, wise, resourceful, by Christian ethical standards often unscrupulous, but never stupidly unscrupulous, persistent in the face of setbacks, courageous in combat. The reciprocal relation of contract is a *moral* one; men must merit the support of the gods, and the gods must merit the support of men. . . .

Achilles is the man all of Homer's listeners would like to be, the man of *aretē*. The untranslatable word comes out in the dictionaries as, among other things, "virtue," but "honor," even "proper pride," come closer. Achilles is young, handsome, the conspicuous and admirable person, the athlete of grace. Agamemnon, leader of the expedition against Troy, in order to appease an offended Apollo, is forced to take a series of steps culminating in a mortal offense to the honor of Achilles. Military ethics forbid Achilles to challenge the old leader to a duel, so Achilles simply withdraws. In his absence his dearest friend, Patroclus, is persuaded to impersonate him in a ritual combat with the Trojan champion Hector, and is killed. Achilles—though he knows from a prophecy that he will die—now follows what *aretē* in such a case demands of the hero. He fights Hector, kills him, drags his body in triumph from his chariot—but dies from a wound in the heel by which his mother had held him when she dipped him as an infant in the waters of the Styx, an immersion she had intended to make him proof against wounds.

Now the *aretē* here brought to a tragic peak is very far from Christian virtue, and almost as far from modern secular, utilitarian morality. It is no trouble at all to outline the story of Achilles in terms, for most of us at least, of strong moral condemnation. The initial offense that outraged the hero was Agamemnon's taking away a concubine from Achilles in a kind of politico-religious deal with Apollo. The hero withdraws, thus endangering the cause of his fellows, his country, the whole expedition, out of jealous pique. He is roused to fight again by a purely personal matter, the death in fair combat of his friend Patroclus, with whom he may have had pederastic relations. He takes a vainglorious revenge on the vanquished Hector. He is moved throughout by vanity; he is about as moral—and as human—as a fighting cock.

The above is, of course, unfair. Homer is setting forth in the framework of the customs of his time a heroic agon, a struggle in which a man who has become what his fellows most admired goes deliberately to what he knows must be his death—to keep that admiration. More nobly put, Achilles sacrifices his life for an ideal, an ideal that has never ceased to be part of Western moral life, though fortunately not often at the frenetic intensity of the Homeric hero's life. We are back again at *aretē*.

It is the virtue of the man, always measuring himself against others, who is determined to do better than they the things they all want to do. In Homer's day those things were the things young, athletic fighting men of a landed aristocracy wanted to do and be. But the element of agon, the ritual struggle, could and would be later in Western history transferred to many other kinds of human activity, a fact that Americans hardly need to be reminded of. The ideal of the Homeric hero can be put pejoratively. He is the obsessively competitive man, always aware of his place in an elaborate order of rank—indeed a human peck order—always trying to move himself up and push someone down, the jealous egalitarian who somehow manages to treat with appropriate differences those above and those below him, the man who must be a success. Perhaps only the archaic dignity of Homer's poetry and the excellence our educational tradition has always found in the Greeks really make the difference between these Homeric competitors and the vulgar big shots of our vulgar business world today. The ultimate prize in the Homeric agon, however, is not mere success, not mere leading the league, any more than it is in business with us. Honor, in a curious way, is its own reward. Achilles followed his father's most Homeric advice, . . . "To be always among the bravest, and hold my head above others," *Iliad*, vi, 208.

After reading this selection, consider these questions:

1. What was the significance of the Homeric epics for Greek civilization?

2. How did the Greeks understand the nature of their gods?

3. What were the central values for the ancient Greeks?

SELECTION 2:

Aretē

Like so many other scholars and even the ancient Greeks themselves, Crane Brinton, in the previous selection, emphasizes the importance of the Homeric poems and especially of The Iliad *in the formation of Greek values, including the Greek conception of the gods. Homer was instrumental in providing the Greeks with a clear sense of divinity, with not just the names but also the powers and characteristics of each of the gods. From the competing local deities of various groups and subgroups of the ancient Greek world, Homer laid the foundations of a common religion. Although Homer did not invent these gods, he defined the major gods of Olympus and provided them with an intersecting series of stories (the myths) that, perhaps more than any other single feature, united various Greek groups and "peoples" into a single nation—however divided politically into separate city-states—and a single civilization.*

Brinton has outlined the story of The Iliad *for us, but we should take a closer look at the text itself to understand the power and brilliance of its images and view of reality. This selection comes from book 16, the climactic moment in which Achilles, still refusing to fight for the Greeks because of an insult to his honor, sends his friend Patroclus to aid in the fight against the on-rushing Trojans. In addition to the ways in which the gods and men interact, we should notice how such notions as honor and* aretē *(excellence), with its related notion of agon (contest), shape these individuals, guide their actions, and provide them with a means of evaluating men and actions, themselves and their own actions included. Warfare in the age of Homer—while including large numbers of lightly armed men— was mainly a contest between individual warriors. From the nature of leadership and the expense of heavy armor, the "heroes"—those of relatively equal class, position, and parentage—were the only ones to decide the course of a battle. From the crowded lines of the light-armed troops, the individual hero was driven in his chariot to the area between the lines. He then dismounted, ascertained the quality of his opponents immediately facing him (refusing to enter a contest with those unworthy of him), and began to fight.*

In The Iliad, *Achilles is the unchallenged hero of the Greeks. As Homer says, he is the "best of the Achaeans (Greeks)" because he is the incom-*

parable "doer of deed and speaker of words." In deeds and words, Achilles seeks eternal glory through the achievement of excellence, aretē. *Excellence functions within a larger moral economy of shame. Shame is not a form of personal guilt but a type of total worthlessness in not living up to the standards of excellence. The value of always striving for excellence in whatever one undertakes and the understanding of this striving as a competitive encounter with all others became the foundation for the Greek conception of life throughout the archaic and classical periods (seventh through fourth centuries B.C.). These values lay the basis of a distinctive Greek notion of competition. In the Olympic Games, as well as in all other athletic contests,* aretē *was tested in the agon.*

But go thou and put on
My well-known armor; lead into the field
My Myrmidons, men that rejoice in war,
Since like a lowering cloud the men of Troy
Surround the fleet, and the Achaians stand
In narrow space close pressed beside the sea,
And all the city of Ilium flings itself
Against them, confident of victory,
Now that the glitter of my helm no more
Flashes upon their eyes. Yet very soon
Their flying host would fill the trenches here
With corpses, had but Agamemnon dealt
Gently with me; and now their squadrons close
Around our army. Now no more the spear
Is wielded by Tydides Diomed
In rescue of the Greeks; no more the shout
Of Agamemnon's hated throat is heard;
But the man-queller Hector, lifting up
His voice, exhorts the Trojans, who, in throngs,
Raising the war-cry, fill the plain, and drive
The Greeks before them. Gallantly lead on
The charge, Patroclus; rescue our good ships;
Let not the enemy give them to the flames,
And cut us off from our desired return.
Follow my counsel; bear my words in mind;
So shalt thou win for me among the Greeks
Great honor and renown, and they shall bring
The beautiful maiden back with princely gifts.
When thou hast driven the assailants from the
    fleet,
Return thou hither. If the Thunderer,

Husband of Juno, suffer thee to gain
That victory, seek no further to prolong
The combat with the warlike sons of Troy,
Apart from me, lest I be brought to shame,
Nor, glorying in the battle and pursuit,
Slaying the Trojans as thou goest, lead
Thy men to Troy, lest from the Olympian mount
One of the ever-living gods descend
Against thee: Phœbus loves the Trojans well.
But come as soon as thou shalt see the ships
In safety; leave the foes upon the plain
Contending with each other. Would to Jove
The All-Father, and to Pallas, and the god
Who bears the bow, Apollo, that of all
The Trojans, many as they are, and all
The Greeks, not one might be reprieved from
    death,
While thou and I alone were left alive
To overthrow the sacred walls of Troy. . . .
    The newly armed, led by their gallant chief,
Patroclus, marched in warlike order forth,
And in high hope, to fall upon the foe.
As wasps, that by the wayside build their cells,
Angered from time to time by thoughtless
    boys,—
Whence mischief comes to many,—if by chance
Some passing traveller should unwittingly
Disturb them, all at once are on the wing,
And all attack him, to defend their young;
So fearless and so fierce the Myrmidons
Poured from their fleet, and mighty was the din.
Patroclus with loud voice exhorted them:—
    "O Myrmidons, companions of the son
Of Peleus, bear in mind, my friends, your fame
For valor, and be men, that we who serve
Achilles, we who combat hand to hand,

From *The Iliad of Homer*, translated by William Cullen Bryant (Boston: Houghton, Osgood, 1879).

May honor him by our exploits, and teach
Wide-ruling Agamemnon how he erred
Slighting the bravest warrior of the Greeks."
    These words awoke the courage and the might
Of all who heard them, and in close array
They fell upon the Trojans. Fearfully
The fleet around them echoed to the sound
Of Argives shouting. When the Trojans saw,
In glittering arms, Menœtius' gallant son
And his attendant, every heart grew faint
With fear; the close ranks wavered; for they
    thought
That the swift son of Peleus at the fleet
Had laid aside his wrath, and was again
The friend of Agamemnon. Eagerly
They looked around for an escape from
    death. . . .
    He ended, and went on; the godlike man
Followed his steps. As when from mountain
    dells
Rises, and far is heard, a crashing sound
Where woodmen fell the trees, such was the
    noise
From those who fought on that wide plain,—the
    din
Of brass, of leather, and of tough bull's-hide
Smitten with swords and two-edged spears. No
    eye,
Although of keenest sight, would then have
    known
Noble Sarpedon, covered as he lay,
From head to foot, with weapons, blood, and
    dust;
And still the warriors thronged around the dead.
As when in spring-time at the cattle-stalls
Flies gather, humming, when the milk is drawn,
Round the full pails, so swarmed around the
    corpse
The combatants; nor once did Jove withdraw
His bright eyes from the stubborn fray, but still
Gazed, planning how Patroclus should be slain.
Uncertain whether, in the desperate strife
Over the great Sarpedon, to permit
Illustrious Hector with his spear to lay
The hero dead, and make his arms a spoil,
Or spare him yet a while, to make the war
More bloody. As he pondered, this seemed best:
That the brave comrade of Achilles first

Should put to flight the Trojans and their chief,
Hector the brazen-mailed, pursuing them
Toward Troy with slaughter. To this end he sent
Into the heart of Hector panic fear,
Who climbed his car and fled, and bade the rest
Flee also, for he saw how Jove had weighed
The fortunes of the day. Now none remained,
Not even the gallant Lycians, when they saw
Their monarch lying wounded to the heart
Among a heap of slain; for Saturn's son
In that day's strife had caused a multitude
To fall in death. Now when the Greeks had
    stripped
Sarpedon of the glittering brazen mail,
The brave son of Menœtius bade his friends
Convey it to the hollow ships. Meanwhile
The Cloud-compeller spake to Phœbus thus:—
    "Go now, beloved Phœbus, and withdraw
Sarpedon from the weapons of the foe;
Cleanse him from the dark blood, and bear him
    thence
And lave him in the river-stream, and shed
Ambrosia o'er him. Clothe him then in robes
Of heaven, consigning him to Sleep and Death,
Twin brothers, and swift bearers of the dead,
And they shall lay him down in Lycia's fields,
That broad and opulent realm. There shall his
    friends
And kinsmen give him burial, and shall rear
His tomb and column,—honors due the dead."
    He spake: Apollo instantly obeyed
His father, leaving Ida's mountain height,
And sought the field of battle, and bore off
Noble Sarpedon from the enemy's spears,
And laved him in the river-stream, and shed
Ambrosia o'er him. Then in robes of heaven
He clothed him, giving him to Sleep and Death,
Twin brothers and swift bearers of the dead,
And they, with speed conveying it, laid down
The corpse in Lycia's broad and opulent realm.
    Meantime Patroclus, urging on his steeds
And charioteer, pursued, to his own hurt,
Trojans and Lycians. Madman! had he then
Obeyed the counsel which Pelides gave,
The bitter doom of death had not been his.
But stronger than the purposes of men
Are those of Jove, who puts to flight the brave,
And takes from them the victory, though he

Impelled them to the battle; and he now
Urged on Patroclus to prolong the fight.
   Who first, when thus the gods decreed thy
     death,
Fell by thy hand, Patroclus, and who last?
Adrastus first, Autonous next, and then
Echeclus; then died Perimus, the son
Of Meges; then with Melanippus fell
Epistor; next was Elasus o'ercome,
And Mulius, and Pylartes. These he slew,
While all the rest betook themselves to flight.
   Then had the Greeks possessed themselves of
     Troy,
With all its lofty portals, by the hand
And valor of Patroclus, for his rage
Was terrible beyond the rage of all
Who bore the spear, had not Apollo stood
On a strong tower to menace him with ill,
And aid the Trojans. Thrice Patroclus climbed
A shoulder of the lofty wall, and thrice
Apollo, striking his immortal hands
Against the glittering buckler, thrust him down;
And when, for the fourth time, the godlike man
Essayed to mount the wall, the archer-god,
Phœbus, encountered him with fearful threats:
"Noble Patroclus, hold thy hand, nor deem
The city of the warlike Trojans doomed
To fall beneath thy spear, nor by the arm
Of Peleus' son, though mightier far than thou."
   He spake; Patroclus, fearful of the wrath
Of the archer-god, withdrew, and stood afar,
While Hector, at the Scæan gates, restrained
His coursers, doubtful whether to renew
The fight by mingling with the crowd again,
Or gather all his host within the walls
By a loud summons. As he pondered thus,
Apollo stood beside him in the form
Of Asius, a young warrior and a brave,
Uncle of Hector, the great horse-tamer,
And brother of Queen Hecuba, and son
Of Dymas, who in Phrygia dwelt beside
The streams of the Sangarius. Putting on
His shape and aspect, thus Apollo said:—
   "Why, Hector, dost thou pause from battle
     thus?
Nay, it becomes thee not. Were I in might
Greater than thou, as I am less, full soon
Wouldst thou repent this shrinking from the war.

Come boldly on, and urge thy firm-paced steeds
Against Patroclus; slay him on the field,
And Phœbus will requite thee with renown."
   He spake, and mingled in the hard-fought
     fray,
While noble Hector bade his charioteer,
The brave Cebriones, ply well the lash,
And join the battle. Phœbus went before,
Entering the crowd, and spread dismay among
The Greeks, and gave the glory of the hour
To Hector and the Trojans. Little heed
Paid Hector to the rest, nor raised his arm
To slay them, but urged on his firm-paced steeds
To meet Patroclus, who, beholding him,
Leaped from his car. In his left hand he held
A spear, and with the other lifting up
A white, rough stone, the largest he could grasp,
Flung it with all its force. It flew not wide,
Nor flew in vain, but smote Cebriones,
The warlike chief who guided Hector's steeds,
A spurious son of Priam the renowned.
The sharp stone smote his forehead as he held
The reins, and crushed both eyebrows in; the
     bone
Resisted not the blow; the warrior's eyes
Fell in the dust before his very feet.
Down from the sumptuous seat he plunged, as
     dives
A swimmer, and the life forsook his limbs.
And this, Patroclus, was thy cruel jest:—
   "Truly a nimble man is this who dives
With such expertness. Were this, now, the sea,
Where fish are bred, and he were searching it
For oysters, he might get an ample store
For many men, in leaping from a ship,
Though in a storm, so skilfully he dives
Even from the chariot to the plain. No doubt
There must be divers in the town of Troy."
   He spake, and sprang upon Cebriones.
With all a lion's fury, which attacks
The stables and is wounded in the breast,
And perishes through his own daring; thus,
Patroclus, didst thou fall upon the slain,
While Hector, hastening also, left his steeds,
And both contended for Cebriones.
As lions for the carcass of a deer
Fight on a mountain summit, hungry both,
And both unyielding, thus two mighty men

Of war, Patroclus Menœtiades
And glorious Hector, eager each to smite
His adversary with the cruel spear,
Fought for Cebriones. The slain man's head
Was seized by Hector's powerful hand, whose
    grasp
Relaxed not, while Patroclus held the foot;
And, thronging to the spot, the other Greeks
And Trojans mingled in the desperate strife.

As when the east wind and the south contend
In the open mountain grounds, and furiously
Assail the deep old woods of beech and ash
And barky cornel, flinging their long boughs
Against each other with a mighty roar,
And crash of those that break, so did the Greeks
And Trojans meet with mutual blows, and slay
Each other; nor had either host a thought
Of shameful flight. Full many a trenchant spear
Went to its mark beside Cebriones,
And many a wingèd arrow that had left
The bowstring; many a massive stone was
    hurled
Against the ringing bucklers, as they fought
Around the dead, while he, the mighty, lay
Stretched on the ground amid the eddying dust,
Forgetful of his art of horsemanship.

While yet the sun was climbing to his place
In middle heaven, the men of either host
Were smitten by the weapons, and in both
The people fell; but when he stooped to the west
The Greeks prevailed, and from that storm of
    darts
And tumult of the Trojans they drew forth
Cebriones, and stripped him of his arms.

Still rushed Patroclus onward, bent to wreak
His fury on the Trojans. Fierce as Mars,
He charged their squadrons thrice with fearful
    shouts
And thrice he laid nine warriors in the dust.
But as with godlike energy he made
The fourth assault, then clearly was it seen,
Patroclus, that thy life was near its end,
For Phœbus terribly in that fierce strife
Encountered thee. Patroclus saw him not
Advancing in the tumult, for he moved
Unseen in darkness. Coming close behind,
He smote, with open palm, the hero's back
Between the ample shoulders, and his eyes

Reeled with the blow, while Phœbus from his
    head
Struck the tall helm, that, clanking, rolled away
Under the horses' feet; its crest was soiled
With blood and dust, though never till that hour
Had dust defiled its horse-hair plume; for once
That helmet guarded an illustrious head,
The glorious brows of Peleus' son, and now
Jove destined it for Hector, to be worn
In battle; and his death was also near.
The spear Patroclus wielded, edged with brass,
Long, tough, and huge, was broken in his hands;
And his broad buckler, dropping with its band,
Lay on the ground, while Phœbus, son of Jove,
Undid the fastenings of his mail. With mind
Bewildered, and with powerless limbs, he stood
As thunderstruck. Then a Dardanian named
Euphorbus, son of Panthoüs, who excelled
His comrades in the wielding of the spear,
The race, and horsemanship, approaching,
    smote
Patroclus in the back with his keen spear,
Between the shoulder-blades. Already he
Had dashed down twenty warriors from their
    cars,
Guiding his own, a learner in the art
Of war.
The first was he who threw a lance
At thee, Patroclus, yet o'ercame thee not;
For, plucking from thy back its ashen stem,
He fled, and mingled with the crowd, nor dared
Await thy coming, though thou wert unarmed,
While, weakened by that wound and by the
    blow
Given by the god, Patroclus turned and sought
Shelter from danger in the Grecian ranks;
But Hector, when he saw the gallant Greek
Thus wounded and retreating, left his place
Among the squadrons, and, advancing, pierced
Patroclus with his spear, below the belt,
Driving the weapon deep. The hero fell
With clashing mail, and all the Greeks beheld
His fall with grief. As when a lion bears
A stubborn boar to earth, what time the twain
Fight on the mountains for a slender spring,
Both thirsty and both fierce, the lion's strength
Lays prone his panting foe, so Priam's son
Slew, fighting hand to hand, the valiant Greek,

Son of Menœtius, who himself had slain
So many. Hector gloried over him
With wingèd words: " Patroclus, thou didst think
To lay our city waste, and carry off
Our women captive in thy ships to Greece.
Madman! in their defence the fiery steeds
Of Hector sweep the battle-field, and I,
Mightiest of all the Trojans, with the spear
Will guard them from the doom of slavery.
Now vultures shall devour thee, wretched youth!
Achilles, mighty though he be, has brought
No help to thee, though doubtless when he sent
Thee forth to battle, and remained within,
He charged thee thus: 'Patroclus, flower of
    knights,
Return not to the fleet until thy hand
Hath torn the bloody armor from the corpse
Of the man-queller Hector.' So he spake,
And filled with idle hopes thy foolish heart."

    Then thou, Patroclus, with a faltering voice,
Didst answer thus: "Now, Hector, while thou
    mayst,
Utter thy boast in swelling words, since Jove
And Phœbus gave the victory to thee.
Easily have they vanquished me; 't was they
Who stripped the armor from my limbs, for else,
If twenty such as thou had met me, all
Had perished by my spear. A cruel fate
O'ertakes me, aided by Latona's son,
The god, and by Euphorbus among men.
Thou who shalt take my spoil art but the third;

Yet hear my words, and keep them in thy
    thought.
Not long shalt thou remain alive; thy death
By violence is at hand, and thou must fall,
Slain by the hand of great Æacides."
    While he was speaking, death stole over him
And veiled his senses, while the soul forsook
His limbs and flew to Hades, sorrowing
For its sad lot, to part from life in youth
And prime of strength. Illustrious Hector thus
Answered the dying man: "Why threaten me,
Patroclus, with an early death? Who knows
That he, thy friend, whom fair-haired Thetis
    bore,
Achilles, may not sooner lose his life,
Slain by my spear?" He spake, and set his heel
Upon the slain, and from the wound drew forth
His brazen spear and pushed the corpse aside,
And with the weapon hurried on to smite
Godlike Automedon, the charioteer
Of swift Æacides; but him the steeds
Fleet-footed and immortal, which the gods
Bestowed on Peleus, swiftly bore away.

    After reading this selection and the previous
one, consider these questions:
    1. What did Homer and the Greeks mean
       by *aretē*?
    2. What was the "shame" system of
       morality? Did it affect Achilles' be-
       havior?
    3. Why do you think *The Iliad* became
       the basis of Greek education?

SELECTION 3:

The Origins of the Polis

The war against Troy, the story told in The Iliad, *probably occurred during the twelfth century B.C. (within what is called the Mycenaean age), but the world—the values and material conditions—depicted in the poem is the world of Homer's own time (probably the eighth century B.C.). The period between the end of the Mycenaean age and the time of Homer is called the Greek Dark Age. It is the time of heroes but also the time when kings ruled over their followers in the style reminiscent of the leadership of warrior chiefs over wandering bands, from which they and their people differed only slightly.*

By the seventh and sixth centuries, things had changed. Instead of individual heroes, entire units of heavily armed men confronted one another on the field of battle. Each of these units was called a phalanx, and the men who formed them were hoplites. The phalanx was to be the major form of land warfare throughout the Hellenic and Hellenistic ages. Only when the phalanx was confronted by the smaller and more mobile Roman maniple did it outlive its military effectiveness. Phalanxes varied in size, some reaching up to three thousand men. More importantly, the phalanx was the military defense of the polis. Upon it depended not just the independence of the polis but the very survival of its citizens, for defeat on the battlefield often resulted in the slaughter of the male population and the sale of women and children into slavery. To make the phalanx an effective military instrument required long hours of physical training, teaching men to move and fight in unison. Heavy shields had to remain locked one to another, long spears had to be positioned so that they formed a nearly impenetrable front to the enemy, and forward and backward movement had to be coordinated. In the case of Sparta after the Messenian wars (seventh century), the life of the citizens was totally dedicated to war and the preparation for war. Although in this organization, Sparta was an exception to the other poleis, it was, nevertheless, a model state for all of Greece, including the very differently organized society of Athens. At its height of power, Sparta had only from eight to ten thousand male citizens, yet it was a dominant power in Greece.

The following poem by the Spartan poet Tyrtaeus, written during the Second Messenian War (the life-and-death struggle between Sparta and its neighbor state between 640 and 630 B.C.), indicates the kind of organization and tactics demanded by the phalanx. It also shows the type of qualities—so different from the highly independent heroes of Homer—called forth by the new mode of combat. Both within the phalanx and within the polis as a whole, a new type of man within a new set of polis values was demanded.

I would not say anything for a man nor take account of him
  for any speed of his feet or wrestling skill he might have,
not if he had the size of a Cyclops and strength to go with it,
  not if he could outrun Bóreas, the North Wind of Thrace,

not if he were more handsome and gracefully formed than Tithónos,
  or had more riches than Midas had, or Kínyras too,
not if he were more of a king than Tantalid Pelops,
  or had the power of speech and persuasion Adrastos had,
not if he had all splendors except for a fighting spirit.
  For no man ever proves himself a good man in war

From *Greek Lyrics*, translated by Richmond Lattimore, 2nd ed. Copyright 1949, 1955, 1960 by Richmond Lattimore. Reprinted by permission of the University of Chicago Press.

unless he can endure to face the blood and the
    slaughter,
    go close against the enemy and fight with his
        hands.
Here is courage, mankind's finest possession,
    here is
    the noblest prize that a young man can
        endeavor to win,
and it is a good thing his city and all the people
    share with him
    when a man plants his feet and stands in the
        foremost spears
relentlessly, all thought of foul flight completely
    forgotten,
    and has well trained his heart to be steadfast
        and to endure,
and with words encourages the man who is
    stationed beside him.
    Here is a man who proves himself to be
        valiant in war.
With a sudden rush he turns to flight the rugged
    battalions
    of the enemy, and sustains the beating waves
        of assault.
And he who so falls among the champions and
    loses his sweet life,
    so blessing with honor his city, his father, and
        all his people,
with wounds in his chest, where the spear that
    he was facing has transfixed
    that massive guard of his shield, and gone
        through his breastplate as well,
why, such a man is lamented alike by the young
    and the elders,
    and all his city goes into mourning and
        grieves for his loss.
His tomb is pointed to with pride, and so are his
    children,

and his children's children, and afterward all
    the race that is his.
His shining glory is never forgotten, his name is
    remembered,
    and he becomes an immortal, though he lies
        under the ground,
when one who was a brave man has been killed
    by the furious War God
    standing his ground and fighting hard for his
        children and land.
But if he escapes the doom of death, the
    destroyer of bodies,
    and wins his battle, and bright renown for the
        work of his spear,
all men give place to him alike, the youth and
    the elders,
    and much joy comes his way before he goes
        down to the dead.
Aging, he has reputation among his citizens. No
    one
    tries to interfere with his honors or all he
        deserves;
all men withdraw before his presence, and yield
    their seats to him,
    the youth, and the men his age, and even
        those older than he.
Thus a man should endeavor to reach this high
    place of courage
    with all his heart, and, so trying, never be
        backward in war.

After reading this selection, consider these
questions:
1. What was the polis?
2. What type of military organization
   was associated with the polis?
3. What values does Tyrtaeus emphasize
   for fighting men in the phalanx?

SELECTION 4:

The Development of Athenian Democracy

The new type of military organization had political consequences as well. The heavily armed men of the phalanx demanded, and in most cases received, the right to make if not all at least the major decisions upon which their lives depended. This process of bringing the hoplites into the government is known as the hoplite franchise. Although many city-states ruled over growing areas surrounding them, the number of active citizens remained relatively small. Not only were women and children excluded from participation in the governing of the polis, also the large number of slaves in the city and the resident alien merchants were not allowed to participate. In addition, under the hoplite franchise full citizenship was restricted to those wealthier individuals who could provide their own heavy armor. The process of governing within the relatively small number of active citizens, most of whom knew each other by sight, led to highly competitive and often destructive politics.

Modern historian Finley Hooper gives an overview of this development. Within this history, Solon (ca. 630–550 B.C.) was the first great democratic reformer of Athenian politics. Accompanying these rapid economic changes came social injustice and even threatened to bring on a civil war. In this time of emergency, Solon received extraordinary powers to begin a process of legal and political reform. In 594 he instituted what he called a "shaking off of obligations" as some sort of reduction or canceling of debts for those whose farms had become encumbered. He did so without, however, actually redistributing land. Solon then divided Athenian society into four classes, based on wealth, which determined eligibility for holding office.

By the fifth century, Athens was the largest and most prosperous city in Greece. News of her wealth and free institutions spread wide, and to her came the writers, sculptors and philosophers whose works, along with those of native citizens, have given Athens a unique place in all of human history. By comparison with the condition of other cities of the ancient world, Athenian cosmopolitanism and democracy were spectacular and startlingly modern. . . .

In Mycenaean times, Attica was divided apparently into a number of small groups of villages, each ruled by a local monarch. According to tradition, the king, whose palace was on the Acropolis at Athens, managed, by conquest or persuasion or both, to unite all Attica under his rule and so gave to the whole area a common citizenship. . . .

How long the monarchy lasted is unknown. Even the name of the last full-fledged king re-

From *Greek Realities: Life and Thought in Ancient Greece*, by Finley Hooper (New York: Scribner's, 1967). Copyright © 1967 by Finley Hooper.

mains undecided, although among ancient writers the popular choice was Codrus. All accounts agree, however, that because of some changes which took place before the seventh century, the kingship was no longer what it once was. While the title *basileus*, king, remained attached to an office on which were entailed the old sacred duties, the real power passed to the nobility who substituted their own privileged rule for that of the monarch. These were of course the same men who had long surrounded the king with advice and, very likely, intrigue.

It is not certain whether the usurpation was carried out by the whole aristocracy acting in concert or by a single powerful clan. By whatever means, the reduction of the kingship took place gradually. Tradition states that the later kings had become weak and effeminate, which, if true, would explain why the first encroachment on the monarchy was a demand by the nobility that a commander-in-chief (*polemarchos*) be elected from among their own ranks. Later the king's civil duties devolved to another elective magistrate, the *archon eponymos*. The title meant that each year would henceforth be recorded in the name of the man who held the office. By subtraction the king was left with only the administration of religious matters, although the office of king was still for life and was retained in the same family.

In time, the magistracy was further expanded by the introduction of new officers who took over some of the routine work, such as recording laws, which formerly belonged to the archon. These lesser officials were also accorded the name archon, and in addition the title was attached to the established offices of polemarch and king. As a consequence, the aristocratic constitution finally included nine archons who made up a kind of executive board headed by the *archon eponymos* who was also the chief judicial officer in the state.

In the familiar tripartite division of government amongst Indo-European societies, there was a king, a council of elders and an assembly of the people. The later Athenian story that their council, the Areopagus, was founded by Athena simply meant that it was very old and nobody knew how it got started. In any event, this body

was left uninjured by the shift in power from king to archons. It had been an aristocratic stronghold even under the monarchy when it was very likely made up of the heads of the noble families. Under the aristocracy all ex-archons were added as members for life. Age, prestige, and experience were built into the council and during its long career at Athens it appears to have performed a task similar to that of the later Senate at Rome. It was the anchor of the state, with a general supervision over all areas of the government; above all it acted as a preserver of custom and public decency. Magistrates were subject to its questioning both during and after their term in office, and it may even have had the right to deny office to anyone elected whom it considered unfit. Furthermore, its traditional role as a court of last appeal gave it an authority in Athenian political life which lasted until the very eve of the popular democracy.

The Assembly of the Athenian people was more of a theory than a practice in earliest times. Consistent with the pattern common to other Indo-European societies, the people were asked to voice their formal support in times of danger, but under the monarchy this earliest Assembly was more akin to a rally of aroused tribesmen than to a meeting of informed citizens prepared to vote.

When the aristocracy assumed control, this folk gathering was replaced by a regularly constituted body which may even have been given some voice in the election of magistrates. It is unlikely that it elected them directly, but it may have nominated men from whom the Areopagus made the final choice or it may simply have met to approve the selection of the Areopagus acting independently. Participation in this Assembly was limited to men with some amount of property, yet the requirement of noble birth continued to exclude the majority of those in the Assembly from holding any office. So the "elections," if there were any, were held by voters who themselves ranked above the poor and who selected the magistrates from among the nobility. Furthermore, only those matters of state which the Areopagus chose to bring before the Assembly would receive its attention. Operating under such restrictions, this body could not have acted as an agency for broadening the base of power below the level of the well-born. The political imbalance in turn reflected the social and economic favoritism within the society. . . .

It is clear that Solon considered the rapaciousness of wealthy landowners to be the greatest evil of the day. He was therefore determined to get the poor out from under their crushing debts. On the other hand, he had distinct reservations about these same much-abused people. He had refused to be moved by their clamor for a redistribution of the land, and he further let it be known that he had no confidence in the judgment of common men who enjoy too much prosperity. When he came to reorganize the government, he says that he gave to the common people only a limited responsibility, as much as he thought they could handle.

Solon was aware that poor men see the rich as hoarding what they do not need, and that rich men see the poor as coveting what they do not deserve. As far as he was concerned, any man—rich or poor—was easily deceived by selfish material interests and was likely to lose sight of more enduring values. This observation and others like it were no more unique then than they are now, yet they helped win Solon a place among the seven wisest men in antiquity. The evidence that he actually practiced what he taught convinces us that he deserved his honors.

Upon taking public office, his first orders were aimed at easing tensions. He writes that he freed the land of those who had fallen into debt slavery both at home and abroad. His statements about these matters are simple and offer no details, for everyone at the time would have known what he meant. He does not explain, for instance, how he managed to buy back men sold abroad for debt. It is possible that the wealthy classes, in addition to their losses from the debt cancellation, were held liable for this cost. The situation may have been critical enough for these men to consider themselves lucky in having avoided the redistribution of land which Solon had blocked. Admittedly, nobody was altogether happy with Solon's arrangements. This, however, would have reassured him; for he insisted that good laws followed a middle course—giving everybody something, but no-

body everything. For the time being at least, he established an accommodation between those with too much and those with too little. In Greece this was not easy to do then, nor has it been since.

In order to open up a wider range for Athenian trade, Solon abandoned the coinage of the Aeginetan standard and shifted to the lighter coins used by Corinth. Athenian products could now more easily enter the markets of the western Mediterranean. The olive oil *amphora* seen on the new coins was itself a clear indication of what Solon had in mind. Although he banned the export of other foodstuffs from Attica during a time of necessity, he never stopped the shipment of olive oil. Pottery was another major product of Attica and Solon saw the need for skilled craftsmen to increase the Athenian output and to provide a better quality of goods. He recruited artisans from Corinth and elsewhere by offering citizenship to all who would come with their families and settle in Attica.

Solon's support and encouragement of the business life of the city had little meaning so long as the government remained largely in the hands of aristocrats whose wealth was in land. It is a testament to his abilities that although he refused to become a tyrant and steadfastly avoided partisanship, he was able to effect changes which tyrants had managed to achieve only with extra-legal force. Solon opened public offices to men of proven ability on the premise that they could not have earned their wealth without some brains. The monopoly of the well-born was abruptly ended. As in the past, however, citizens were assigned to classes based on income and the assessment was still stated in archaic terms of bushels of produce. The wealthiest citizens were called "five-hundred bushel men" while those of the lowest class produced less than two hundred.

All men were admitted to some degree of participation in the government, although responsibilities were still heavily weighted from the top brackets down. How this principle worked itself out in every detail is not known but the overall intention seems clear. It is apparent that offices were on a graded scale with the nine archons, for instance, being chosen only from the first class. Lesser magistrates were elected from the second and third classes, but the poorest citizens were excluded from the magistracy altogether. Solon's decision to bar the most numerous class from public office was balanced, however, by his admission of all citizens to serve as jurymen. In effect, decisions by magistrates belonging to the upper classes could now be challenged by an appeal to popular judgment.

A new Council of 400, open to members of the top three classes, was created for the purpose of directing the day-to-day business of the state. It discussed and weighed all policy questions and proposed laws, and decided which matters were to be brought to the Assembly of all citizens for a vote. As such it took over the prerogative which the Areopagus had had during the time of aristocratic domination. Since the Council was in the hands of the upper three classes, the fourth class of poorest citizens still had no chance for radicalism. In other respects too, so far as both the Assembly and the courts were concerned, what the poorer citizens had been given in theory was very likely different from what they had in practice. For one thing, they would be the least likely to spare the time from making a living to come into the city and participate in government business. Their lack of experience in public affairs, their

depressed circumstances, and their inability to afford any education must also have discouraged large numbers of them from taking steps to claim their rights. Indeed, under the Solonian constitution it was apparently not expected that they would. While Solon has always been credited with giving the common people a place, it has been plain that he intended them to have only a limited role in the government and did not by any means intend that they should have the last word. More than a century would pass before a more experienced and better-informed majority would take the ultimate power for themselves. It was as though Solon had invited the hired hands into the house—and at first few of them knew how to behave but after several generations they owned it! Democracy was not a sudden invention.

After reading this selection, consider these questions:
1. What was the geographic extent of the polis of Athens?
2. What was the original form of government of Athens?
3. What reforms did Solon introduce into Athenian government and why?

SELECTION 5:
Pericles' Funeral Oration

The basis for an even more radical form of democracy was ushered in under Pericles in the fifth century B.C. Now all free men in Athens and its surrounding territories had the right to participate in the assembly and serve as jurors in the law courts. As with the hoplite franchise, citizenship was related to military service. Since the success of the Athenian navy in the wars against Persia (480–479 B.C.), the fleet was Athens's first line of military defense. Most of the new citizens were so poor that they could not arm themselves for the phalanx, but they could serve as rowers in the fleet. The period after the Persian wars (479–431) witnessed the growth of Athenian dominance over large sections of mainland Greece and the Aegean islands and coastline. It was also the period called the "classical" period of Greek civilization. The democratic spirit and the ways in which the earlier values of competition and the striving for excellence were joined to it resulted in the development of one of the most remarkably creative periods in world history. In the poetic arts (especially drama), architecture (the Parthenon), sculpture (both Phidias and Myron were active), and philosophy (Protagoras, Socrates, Plato), Athens became not just "the school of Hellas," as Pericles claimed, but the dominant model for much of subsequent Western civilization.

In his History of the Peloponnesian War, *the Athenian soldier and historian Thucydides captures both the mood of the times and the high quality of life that participation in the polis of Athens produced for its citizens. On the occasion of the state funeral for soldiers lost after the first year of war with Sparta (431–404), Pericles praised the dedication of all Athenians to the highest ideals of the polis. Through an often unstated series of contrasts with life among the Spartans, Pericles demonstrates that the Athenians possessed all the traditional virtues for which the Spartans were considered to be the best example, but the Athenians also possessed something more, which made them unrivaled among the Greeks. Pericles' oration is excerpted from Thucydides' history.*

Our form of government does not enter into rivalry with the institutions of others. We do not copy our neighbours, but are an example to them. It is true that we are called a democracy, for the administration is in the hands of the many and not of the few. But while the law secures equal justice to all alike in their private disputes, the claim of excellence is also recognised; and when a citizen is in any way distinguished, he is preferred to the public service, not as a matter of privilege, but as the reward of merit. Neither is poverty a bar, but a man may benefit his country whatever be the obscurity of his condition. There is no exclusiveness in our public life, and in our private intercourse we are not suspicious of one another, nor angry with our neighbour if he does what he likes; we do not put on sour looks at him which, though harmless, are not pleasant. While we are thus unconstrained in our private intercourse, a spirit of reverence pervades our public acts; we are prevented from doing wrong by respect for authority and for the laws, having an especial regard to those which are ordained for the

protection of the injured as well as to those unwritten laws which bring upon the transgressor of them the reprobation of the general sentiment.

And we have not forgotten to provide for our weary spirits many relaxations from toil; we have regular games and sacrifices throughout the year; at home the style of our life is refined; and the delight which we daily feel in all these things helps to banish melancholy. Because of the greatness of our city the fruits of the whole earth flow in upon us; so that we enjoy the goods of other countries as freely as of our own.

Then, again, our military training is in many respects superior to that of our adversaries. Our city is thrown open to the world, and we never expel a foreigner or prevent him from seeing or learning anything of which the secret if revealed to an enemy might profit him. We rely not upon management or trickery, but upon our own hearts and hands. And in the matter of education, whereas they from early youth are always undergoing laborious exercises which are to make them brave, we live at ease, and yet are equally ready to face the perils which they face. And here is the proof. The Lacedaemonians [Spartans] come into Attica not by themselves, but with their whole confederacy following; we go alone into a neighbour's country; and although our opponents

From *Thucydides*, translated by B. Jowett (Oxford: Clarendon Press, 1881).

are fighting for their homes and we on a foreign soil, we have seldom any difficulty in overcoming them. Our enemies have never yet felt our united strength; the care of a navy divides our attention, and on land we are obliged to send our own citizens everywhere. But they, if they meet and defeat a part of our army, are as proud as if they had routed us all, and when defeated they pretend to have been vanquished by us all.

If then we prefer to meet danger with a light heart but without laborious training, and with a courage which is gained by habit and not enforced by law, are we not greatly the gainers? Since we do not anticipate the pain, although, when the hour comes, we can be as brave as those who never allow themselves to rest; and thus too our city is equally admirable in peace and in war. For we are lovers of the beautiful, yet simple in our tastes, and we cultivate the mind without loss of manliness. Wealth we employ, not for talk and ostentation, but when there is a real use for it. To avow poverty with us is no disgrace; the true disgrace is in doing nothing to avoid it. An Athenian citizen does not neglect the state because he takes care of his own household; and even those of us who are engaged in business have a very fair idea of politics. We alone regard a man who takes no interest in public affairs, not as a harmless, but as a useless character; and if few of us are originators, we are all sound judges of a policy. The great impediment to action is, in our opinion, not discussion, but the want of that knowledge which is gained by discussion preparatory to action. For we have a peculiar power of thinking before we act and of acting too, whereas other men are courageous from ignorance but hesitate upon reflection. And they are surely to be esteemed the bravest spirits who, having the clearest sense both of the pains and pleasures of life, do not on that account shrink from danger.

After reading this selection, consider these questions:

1. What, according to Pericles, are the distinctive values of the Athenians?
2. What does Pericles consider to be the major differences between Athens and Sparta?
3. How does Pericles understand the relationship between these Athenian values and its form of government?

SELECTION 6:

Greek Values

Although innovative in its governmental forms, Athens drew heavily on the Greek aristocratic heritage. In fact, Athenian democracy represented less an opening of power to all free adult male citizens than it was a bold experiment in raising even the poorest of these citizens to the level of being economically independent and, therefore, fully human individuals. The modern historian A.W.H. Adkins describes how the values associated with the striving for aretē continued to shape Greek values throughout the classical period. These values were confined, however, to those people who were considered noble (agathos; pl. agathoi), but the number of individuals who could achieve this status increased in the fifth century B.C. Adkins defines the difference between the agathoi and those who were not noble, the kakoi (singular kakos) within democratic Athens.

The *agathos* traditionally is he who is held to be most effective in assuring the security, stability and well-being of the social unit, in war and in peace. It will be convenient to examine the use of *agathos* and *arete* in the earlier fifth century separately in war and in peace. The purpose is merely to make the exposition clearer: the words of course commend a complete view of life.

In war, the *agathos* is still the effective fighter; and it remains *kalon* to succeed, *aischron* to fail. . . .

This is both a results-culture, whose values are deeply influenced by the absolute demand that certain goals be successfully attained, and a shame-culture, whose sanction, in addition to the disastrous nature of certain failures in themselves, is *overtly* 'what people will say'. Sometimes, as in failure to win in the games, there is little material loss; but failure is *aischron* nonetheless, and will be mocked, by one's *echthroi* [equals] at all events. Nevertheless, the results-culture is more basic: it is the need for success in maintaining the prosperity and stability of the city-state that most powerfully influences the nature of *arete* and the *agathos*, and consequently what is held to be *aischron*. . . .

This being the case, those who are held to be most effective fighters on such level ground, the heavy-armed infantry, the hoplites, will evidently be held to contribute most to the well-being and indeed the continued existence of the city; so that it is not surprising to find them commended as *agathoi*. In such commendation of the hoplites a social class is commended. Citizens must buy their own armour; hoplite armour is expensive; so that only comparatively wealthy citizens can be effective in war, and so *agathoi*. To be brave, to have a strong right arm, is of little use in such infantry warfare if one has no armour.

On the other hand, though wealth is necessary, it is not sufficient; and here we may begin to consider the range of *agathos* and *arete* in peacetime. . . .

The *esthlos*, the man of adequate wealth who undertakes the approved rôles in war and in

From *Moral Values and Political Behaviour in Ancient Greece: From Homer to the End of the Fifth Century*, by A.W.H. Adkins. Copyright © 1972 by A.W.H. Adkins. Reprinted by permission of W.W. Norton & Company, Inc., and the Estate of A.W.H. Adkins.

peace, is most admirable; but even if he does not take part in games as an *esthlos* should—in Athens, at all events, he would have to serve as a hoplite—the man of mere money makes a contribution that must be acknowledged, and highly: [the ancient poet] Bacchylides treats the possession of wealth as less *kalon*, but its possessor is useful, *chrestos*; and *chrestos* used absolutely of persons is a virtual synonym of *agathos* and *esthlos*, and has similar commendatory power. . . .

Agathos and *arete*, then, commend the activities in war and in peace of those who are held to make most contribution to the prosperity and stability of the state, together with other activities which also require money and leisure, and which, being not available, or less available, to other members of society, consequently enjoy high prestige. Membership of this favoured group will vary from city to city in accordance with its history and constitution. . . .

To be an *agathos* is to be a good specimen of human being, to be a human being at his best; to be a *kakos* is to be the reverse. It would be very difficult for one termed *kakos*, who could not fail to observe the contribution to the well-being of the city made by the *agathos* in virtue of his wealth, to deny that he himself was of less value, was an inferior specimen of human being; and how could he then claim to be more fitted to rule, or to take part in any other admired activity, than the *agathos*? Even when a state enjoys a democratic constitution, the *kakoi* are likely to be deterred from speaking in the assembly, and unlikely to be elected to office, though they can of course vote. In fifth-century Athens not merely wealthy citizens but members of aristocratic families continue to be elected to the highest offices long after the democratisation of Athens' institutions. . . . There is, accordingly, some difficulty, even in a Greek democracy, for wealth unaccompanied by 'good family' to be acknowledged as *arete*, at all events where that *arete* is to be translated into political influence. . . .

The *kakos*, then, has great difficulty in maintaining his claims to just treatment against the *agathos*. It would be difficult to enumerate any 'undoubted rights' that he possesses. Certainly he possesses none merely in virtue of his being human; what rights he has, he has in virtue of his membership of a particular group; and if the group to which he belongs accords few effective rights to the *kakos*, he has few effective rights. In Athens, the state made certain forms of financial relief available to poor citizens, which increased in size and number as the fifth century progressed; but his redress in law, should he be wronged by an *agathos*, was . . . much more difficult to secure than might be expected in what was in name a democracy governed by law, according, it was claimed, equal rights before that law to all of its citizens.

After reading this selection, consider these questions:
1. What was the military and economic condition of the *agathoi*?
2. What does Adkins mean by "results-culture"?
3. How were the *kakoi* defined?

SELECTION 7:
Slavery in the Classical World

Even with the greatness associated with Athenian democracy and its cultural achievements, modern historians point out that economically and socially Athens was based on slavery. Slaves not only performed most of the menial tasks within individual households but also did all the most grueling work within Athenian industries and mining operations. While slavery was widely pervasive throughout most of the Greek city-states, other types of enforced labor also existed in the Greek world. Modern historian M.I. Finley investigates the origins of slavery in the ancient classical world and then compares the role of slaves in Greek and Roman societies.

As a commodity, the slave is property. At least since [philosopher Edward] Westermarck writing at the beginning of the [twentieth] century, some sociologists and historians have persistently tried to deny the significance of that simple fact, on the ground that the slave is also a human being or that the owner's rights over a slave are often restricted by the law. All this seems to me to be futile: the fact that a slave is a human being has no relevance to the question whether or not he is also property; it merely reveals that he is a peculiar property, Aristotle's 'property with a soul'. Reciprocally,

the old Latin word *erus* also implies the peculiarity of a slave-property. Defined in the Oxford Latin Dictionary as 'a man in relation to his servants, master', *erus* was regularly and frequently used by slaves in the comedies of Plautus and even of Terence, in preference to *dominus*. Later poets continued to employ the word as an occasional archaism, but they extended it to mean also the owner of an animal or other property, thus sacrificing the original implication that the slave-master relationship was odd, indeed unique, among property relations.

Legal restrictions on the rights of a slaveowner are also a side-issue: in modern sociological and juridical theories of any school, all property is understood to be a matrix of rights, rarely if ever unlimited. The precise rights that constitute the matrix vary with kinds of property and kinds of society. Property, in other words, is an historical category, and that is one more commonplace that I must regretfully enunciate in order to remove the confusions that still prevail on the subject. When Roman lawyers defined a slave as someone who was in the *dominium* of another, they used the quintessential property-term *dominium*. They were not dissuaded by the slave's human quality (not even when they used the word *homo* to refer to a slave, as they did frequently). Nor were the millions of slaveowners who bought and sold slaves, overworked them, beat and tortured them, and sometimes put them to death, precisely as millions of horse-owners have done throughout history. Other millions did not exercise their rights to the full in this way: that is interesting, even important, but it does not undermine the slave-property link conceptually.

The failure of any individual slaveowner to exercise all his rights over his slave-property was always a unilateral act on his part, never binding, always revocable. That is a critical fact. So is its reverse, the equally unilateral, always revocable grant by a slaveowner of a specific privilege or benevolence. As for promises, one of Plautus' slaves succinctly exposed their standing: no master can be brought to court over a promise to a slave. Even the act of manumission could be, and frequently was, qualified in a multitude of ways. Failure to appreciate the fundamental significance of this unilaterality—as when [German historian] Eduard Meyer compared the chances of ancient slaves and modern wage-earners to achieve wealth and social position—destroys the possibility of fixing and comprehending the nature and history of slavery within any given society.

Paradoxically, it was precisely this quality of the slave, as property, that offered the owning class flexibility (to which I shall return shortly) not available with other forms of compulsory labour. That is one reason why I stress what is a juristic category and therefore of itself not a sufficient 'definition' of the slave. How individual owners chose to treat their peculiar property was normally not a matter of mere whim or of differences in personality. Owners frequently offered slaves the incentive of eventual manumission through various arrangements which automatically brought into being a chain of behaviour and expectations that affected the master, too. Although in law and in fact he could always revoke the offer, the material gains to be derived from slavery would have been sharply reduced if such arrangements were not as a rule honoured.

The slaveowner's rights over his slave-property were total in more senses than one. The slave, by being a slave, suffered not only 'total loss of control over his labour' but total loss of control over his person and his personality: the uniqueness of slavery, I repeat, lay in the fact that the labourer himself was a commodity, not merely his labour or labour-power. His loss of control, furthermore, extended to the infinity of time, to his children and his children's children—unless, again, the owner by a unilateral act broke the chain through unconditional manumission. And even then, only children born subsequently were beneficiaries, not those already in existence at the moment of manumission. There is indeed ample evidence that manumission was not rarely withheld until a slave had progeny who could replace him (or her) in servitude, though there is no way of determining how frequent a practice this was, or whether it was largely restricted to certain categories of slaves, such as those in the Roman imperial employ.

This totality of the slaveowner's rights was facilitated by the fact that the slave was always a deracinated outsider—an outsider first in the sense that he originated from outside the society into which he was introduced as a slave, second in the sense that he was denied the most elementary of social bonds, kinship. '*Quem patrem, qui servos est?*' 'What father, when he is a slave?' The contrast with Spartan helots, Thessalian *penestai* or the *clientes* of early Rome provides the clearest delineation, as has already been suggested: never did the master-class need or attempt to replenish the supply of dependent labour of this kind from outside. In stressing the kinlessness of slaves, I am concerned less with the juridical position, primarily the exclusion of slaves from legally recognized marriage (hence the Roman insistence on the word *contubernium*) than with the *de facto* position. There were slave unions and slave families, beyond a doubt, but they counted among the privileges that could be granted unilaterally by a slaveowner, and withdrawn unilaterally. The very possibility could be totally withdrawn by castration. As the poet Statius wrote in praise of Domitian's (ineffectual) prohibition of the practice, 'nor by a harsh law are slave mothers fearful of the burden of sons'.

Complete and brutal withdrawal of the kinship privilege also took the form of dispersing a slave family through sale. In A.D. 325 Constantine ordered an official to stop the break-up of slave families on imperial estates in Sardinia which he had transferred to private ownership, and that was almost certainly the earliest governmental interference with the practice. A little earlier the jurists were ruling that in an intestate succession or in certain other situations in which the contrary intention was not made explicit, slave families should not be broken up. That reflects a humane tendency, no doubt, but the more significant point is the stress on intent: the slaveowner's freedom in this respect was not being challenged as late as the third century. . . .

A priori these three components of slavery— the slave's property status, the totality of the power over him, and his kinlessness—provided powerful advantages to the slaveowner as against other forms of involuntary labour: he had greater control and flexibility in the employment of his labour force and far more freedom to dispose of unwanted labour. In consequence, a hierarchy arose within the slave population. One need only think of the following contemporaries: the slaves in the Spanish gold and silver mines or in the chain-gangs on Italian estates, the slaves in the imperial civil service, the slave overseers and stewards on the land, the urban slaves conducting their own commercial and manufacturing establishments in Rome and the other cities of Italy through the device of the *peculium* (to which we shall return). The slaves, in other words, constituted a type within the larger class of involuntary labour, but they were at the same time significantly divisible into sub-types. Stated differently, the slaves were a logical class and a juridical class but not, in any usual sense of that term, a social class.

Yet, for all the advantages (or apparent advantages), slavery was a late and relatively infrequent form of involuntary labour, in world history generally and in ancient history in particular. Advantages and disadvantages are not essences but historical attributes that come and go under changing social and economic conditions. The critical question in the development and decline of ancient slavery can therefore be examined only by an inquiry into the necessary and sufficient conditions. What, in other words, brought about the transformation from the 'primordial fact' of individual slaves to the existence of slave societies, and what subsequently brought about a reversal of that process?

The process was not only complex, but uneven and in a sense incomplete. Free labour was never eliminated, not only incidental hired labour but the central labour of the independent peasants and artisans. The coexistence of free and slave labour, furthermore, was more than a coincidence in time and place; it was often a symbiosis, as in Italian agriculture where an adequate supply of free seasonal labour was a necessary condition for both the proper operation of slave *latifundia* and the economic survival of the free peasantry. That is straightforward enough, unlike the survival of non-slave forms of involuntary labour. The latter opens up the very large question of the unity we implicitly posit when we speak of the Graeco-Roman world, a question I cannot discuss except in the one aspect immediately relevant to the matter of involuntary labour. . . .

It is conventional to begin the analysis by what I have repeatedly called the 'numbers game'. I shall not join in, both because it has long been clear that the evidence does not permit genuine quantification and because most of the players start from the false assumption that they must either produce astronomical figures in order to justify the label 'slave society' or, in opposition, that they somehow eliminate a slave society by demolishing the extreme figures. In 1860 the slaves made up 33% of the population in the southern states of the United States, a slightly lower percentage in Cuba and Brazil. On conservative estimates—60,000 slaves in Athens at the end of the fifth century B.C., 2,000,000 in Italy at the end of the Republic—the comparable percentages are in precisely the same range, about 30 and 35%, respectively. That is more than sufficient, especially since the signs all say that slaveowners in antiquity were found considerably lower in the social and economic scale than in the New World, and since this proportion of slaves was retained in antiquity over a long period of time: the entire history of slavery in the United States lasted no more than the period from Augustus to Septimius Severus [27 B.C.–A.D. 211]. . . .

I have cited these few, admittedly outsize figures as a prelude to the general point that an assessment of the place of slaves in a society is not a matter of their totals, given a reasonably large number, but of their location, in two senses—first, who their owners were; secondly, what role they played, in the economy but not only in the economy. There were no slave employments, apart from mining as a general rule and domestic service, the latter defined as service in households other than those of one's immediate family. Equally there were no free employments, other than law and politics (as distinct from administration) and normally the army (but not the navy, and excluding the servants of individual soldiers). In practice, however, moralists such as Aristotle or Cicero may have evaluated the work, all other occupations were shared by slaves and free men, often working side by side on identical tasks. Xenophon's remark that 'those who can do so buy slaves so that they may have fellow workers' is not mere sententiousness. The ratios between slaves and free men in any occupation varied greatly in time and place: one need only contrast the normally free, respected physicians of Greece and their often unfree, always low-status counterparts in Rome and Italy. Such distinctions are interesting but marginal. The location of slavery cannot be determined by occupational tests.

One fundamental nuance in Xenophon's remark is that the fellow-workers were a slaveowner together with his slave or slaves, not slaves alongside hired free labour. In all Greek or Roman establishments larger than the family unit, whether on the land or in the city, the *permanent* work force was composed of slaves (or of other kinds of involuntary labour where that regime survived). I stress the word 'permanent',

for, as I have already indicated, free casual and temporary hired labour was common enough, and indeed indispensable, in agriculture and in such abnormal activities as temple building. Not many generalizations about the ancient world can be substantiated with such certainty, with so few exceptions in the documentation. Farm tenancy, which is often adduced as an alternative to agricultural slavery, was no exception to this rule. Tenants were not employees: they either took on family-size farms which they worked without additional labour or they leased larger holdings and themselves employed slaves. Either way they did not breach the normal structure of labour on the land. Nor was there a slave 'level' of work: in the larger establishments, urban and rural, slaves performed all tasks from the most menial to the professional and managerial.

We may therefore locate slavery neatly and simply. With one exception which I shall clarify in a moment, free men dominated small-scale farming, much of it subsistence farming, as well as petty commodity production and small-scale trading in the cities; slaves dominated, and virtually monopolized, large-scale production in both the countryside and the urban sector. It follows that slaves provided the bulk of the immediate income from property (that is, income from other than political sources, such as the vast sums pocketed by Roman Republican commanders and provincial officials or tax-farmers, and other than the secondary income obtained by the rich from moneylending) of the élites, economic, social and political. The exception I mentioned is primarily a procedural one: the practice, probably much more common in Italy than in Greece, whereby slaves enriched their owners by working as 'independent' craftsmen, shopkeepers and 'businessmen'—through what the Romans called *peculium*—was merely a variant procedure for the benefit of the élite; in one sense it led to considerable slave participation in petty commodity production, with important social consequences, but economically it did not disturb the location of slavery as the basic source of élite income. Manumission, finally, was often but a further extension of the *peculium*-idea.

I have of course been referring only to those

'central' areas in which other forms of involuntary labour were displaced by slavery. They were the slave societies of Graeco-Roman antiquity, and they were that precisely because of the location of slavery within them. And so the time has come to consider how and why that rare phenomenon came into being. The conventional starting-point has almost always been the 'natural' state of war that has supposedly existed in early times and in simple societies among different tribes and peoples. Already in antiquity, and in modern times ever since the international lawyers of the sixteenth and seventeenth centuries, it has been repeated like a litany that slavery was in the first instance a mitigation of barbarian modes of warfare. That was [French historian Numa-Denis] Fustel's 'primordial fact'.

Historians of antiquity have then gone a step further, and insisted on war and conquest as the necessary condition for the creation of a slave society. I must demur at some length. The fallacy arises from a view of Roman history that is so dazzled by the vastness of the conquests and enslavements of the last two centuries before Christ that it is blind to the unmistakable, considerably earlier growth of slavery in Rome. No one will deny the enormous leap that occurred after the second Punic War. A similar leap occurred in the course of American history, for different reasons, but that does not invalidate the view that the southern states were already a slave society in the first half of the eighteenth century. So was Rome not later than the third century B.C. All vigorous new institutions develop and expand, but that process follows their introduction and cannot be confused with the latter.

After reading this selection, consider these questions:
1. What, according to Finley, was the origin of slavery in the ancient classical world?
2. What were the differences between slavery in Greece and Rome?
3. According to Finley, what were the percentages of slaves in the populations of Greece and Rome?

SELECTION 8:

Greek Philosophy

Within this world, philosophy came to be defined not just as an academic pursuit or the basis of scientific research, it became a way in which individuals sought personal happiness. Although the older beliefs in the Olympian gods continued, a whole new series of mystery cults and oriental religions entered this essentially Greek civilization; philosophy rather than religion was the way through which many educated persons sought the meaning of their existence.

The development of Greek philosophy and its full realization within a number of schools of philosophy in the Hellenistic period mark a transformation and culmination of earlier Greek values. Greek thought became one of the main ways in which ancient Hellenic civilization was handed down to subsequent ages becoming one of the main contributions of the Greeks to the civilization of the West. Philosophy arose in the archaic period of the seventh century B.C. When the world was no longer understood *as the chance and arbitrary actions of the gods (for which the various myths were explanations in the form of stories) but as an ordered cosmos, the early nature philosophers of Ionia* claimed that the human mind was capable of comprehending this order. The motion of heavenly bodies, the changes in the weather, the fluctuations of human health and well-being now were to be understood in terms of this order and its intelligibility.*

As philosopher William Barrett makes clear in the following selection, this basic philosophy about life—of what are the significant values in human life, of the nature of the social bond, and the underlying sense of the real—is radically different from that of the Hebrews. In drawing out these differences and indicating how they have continued to provide the two pillars of Western civilization, Barrett concludes by showing how Aristotle culminates a philosophic tradition that dates back to the archaic period and hands over to the future one of the major philosophical traditions of the West.

*Ionia is the eastern shore of the Aegean Sea, in ancient times home to many Greek poleis. Today it is the western coast of Turkey.

Hebraism contains no eternal realm of essences, which Greek philosophy was to fabricate, through Plato, as affording the intellectual deliverance from the evil of time. Such a realm of eternal essences is possible only for a *detached* intellect, one who, in Plato's phrase, becomes a "spectator of all time and all existence." This ideal of the philosopher as the highest human type—the theoretical intellect who from the vantage point of eternity can survey all time and existence—is altogether foreign to the Hebraic concept of the man of faith who is passionately committed to his own mortal being. Detachment was for the Hebrew an impermissible state of mind, a vice rather than a virtue; or rather it was something that Biblical man was not yet even able to conceive, since he had not reached the level of rational abstraction of the Greek. His existence was too earth-bound, too laden with the oppressive images of mortality, to permit him to experience the philosopher's detachment. The notion of the immortality of the soul as an intellectual substance (and that that immortality might even be demonstrated rationally) had not dawned upon the mind of Biblical man. If he hoped at all to es-

cape mortality it was on the basis of personal trust that his Creator might raise him once again from the dust. . . .

To sum up:

(1) The ideal man of Hebraism is the man of faith; for Hellenism, at least as it came to ultimate philosophic expression in its two greatest philosophers, Plato and Aristotle, the ideal man is the man of reason, the philosopher who as a spectator of all time and existence must rise above these.

(2) The man of faith is the concrete man in his wholeness. Hebraism does not raise its eyes to the universal and abstract; its vision is always of the concrete, particular, individual man. The Greeks, on the other hand, were the first thinkers in history; they discovered the universal, the abstract and timeless essences, forms, and ideas. The intoxication of this discovery (which marked nothing less than the earliest emergence and differentiation of the rational function) led Plato to hold that man lives only insofar as he lives in the eternal.

(3) There follows for the Greek the ideal of *detachment* as the path of wisdom which only the philosopher can tread. The word "theory" derives from the Greek verb *theatai*, which means to behold, to see, and is the root of the word theater. At a theater we are spectators of an action in which we ourselves are not involved. Analogously, the man of theory, the philosopher or pure scientist, looks upon existence with detachment, as we be-

hold spectacles at the theater; and in this way he exists, to use [Danish philosopher Søren] Kierkegaard's expression, only upon the aesthetic level of existence.

The Hebraic emphasis is on *commitment,* the passionate involvement of man with his own mortal being (at once flesh and spirit), with his offspring, family, tribe, and God; a man abstracted from such involvements would be, to Hebraic thought, but a pale shade of the actual existing human person.

(4) The eternal is a rather shadowy concept for the Hebrew except as it is embodied in the person of the unknowable and terrible God. For the Greek eternity is something to which man has ready and continuous access through his intellect.

(5) The Greek invented logic. His definition of man as the rational animal is literally as the logical animal, *to zoon logikon*; or even more literally the animal who has language, since logic derives from the verb *legein*, which means to say, speak, discourse. Man is the animal of connected logical discourse.

For the Hebrew the status of the intellect is rather typified by the silly and proud babbling of Job's friends, whose arguments never touch the core of the matter. Intellect and logic are the pride of fools and do not touch the ultimate issues of life, which transpire at a depth that language can never reach, the ultimate depth of faith. Says Job at the end of the Book: "I have heard of thee by the hearing of the ear: but now mine eye seeth thee."

(6) The Greek pursues beauty and goodness as things that are identical or at least always coincident; in fact he gives them a single name, the beautiful-and-good, *to kalokagathia.* The Hebraic sense of sin . . . is too much aware of the galling and refractory aspects of human existence to make this easy identification of the good and the beautiful. The sense of the sinfulness of Biblical man is the sense of his radical finitude in its aspect of imperfection. Hence his good must sometimes wear an ugly face, just as beauty for him may be the shining mask of evil and corruption. . . .

When we come to the end, with Aristotle, of the great historical cycle that began with the pre-Socratics, philosophy had become a purely theoretical and objective discipline. The main branches of philosophy, as we know it today as an academic subject, had been laid out. Wisdom is identified as Metaphysics, or "First Philosophy," a detached and theoretical discipline: the ghost of the existential Socrates had at last been put to rest. . . . The foundations of the sciences, as the West has known them, had been laid, and this was only possible because reason had detached itself from the mythic, religious, poetic impulses with which it had hitherto been mixed so that it had no distinguishable identity of its own.

The West has thought in the shadow of the Greeks; even where later Western thinkers have rebelled against Greek wisdom, they have thought their rebellion through in the terms which the Greeks laid down for them. . . . A young Greek who felt a disposition toward both poetry and theory, and wanted to choose one for a career, would want to know which was the better life, and Plato and Aristotle would have made no bones about their reply: the theoretical life is higher than the life of the artist or that of the practical man of politics—or of the saint, for that matter, though they did not yet know of this kind of existence. In his *Nicomachean Ethics* Aristotle gives us a remarkably flexible and well-rounded picture of human nature and the many different kinds of goals, or goods, at which it may aim; but the ethical question still seems unanswered for him until he has declared which of all possible goods is the best, and in the tenth and final book of this work he expresses his own preference (stated, of course, as an objective truth) for the life of pure reason, the life of the philosopher or theoretical scientist, as the highest life. . . .

Reason, Aristotle tells us, is the highest part of our personality: that which the human person truly is. One's reason, then, is one's real self, the center of one's personal identity. This is rationalism stated in its starkest and strongest terms— *that one's rational self is one's real self*—and as such held sway over the views of Western philosophers up until very modern times. Even the Christianity of the Middle Ages, when it assimilated Aristotle, did not displace this Aristotelian principle: it simply made an uneasy alliance between faith as the supernatural center of the personality and reason as its natural center;

the natural man remained an Aristotelian man, a being whose real self was his rational self.

After reading this selection, consider these questions:
1. What are the key values of Hebrew religion for Barrett?
2. How did these values differ from those of the Greek philosophers?
3. What was the relationship of Aristotle to earlier Greek philosophers?

SELECTION 9:
The Nicomachean Ethics of Aristotle

Aristotle's ethical writings are a case in point. The following selection from the Nicomachean Ethics *indicates how the older Greek values of striving for excellence and the moral basis of friendship continued. They were, however, subsumed within a striving for philosophical enlightenment. In ways already indicated by Socratic questioning and Platonic thought, the active life that was demanded by life in the polis had become subordinated to the theoretical and contemplative life.*

If happiness is activity in accordance with virtue, it is reasonable that it should be in accordance with the highest virtue; and this will be that of the best thing in us. Whether it be reason or something else that is this element which is thought to be our natural ruler and guide and to take thought of things noble and divine, whether it be itself also divine or only the most divine element in us, the activity of this in accordance with its proper virtue will be perfect happiness. That this activity is contemplative we have already said.

Now this would seem to be in agreement both with what we said before and with the truth. For, firstly, this activity is the best (since not only is reason the best thing in us, but the objects of rea-son are the best of knowable objects); and, secondly, it is the most continuous, since we can contemplate truth more continuously than we can *do* anything. And we think happiness has pleasure mingled with it, but the activity of philosophic wisdom is admittedly the pleasantest of virtuous activities; at all events the pursuit of it is thought to offer pleasures marvellous for their purity and their enduringness, and it is to be expected that those who know will pass their time more pleasantly than those who inquire. And the self-sufficiency that is spoken of must belong most to the contemplative activity. For while a philosopher, as well as a just man or one possessing any other virtue, needs the necessaries of life, when they are sufficiently equipped with things of that sort the just man needs people towards whom and with whom he shall act justly, and the temperate man, the brave man, and each of the others is in the same case, but the philosopher, even when by himself, can contemplate

From *The Basic Works of Aristotle*, edited by Richard McKeon (New York: Random House, 1941.)

truth, and the better the wiser he is; he can perhaps do so better if he has fellow-workers, but still he is the most self-sufficient. And this activity alone would seem to be loved for its own sake; for nothing arises from it apart from the contemplating, while from practical activities we gain more or less apart from the action. And happiness is thought to depend on leisure; for we are busy that we may have leisure, and make war that we may live in peace. Now the activity of the practical virtues is exhibited in political or military affairs, but the actions concerned with these seem to be unleisurely. Warlike actions are completely so (for no one chooses to be at war, or provokes war, for the sake of being at war; any one would seem absolutely murderous if he were to make enemies of his friends in order to bring about battle and slaughter); but the action of the statesman is also unleisurely, and—apart from the political action itself—aims at despotic power and honours, or at all events happiness, for him and his fellow citizens—a happiness different from political action, and evidently sought as being different. So if among virtuous actions political and military actions are distinguished by nobility and greatness, and these are unleisurely and aim at an end and are not desirable for their own sake, but the activity of reason, which is contemplative, seems both to be superior in serious worth and to aim at no end beyond itself, and to have its pleasure proper to itself (and this augments the activity), and the self-sufficiency, leisureliness, unweariedness (so far as this is possible for man), and all the other attributes ascribed to the supremely happy man are evidently those connected with this activity, it follows that this will be the complete happiness of man, if it be allowed a complete term of life (for none of the attributes of happiness is *in*complete).

But such a life would be too high for man; for it is not in so far as he is man that he will live so, but in so far as something divine is present in him; and by so much as this is superior to our composite nature is its activity superior to that which is the exercise of the other kind of virtue. If reason is divine, then, in comparison with man, the life according to it is divine in comparison with human life. But we must not follow those who advise us, being men, to think of human things, and, being mortal, of mortal things, but must, so far as we can, make ourselves immortal, and strain every nerve to live in accordance with the best thing in us; for even if it be small in bulk, much more does it in power and worth surpass everything. This would seem, too, to be each man himself, since it is the authoritative and better part of him. It would be strange, then, if he were to choose not the life of his self but that of something else. And what we said before will apply now; that which is proper to each thing is by nature best and most pleasant for each thing; for man, therefore, the life according to reason is best and pleasantest, since reason more than anything else *is* man. This life therefore is also the happiest.

After reading the selection, consider these questions:

1. How does Aristotle define happiness?
2. How does he define reason in relation to happiness?
3. Is Aristotle's definition of excellence (*aretē*) different from earlier ones?

CHAPTER 5
The Roman World: Individual Piety and Civic Virtue

The ancient Greeks and their civilization were to provide one of the two foundations of the civilization of the West. But it was the further adoption and adaptations of Greek civilization by the Romans that provided the specific form in which the classical tradition was to be handed down to the modern West. The enormous empire the Romans eventually established around the Mediterranean basin stretched from Britain to Persia and back across North Africa, absorbing mainland Greece and the various Hellenistic kingdoms of the East. Within this imperial structure, the major traditions of the Near East and Greece were not just transformed but also transferred to outlying areas such as northern and western Europe and North Africa.

On the other side of the Mediterranean, Rome was also to adopt and shape the other major tradition of the West. Arising as a sect within Judaism, Christianity had its origins in Roman-dominated Palestine and developed into a separate religion with its own rituals and values. Within the confines of this empire, Christianity would spread, eventually becoming the official state religion. In this way, Roman civilization influenced the dominant religion of the West. In terms of the various traditions that would make up the civilization of the West, all converged in Rome.

Who were the Romans? In a general sense, their political forms were not that different from those of the Greeks of the Hellenic period. Rome originated as a city-state in central Italy; 753 B.C. is the traditional date of its founding. It was surrounded by competing city-states to the east, to the north (the Etruscan cities), and to the south (the Greek cities of Italy). Its early history is the story of seemingly unending conflicts with these other Italian cities. Also, in ways not totally dissimilar to the poleis of Greece, conflicts outside the state led to conflicts within, as various social groups vied for power. Eventually a type of shared rule among the aristocratic families and the nonaristocrats achieved a workable political and social structure. This political settlement allowed Rome to first conquer central Italy, then to dominate the entire peninsula. After the war with Carthage in North Africa (the Punic Wars, 264–146 B.C.), Rome also controlled large areas outside Italy around the western Mediterranean.

This overview of political and constitutional history may suggest similarities to the city-states of Greece, but Rome achieved something that escaped the Greeks. It created an empire that lasted at least until the sixth century A.D. in the West and (remarkable as it may seem) until the fifteenth century in the East. What were the reasons for Rome's longevity? The extent of the empire and its long life belie any explanation that emphasizes mere chance or sheer luck in its creation and endurance. Roman political institutions and military organization had much to do with explaining this notable achievement, although these had to be modified as the government of the small city-state became the ruler of a vast empire. Beyond these military and political formations and transformations, and indeed behind them, lay a distinctive Roman attitude toward the world. In this the Romans were decidedly different from the Greeks and especially from the Athenians and even from the Spartans. For the most part, the Greeks of the Hellenic and Hellenistic periods valued wit, spontaneity, the cunning of correctly sizing up a situation and taking advantage of it, and the play of language and thought. Romans valued other things.

The Roman sense of *pietas* (piety) connoted a sense of devotion and duty. This quality was grounded in a sense of duty to the gods of the state religion but also found its source in the family and the ancestors of the family. These values were given expression in the respect paid to the gods. These were the Lares (the spirits of the ancestors), whose images, first in wax models and then in marble busts, were given a place of honor in every Roman household. These gods were also thought to participate in current activities. The Penates (the spirits of the pantry), together with the Lares, were connected with keeping the family well and its traditions alive. Maintaining these traditions of the household and family and the moral attitudes arising from them was the responsibility of the parents, especially of the mother. This moral code thus stressed the importance of the women in the education of their children. Unlike the almost totally secluded position of women within Greek households, women of good birth in Rome were considered the centers, if not the leaders, of the family. Children, including grown men and women, remained tied to their families throughout their lives. The shame of not living up to these traditions of the family both in private and in public life presented more of a threat and thus offered more of a deterrent to immoral behavior than did impersonal legal or divine punishment.

The Roman state was built on these same foundations and was considered an extension of these family-based values. Politics, then, was not seen as a place for innovation. Even in the face of new situations, continuity with the past—with the customs of the ancients—was primary. Innovations, when demanded, were instituted through reference to a return to the ways of the ancestors. This sense of tradition gave stability to the state and to politics.

SELECTION 1:

Roman Values

British historian R.H. Barrow analyzes those specifically Roman virtues that came forth early in their history and continued to shape Roman attitudes throughout the imperial period and even into the years of decline.

Throughout their history the Romans were acutely aware that there is 'power' outside man, individually or collectively, of which man must take account. He must subordinate himself to something. If he refuses, he invites disaster; if he subordinates himself unwillingly, he becomes the victim of superior force; if willingly, he finds that he may be raised to the rank of cooperator; by cooperation he can see something of the trend, even the purpose, of that superior power. Willing cooperation gives a sense of dedication; the purposes become clearer, and he feels he is an agent or an instrument in forwarding them; at a higher level he becomes conscious of a vocation, of a mission for himself and for men like him, who compose the state. When the Roman general celebrated his 'triumph' after a victorious campaign, he progressed through the city from the gates to the temple of Jupiter (later in imperial times to the temple of Mars Ultor) and there offered to the god 'the achievements of Jupiter wrought *through* the Roman people'.

From the earliest days of Rome we can detect in the Roman a sense of dedication, at first crude and inarticulate and by no means unaccompanied by fear. In later days it is clearly expressed and is often a mainspring of action. In the latest days the mission of Rome is clearly proclaimed; it is often proclaimed most loudly by men who strictly were not Romans, and most insistently at the very time when in its visible expression the mis-

sion was accomplished. The sense of dedication at first reveals itself in humble forms, in the household and in the family; it is enlarged in the city-state and it finds its culmination in the imperial idea. From time to time it employs different categories of thought and modes of expression; but in its essence it is religious, for it is a leap beyond experience. When the mission is accomplished, its basis changes.

This is the clue to Roman character and to Roman history.

The Roman mind is the mind of the farmer and soldier; not farmer, nor soldier, but farmer-soldier; and this is true on the whole even in the later ages when the Roman might be neither farmer nor soldier. 'Unremitting work' is the lot of the farmer, for the seasons wait for no man. Yet his own work by itself will achieve nothing; he may plan and prepare, till and sow; in patience he must await the aid of forces which he cannot understand, still less control. If he can make them favourable, he will; but most often he can only cooperate, and he places himself in line with them that they may use him as their instrument, and so he may achieve his end. Accidents of weather and pest may frustrate him; he must accept compromise and be patient. Routine is the order of his life; seed-time, growth, and harvest follow in appointed series. The life of the fields is his life. If as a citizen he is moved to political action at last, it will be in defence of his land or his markets or the labour of his sons. To him the knowledge born of experience is worth more than speculative theory. His virtues are honesty and thrift, forethought and patience, work and endurance and courage, self-reliance, simplicity, and humility in the face of what is greater than himself.

Such also are the virtues of the soldier. He too will know the value of routine, which is a part of discipline, for he must respond as by instinct to a sudden call. He must be self-reliant. The strength and endurance of the farmer serve the soldier; his practical skill helps him to become what the Roman soldier must be, a builder and a digger of ditches and maker of roads and ramparts. He lays out a camp or a fortification as well as he lays out a plot or a system of drains. He can live on the land, for that is what he has done all his life. He too knows the incalculable element which may upset the best of dispositions. He is conscious of unseen forces, and he attributes 'luck' to a successful general whom some power—destiny or fortune—uses as an instrument. He gives his loyalty to persons and to places and to friends. If he becomes politically violent, he will be violent to secure, when the wars are over, land to till and a farm to live in; and still greater loyalty rewards the general champions his cause. He has seen many men and many places, and with due caution he will imitate what he has seen to work; but for him 'that corner of the earth smiles above all others', his home and native fields, and he will not wish to see them changed.

The study of Roman history is, first, the study of the process by which Rome, always conscious of her dedication, painfully grew from being the city-state on the Seven Hills until she became mistress of the world; secondly, the study of the means by which she acquired and maintained that dominion; the means was her singular power of turning enemies into friends, and eventually into Romans, while yet they remained Spaniards or Gauls, or Africans. From her they derived 'Romanitas', their 'Roman-ness'. 'Romanitas' is a convenient word used by the Christian Tertullian to mean all that a Roman takes for granted; the Roman point of view and habit of thought. . . .

First in every catalogue of virtues comes some recognition that a man should admit his subordination to something external which has a 'binding-power' upon him, and the term for this, *religio*, has a wide application. For a 'religious man' the phrase is usually 'a man of the highest *pietas*', and *pietas* is part of that subordination of

which we have spoken. You are *pius* to the gods if you admit their claims: you are *pius* to your parents and elders, and children and friends, and country and benefactors, and all that excites, or should excite, your regard and perhaps affection, if you admit their claims on you, and discharge your duty accordingly; the claims exist because the relationships are sacred. The demands of *pietas* and of *officium* (duty and services, as in 'tender offices') constituted in themselves a massive and unwritten code of feeling and behaviour which was outside the law, and was so powerful as to modify in practice the harsh rules of private law, which were only a last resort.

Gravitas means 'a sense of the importance of the matters in hand', a sense of responsibility and earnestness. It is a term to apply at all levels—to a statesman or a general as he shows appreciation of his responsibilities, to a citizen as he casts his vote with consciousness of its importance, to a friend who gives his advice based on his experience and on regard for your welfare; Propertius uses it when assuring his mistress of 'the seriousness of his intentions'. It is the opposite of *levitas*, a quality the Romans despised, which means trifling when you should be serious; flippancy, instability. *Gravitas* is often joined with *constantia*, firmness of purpose, or with *firmitas*, tenacity; it may be seasoned with *comitas*, which means the relief given to over-seriousness by ease of manner, good humour, and humour. *Disciplina* is the training which produces steadiness of character; *industria* is hard work; *virtus* is manliness and energy; *clementia* the willingness to forgo one's rights; *frugalitas*, simple tastes.

These are some of the qualities which Romans most admired. They are moral qualities; they may even be dull and unexciting. There is nothing among them to suggest that intellectual power, or imaginativeness, or sense of beauty, or versatility, or charm—that hard-worked word nowadays—appealed to them as a high ideal. The qualities which served the Roman in his early struggles with Nature and with neighbours remained for him the virtues above all others. To them he owed it that his city-state had risen superior to the older civilisation which surrounded it—a civilisation which appeared to him to be limp and nerveless unless stiffened by the very virtues which he himself had painfully cultivated. Perhaps they can be summed up under *severitas*, which means being stern with oneself.

The manner of life and the qualities of character here described make up the *mores maiorum*, the manners of one's ancestors, which are among the most potent forces in Roman history. In the broadest sense the phrase may include the political constitution and the legal framework of the state, though generally such words as *instituta*, institutions, and *leges*, laws, are added. In the narrower sense the phrase means the outlook on life, the moral qualities, together with the unwritten rules and precedents of duty and behaviour, which combined to form a massive tradition of principle and usage. To this tradition appeal was made when revolutionaries laid violent hand on political practice, on religious custom, or on standards of morality or taste. The constancy of this appeal, made by orator and poet, soldier and statesman, showed that it had not lost its force even in the most troubled times or in the latest ages. Reformers might ignore tradition, but they could not deride it; and no roman dreamed of destroying what was old merely because it was old.

After reading this selection, consider these questions:

1. What are the characteristic values of the Romans, according to Barrow?
2. What were *pietas* and *gravitas* for the Romans?
3. What did the Romans mean by *mores maiorum*?

SELECTION 2:

The Story of Cincinnatus

With *this sense of the past and the tradition of their ancestors, the Romans looked to history both as a justification of their political institutions and as a set of models for individual and collective action in public life. The stories of early Rome and early Romans provided inspiration and guidance for centuries. The first-century Roman historian Titus Livius—Livy, as he is known in English—was perhaps the most successful in presenting images of a vast array of early Romans. In the following selection from his book* The History of Rome, *Livy relates the story of Cincinnatus (fifth century B.C.), who, perhaps more than any other noble Roman, illustrated the core political virtues. From the harsh conditions of small-scale farming, Cincinnatus became a successful military commander in a time of crisis. Cincinnatus represented another important Roman value,* virtus. *Virtus—virtue—combined the primarily masculine values of strength, courage, and loyalty. And it also included wisdom, moral purity, and dedication to the state over one's own interests. This selection from Livy opens with the breaking of a peace treaty and the beginning of yet another war with the near-by cities of Aequina and Sabina. Rome's enemies were initially successful, throwing Rome into a panic. As in other crisis situations, Roman citizens elected a temporary leader with extraordinary powers. This individual was called the dictator.*

Nothing could have happened so unexpected, or so contrary to the people's hopes; and the fright and consternation, in consequence of it, were not less than if the city were surrounded and threatened, instead of the camp. They sent for the consul Nautius, yet not supposing him capable of affording them sufficient protection, resolved that a dictator should be chosen to extricate them from this distress, and Lucius Quintius Cincinnatus was accordingly appointed with unanimous approbation. Here they may receive instruction who despise every quality which man can boast, in comparison with riches; and who think, that those who possess them can alone have merit, and to such alone honours and distinctions belong. Lucius Quintius, the now sole hope of the people, and of the empire of Rome, cultivated a farm of four acres on the other side of the Tiber, at this time called the Quintian meadows, opposite to the very spot where the dock-yard stands. There he was found by the deputies, either leaning on a stake, in a ditch which he was raking, or ploughing; in some work of husbandry he was certainly employed. After mutual salutations, and wishes on the part of the commissioners, "that it might be happy both to him and the commonwealth," he was requested to "put on his gown, and hear a message from the senate." Surprised, and asking if "all was well?" he bade his wife Racilia bring out his gown quickly from the cottage. When he had put it on, after wiping the sweat and dust from his brow, he came forward, when the deputies congratulated him, and saluted him dictator; requested his presence in the city, and informed him of the alarming situation of the army. A vessel had been prepared for Quintius by order of government, and on his landing on the other side, he was received by his three sons, who came out to meet him; then by his other relations and friends, and afterwards by the greater part of the patricians. Surrounded by this numerous attendance, and the lictors marching before him, he was conducted to his residence. The plebeians

likewise ran together from all quarters; but they were far from beholding Quintius with equal pleasure, for they thought the powers annexed to his office too unlimited, and the man still more arbitrary. During that night, no farther steps were taken than to post watches in the city.

Next day, the dictator coming into the forum before it was light, named Lucius Tarquitius master of the horse; he was of a patrician family, but though, by reason of the narrowness of his circumstances, he had served among the foot, yet he was accounted by many degrees the first in military merit among all the young men of Rome. Attended, then, by his master of the horse, Quintius came to the assembly of the people, proclaimed a cessation of civil business, ordered the shops to be shut in all parts of the city, and that no one should attend to any private affairs. He then issued orders that all who were of the military age should attend, under arms, in the field of Mars, before sunset, with victuals for five days, and twelve palisades each and that those whose age rendered them unfit for service, should dress that victuals for the soldiers who lived near them, while they were preparing their arms, and procuring the military pales. Immediately the young men ran different ways to look for palisades, which every one without molestation took, wherever he could find them; and they all attended punctually according to the dictator's order. The troops being then formed in such a manner as was not only proper for a march, but for an engagement also, if occasion should require it, the dictator set out at the head of the legions, and the master of the horse at the head of his cavalry. In both bodies such exhortations were used, as the juncture required; that "they should quicken their pace; that there was a necessity for expedition, in order to reach the enemy in the night; that the Roman consul and his army were besieged; that this was the third day of their being invested; that no one could tell what any one night or day might produce; that the issue of the greatest affairs often depended on a moment of time." The men too, to gratify their leaders, called to each other, "standard-bearer, advance quicker; soldiers, follow." At midnight they arrived at Algidum, and when they found themselves, near the enemy, halted.

From *The History of Rome*, by Titus Livius, translated by George Baker (New York: Derby, 1861).

The dictator then having rode about, and examined as well as he could in the night, the situation and form of the enemy's camp, commanded the tribunes of the soldiers to give orders that the baggage should be thrown together in one place; and then that the soldiers, with their arms and palisades, should return into the ranks. These orders were executed; and then with the same regularity in which they had marched, he drew the whole army in a long column, and directed that, on a signal being given, they should all raise a shout, and that on the shout being raised, every man should throw up a trench in front of his post, and fix his palisades. As soon as these orders were communicated, and the signal given, the soldiers performed what they were commanded: the shout resounded on every side of the enemy, and reaching beyond their camp, was heard in that of the consul, exciting terror in the one, and the greatest joy in the other. The Romans observing to each other, with exultation, that this was the shout of their countrymen, and that assistance was at hand, took courage, and from their watch-guards and out-posts issued threats. The consul likewise declared, that "they ought not to lose time, for that the shout then heard was a signal, not only that their friends were arrived, but that they had entered upon action; and they might take it for granted, that the camp was attacked on the outside." He therefore ordered his men to take arms, and follow him; these falling on the enemy before it was light, gave notice by a shout to the dictator's legions, that on their side also the action was begun. The Æquans were now preparing measures to hinder themselves from being surrounded with works; when being attacked within, they were obliged, lest a passage might be forced through the midst of their camp, to turn their attention from those employed on the fortifications, to the others who assailed them on the inside; and thus left the former at leisure, through the remainder of the night, to finish the works, and the fight with the consul continued until morn appeared. At the break of day, they were entirely encompassed by the dictator's works, and while they were hardly able to support the fight against one army, their trenches were assaulted by Quintius's troops, who instantly, on completing those

works, had returned to their arms. Thus they found themselves obliged to encounter a new enemy, and the former never slackened their attack. Being thus closely pressed on every side, instead of fighting, they had recourse to entreaties, beseeching the dictator on one side, and the consul on the other, to be content with the victory without their entire destruction, and to permit them to retire without arms. By the consul they were referred to the dictator, and he, highly incensed against them, added ignominy to their defeat. He ordered their general, Gracchus Clœlius, and the other leaders, to be brought to him in chains, and the town of Corbie to be evacuated; then told them, that "he wanted not the blood of the Æquans; that they were at liberty to depart; but he would send them under the yoke, as an acknowledgment, at length extorted, that their nation was conquered and subdued." The yoke is formed of three spears, two being fixed upright in the ground, and the other tied across between the upper ends of them. Under this yoke the dictator sent the Æquans.

Having possessed himself of the enemy's camp, which was filled with plenty, for he had sent them away naked, he distributed the entire booty among his own troops. Reprimanding the consular army and the consul himself, he said to them, "Soldiers, ye shall share no part of the spoil of that enemy, to whom ye were near becoming a prey; and as to you, Lucius Minucius, until you begin to show a spirit becoming a consul, you shall command those legions, with the rank of lieutenant-general only." Accordingly Minucius resigned the consulship, and, in obedience to orders, remained with the army. But so well were people then disposed to obey, without repining, the commands of superiors, that this army regarding more the benefit which he had conferred, than the disgrace which he had inflicted on them, not only voted a golden crown of a pound weight to the dictator, but at his departure saluted him as their patron. At Rome, the senate, being convened by Quintus Fabius, prefect of the city, ordered that Quintius on his arrival should enter the city in triumph, without changing his order of march. The generals of the enemy were led before his chariot, the military ensigns carried before him, and his army followed, laden with spoil. It is said that tables were laid out with provisions before every house, and that the troops, partaking of the entertainment, singing the triumphal hymn, and throwing out their customary jests, followed the chariot like revellers at a feast.

After reading this selection, consider these questions:

1. What were the virtues exhibited in the story of Cincinnatus?
2. What does Livy's account tell us about early Roman history?
3. How does this account of Cincinnatus relate to the Roman notion of *mores maiorum*?

Selection 3:

The Challenge of Greek Culture

With his simple ways and ultimate dedication to the Roman Republic, Cincinnatus was one of the highest models of the good citizen-soldier, which the Romans would continue to honor throughout their long history. He represented the values of solemn dedication to family, city, and the gods—of pietas and gravitas—which, on their positive sides, sought simplicity and respect for ancestors and "the old ways," but, on their negative sides, remained suspicious of alien ways and of innovation.

Problems for this value system arose once Rome came into contact with other peoples. Whereas the origins of Roman civilization were intimately connected to that of the Etruscans to their immediate north, the various peoples to the north and east of the Romans on the Italian peninsula presented little challenge to their basic way of life. When, however, the Romans turned farther south and east, to the Greek cities of Italy and the Greek mainland, things were different. Here, Romans encountered a type of sophistication in culture, a level of wealth, and an ideal of what constituted the good life, which seemed both higher than their own and irresistible. As the empire expanded eastward, even under the Roman Republic, Greek art and literature, philosophy and rhetoric, and values of intelligence and sophistication all set a new model for many Romans.

As with all such cultural adoptions and transformations, the absorption of Greek values was neither total nor complete. Roman virtues merged with those of the Greeks to form something new—both Roman and Greek. Since the fifteenth and sixteenth centuries, the term classical has been used when referring to this complex merging of heritages. When, however, the Romans first came into contact with Greek civilization, there was no guarantee that Greek models would be accepted or that they would be

merged with traditional Roman values. In fact, when the politically pow-
erful Roman clan of the Scipios—which included the conqueror of
Carthage—became the major proponents of Greek civilization in the
Rome of the first century B.C., there were equally powerful families and in-
dividuals who opposed them, and opposed them in the name of "good
old" Roman simplicity. This group of traditionalists was headed by Cato
the Elder. Cato wrote a history of Rome praising its simple, sturdy values,
The Origins *(written between 168 and 149 B.C.), and a treatise on man-*
aging a large farm, On Agriculture *(160 B.C.). In the following selection*
from Plutarch's Life of Cato the Elder, *the ancient biographer and moral-*
ist describes Cato's reasons for attacking these new Greek attitudes.

When he [Cato] was now well on in years, there came as ambassadors from Athens to Rome, Carneades the Academic, and Diogenes the Stoic philosopher, to beg the reversal of a certain decision against the Athenian people, which imposed upon them a fine of five hundred talents. The people of Oropus had brought the suit, the Athenians had let the case go by default, and the Sicyonians had pronounced judgment against them. Upon the arrival of these philosophers, the most studious of the city's youth hastened to wait upon them, and became their devoted and admiring listeners. The charm of Carneades especially, which had boundless power, and a fame not inferior to its power, won large and sympathetic audiences, and filled the city, like a rushing mighty wind, with the noise of his praises. Report spread far and wide that a Greek of amazing talent, who disarmed all opposition by the magic of his eloquence, had infused a tremendous passion into the youth of the city, in consequence of which they forsook their other pleasures and pursuits and were "possessed" about philosophy. The other Romans were pleased at this, and glad to see their young men lay hold of Greek culture and consort with such admirable men. But Cato, at the very outset, when this zeal for discussion came pouring into the city, was distressed, fearing lest the young men, by giving this direction to their ambition, should come to love a reputation based on mere words more than one achieved by

martial deeds. And when the fame of the visiting philosophers rose yet higher in the city, and their first speeches before the Senate were interpreted, at his own instance and request, by so conspicuous a man as Gaius Acilius, Cato determined, on some decent pretext or other, to rid and purge the city of them all. So he rose in the Senate and censured the magistrates for keeping in such long suspense an embassy composed of men who could easily secure anything they wished, so persuasive were they. "We ought," he said, "to make up our minds one way or another, and vote on what the embassy proposes, in order that these men may return to their schools and lecture to the sons of Greece, while the youth of Rome give ear to their laws and magistrates, as heretofore."

This he did, not, as some think, out of personal hostility to Carneades, but because he was wholly averse to philosophy, and made mock of all Greek culture and training, out of patriotic zeal. He says, for instance, that Socrates was a mighty prattler, who attempted, as best he could, to be his country's tyrant, by abolishing its customs, and by enticing his fellow citizens into opinions contrary to the laws. He made fun of the school of Isocrates, declaring that his pupils kept on studying with him till they were old men, as if they were to practise their arts and plead their cases before Minos in Hades. And seeking to prejudice his son against Greek culture, he indulges in an utterance all too rash for his years, declaring, in the tone of a prophet or a seer, that Rome would lose her empire when she had become infected with Greek letters. But time has certainly shown the emptiness of this ill-boding speech of his, for while the city was at the zenith

From *Plutarch's Lives*, translated by Bernadotte Perrin (London: Heinemann, 1914).

of its empire, she made every form of Greek learning and culture her own.

After reading this selection, consider these questions:

1. According to Plutarch, what led to Cato's attack on Greek values?
2. What did Cato propose should be done to all Greek philosophers in Rome?
3. What was Cato's objection to Greek learning?

SELECTION 4:
The Problem of Luxury

Not only Greek art, literature, ideals of intelligence, and sophistication came into Rome beginning in the second century B.C. Wealth, too, poured into Rome at this time from the East, bringing both the possibility of the good life to some and crudeness and overindulgence to others. Even with this recognition of the excesses of wealth, and in the face of traditional Roman values that were challenged by the appeal of riches, what could the Romans do? The great Roman historian Tacitus, writing in the first century A.D., relates a story of the emperor Tiberius, the heir of Augustus.

The consulate of Gaius Sulpicius and Decimus Haterius followed [A.D. 22]: a year of quiet abroad, though at home there was uneasiness at the prospect of stern measures against the luxury which had broken all bounds and extended to every object on which money can be squandered. But other extravagances, though actually more serious, could as a rule be kept private by concealing the prices paid: it was the apparatus of gluttony and intemperance which had become the eternal theme of gossip and had awakened anxiety lest a prince of old-world thriftiness might adopt too harsh measures. For, when the point was mooted by Gaius Bibulus, it had been maintained by his fellow-aediles also that the sumptuary law was a dead letter; that the prohibited prices for articles of food were rising daily; and that the advance could not be checked by moder-

ate methods. The senate, too, when consulted, had referred the question without any discussion to the emperor. But Tiberius, after debating with himself repeatedly whether it was possible to arrest these uncurbed passions, whether such an arrest might not prove an even greater national evil, and what would be the loss of dignity should he attempt a reform which could not be enforced, or, if enforced, would demand the degradation and disgrace of his most illustrious subjects, finally composed a letter to the senate, the drift of which was as follows:—

"On other occasions, Conscript Fathers, it is perhaps preferable that, if my opinion is needed on a matter of public policy, the question should be put and answered when I am present; but in this debate it was better that my eyes should be withdrawn; otherwise, through your indicating the anxious features of members who might be charged with indecent luxury, I too might see and, so to speak, detect them. If our active aediles had taken me into their counsels beforehand, I am not sure but that I should have advised them to

From *The Histories*, by Tacitus, translated by Clifford H. Moore (London: Heinemann, 1931).

leave vigorous and full-blown vices alone, rather than force matters to an issue which might only inform the world with what abuses we were powerless to cope. Still, they have done their duty—and I could wish to see every other magistrate as thorough in the discharge of his office. But for myself it is neither honourable to be silent nor easy to be outspoken, because it is not the part of aedile or praetor or consul that I act. Something greater and more exalted is demanded from a prince; and, while the credit of his successes is arrogated by every man to himself, when all err it is one alone who bears the odium. For on what am I to make my first effort at prohibition and retrenchment to the ancient standard? On the infinite expanse of our villas? The numbers—the nations—of our slaves? The weight of our silver and gold? The miracles of bronze and canvas? The promiscuous dress of male and female—and the specially female extravagance by which, for the sake of jewels, our wealth is transported to alien or hostile countries?

"I am aware that at dinner-parties and social gatherings these things are condemned, and the call is for restriction; but let any one pass a law and prescribe a penalty, and the same voices will be uplifted against 'this subversion of the state, this death-blow to all magnificence, this charge of which not a man is guiltless'! And yet even bodily ailments, if they are old and inveterate, can be checked only by severe and harsh remedies; and, corrupted alike and corrupting, a sick and fevered soul needs for its relief remedies not less sharp than the passions which inflame it. All the laws our ancestors discovered, all which the deified Augustus enacted, are now buried, those in oblivion, these—to our yet greater shame—in contempt. And this it is that has given luxury its greater boldness. For if you covet something which is not yet prohibited, there is always a fear that prohibition may come; but once you have crossed forbidden ground with impunity, you have left your tremors and blushes behind.—Then why was frugality once the rule?—Because every man controlled himself; because we were burghers of a single town; nor were there even the same temptations while our empire was confined to Italy. By victories abroad we learned to waste the substance of others; by victories at home, our own."

After reading this selection, consider these questions:

1. How did the expansion of the empire directly affect life in the city of Rome?
2. How did the increase in wealth threaten traditional Roman values?
3. According to Tacitus, what was the emperor Tiberius's stance on luxury?

CHAPTER 6
The Birth of Christianity

The most remarkable "event" in the later history of Rome was the adoption of Christianity as the empire's official religion. From a small sect within Judaism, Christianity spread to become an independent religion in the first, second, and third centuries A.D. The conversion of many souls to Christianity is a complex story, involving missionary activities, inspirational tales of individual and collective martyrdom, and "philosophical" conversions. But Christianity was not the only belief system contending for the attention of the great numbers and wide varieties of peoples who made up the Roman Empire in this period. Stoicism and Epicureanism continued to be popular among the Roman elites, but their impact was limited. Older forms of polytheism remained the major religion of the majority as well as the official religion. Through its syncretic nature, polytheism could merge fairly easily with other religions, Judaism and Christianity being the only notable exceptions.

There were, however, other types of beliefs that, even when their adherents gave allegiance to the official religion, still moved them to value other notions of divinity and to value other moral attitudes. Like Christianity and Judaism, these religions came from the East. Predominant among them were the revival of the worship of the Egyptian goddess Isis, a separate cult to Osiris (Sarapis), and the cult of the Persian god Mithras. Whatever form these religions took, they shared a number of common features. They all emphasized ways in which, through ritualistic observations, one could deal with the blows of fate. They also guaranteed an ultimate form of divine justice in the afterlife. In this sense, they stressed the plight of the individual, not dedication to the common values of preserving the polis, the republic, or any other public institution. By the second century B.C. political life, even on the local level, was either entirely extinct, as in the Hellenistic kingdoms, or merely window dressing for the real exercise of power, as in Rome. Although directed to the individual, these religions were also social, in the sense that the individual believers sought a community—a nonpolitical community—in which his or her faith could be guided, encouraged, and shared.

How did Christianity "triumph" over these other religions? The causes of this phenomenon are difficult to understand in any simple sense; but the consequences for the West are not. Christianity shaped and continues to shape the basic values of the West. We still can speak meaningfully of the two foundations of the West in Hebrew and Greek civilization. But it is the particular ways in which these traditions were modified first under Roman rule and then, as the Roman Empire became a Christian empire, transformed into Christian forms that made them distinctly Western. Christianity originally arose from Jewish roots, and this origin resulted in the continuity of many of the basic beliefs of this religion into the civilization of the West. The notion of divinity, the understanding of divine providence working in the individual and throughout world history, the acceptance of the ethical code of the Ten Commandments—all these derive from Hebrew sources and continue to influence the West. But there were other sources that led to the formation of what we know as Christian values and beliefs. The Persian religion of Zoroastrianism added or strengthened the value of otherworldliness and an understanding of the cosmos as an eternal conflict between good and evil, light and dark. Within the empire, the growing cult of Mithras added notions of baptism and the use of holy water as well as the identification of Sundays as the sabbath. Hellenistic philosophies, as they continued through the imperial period, also had their influences. Stoicism placed emphasis on asceticism, cosmopolitanism, and the idea of the brotherhood of all mankind. And Gnosticism brought out, within Christian doctrine, the belief in the importance of revelation and the idea of a god-man becoming incarnate in human form. Although there would be other components that contribute to this complex mix that is the modern West, Christianity as it developed within the Roman Empire already represented a remarkable combination of many of the traditions of the ancient world.

The complexity of values in early Christianity was already there at the site of origins. Jesus of Nazareth began his career as teacher and preacher within a particular moment in the development of Judaism. Ancient Hebrew religion itself had been heavily influenced (once again) by the great civilizations of the East through the conquest and subsequent exile of its political and religious leaders to Babylon in the seventh century B.C. Once the religion was allowed to reestablish itself in Judaea under the rule of the Persians, Judaism both reinterpreted its own past and introduced a new emphasis on the role of prophecy within the continuity of its traditions. Into this new mix came first Greek domination and Hellenistic values in the fourth century B.C. and ultimately Roman rule and Roman values in the first century. Throughout, the Jews attempted to preserve their ancient religion in the face of alien gods and foreign ways as well as the obvious attractions of Hellenistic learning and philosophy. The history of Judaism is very much the account of the vicissitude of maintaining this distinctive mode of life. Into this contrasting and conflicting world of political powers and religious affiliations, Jesus was born in Roman Palestine at the end of the first century.

From within Judaism, and drawing out certain of its central features in new ways, Jesus preached the fatherhood of God and the brotherhood of man, the forgiveness of sin and the love of one's neighbors, the resurrection of the dead in the afterworld and the rejection of greed, hypocrisy, and ceremony in this one. Viewed as a challenge to the religious authority of the Jewish religious community and as a threat to Roman political domination, Jesus was executed around A.D. 30. According to those who continued to believe in Jesus as the savior of the world (the Messiah) and in his message of the fatherly love of God, Jesus overcame death, was resurrected, and returned to heaven, which both proved his status as the Messiah and provided a means for others to triumph over death and this world. Only in the Gospel of John (ca. A.D. 90)—as opposed to the earlier Epistles of Paul and the Synoptic gospels—is the divinity of Jesus Christ affirmed as the word, the *logos*, of God.

With the conversion to Christianity of Emperor Constantine, the Christian church was established as the official religion of the empire by the Edict of Milan in A.D. 313. This adoption of Christianity had a number of unintended consequences. The movement from a sect to a world religion involved changes from the commitments of a small group of intense believers within a larger and often hostile world (only 5 to 20 percent of the population of the empire in A.D. 300) to the official and highly institutionalized religion of an empire of tens of millions. But what was Christianity in the third, fourth, and fifth centuries? It is not always clear. Without an established hierarchy or direct lines of authority before the fourth century, Christianity was open to various interpretations by the growing numbers who claimed to be its true followers. Interpretations that would later be labeled heretical by the official church included Arianism and Nestorianism. Both these forms of Christianity refused to accept the doctrine of the Trinity—the equality of Father, Son, and Holy Spirit within a single Godhead. Under the influence of Greek philosophical thought, the Arians claimed that God created the Son; and therefore, the Son was not coeternal with the Father. The Nestorians maintained that Christ had two natures, human and divine. Nestorians, therefore, rejected the idea that Mary should be called the mother of God, implying that Christ participated in a lesser way than God in divinity. Mystical forms of Christianity and its offshoots continued as well: thus Gnosticism and Manichaeanism rejected the idea that there was any rational understanding of God. Faith came through revelation. They were also suspicious of worldliness—worldly wealth and power—not just as antagonistic to true religious belief but also as an expression of evil. The establishment of Christianity as the empire's official religion not only ended persecution but also made the church a political power and a recipient of the empire's tremendous wealth. Gnostics and Manichaeans inveighed against this growing political and economic power of the official church.

SELECTION 1:

The Teachings of Jesus

Although it is not clear that the first generations of Christians held to the teachings of Jesus, they were most succinctly expressed in the Sermon on the Mount. The following selection is taken from the Gospel According to St. Matthew.

And [Jesus] went about all Galilee, teaching in their synagogues and preaching the gospel of the kingdom and healing every disease and every infirmity among the people. So his fame spread throughout all Syria, and they brought him all the sick, those afflicted with various diseases and pains, demoniacs, epileptics, and paralytics, and he healed them. And great crowds followed him from Galilee and the Decap'olis and Jerusalem and Judea and from beyond the Jordan.

Seeing the crowds, he went up on the mountain, and when he sat down his disciples came to him. And he opened his mouth and taught them, saying:

"Blessed are the poor in spirit, for theirs is the kingdom of heaven.

"Blessed are those who mourn, for they shall be comforted.

"Blessed are the meek, for they shall inherit the earth.

"Blessed are those who hunger and thirst for righteousness, for they shall be satisfied.

"Blessed are the merciful, for they shall obtain mercy.

Matthew 4:23–5:48 from *The New Oxford Annotated Bible with the Apocrypha*, edited by Herbert G. May and Bruce M. Metzger (New York: Oxford University Press, 1977). Copyright 1973, 1977 by Oxford University Press, Inc.

"Blessed are the pure in heart, for they shall see God.

"Blessed are the peacemakers, for they shall be called sons of God.

"Blessed are those who are persecuted for righteousness' sake, for theirs is the kingdom of heaven.

"Blessed are you when men revile you and persecute you and utter all kinds of evil against you falsely on my account. Rejoice and be glad, for your reward is great in heaven, for so men persecuted the prophets who were before you.

"You are the salt of the earth; but if salt has lost its taste, how shall its saltness be restored? It is no longer good for anything except to be thrown out and trodden under foot by men.

"You are the light of the world. A city set on a hill cannot be hid. Nor do men light a lamp and put it under a bushel, but on a stand, and it gives light to all in the house. Let your light so shine before men, that they may see your good works and give glory to your Father who is in heaven.

"Think not that I have come to abolish the law and the prophets; I have come not to abolish them but to fulfil them. For truly, I say to you, till heaven and earth pass away, not an iota, not a dot, will pass from the law until all is accomplished. Whoever then relaxes one of the least of these commandments and teaches men so, shall be called least in the kingdom of heaven; but he who does them and teaches them shall be called great in the kingdom of heaven. For I tell you, unless your righteousness exceeds that of the scribes and Pharisees, you will never enter the kingdom of heaven.

"You have heard that it was said to the men of old, 'You shall not kill; and whoever kills shall be liable to judgment.' But I say to you that every one who is angry with his brother shall be liable to judgment; whoever insults his brother shall be liable to the council, and whoever says, 'You fool!' shall be liable to the hell of fire. So if you are offering your gift at the altar, and there remember that your brother has something against you, leave your gift there before the altar and go; first be reconciled to your brother, and then come and offer your gift. Make friends quickly with your accuser, while you are going with him to court, lest your accuser hand you over to the judge, and the judge to the guard, and you be put in prison; truly, I say to you, you will never get out till you have paid the last penny.

"You have heard that it was said, 'You shall not commit adultery.' But I say to you that every one who looks at a woman lustfully has already committed adultery with her in his heart. If your right eye causes you to sin, pluck it out and throw it away; it is better that you lose one of your members than that your whole body be thrown into hell. And if your right hand causes you to sin, cut it off and throw it away; it is better that you lose one of your members than that your whole body go into hell.

"It was also said, 'Whoever divorces his wife, let him give her a certificate of divorce.' But I say to you that every one who divorces his wife, ex-cept on the ground of unchastity, makes her an adulteress; and whoever marries a divorced woman commits adultery.

"Again you have heard that it was said to the men of old, 'You shall not swear falsely, but shall perform to the Lord what you have sworn.' But I say to you, Do not swear at all, either by heaven, for it is the throne of God, or by the earth, for it is his footstool, or by Jerusalem, for it is the city of the great King. And do not swear by your head, for you cannot make one hair white or black. Let what you say be simply 'Yes' or 'No'; anything more than this comes from evil.

"You have heard that it was said, 'An eye for an eye and a tooth for a tooth.' But I say to you, Do not resist one who is evil. But if any one strikes you on the right cheek, turn to him the other also; and if any one would sue you and take your coat, let him have your cloak as well; and if any one forces you to go one mile, go with him two miles. Give to him who begs from you, and do not refuse him who would borrow from you.

"You have heard that it was said, 'You shall love your neighbor and hate your enemy.' But I say to you, Love your enemies and pray for those who persecute you, so that you may be sons of your Father who is in heaven; for he makes his sun rise on the evil and on the good, and sends rain on the just and on the unjust. For if you love those who love you, what reward have you? Do not even the tax collectors do the same? And if you salute only your brethren, what more are you doing than others? Do not even the Gentiles do the same? You, therefore, must be perfect, as your heavenly Father is perfect."

SELECTION 2:
Women in the Early Church

Although Jesus' followers continued to believe in the truth of his message, they soon divided over whether Jesus the Messiah had come to save just the Jews or all mankind. St. Peter sought the conversion of the Jews; St. Paul moved to an international ministry, preaching to all the peoples of the Roman world. Conversion from both within and outside Judaism was most often achieved by preaching. Through his preaching and writings (an extension of his mission as preacher), Paul explained that his own conversion to Christianity came with a new interpretation of the crucifixion of Jesus. Jesus was not only the Christ, the Messiah of Jewish tradition, but also the Savior of mankind. His death was the ultimate sacrifice, removing sin from the world. Righteousness and ultimately salvation meant accepting this definition of Christ. Faith in Jesus and not Jewish law or Jewish ritual was therefore all-important.

As Christianity slowly grew in the cities of the eastern Mediterranean, it attracted slaves and women disproportionately to their numbers in the general population. The reasons are not difficult to comprehend. Not only was the message of hope and salvation popular with those who had little or no prestige in this world, but the dominant culture was essentially elitist male and competitive in its values. The Roman world—as was the Greek—was dominated by a small group of males competing for dominance. In attracting women, Christianity clashed with the established social structures as well as with the dominant system of values. In various epistles written to the newly organized Christian communities throughout the empire, Paul found it necessary to give a Christian definition to marriage and the position of women generally. In his first letter to the Corinthians, he credits the unmarried state as higher than the married for both men and women. Within marriage, Paul definitely tells women to subordinate themselves to their husbands. This position confirmed Roman as well as Jewish traditions. Paul argued, though, from a new understanding of the meaning of the secondary status of women within God's creation. With its appeal to the equality of women on the one hand and Paul's insistence on their subordination on the other, Christianity provided a rather ambiguous definition of the role of women in church and in society.

Now concerning the matters about which you wrote. It is well for a man not to touch a woman. But because of the temptation to immorality, each man should have his own wife and each woman her own husband. The husband should give to his wife her conjugal rights, and likewise the wife to her husband. For the wife does not rule over her own body, but the husband does; likewise the husband does not rule over his own body, but the wife does. Do not refuse one another except perhaps by agreement for a season, that you may devote yourselves to prayer; but then come together again, lest Satan tempt you through lack of self-control. I say this by way of concession, not of command. I wish that all were as I myself am. But each has his own special gift from God, one of one kind and one of another.

To the unmarried and the widows I say that it is well for them to remain single as I do. But if they cannot exercise self-control, they should marry. For it is better to marry than to be aflame with passion,

To the married I give charge, not I but the Lord, that the wife should not separate from her husband (but if she does, let her remain single or else be reconciled to her husband)—and that the husband should not divorce his wife.

1 Corinthians 7:1–40; 11:1–16, from *The New Oxford Annotated Bible with the Apocrypha*, edited by Herbert G. May and Bruce M. Metzger (New York: Oxford University Press, 1977). Copyright 1973, 1977 by Oxford University Press, Inc.

To the rest I say, not the Lord, that if any brother has a wife who is an unbeliever, and she consents to live with him, he should not divorce her. If any woman has a husband who is an unbeliever, and he consents to live with her, she should not divorce him. For the unbelieving husband is consecrated through his wife, and the unbelieving wife is consecrated through her husband. Otherwise, your children would be unclean, but as it is they are holy. But if the unbelieving partner desires to separate, let it be so; in such a case the brother or sister is not bound. For God has called us to peace. Wife, how do you know whether you will save your husband? Husband, how do you know whether you will save your wife?

Only, let every one lead the life which the Lord has assigned to him, and in which God has called him. This is my rule in all the churches. Was any one at the time of his call already circumcised? Let him not seek to remove the marks of circumcision. Was any one at the time of his call uncircumcised? Let him not seek circumcision. For neither circumcision counts for anything nor uncircumcision, but keeping the commandments of God. Every one should remain in the state in which he was called. Were you a slave when called? Never mind. But if you can gain your freedom, avail yourself of the opportunity. For he who was called in the Lord as a slave is a freedman of the Lord. Likewise he who was free when called is a slave of Christ. You were bought with a price; do not become slaves of men. So, brethren, in whatever state each was called, there let him remain with God.

Now concerning the unmarried, I have no command of the Lord, but I give my opinion as one who by the Lord's mercy is trustworthy. I think that in view of the present distress it is well for a person to remain as he is. Are you bound to a wife? Do not seek to be free. Are you free from a wife? Do not seek marriage. But if you marry, you do not sin, and if a girl marries she does not sin. Yet those who marry will have worldly troubles, and I would spare you that. I mean, brethren, the appointed time has grown very short; from now on, let those who have wives live as though they had none, and those who mourn as though they were not mourning, and those who

rejoice as though they were not rejoicing, and those who buy as though they had no goods, and those who deal with the world as though they had no dealings with it. For the form of this world is passing away.

I want you to be free from anxieties. The unmarried man is anxious about the affairs of the Lord, how to please the Lord; but the married man is anxious about worldly affairs, how to please his wife, and his interests are divided. And the unmarried woman or girl is anxious about the affairs of the Lord, how to be holy in body and spirit; but the married woman is anxious about worldly affairs, how to please her husband. I say this for your own benefit, not to lay any restraint upon you, but to promote good order and to secure your undivided devotion to the Lord.

If any one thinks that he is not behaving properly toward his betrothed, if his passions are strong, and it has to be, let him do as he wishes: let them marry—it is no sin. But whoever is firmly established in his heart, being under no necessity but having his desire under control, and has determined this in his heart, to keep her as his betrothed, he will do well. So that he who marries his betrothed does well; and he who refrains from marriage will do better.

A wife is bound to her husband as long as he lives. If the husband dies, she is free to be married to whom she wishes, only in the Lord. But in my judgment she is happier if she remains as she is. And I think that I have the Spirit of God. . . .

Be imitators of me, as I am of Christ.

I commend you because you remember me in everything and maintain the traditions even as I have delivered them to you. But I want you to understand that the head of every man is Christ, the head of a woman is her husband, and the head of Christ is God. Any man who prays or prophesies with his head covered dishonors his head, but any woman who prays or prophesies with her head unveiled dishonors her head—it is the same as if her head were shaven. For if a woman will not veil herself, then she should cut off her hair; but if it is disgraceful for a woman to be shorn or shaven, let her wear a veil. For a man ought not to cover his head, since he is the image and glory of god; but woman is the glory of man. (For man was not made from woman, but woman from man. Neither was man created for woman, but woman for man.) That is why a woman ought to have a veil on her head, because of the angels. (Nevertheless, in the Lord woman is not independent of man nor man of woman; for as woman was made from man, so man is now born of woman. And all things are from God.) Judge for

yourselves; is it proper for a woman to pray to God with her head uncovered? Does not nature itself teach you that for a man to wear long hair is degrading to him, but if a woman has long hair, it is her pride? For her hair is given to her for a covering. If any one is disposed to be contentious, we recognize no other practice, nor do the churches of God.

SELECTION 3:
A New Sense of Community

A modern historian of late antiquity, Peter Brown emphasizes the role that community played in early Christianity. In what was increasingly seen as an alien and corrupt world, Christianity provided a new sense of belonging as well as a means of overcoming this world. Brown begins by contrasting the development of the Christian communities with those of the Jews within the Roman Empire. He then explores the reasons for the spread of the Christian faith in the years before the official Roman toleration of Christianity at the beginning of the fourth century.

When we talk of the rise of Christianity in the cities of the Mediterranean, we are speaking of the destiny of an exceptionally labile and structurally unstable fragment of sectarian Judaism. The mission of Saint Paul (from about A.D. 32 to about A.D. 60) and of similar apostles had consisted of gathering the Gentiles into a new Israel, made available to them at the end of time by the messiahship of Jesus. In practice, this new Israel was formed among pagans who had been attracted, with varying degrees of commitment, to the influential Jewish communities of the cities of Asia Minor and the Aegean and to the large Jewish community in Rome. In its view of itself, the new Israel was a "gathering in": Jesus, as Messi-

ah, had broken down previous "walls of division." Paul in his letters recited the traditional catalogues of opposed groups of persons—Jew and Gentile, slave and freeman, Greek and barbarian, male and female—in order to declare that such categories had been eradicated within the new community. The sole initiation into the group—a single purificatory bath—was presented by Paul as a stripping away of the garments of all previous social and religious categories, and the putting on of Christ, by which Paul meant the gaining by each believer of a single, uncompartmented identity, common to all members of the community, as befitted "sons of God" newly adopted "in Christ."

This potent mirage of solidarity flickered on the horizons of bodies of men and women whose position in Roman society made the achievement of such solidarity a hope destined to remain forever unfulfilled and, for that reason, all the more poignantly central to their moral concerns. The

Reprinted by permission of the publisher from *A History of Private Life: From Pagan Rome to Byzantium*, edited by Paul Veyne, translated by Arthur Goldhammer (Cambridge, MA: Belknap Press of Harvard University Press). Copyright © 1987 by the President and Fellows of Harvard College.

early Christian converts lacked the social situation that would have made Paul's mighty ideal of undifferentiated solidarity "in Christ" possible. The patrons and disciples of Paul and his successors were not simple souls, nor were they the humble and oppressed of modern romantic imagination. Had they been so, his ideals might have been realized more easily. Rather, they were moderately wealthy and frequently well traveled. As a result, they were exposed to a range of social contacts, of opportunities for choice and hence for potential double-hearted conflict, on many more issues than were, for instance, the rural poor of the "Jesus Movement" of Palestine or the members of the sedentary and enclosed Jewish settlement at Qumran. To "follow Jesus" by moving from village to village in Palestine and Syria, to "choose the Law" by abandoning "the will of their own spirit" in a monastic grouping perched on the edge of the Judaean wilderness, exposed believers to a range of choices mercifully more restricted than those experienced by the men and women of the "gatherings of the saints" in large and prosperous cities such as Corinth, Ephesus, and Rome. In the history of the Christian churches in the first and second centuries A.D. we are looking along a rich vein of human material notably different from that known to us either among the wellborn of the cities or among the villagers of the Gospels. . . .

It was a morality of the socially vulnerable. In modestly well-to-do households the mere show of power was not available to control one's slaves or womenfolk. As a result, concern for intimate order, for intimate restraints on behavior, for fidelity between spouses and obedience within the household acted out "in singleness of heart, fearing God," tended to be that much more acute. Obedience on the part of servants, fair dealings between partners, and the fidelity of spouses counted for far more among men more liable to be fatally injured by sexual infidelity, by trickery, and by the insubordination of their few household slaves than were the truly wealthy and powerful. Outside the household a sense of solidarity with a wider range of fellow city-dwellers had developed, in marked contrast to the civic notables, who continued throughout the period to view the world through the narrow slits of their traditional "civic" definition of the urban community. A sense of solidarity was a natural adjunct of a morality of the socially vulnerable. There was, therefore, nothing strange, much less specifically Christian, in the inscription on the undoubtedly pagan tomb of an immigrant Greek pearl merchant on Rome's Via Sacra: "[Here] lie contained the bones of a good man, a man of mercy, a lover of the poor.". . .

The Christian church caused this new morality to undergo a subtle process of change by rendering it more universal in its application and far more intimate in its effect of the private life of the believer. Among Christians a somber variant of popular morality facilitated the urgent search for new principles of solidarity that aimed to penetrate the individual ever more deeply with a sense of the gaze of God, with a fear of His judgment, and with a sharp sense of commitment to the unity of the religious community.

To appreciate the extent of the changes in moral ideals brought about within the churches we need only consider the structures of marriage and sexual discipline that developed in Christian households during the course of the second and third centuries. [The Greek physician] Galen was struck by the sexual austerity of the Christian communities in the late second century: "Their contempt of death is patent to us every day, and likewise their restraint in cohabitation. For they include not only men but also women who refrain from cohabiting all their lives; and they also number individuals who, in self-discipline and self-control, have attained a pitch not inferior to that of genuine philosophers."

On the surface the Christians practiced an austere sexual morality, easily recognizable and acclaimed by outsiders: total sexual renunciation by the few; marital concord between the spouses (such as had begun to permeate the public behavior of the elites, if for very different reasons); strong disapproval of remarriage. This surface was presented openly to outsiders. Lacking the clear ritual boundaries provided in Judaism by circumcision and dietary laws, Christians tended to make their exceptional sexual discipline bear the full burden of expressing the difference between themselves and the pagan world. The message of the Christian apologists was similar to that of later admirers of clerical celibacy, as described by [the nineteenth-century philosopher Friedrich] Nietzsche. They appealed to "the faith that a person who is an exception on this point will be an exception in other respects as well."

It is important to understand the new inner structures that supported what on the surface seemed no more than a dour morality, readily admired by the average man. The commonplace facts of sexual discipline were supported by a deeper structure of specifically Christian concerns. From Saint Paul onward, the married couple had been expected to bear in their own persons nothing less than an analogue in microcosm of the group's single-hearted solidarity. Even if these might be dangerously confused by the workings of the Holy Spirit, in the undifferentiated "gatherings of the saints" the proper relations of husbands and wives, of masters and slaves, were reasserted in no uncertain manner within the Christian household. These relations were invested with a sense that such fidelity and obedience manifested in a peculiarly transparent manner the prized ideal of unfeigned singleness of heart. With the moral gusto characteristic of a group that courted occasions on which to test its will to cohesion, Christian urban communities even abandoned the normal means which Jewish and pagan males had relied upon to discipline and satisfy their wives. They rejected divorce, and they viewed the remarriage of widows with disapproval. The reasons they came to give, often borrowed from the maxims of the philosophers, would have pleased Plutarch. This exceptional marital morality, practiced by modestly well-to-do men and women, betrayed an exceptional will for order: "A man who divorces his wife admits that he is not even able to govern a woman."

It was quite possible for Christian communities to settle down into little more than that. Marital morality could have been presented as a particularly revealing manifestation of the will of the group to singleness of heart. Adultery and sexual scheming among married couples could have been presented as the privileged symptoms of the "zone of negative privacy" associated with dou-

bleness of heart. Without the tolerant space accorded by the ancient city to the upper-class males in which to work off their adolescent urges in relatively free indulgence in sexuality, young people would have married early, as close to puberty as possible, in order to mitigate through lawful wedlock the disruptive tensions of sexual attraction. Women and, it was occasionally hoped, even men would be disciplined by early marriage and by a sense of the piercing gaze of God penetrating into the recesses of the bedchamber. By avoiding remarriage the community could assure for itself a constant supply of venerable widows and widowers able to devote time and energy to the service of the church. Less exposed than notables to the tensions associated with the exercise of real power—bribery, perjury, hypocrisy, violence, and anger—these quiet citizens "of the middling condition" could show their concern for order and cohesion in the more domestic sphere of sexual self-discipline.

The disturbing ease with which the sexes mingled at ritual gatherings of Christians remained distasteful to respectable pagans, and strangers avoided speaking to Christians for that reason. A Christian contemporary of Galen actually petitioned the governor of Alexandria for permission to allow himself to be castrated, for only by such means could he clear himself and his correligionists from the charge of promiscuity! On a more humble level, the difficulties in arranging matches for young people, especially for Christian girls, in a community anxious to avoid marriage with pagans ensured that issues of sexual control would be treated with an intensity greater than that of more settled communities. It also meant that the resulting morality would be much more apparent to outsiders and applied much more rigorously to believers.

Such pressures go a long way to explain the moral tone of the average late antique Christian community. What they cannot explain is the further revolution by which sexual renunciation—virginity from birth, or continence vowed at baptism, or continence adopted by married couples or widowers—became the basis of male leadership in the Christian church. In this, Christianity had made *il gran rifiuto* (the great renunciation). In the very centuries when the rabbinate rose to prominence in Judaism by accepting marriage as a near-compulsory criterion of the wise, the leaders of the Christian communities moved in the diametrically opposite direction: access to leadership became identified with near-compulsory celibacy. Seldom has a structure of power risen with such speed and sharpness of outline on the foundation of so intimate an act of renunciation. What Galen had perceived at the end of the second century would distinguish the Christian church in later centuries from both Judaism and Islam.

It is claimed that a disgust for the human body was already prevalent in the pagan world. It is then assumed that when the Christian church moved away from its Jewish roots, where optimistic attitudes toward sexuality and marriage as part of God's good creation had prevailed, Christians took on the bleaker colors of their pagan environment. Such a view is lopsided. The facile contrast between pagan pessimism and Jewish optimism overlooks the importance of sexual renunciation as a means to singleness of heart in the radical Judaism from which Christianity emerged. The possible origins of this renunciation may be diverse in the extreme, but they do not in themselves explain why sexual renunciation rapidly became a badge of specifically male leadership in the Christian communities of the second and third centuries.

We must ask not why the human body could have come to be treated with such disquiet in late antiquity, but the exact opposite. Why is the body singled out by being presented so consistently in sexual terms—as the locus of imagined recesses of sexual motivations and the center of social structures thought of sexually—as being formed originally by a fateful sexual drive to marriage and childbirth? Why was this particular constel-lation of perceptions about the body allowed to carry so huge a weight in early Christian circles? It is the intensity and the particularity of the charge of significance that counts, not the fact that this significance often was expressed in terms so harshly negative as to rivet the attention of the modern reader, who is understandably bruised by such language.

The division between Christianity and Judaism was sharpest in this. As the rabbis chose to present it, sexuality was an enduring adjunct of the personality. Though potentially unruly, it was amenable to restraint—much as women were both honored as necessary for the existence of Israel, and at the same time were kept from intruding on the serious business of male wisdom. It is a model based on the control and segregation of an irritating but necessary aspect of existence. Among the Christians the exact opposite occurred. Sexuality became a highly charged symbolic marker precisely because its disappearance in the committed individual was considered possible, and because this disappearance was thought to register, more significantly than any other human transformation, the qualities necessary for leadership in the religious community. The removal of sexuality—or, more humbly, removal from sexuality—stood for a state of unhesitating availability to God and one's fellows, associated with the ideal of the single-hearted person.

After reading this selection and the previous one, consider these questions:

1. What role did Paul play in the development of early Christianity?
2. What were the main Christian values in this period, according to Brown?
3. How did Christian communities differ from those of the Jews?

SELECTION 4:

The Christians in Roman Eyes

As Peter Brown points out, by the end of the third century A.D., Christianity was firmly established within the Roman Empire, with its own clearly defined communal organization and "spiritual" identity. This development is the more remarkable since Roman policy became increasingly antagonistic in the third century. With the exception of a few crucifixions of religious leaders and such sporadic persecutions as the emperor Nero's scapegoating of this small sect for the great fire in Rome in A.D. 64, Christians continued to live undisturbed and even anonymously for the first two centuries of the religion's existence. To the imperial elite, the Christians were hardly noticeable.

Perhaps the first official mention of Christianity was made by the writer and naturalist Pliny the Younger. When Pliny was governor of Bithynia-Pontus (in northern Anatolia) in the years A.D. 111–113, he wrote to the emperor Trajan asking what to do with this strange sect. Not only did Pliny seem not to have known anything about the Christians before he moved to the East but he also appears to have been confused on how to deal with the complaints others were bringing against them.

It is a rule, Sir, which I inviolably observe, to refer myself to you in all my doubts; for who is more capable of guiding my uncertainty or informing my ignorance? Having never been present at any trials of the Christians, I am unacquainted with the method and limits to be observed either in examining or punishing them. Whether any difference is to be made on account of age, or no distinction allowed between the youngest and the adult; whether repentance admits to a pardon, or if a man has been once a Christian it avails him nothing to recant; whether the mere profession of Christianity, albeit without crimes, or only the crimes associated therewith are punishable—in all these points I am greatly doubtful.

In the meanwhile, the method I have observed towards those who have been denounced to me as Christians is this: I interrogated them whether they were Christians; if they confessed it I repeated the question twice again, adding the threat of capital punishment; if they still persevered, I ordered them to be executed. For whatever the nature of their creed might be, I could at least feel no doubt that contumacy and inflexible obstinacy deserved chastisement. There were others also possessed with the same infatuation, but being citizens of Rome, I directed them to be carried thither.

These accusations spread (as is usually the case) from the mere fact of the matter being investigated and several forms of the mischief came to light. A placard was put up, without any signature, accusing a large number of persons by name. Those who denied they were, or had ever been, Christians, who repeated after me an invocation to the Gods, and offered adoration, with wine and frankincense, to your image, which I had ordered to be brought for that purpose, together with those of the Gods, and who finally cursed Christ—none of which acts, it is said,

From *Letters*, by Pliny (the Younger), translated by William Melmouth (London: Heinemann, 1915).

those who are really Christians can be forced into performing—these I thought it proper to discharge. Others who were named by that informer at first confessed themselves Christians, and then denied it; true, they had been of that persuasion but they had quitted it, some three years, others many years, and a few as much as twenty-five years ago. They all worshipped your statue and the images of the Gods, and cursed Christ.

They affirmed, however, the whole of their guilt, or their error, was, that they were in the habit of meeting on a certain fixed day before it was light, when they sang in alternate verses a hymn to Christ, as to a god, and bound themselves by a solemn oath, not to any wicked deeds, but never to commit any fraud, theft or adultery, never to falsify their word, nor deny a trust when they should be called upon to deliver it up; after which it was their custom to separate, and then reassemble to partake of food—but food of an ordinary and innocent kind. Even this practice, however, they had abandoned after the publication of my edict, by which, according to your orders, I had forbidden political associations. I judged it so much the more necessary to extract the real truth, with the assistance of torture, from two female slaves, who were styled *deaconesses*: but I could discover nothing more than depraved and excessive superstition.

I therefore adjourned the proceedings, and betook myself at once to your counsel. For the matter seemed to me well worth referring to you,—especially considering the numbers endangered. Persons of all ranks and ages, and of both sexes are, and will be, involved in the prosecution. For this contagious superstition is not confined to the cities only, but has spread through the villages and rural districts; it seems possible, however, to check and cure it. 'Tis certain at least that the temples, which had been almost deserted, begin now to be frequented; and the sacred festivals, after a long intermission, are again revived; while there is a general demand for sacrificial animals, which for some time past have met with but few purchasers. From hence it is easy to imagine what multitudes may be reclaimed from this error, if a door be left open to repentance.

After reading this selection, consider these questions:

1. What problems have the Christians caused in Bythinia-Pontus?
2. What did Pliny understand as Christian beliefs and practices?
3. What were Pliny's chief concerns in dealing with the Christians?

SELECTION 5:

The Persecution of Christians

Pliny executed the Christians not because he found them guilty of any crimes but because they refused to surrender their religion and honor the gods of the state. The empire had no policy against the Christians and only moved against them when local communities raised complaints. In general, as in this case, objections arose because in refusing to sacrifice to the gods of the empire, to participate in official sacrifices, and to take public oaths, Christians threatened the traditional pax deorum *("the peace of the gods"), the fundamental religious bond that joined families and the state to the gods. Such violations were seen as angering the gods and challenging the traditional Roman values of* pietas. *The practice of*

Christianity thus opened the community and even the empire as a whole to catastrophe.

Under Emperor Diocletian (reigned 284–305), persecution of Christianity became widespread and intense. The reasons seem to have been more political and social than religious. This policy was part of a major bureaucratic reorganization of the imperial government as well as an attempt to restore traditional Roman values. By their refusal to take the customary oaths of allegiance in civil courts and to participate in the official state religion, Christians were viewed with increasing hostility.

Imperial persecution backfired. Instead of destroying or even weakening Christianity, the renewed examples of struggle against adversity and the witness of martyrdom to the truth of the faith and the triumph over death only enhanced the prestige of Christianity. Martyrdom became a central feature of Christianity in the third and early fourth centuries. As the third-century Christian theologian Tertullian claimed, "the blood of the martyrs is the seed of the church." Not only against the worldly values of "flesh," as Paul phrases it, but also in the face of imprisonment and even death by the Roman authorities, individuals confirmed the depth of their own beliefs and signaled to others that even confronted with beasts in the arena, the truth of Christianity lay beyond this world.

One of the great documents of such faith is The Passion of Saints Perpetua and Felicity. *St. Perpetua was a young married Roman woman (twenty-two years old) who suffered arrest, loss of her family, and martyrdom all for her faith. She was executed in the arena in Carthage on March 7, 203. The account of her martyrdom is not only written for the most part by herself but also represents one of the first accounts by a woman of her experience of the Christian faith. Perpetua records in her own words the events of her arrest and the various visions she had confirming her faith. In the final section, a narrator tells the story of her death in the arena.*

"Another day, while we were at dinner, we were suddenly taken away to be heard, and we arrived at the town-hall. At once the rumour spread through the neighbourbood of the public place, and an immense number of people were gathered together. We mount the platform. The rest were interrogated, and confessed. Then they came to me, and my father immediately appeared with my boy, and withdrew me from the step, and said in a supplicating tone, 'Have pity on your babe.' And Hilarianus the procurator, who had just received the power of life and death in the place of the proconsul Minucius Timinianus, who was deceased, said, 'Spare the grey hairs of your father, spare the infancy of your boy, offer sacrifice for the well-being of the emperors.' And I replied, 'I will not do so.' Hilarianus said, 'Are you a Christian?' And I replied, 'I am a Christian.' And as my father stood there to cast me down [from the faith], he was ordered by Hilarianus to be thrown down, and was beaten with rods. And my father's misfortune grieved me as if I myself had been beaten, I so grieved for his wretched old age. The procurator then delivers judgement on all of us, and condemns us to the wild beasts, and we went down cheerfully to the dungeon. Then, because my child had been used to receive suck from me, and to stay with me in the prison, I send Pomponius the deacon to my father to ask for the infant,

From *The Writings of Cyprian, Bishop of Carthage*, vol. 2, translated by Robert Ernest Wallis (Edinburgh: T&T Clark, 1873).

but my father would not give it him. And even as God willed it, the child no longer desired the breast, nor did my breasts cause me uneasiness, lest I should be tormented by care for my babe and by the pain of my breasts at once. . . .

"Again, after a few days, Pudens, a soldier, an assistant overseer of the prison, who began to regard us in great esteem, perceiving that the great power of God was in us, admitted many brethren to see us, that both we and they might be mutually refreshed. And when the day of the exhibition drew near, my father, worn out with suffering, came in to me, and began to tear out his beard, and to throw himself on the earth, and to cast himself down on his face, and to reproach his years, and to utter such words as might move all creation. I grieved for his unhappy old age.

"The day before that on which we were to fight, I saw in a vision that Pomponius the deacon came hither to the gate of the prison, and knocked vehemently. I went out to him, and opened the gate for him; and he was clothed in a richly ornamented white robe. . . . And he said to me, 'Perpetua, we are waiting for you; come!' And he held his hand to me, and we began to go through rough and winding places. Scarcely at length had we arrived breathless at the amphitheatre, when he led me into the middle of the arena, and said to me, 'Do not fear, I am here with you, and I am labouring with you;' and he departed. And I gazed upon an immense assembly in astonishment. And because I knew that I was given to the wild beasts, I marvelled that the wild beasts were not let loose upon me. Then there came forth against me a certain Egyptian, horrible in appearance, with his backers, to fight with me. And there came to me, as my helpers and encouragers, handsome youths; and I was stripped, and became a man. Then my helpers began to rub me with oil, as is the custom for contest; and I beheld that Egyptian on the other hand rolling in the dust. And a certain man came forth, of wondrous height, so that he even overtopped the top of the amphitheatre; and he wore a loose tunic and a purple robe between two bands over the middle of the breast; . . . and he carried a rod, as if he were a trainer of gladiators, and a green branch upon which were apples of gold. And he called for silence, and said, 'This Egyptian, if he

should overcome this woman, shall kill her with the sword; and if she shall conquer him, she shall receive this branch.' Then he departed. And we drew near to one another, and began to deal out blows. He sought to lay hold of my feet, while I struck at his face with my heels; and I was lifted up in the air, and began thus to kick at him as if spurning the earth. But when I saw that there was some delay, I joined my hands so as to twine my fingers with one another; and I took hold upon his head, and he fell on his face, and I trod upon his head. And the people began to shout, and my backers to exult. And I drew near to the trainer and took the branch; and he kissed me, and said to me, 'Daughter, peace be with you:' and I began to go gloriously to the Sanavivarian gate [by which the victims spared by the popular clemency escaped from the ampitheatre]. Then I awoke, and perceived that I was not to fight with beasts, but against the devil. Still I knew that the victory was awaiting me. This, so far, I have completed several days before the exhibition; but what passed at the exhibition itself let who will write.". . .

The day of their victory shone forth, and they proceeded from the prison into the ampitheatre, as if to an assembly, joyous and of brilliant countenances; if perchance shrinking, it was with joy, and not with fear. Perpetua followed with placid look, and with step and gate as a matron of Christ, beloved of God; casting down the lustre of her eyes from the gaze of all. Moreover, Felicitas rejoicing that she had safely brought forth, so that she might fight with the wild beasts; from the blood and from the midwife to the gladiator, to wash after childbirth with a second baptism. And when they were brought to the gate, and were being constrained to put on the clothing—the men, that of the priests of Saturn, and the women, that of those who were consecrated to Ceres— that noble-minded woman resisted even to the end with constancy. For she said, "We have come thus far of our own accord, for this reason, that our liberty might not be restrained. For this reason we have yielded our minds, that we might not do any such thing as this: we have agreed on this with you." Injustice acknowledged the justice; the tribune yielded to their being brought as simply as they were. Perpetua sang psalms, already treading under foot the head of the Egyptian; Re-vocatus, and Saturninus, and Saturus uttered threatenings against the gazing people about this martyrdom. When they came within sight of Hi-larianus, by gesture and nod, they began to say to Hilarianus, "Thou judgest us," say they, "but God will judge thee." At this the people, exasperated, demanded that they should be tormented with scourges as they passed along the rank of the *ve-natores* [a row of men drawn up to scourge them as they passed along]. And they indeed rejoiced that they should have incurred any one of their Lord's passions.

But He who had said, "Ask, and ye shall re-ceive," gave to them when they asked, that death which each one had wished for. For when at any time they had been discoursing among them-selves about their wish in respect of their martyr-dom, Saturninus indeed had professed that he wished that he might be thrown to all the beasts; doubtless that he might wear a more glorious crown. Therefore in the beginning of the exhibi-tion, he and Revocatus made trial of the leopard, and moreover upon the scaffold they were ha-rassed by the bear. Saturus, however, held noth-ing in greater abomination than a bear; but he imagined that he would be put an end to with one bite of a leopard. Therefore, when a wild boar was supplied, it was the huntsman rather who had supplied that boar who was gored by that same beast, and died the day after the shows. Saturus only was drawn out; and when he had been bound on the floor near to a bear, the bear would not come forth from his den. And so Saturus for the second time is recalled unhurt.

Moreover, for the young women the devil pre-pared a very fierce cow, provided especially for that purpose contrary to custom, rivalling their sex also in that of the beasts. And so, stripped and clothed with nets, they were led forth. The popu-lace shuddered as they saw one young woman of delicate frame, and another with breasts still drop-ping from her recent childbirth. So, being recalled, they are unbound. Perpetua is first led in. She was tossed, and fell on her loins; and when she saw her tunic torn from her side, she drew it over her as a veil for her middle, rather mindful of her modesty than her suffering. Then she was called for again,

and bound up her dishevelled hair; for it was not becoming for a martyr to suffer with dishevelled hair, lest she should appear to be mourning in her glory. So she rose up; and when she saw Felicitas crushed, she approached and gave her her hand, and lifted her up. And both of them stood together; and the brutality of the populace being appeased, they were recalled to the Sanavivarian gate. Then Perpetua was received by a certain one who was still a catechumen, Rusticus by name, who kept close to her; and she, as if aroused from sleep, so deeply had she been in the Spirit and in an ecstasy, began to look round her, and to say to the amaze-ment of all, "I cannot tell when we are to be led out to that cow." And when she had heard what had al-ready happened, she did not believe it until she had perceived certain signs of injury in her body and in her dress, and had recognised the catechumen. Af-terwards causing that catechumen and her brother to approach, she addressed them, saying, "Stand fast in the faith, and love one another, all of you, and be not offended at my sufferings."

The same Saturus at the other entrance exhort-ed the soldier Pudens, saying, "Assuredly here I am, as I have promised and foretold, for up to this moment I have felt no beast. And now believe with your whole heart. Lo, I am going forth to that beast, and I shall be destroyed with one bite of the leopard." And immediately at the conclusion of the exhibition he was thrown to the leopard; and with one bite of his he was bathed with such a quantity of blood, that the people shouted out to him as he was returning, the testimony of his sec-ond baptism, "Saved and washed, saved and washed." Manifestly he was assuredly saved who had been glorified in such a spectacle. Then to the soldier Pudens he said, "Farewell, and be mindful of my faith; and let not these things disturb, but confirm you." And at the same time he asked for a little ring from his finger, and returned it to him bathed in his wound, leaving to him an inherited token and the memory of his blood. And then life-less he is cast down with the rest, to be slaugh-tered in the usual place. And when the populace called for them into the midst, that as the sword penetrated into their body they might make their eyes partners in the murder, they rose up of their own accord, and transferred themselves whither the people wished; but they first kissed one another, that they might consummate their martyrdom with the kiss of peace. The rest indeed, immoveable and in silence, received the sword-thrust; much more Saturus, who also had first ascended the ladder, and first gave up his spirit, for he also was waiting for Perpetua. But Perpetua, that she might taste some pain, being pierced between the ribs, cried out loudly, and she herself placed the wavering right hand of the youthful gladiator to her throat. Possibly such a woman could not have been slain unless she herself had willed it, because she was feared by the impure spirit.

O most brave and blessed martyrs! O truly called and chosen unto the glory of our Lord Jesus Christ! whom whoever magnifies, and honours, and adores, assuredly ought to read these examples for the edification of the church, not less than the ancient ones, so that new virtues also may testify that one and the same Holy Spirit is always operating even until now, and God the Father Omnipotent, and His Son Jesus Christ our Lord, whose is the glory and infinite power for ever and ever. Amen.

After reading this selection, consider these questions:

1. Why was Perpetua persecuted as a Christian?
2. What proof did she find for her faith while in prison?
3. How did Perpetua accept her impending death?

SELECTION 6:

The Act of Toleration

As the values and institutions upon which the empire was founded were decaying, and as emperor after emperor attempted to salvage its institutions and its sustaining spirit, this hostility became official state policy. Diocletian divided the empire into two parts and restructured its smaller administrative units into dioceses. To help him rule, he appointed Maximian as his coemperor and Constantius I (the father of Constantine) and Galerius as caesars (subemperors). When the "sect" of Christianity was too large and too strong to be wiped out by persecution (when it was becoming a religion in the full sense of the term), the emperor Galerius issued an edict of toleration in A.D. 311.

Among other arrangements which we are always accustomed to make for the prosperity and welfare of the republic, we had desired formerly to bring all things into harmony with the ancient laws and public order of the Romans, and to provide that even the Christians who had left the religion of their fathers should come back to reason; since, indeed, the Christians themselves, for some reason, had followed such a caprice and had fallen into such a folly that they would not obey the institutes of antiquity, which perchance their own ancestors had first established; but at their own will and pleasure, they would thus make laws unto themselves which they should observe and would collect various peoples in di-

From the Edict of Toleration of Galerius, in *De Mortibus Persecutorum*, by Lactantius, edited by O.F. Fritsche (Leipzig, 1844).

verse places in congregations. Finally when our law had been promulgated to the effect that they should conform to the institutes of antiquity, many were subdued by the fear of danger, many even suffered death. And yet since most of them persevered in their determination, and we saw that they neither paid the reverence and awe due to the gods nor worshipped the God of the Christians, in view of our most mild clemency and the constant habit by which we are accustomed to grant indulgence to all, we thought that we ought to grant our most prompt indulgence also to these, so that they may again be Christians and may hold their conventicles, provided they do nothing contrary to good order. But we shall tell the magistrates in another letter what they ought to do.

Wherefore, for this our indulgence, they ought to pray to their God for our safety, for that of the republic, and for their own, that the republic may continue uninjured on every side, and that they may be able to live securely in their homes.

This edict is published at Nicomedia on the day before the Kalends of May, in our eighth consulship and the second of Maximinus.

SELECTION 7:

The Edict of Milan

The "conversion" of the emperor Constantine (reigned 310–337) in the third decade of the fourth century marked the important turning point in the process of Christianizing the empire. In 313, in the famous Edict of Milan, the emperors Constantine and Licinius proclaimed their own official policy. It did not make Christianity the official religion of the empire, but it did end persecution.

When I, Constantine Augustus, as well as I, Licinius Augustus, fortunately met near Mediolanurn (Milan), and were considering everything that pertained to the public welfare and security, we thought, among other things which we saw would be for the good of many, those regulations pertaining to the reverence of the Divinity ought certainly to be made first, so that we might grant to the Christians and others full authority to observe that religion which each preferred; whence any Divinity whatsoever in the seat of the heavens may be propitious and kindly disposed to us and all who are placed under our rule. And thus by this wholesome counsel and most upright provision we thought to arrange that no one whatsoever should be denied the opportunity to give his heart to the observance of the Christian religion, of that religion which he should think best for himself, so that the Supreme Deity, to whose worship we freely yield our hearts may show in all things His usual favor and benevolence. Therefore, your Worship should know that it has pleased us to remove all conditions whatsoever, which were in the rescripts formerly given to you officially, concerning the Christians and now any one of these who wishes to observe Christian religion may do so freely and openly, without molestation. We thought it fit to commend these things most fully to your care that you may know that we have given to those Christians free and unrestricted opportunity of religious worship.

From the Edict of Milan of Constantine I, in *De Mortibus Persecutorum*, by Lactantius, edited by O.F. Fritsche (Leipzig, 1844).

When you see that this has been granted to them by us, your Worship will know that we have also conceded to other religions the right of open and free observance of their worship for the sake of the peace of our times, that each one may have the free opportunity to worship as he pleases; this regulation is made that we may not seem to detract from any dignity or any religion.

Moreover, in the case of the Christians especially we esteemed it best to order that if it happens anyone heretofore has bought from our treasury from anyone whatsoever, those places where they were previously accustomed to assemble, concerning which a certain decree had been made and a letter sent to you officially, the same shall be restored to the Christians without payment or any claim of recompense and without any kind of fraud or deception. Those, moreover, who have obtained the same by gift, are likewise to return them at once to the Christians. Besides, both those who have purchased and those who have secured them by gift, are to appeal to the vicar if they seek any recompense from our bounty, that they may be cared for through our clemency. All this property ought to be delivered at once to the community of the Christians through your intercession, and without delay. And since these Christians are known to have possessed not only those places in which they were accustomed to assemble, but also other property, namely the churches, belonging to them as a corporation and not as individuals, all these things which we have included under the above law, you will order to be restored, without any hesitation or controversy at all, to these Christians, that is to say to the corporations and their conventicles: providing, of course, that the above arrangements be followed so that those who return the same without payment, as we have said, may hope for an indemnity from our bounty. In all these circumstances you ought to tender your most efficacious intervention to the community of the Christians, that our command may be carried into effect as quickly as possible, whereby, moreover, through our clemency, public order may be secured. Let this be done so that, as we have said above, Divine favor towards us, which, under the most important circumstances we have already experienced, may, for all time, preserve and prosper our successes together with the good of the state. Moreover, in order that the statement of this decree of our good will may come to the notice of all, this rescript, published by your decree, shall be announced everywhere and brought to the knowledge of all, so that the decree of this, our benevolence, cannot be concealed.

After reading this selection and the previous one, consider these questions:

1. What were the provisions of the Act of Toleration?
2. What were the provisions of the Edict of Milan?
3. How does Constantine define his relation to Christianity in the Edict of Milan?

SELECTION 8:

Constantine and the Church

The early history of the established church is the story of the organization of an ecclesiastical government on the one hand and of the clarification of official Catholic Christian doctrines against "heretical" positions on the other. In both, the role of the emperor proved crucial. Through direct imperial control and patronage, the emperor assumed a new position as head of the church. These processes of constituting an official church government and official church doctrine were complex and confusing; and the evolving role of the emperor in relation to them was far from straightforward.

Constantine's new role within the church was clearly related to his summoning of and active participation in a number of church councils. The most important of these was held at Nicaea in 325, condemning the Arian form of Christianity, the Council of Nicaea clearly articulated the belief in the equality of Jesus with the Father and the Holy Ghost. Although discussions would continue throughout the succeeding centuries over the specific relationship between the human and the divine natures of Jesus, the Nicene Creed confirmed that Jesus was divine and thus of equal status within the Trinity. Only with slight variations, this creed remains the accepted basis of the Christian faith.

We believe in one God, the Father Almighty, maker of all things visible and invisible; and in one Lord Jesus Christ, the Son of God, the only-begotten of his Father, of the substance of the Father, God of God, Light of Light, very God of very God, begotten, not made, being of one substance with the Father. By whom all things were made, both which be in heaven and in earth. Who for us men and for our salvation came down [from heaven] and was incarnate and was made man. He suffered and the third day he rose again, and ascended into heaven. And he shall come again to judge both the quick and the dead. And [we believe] in the Holy Ghost. And whosoever shall say that there was a time when the Son of God was not, or that before he was begotten he was not, or that he was made of things that were not, or that he is of a different substance or essence [from the Father] or that he is a creature, or subject to change or conversion—all that so say, the Catholic and Apostolic Church anathematizes them.

After reading this selection, consider these questions:

1. How does the Nicene Creed define the relationship of God to Jesus?
2. Why does the Nicene Creed place so much emphasis on this relationship?
3. What is a creed?

From *The Oecumenical Documents of the Faith,* edited by Herbert T. Bindley (London: Methuen, 1899).

SELECTION 9:

The Foundations of Western Theology

With the conversion of Augustine of Hippo (354–430), the Christian community acquired a mind of the first order. Born in a small town in North Africa, Augustine rose to become a famous teacher of rhetoric and *chief rhetorician of the empire. Although exposed to Christian beliefs from childhood by the strong faith of his mother, Monica, Augustine did not find his way to Christianity until much later in life. Trained in the logical and rhetorical traditions of the ancient classical world, he had great difficulties in understanding the Bible both as the account of creation and as the story of God's providential plan for the world. Only when he came under the influence of the remarkable early churchman St. Ambrose did Augustine learn how to interpret Scriptures on a symbolic rather than a literal level. Augustine was quickly consumed by the truth of the Bible and the meaning of the Christian message. In the following selection from Augustine's extraordinary account of his process of conversion,* The Confessions, *he describes how he learned to interpret the Bible. Augustine's subsequent writings, including those dealing with the symbolic reading of Scriptures, became foundational for Latin Christianity.*

Ignorant then how this Thy image should subsist, I should have knocked and proposed the doubt, how it was to be believed, not insultingly opposed it, as if believed. Doubt, then, what to hold for certain, the more sharply gnawed my heart, the more ashamed I was, that so long deluded and deceived by the promise of certainties, I had with childish error and vehemence, prated of so many uncertainties. For that they were falsehoods, became clear to me later. However I was certain that they were uncertain, and that I had formerly accounted them certain, when with a blind contentiousness, I accused Thy Catholic Church, whom I now discovered, not indeed as yet to teach truly, but at least not to teach that, for which I had grievously censured her. So I was confounded, and converted: and I joyed, O my God, that the One Only Church, the body of Thine Only Son, (wherein the name of Christ had been put upon me as an infant,) had no taste for infantine conceits; nor in her sound doctrine, maintained any tenet which should confine Thee, the Creator of all, in space, however great and large, yet bounded every where by the limits of a human form.

I joyed also, that the old Scriptures of the Law and the Prophets, were laid before me, not now to be perused with that eye to which before they seemed absurd, when I reviled Thy holy ones for so thinking, whereas indeed they thought not so: and with joy I heard Ambrose in his sermons to the people, oftentimes most diligently recommend this text for a rule, *The letter killeth, but the Spirit giveth life*; whilst he drew aside the mystic veil, laying open spiritually what according to the letter, seemed to teach something unsound; teaching herein nothing that offended me, though he taught what I knew not as yet, whether it were true. For I kept my heart from assenting to any thing, fearing to fall headlong; but by hanging in suspense I was the worse killed. For I wished to be as assured of the things I saw not, as I was that seven and three are ten. For I was not so mad, as to think that even this could not be comprehended; but I desired to have other things as clear as this, whether things corporeal, which were not present to my senses, or spiritual, whereof I knew not how to conceive, except corporeally. And by believing might I have been cured, that so the eyesight of my soul being cleared, might in some way be directed to Thy truth, which abideth always, and in no part faileth. But as it happens that one, who has tried a bad physician, fears to trust himself with a good one, so was it with the health of my soul, which could not be healed but by believing, and lest it should believe falsehoods, refused to be cured; resisting Thy hands, who hast prepared the medicines of faith, and hast applied them to the diseases of the whole world, and given unto them so great authority.

Being led, however, from this to prefer the

From *The Confessions of St. Augustine,* translated by E.B. Pusey (London: J.M. Dent, 1907).

Catholic doctrine, I felt that her proceeding was more unassuming and honest, in that she required to be believed things not demonstrated, (whether it was that they could in themselves be demonstrated but not to certain persons, or could not at all be,) whereas among the Manichees [Manichaeans] our credulity was mocked by a promise of certain knowledge, and then so many most fabulous and absurd things were imposed to be believed, because they could not be demonstrated. Then Thou, O Lord, little by little with most tender and most merciful hand, touching and composing my heart, didst persuade me—considering what innumerable things I believed, which I saw not, nor was present while they were done, as so many things in secular history, so many reports of places and of cities, which I had not seen; so many of friends, so many of physicians, so many continually of other men, which unless we should believe, we should do nothing at all in this life; lastly, with how unshaken an assurance I believed, of what parents I was born, which I could not know, had I not believed upon hearsay—considering all this, Thou didst persuade me, that not they who believed Thy Books, (which Thou hast established in so great authority among almost all nations,) but they who believed them not, were to be blamed; and that they were not to be heard, who should say to me, "How knowest thou those Scriptures to have been imparted unto mankind by the Spirit of the one true and most true God?" For this very thing was of all most to be believed, since no contentiousness of blasphemous questionings, of all that multitude which I had read in the self-contradicting philosophers, could wring this belief from me, "That Thou art" whatsoever Thou wert, (what I knew not,) and "That the government of human things belongs to Thee."

This I believed, sometimes more strongly, more weakly other-whiles; yet I ever believed both that Thou wert, and hadst a care of us;

though I was ignorant, both what was to be thought of Thy substance, and what way led or led back to Thee. Since then we were too weak by abstract reasonings to find out truth: and for this very cause needed the authority of Holy Writ; I had now begun to believe, that Thou wouldest never have given such excellency of authority to that Writ in all lands, hadst Thou not willed thereby to be believed in, thereby sought. For now what things, sounding strangely in the Scripture, were wont to offend me, having heard divers of them expounded satisfactorily, I referred to the depth of the mysteries, and its authority appeared to me the more venerable, and more worthy of religious credence, in that, while it lay open to all to read, it reserved the majesty of its mysteries within its profounder meaning, stooping to all in the great plainness of its words and lowliness of its style, yet calling forth the intensest application of such as are not light of heart; that so it might receive all in its open bosom, and through narrow passages waft over towards Thee some few, yet many more than if it stood not aloft on such a height of authority, nor drew multitudes within its bosom by its holy lowliness. These things I thought on, and Thou wert with me; I sighed, and Thou heardest me; I wavered, and Thou didst guide me; I wandered through the broad way of the world, and Thou didst not forsake me.

After reading this selection, consider these questions:

1. What led Augustine to accept Christianity?
2. What specific problems did Augustine originally have in accepting Christian beliefs?
3. In what ways did Augustine learn to read the Bible?

UNIT 2

The Medieval Heritage

CONTENTS

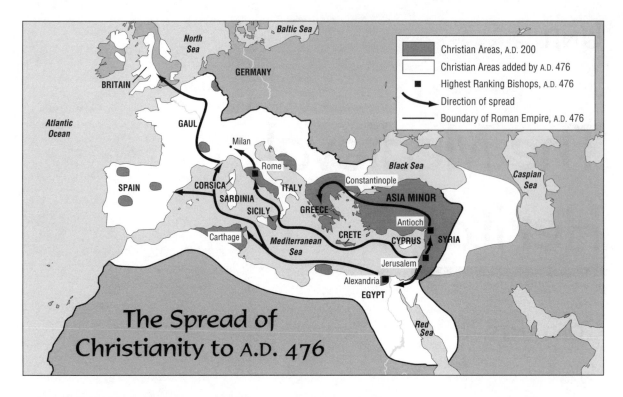

The Spread of Christianity to A.D. 476

Christian Areas, A.D. 200
Christian Areas added by A.D. 476
Highest Ranking Bishops, A.D. 476
Direction of spread
Boundary of Roman Empire, A.D. 476

Medieval Europe

CHAPTER 7
The Origins of Medieval Europe

The term *Middle Ages,* denoting the time span between the end of the ancient world and the beginning of "modern" Europe, is vague in its chronological limits, its internal content, and its historical meaning. In other words, there is no total break between the civilization of late antiquity in the West and the emergence of other forms of social and political institutions in the fifth, sixth, and seventh centuries A.D. Nor is there any absolute break between the late Middle Ages and the beginnings of modernity in the fifteenth, sixteenth, and seventeenth centuries. In each case there can be seen the decay and dissolution of certain features of the preceding eras as well as continuity and transformation of others. This continuity, in all its complexities and inner contradictions, we call the tradition of the West.

The modern West inherited and was influenced by a number of central values and key institutions from the Middle Ages, including the ways of relating to and interpreting the inheritance of the ancient world. With varying degrees of mastery and knowledge, the Middle Ages perpetuated the classical traditions of learning. Of course, there was nothing like an unbroken continuity of the various schools of thought of antiquity. But even in the early Middle Ages, some knowledge of classical learning survived. From this thin thread evolved a world of scholarship, the recovery of lost philosophy (especially Aristotle's), and innovations in theology. These developments called for a new type of institutional structure, designed both for teaching and for furthering knowledge and thought itself: the university, as we have come to know it in the modern West. Medieval universities were invariably located in towns and cities, themselves of medieval origin, which continue into our own world. Unlike the consumption centers of the ancient world, the medieval town was both a production and a consumption center. From the production and distribution of production arose a new class—the bourgeoisie (originally the free citizens of the incorporated towns)—out of which grew the modern middle classes. Although these middle classes eventually looked to the political forms and language of classical antiquity for their own institutions, the idea of the nation and of the legitimation of political power based on the nation, as well as the specific identities of the nations of modern Europe, all derive from the Middle Ages.

The transition from the ancient to the medieval world saw certain features of late antiquity continued and transformed and others lost and forgotten. Unlike the move to modernity, however, this earlier transformation was in many ways more dramatic and more threatening for the survival of the civilization. The Germanic invasions of the fifth, sixth, and seventh centuries, followed by the Viking invasions of the eighth and ninth centuries, resulted in the effective end of Roman political, military, and legal domination of its former provinces in the West. Rather than a complete break, however, the West gradually merged Roman imperial law and notions of political power with the barbarian law codes and political institutions. Classical learning, though descending to low levels and restricted to only the smallest number of individuals, was never entirely lost— if only in memory and not in practice. Intimately connected to this preservation of ancient political authority and classical learning was the Catholic Church, which continued to exist throughout this period. As it became organized and institutionalized under the papacy in Rome, the church in the West was the most direct tie to the ancient world. It was the bishops within the various and often declining ancient cities of the Roman Empire who provided the religious and even the political ties not only to the papacy but also to the Christianity of the ancient world. Again, with the admixture of many barbarian components, there eventually evolved a unique civilization that gave meaning to itself and found its basic values in Christian notions of love, selflessness, and the divine governance of the world.

It was not only the activities of the bishops and the organization of the papacy that provided the conditions of continuity; the early Middle Ages witnessed the development of new institutions and new ways of organizing men and women. Specifically Western forms of monasticism evolved, which provided havens in a violent, lawless, and increasingly disorganized world. Monasteries emerged as centers of faith and learning. In addition, town life itself, both in overall organization and in the forms given to manufacturing and commercial enterprises through guilds and other corporations, provided new ways of organizing communal life. Finally, feudalism and the great feudal monarchies of the High Middle Ages (eleventh through thirteenth centuries) represented attempts to structure effective military, political, and legal relations on the local level. As feudalism became entwined with collective efforts at farming— with the basic economic conditions of subsistence within lawless and economically precarious times—manorialism also took root.

SELECTION 1:

The Conversion of the Franks

In the History of the Franks, *Gregory, the bishop of Tours (539–594), recounts the conversion of Clovis, king of the Germanic tribe of Salian Franks in the year 496. Clovis's rule marks the beginning of effective military and governmental control over the former Roman province of Gaul. Eventually Gaul became known as France, and Clovis's line of kings became the origins of the Merovingian dynasty of French monarchs.*

[Clovis] had a first-born son by queen Clotilda, and as his wife wished to consecrate him in baptism, she tried unceasingly to persuade her husband, saying: "The gods you worship are nothing, and they will be unable to help themselves or any one else. For they are graven out of stone or wood or some metal. And the names you have given them are names of men and not of gods, as Saturn, who is declared to have fled in fear of being banished from his kingdom by his son; as Jove himself, the foul perpetrator of all shameful crimes, committing incest with men, mocking at his kinswomen, not able to refrain from intercourse with his own sister. . . . What could Mars or Mercury do? They are endowed rather with the magic arts than with the power of the divine name. But he ought rather to be worshipped who created by his word heaven and earth, the sea and all that in them is out of a state of nothingness, who made the sun shine, and adorned the heavens with stars, who filled the waters with creeping things, the earth with living things and the air with creatures that fly, at whose nod the earth is decked with growing crops, the trees with fruit, the vines with grapes, by whose hand mankind was created, by whose generosity all that creation serves and helps man whom he created as his own." But though the queen said

this the spirit of the king was by no means moved to belief, and he said: "It was at the command of our gods that all things were created and came forth, and it is plain that your God has no power and, what is more, he is proven not to belong to the family of the gods.". . .

The queen did not cease to urge him to recognize the true God and cease worshipping idols. But he could not be influenced in any way to this belief, until at last a war arose with the Alamanni, in which he was driven by necessity to confess what before he had of his free will denied. It came about that as the two armies were fighting fiercely, there was much slaughter, and Clovis's army began to be in danger of destruction. He saw it and raised his eyes to heaven, and with remorse in his heart he burst into tears and cried: "Jesus Christ, whom Clotilda asserts to be the son of the living God, who art said to give aid to those in distress, and to bestow victory on those who hope in thee, I beseech the glory of thy aid, with the vow that if thou wilt grant me victory over these enemies, and I shall know that power which she says that people dedicated in thy name have had from thee, I will believe in thee and be baptized in thy name. For I have invoked my own gods but, as I find, they have withdrawn from aiding me; and therefore I believe that they possess no power, since they do not help those who obey them. I now call upon thee, I desire to believe thee only let me be rescued from my adversaries." And when he said thus, the Alamanni turned their backs, and began to disperse in

From *History of the Franks*, by Gregory of Tours, translated by Ernest Brehaut (New York: Columbia University Press, 1916).

flight. And when they saw that their king was killed, they submitted to the dominion of Clovis, saying: "Let not the people perish further, we pray; we are yours now." And he stopped the fighting, and after encouraging his men, retired in peace and told the queen how he had had merit to win the victory by calling on the name of Christ. This happened in the fifteenth year of his reign.

Then the queen asked saint Remi, bishop of Rheims, to summon Clovis secretly, urging him to introduce the king to the word of salvation. And the bishop sent for him secretly and began to urge him to believe in the true God, maker of heaven and earth, and to cease worshipping idols, which could help neither themselves nor any one else. But the king said: "I gladly hear you, most holy father; but there remains one thing: the people who follow me cannot endure to abandon their gods; but I shall go and speak to them according to your words." He met with his followers, but before he could speak the power of God anticipated him, and all the people cried out together: "O pious king, we reject our mortal gods, and we are ready to follow the immortal God whom Remi preaches." This was reported to the bishop, who was greatly rejoiced, and bade them get ready the baptismal font. The squares were shaded with tapestried canopies, the churches adorned with white curtains, the baptistery set in order, the aroma of incense spread, candles of fragrant odor burned brightly, and the whole shrine of the baptistery was filled with a divine fragrance: and the Lord gave such grace to those who stood by that they thought they were placed amid the odors of paradise. And the king was the first to ask to be baptized by the bishop. Another Constantine advanced to the baptismal font, to terminate the disease of ancient leprosy and wash away with fresh water the foul spots that had long been borne. And when he entered to be baptized, the saint of God began with ready speech: "Gently bend your neck, Sigamber; worship what you burned; burn what you worshipped." The holy bishop Remi was a man of excellent wisdom and especially trained in rhetorical studies, and of such surpassing holiness that he equalled the miracles of [saint] Silvester. For there is extant a book of his life which tells that he raised a dead man. And so the king confessed all-powerful God in the Trinity, and was baptized in the name of the Father, Son and holy Spirit, and was anointed with the holy ointment with the sign of the cross of Christ. And of his army more than 3,000 were baptized. His sister also, Albofled, was baptized, who not long after passed to the Lord. And when the king was in mourning for her, the holy Remi sent a letter of consolation which began in this way: "The reason of your mourning pains me, and pains me greatly, that Albofled your sister, of good memory, has passed away. But I can give you this comfort, that her departure from the world was such that she ought to be envied rather than mourned." Another sister also was converted, Lanthechild by name, who had fallen into the heresy of the Arians, and she confessed that the Son and the holy Spirit were equal to the Father, and was anointed. . . .

Clovis received an appointment to the consulship from the emperor Anastasius, and in the church of the blessed [saint] Martin he clad himself in the purple tunic and chlamys, and placed a diadem on his head. Then he mounted his horse, and in the most generous manner he gave gold and silver as he passed along the way which is between the gate of the entrance [of the church of St. Martin] and the church of the city, scattering it among the people who were there with his own hand, and from that day he was called consul or *Augustus*. Leaving Tours he went to Paris and there he established the seat of his kingdom.

After reading this selection, consider these questions:
1. Describe the conditions of Europe after the collapse of effective military and political control by Rome.
2. What were the origins of the kingdom of France?
3. Why, according to Gregory, did Clovis convert to Christianity?

SELECTION 2:

The Conversion of the English

In other instances, the conversion of the various Germanic and Norse tribes was carried out by the papacy itself. In the late sixth century, England was, for the most part, ruled by the descendants of invading Germanic tribes, the Angles, Jutes, and Saxons. They did not believe in Christianity and had driven the native Celtic Britons (who were Christian) into Scotland, Wales, Cornwall, and Ireland (or to Brittany in northern France). In 596 Gregory sent a group of Benedictine monks, led by a Roman named Augustine, to convert the Anglo-Saxons. The expedition landed in southeastern England in the kingdom of Kent. Augustine managed to convert Ethelbert, the king of Kent, who in turn allowed Augustine to establish a church and a Benedictine monastery at Canterbury. In the following letter, Pope Gregory I (ca. 540–604) writes to Abbot Mellitus who is about to join Augustine on his mission.

Tell Augustine that he should by no means destroy the temples of the gods but rather the idols within those temples. Let him, after he has purified them with holy water, place altars and relics of the saints in them. For, if those temples are well built, they should be converted from the worship of demons to the service of the true God. Thus, seeing that their places of worship are not destroyed, the people will banish error from their hearts and come to places familiar and dear to them in acknowledgement and worship of the true God.

Further, since it has been their custom to slaughter oxen in sacrifice, they should receive some solemnity in exchange. Let them therefore, on the day of the dedication of their churches, or on the feast of the martyrs whose relics are preserved in them, build themselves huts around their one-time temples and celebrate the occasion with religious feasting. They will sacrifice and eat the animals not any more as an offering to the devil, but for the glory of God to whom, as the giver of all things, they will give thanks for having been satiated. Thus, if they are not deprived of all exterior joys, they will more easily taste the interior ones. For surely it is impossible to efface all at once everything from their strong minds, just as, when one wishes to reach the top of a mountain, he must climb by stages and step by step, not by leaps and bounds. . . .

Mention this to our brother the bishop, that he may dispose of the matter as he sees fit according to the conditions of time and place.

From Pope Gregory I, letter to Abbot Mellitus, in *Patrologia Latina*, vol. 76, edited by J.P. Migne, translated by Ernest F. Henderson, in *Select Historical Documents of the Middle Ages* (London: George Bell, 1910).

SELECTION 3:

The Decline of Learning

Pope Gregory I (pope from 590–604) was to become a father of the Western church. He wrote some of the most influential works interpreting Scripture, recording the lives of saints, and providing instructions for priests. Through both his writings and his attempts to organize the governance of the church from Rome, Gregory was instrumental in establishing the spiritual and institutional superiority of the Roman church in the West. He began life as the son of a noble Roman family, who took the vows of a monk. Although refusing promotion within the church, he eventually was cajoled into becoming pope at a time when effective military and governmental control over Italy by the emperors in Constantinople had collapsed. Gregory refused to grant precedence to the patriarch of Constantinople and thus precipitated a split between the Western and Eastern Christian churches.

In writing an intellectual biography of Gregory, modern historian G.R. Evans describes the extent of the decline in classical learning and the general decay of all forms of life in Rome during the late sixth and early seventh centuries.

This was a world where the materials of Christian scholarship could not be taken for granted, and where Gregory can be seen to be making use of authorities in a way peculiarly of his time. He takes the Bible as his supreme authority and it provided him with material for the bulk of what he wrote and preached. Beneath it stand statements made by the ecumenical Councils, which he takes as the foundation of catholic formulations of doctrine. For the rest, he draws on whatever has been said by earlier Christian authors as he needs it, but so often without acknowledgement that the question of his knowledge of many individual authors remains uncertain. His method was to write in his own words rather than to quote the words of others, because the earlier Fathers did not yet have the status for him that they were to have for later

generations. (He was himself to become one of the last of those to whom it was natural to refer as Fathers.) Yet he was not obliged to do so much pioneering thinking as Augustine, and we do not find him struggling with a problem as Augustine does. There is a calmer air, an air of exposition rather than investigation. Gregory could take for granted, if not a library of source-materials, at least an established body of teaching, a full theology whose principles can safely be subsumed in his writings because he can expect his readers and listeners to grasp their essentials.

Secular learning raised a difficulty for those who were the leaders of thought in the Church. Cassiodorus (c. 485–c. 582) recognised great enthusiasm for it; most people believed that it would make them knowledgeable and advance them in life. It grieved him to think that no Christian teaching went on in the public schools of Rome when secular authors were being given such distinguished exposition. He himself wanted to see Christian schools where those who studied would

From *The Thought of Gregory the Great*, by G.R. Evans. Copyright © Cambridge University Press 1986. Reprinted with the permission of Cambridge University Press.

be helped to a heavenly not an earthly wisdom. He hoped for a time to be able to raise money by subscription to bring such schools into existence, but he failed to gain enough support. His solution in the end was to set up a school of his own in old age, in his monastery of Vivarium, where he provided for the study of both secular and Christian materials. For him there was perhaps no real conflict of purpose between the two. He simply wanted to redress a balance and give Christian teaching its proper place, as something far more important than secular learning, and deserving a substantial section of his encyclopaedia the *Institutiones* to itself. . . .

Greek philosophical ideas entered the Latin West by a number of routes. Roman education had long aspired to the Greek in matters of philosophy (taken in the widest sense to include natural science, astronomy and medicine). Cicero had insisted that Latin was, in his own day, already an adequate vehicle for philosophical discourse, against some who doubted it; he believed that Latin now had a vocabulary to match that of Greek. From at least the late second century, Greek thought was being brought together in a series of handbooks and encyclopaedias. As a result of these developments, some general knowledge of Greek philosophical ideas was the common stock of educated Romans from at least Cicero's day. Groups of enthusiasts, like those in Milan in the fourth century when Augustine met them, sought out platonic writings for study and discussion: Manlius Theodorus gave Augustine some of [the Roman philosopher] Plotinus' *Enneads* to read, and [the Greek scholar and philosopher] Porphyry's *De Regressu Animae*. With the decay of Greek in the West some scholars saw a need for translations; Jerome and Rufinus, and later Boethius, did their best to meet it. The question of the extent of Gregory's knowledge of Greek remains a vexed one, but there can be no doubt that he held Christian Greek thought to be important. When he had to combat the Eudoxian heresy he sent to Eulogius of Alexandria, who provided him with extracts from the Cappadocian Fathers who had crushed this heresy in the past. It was at least in part by way of Christian authors that Gregory got his Greek philosophical notions, although he may be supposed to have had access to some at least of the Latin authors who had written about Greek thought: Cicero in the *De Natura Deorum*; Seneca's *Letters* (56, 65); Aulus Gellius' notes in the *Noctes Atticae*; Valerius Maximus' collection of *Facta et Dicta Memorabilia*; Apuleius' *De Deo Socratis* and *De Platone et Eius Dogmate*; Macrobius, whose circle in the *Saturnalia* pride themselves on their philosophical culture like the Milan circle of Manlius Theodorus, and whose commentary on *Scipio's Dream* is crammed with Plotinus. Among Christian authors, Augustine was able to describe various philosophical schools in Book VIII of *The City of God*. Claudianus Mamertus can list the great philosophical schools of the Greek past; he mentions Plato's Ideas, the New Academy and its scepticism, Epicurus' atomic theory. Hilary of Poitiers (c. 315–67), too, can readily list the various views held about God by the *antiqui*. Ambrose of Milan, adapting Basil's *Hexaemeron*, talks about Plato's three *principia* (*deus, exemplar, materia*), in his own *Hexaemeron*. From the Greek Fathers Rufinus imported into Latin Origen's Christian Platonism and parts of the *Orationes* of Gregory Nazianzen. . . .

Gregory's world of thought is, then, that of an educated Roman, but it is also—as far as he was able to enter into their difficulties—that of every Christian in his charge. In presenting Augustine's ideas in a framework of stories or pictures he sometimes diminished him. But he made him available to many. He did the same for the philosophers. And he brought popular superstition up to a level of commonsense piety.

After reading this selection and the previous one, consider these questions:
1. Why did Gregory send a missionary to King Ethelbert?
2. How did Gregory define legitimate political power?
3. What survived of classical learning in the sixth and seventh centuries?

SELECTION 4:

Western Monasticism

In the face of intellectual decline and the general lawlessness of the times, Gregory encouraged monasticism. Monasteries not only provided havens from the violence of the surrounding world but also allowed individuals to pursue a fully Christian life. Although Gregory helped establish the Roman church and sent missionaries to convert the barbarian pagans, he himself (as many in this age) found the highest expression of Christian values in withdrawal from this godforsaken world and in the dedication of life on the earth to the preparation of eternal life in heaven. Monks voluntarily withdrew from worldly existence and accepted the ascetic values by renouncing sexual relations, indulgence in food and drink, and the comforts of life in general.

From our modern perspective, Gregory and his contemporaries put little worth on establishing a lasting Christian civilization. Probably they would have considered the phrase internally contradictory. Civilization in the sense of a lasting commitment to the values and institutions of this world appeared, in fact, to be inimical to early medieval Christianity. And yet, paradoxically, it was the result of this otherworldly commitment of the monks in the West that a distinctly medieval civilization eventually evolved and through which the modern West was to be linked to the classical past.

*David Knowles, a renowned historian of medieval Christianity and himself a Benedictine monk, provides a picture of the development of monasticism in the West through the early Middle Ages. Although the earliest monks had lived in isolation or within small, simple communities, there arose a need for greater organization. In creating a Christian community of individuals living under a rule (*regula, *hence "regular clergy"), Basil of Caesarea (ca. 330–379) provided a severe model for the monasteries of the Eastern church. As Knowles points out, Benedict of Nursia (ca. 480–553) served a similar function in the West, founding the most important religious order of the early Middle Ages, the Benedictines.*

The rule of St. Benedict was written at a moment of change. The compendium of almost three centuries of monastic experience, it was to become the only code for monks during some six hundred years. Artificial as is all division of human history into periods, it is not altogether fanciful to say that between the birth and the death of Benedict Italy, at least, passed from the twilight of the ancient world into the darkness that preceded the dawn of medieval civilisation. In his boyhood the government and culture of Rome was still a shadow of the past; when he died, the Rome of the papal power was being born. The fragmentation of Europe, the disappearance of political and economic unity and control, the rift between the east-

From *Christian Monasticism*, by David Knowles (New York: World University Library, 1969). Copyright © 1969 David Knowles. Reprinted by permission of the Orion Publishing Group, Ltd.

THE ORIGINS OF MEDIEVAL EUROPE 141

ern empire and the western kingdoms were widening. In the chaos and turmoil of the age that followed, the monasteries of western Europe, from being places of withdrawal from a world that was seething with political and social activity, gradually became centres of light and life in a simple, static, semibarbarian world, preserving and later diffusing what remained of ancient culture and spirituality. In the course of this process they became a part, indeed an integral and important part, of society and of its economy. While kingdoms changed hands and great estates were broken up, the monastery, self-supporting and self-sufficient, could often remain. It became a nucleus that could escape destruction when towns were destroyed, and that could receive gifts and prosper in times of peace.

In the two centuries between the age of Benedict (*c.* 550) and the rise of Charlemagne (770) the typical monastery of western Europe changed entirely both in outward appearance and in social significance. From being a small building housing a dozen or twenty men 'the world forgetting, by the world forgot', the monastery became a large complex built round one or more open courts and containing, besides a large church and the necessary accommodation for the monks, their novices and their infirm and elderly members, offices for the administration and exploitation of large estates, guest-houses and rooms for servants and labourers. In its most extensive form, as in the monasteries of southern Germany and Burgundy, a monastery became a miniature civic centre, with almonry, hospital, school and halls for meetings of its dependents and civil and criminal lawsuits. Around it there often grew up a small borough composed entirely of those to whom it gave livelihood either by wages or by the purchase of goods. At the same time the church, from being the simple oratory of the Benedictine rule, was becoming a storehouse of relics and objects of art, visited by crowds of pilgrims, while in the cloister were stored illuminated service books, manuscripts and liturgical treasures. On the religious level also there had been a change. The early monks had gone into the desert

and the mountains leaving behind them a highly developed urban Christian society with a traditional piety and observance. Now, in the wholly agrarian Europe west and north of Italy, Christian life was reduced to the simplicity of a small rural parish with a priest of peasant, if not servile, birth. The monastic life was both for men and women the only form of instructed, organised devotion. Consequently monks, from being a class of non-social individuals, became a class of 'twice-born' Christians, interceding for the rest of mankind with God and representing the only clear way of salvation. The majority were now in orders, at least by middle life, and were on the way to becoming a branch of the clerical estate. For such, manual work was unfitting, and the cloister, with its facilities for writing, reading, painting and artistic craft-work, became the centre of European cultural life. The liturgy was greatly increased in bulk and in solemnity, as the monks adored God vicariously for contemporaries 'in the world'. The 'monastic centuries' had begun. At the beginning of this epoch, as we have seen, monasteries deriving their inspiration from the east had varied customs of their own settled largely by their abbot, while those of the Celtic tradition had quite different practices embodying the rule of Columbanus [an Irish missionary who established a monastic rule], which was principally a penal code. Gradually the rule of St Benedict made its way, solely by reason of its practical and spiritual excellence, at first alongside other rules, later standing alone as the rule *par excellence*. As time went on, what had actually happened was forgotten and the myth grew up that all existing monasteries had in one way or another derived from the monastery of St Benedict. The legend of the mission of Maurus (St. Maur), Benedict's disciple, to Glanfeuil-sur-Loire to become the father of monasticism in Gaul, was a projection of this myth. By the age of Charlemagne the position of the rule and of St Benedict had become so firmly established that the emperor could ask if any other rule was in use, and others could wonder if there had been monks at all in Europe before Benedict.

SELECTION 5:

The Rule of St. Benedict

As David Knowles makes clear, the Rule of St. Benedict (ca. 530) be-came a model for all of Western monasticism. The following selection pre-sents excerpts from his rule, clearly itemizing the way of life and the val-ues of a Christian.

Prologue. We are about to found therefore a school for the Lord's service; in the organization of which we trust that we shall ordain nothing se-vere and nothing burdensome. But even if, the demands of justice dictating it, something a little irksome shall be the result, for the purpose of amending vices or preserving charity;—thou shalt not therefore, struck by fear, flee the way of salvation, which can not be entered upon except through a narrow entrance. But as one's way of life and one's faith progresses, the heart becomes broadened, and, with the unutterable sweetness of love, the way of the mandates of the Lord is traversed. Thus, never departing from His guid-ance, continuing in the monastery in his teaching until death, through patience we are made par-takers in Christ's passion, in order that we may merit to be companions in His kingdom. . . .

Concerning Humility. The sixth grade of hu-mility is, that a monk be contented with all low-liness or extremity, and consider himself, with re-gard to everything which is enjoined on him, as a poor and unworthy workman; saying to himself with the prophet: "I was reduced to nothing and was ignorant; I was made as the cattle before thee, and I am always with thee." The seventh grade of humility is, not only that he, with his tongue, pronounce himself viler and more worth-less than all; but that he also believe it in the inner-most workings of his heart; humbling him-

From *Regula Monachorum* (*Rule of Monks*) of Benedict of Nursia, in *Patrologia Latina*, vol. 66, edited by J.P. Migne, translated by Ernest F. Henderson, in *Select Historical Documents of the Middle Ages* (London: George Bell, 1910).

self and saying with the prophet, etc. The eighth degree of humility is that a monk do nothing ex-cept what the common rule of the monastery, or the example of his elders, urges him to do. The ninth degree of humility is that a monk restrain his tongue from speaking; and, keeping silence, do not speak until he is spoken to. The tenth grade of humility is that he be not ready, and eas-ily inclined, to laugh. . . . The eleventh grade of humility is that a monk, when he speaks, speak slowly and without laughter, humbly with gravi-ty, using few and reasonable words; and that he be not loud of voice. . . . The twelfth grade of hu-mility is that a monk shall, not only with his heart but also with his body, always show humility to all who see him: that is, when at work, in the or-atory, in the monastery, in the garden, on the road, in the fields. And everywhere, sitting or walking or standing, let him always be with head inclined, his looks fixed upon the ground; re-membering every hour that he is guilty of his sins. Let him think that he is already being pre-sented before the tremendous judgment of God, saying always to himself in his heart what the publican of the gospel, fixing his eyes on the earth, said: "Lord I am not worthy, I a sinner, so much as to lift mine eyes unto Heaven."

Concerning the Divine Offices at Night. In the winter time, that is from the Calends [first day] of November until Easter, according to what is rea-sonable, they must rise at the eighth hour of the night, so that they rest a little more than half the night, and rise when they have already digested. But let the time that remains after vigils be kept for meditation by those brothers who are in any way behind hand with the psalter or lessons. From Easter, moreover, until the aforesaid Calends of November, let the hour of keeping vigils be so arranged that, a short interval being observed in which the brethren may go out for the necessities of nature, the matins [morning prayer], which are always to take place with the dawning light, may straightway follow.

How Many Psalms Are to Be Said at Night. In the winter first of all the verse shall be said: "Make haste oh God to deliver me; make haste to help me oh God." Then, secondly, there shall be said three times: "Oh Lord open Thou my lips and my mouth shall show forth Thy praise." To which is to be subjoined the third psalm and the Gloria. After this the ninety-fourth psalm is to be sung antiphonally or in unison. The Ambrosian chant shall then follow: then six psalms antiphonally. These having been said, the abbot shall, with the verse mentioned, give the blessing. And all being seated upon the benches, there shall be read in turn from the Scriptures—following out the analogy—three lessons; between which also three responses shall be sung. Two responses shall be said without the Gloria; but, after the third lesson, he who chants shall say the Gloria. And, when the cantor begins to say this, all shall straightway rise from their seats out of honour and reverence for the holy Trinity. Books, moreover, of the old as well as the New Testament of Divine authority shall be read at the Vigils; but also expositions of them which have been made by the most celebrated orthodox teachers and catholic Fathers. Moreover, after these three lessons with their responses, shall follow other six psalms to be sung with the Alleluia. After this a lesson of the Apostle shall follow, to be recited by heart; and verses and the supplication of the Litany, that is the Kyrie eleison: and thus shall end the nocturnal vigils. . . .

Whether the Monks Should Have Anything of Their Own. More than anything else is this special vice to be cut off root and branch from the monastery, that one should presume to give or receive anything without the order of the abbot, or should have anything of his own. He should have absolutely not anything: neither a book, nor tablets, nor a pen—nothing at all.—For indeed it

is not allowed to the monks to have their own bodies or wills in their own power. But all things necessary they must expect from the Father of the monastery; nor is it allowable to have anything which the abbot did not give or permit. All things shall be common to all, as it is written: "Let not any man presume or call anything his own." But if any one shall have been discovered delighting in this most evil vice: being warned once and again, if he do not amend, let him be subjected to punishment. . . .

Concerning the Amount of Food. We believe, moreover, that, for the daily refection of the sixth as well as of the ninth hour, two cooked dishes, on account of the infirmities of the different ones, are enough for all tables: so that whoever, perchance, can not eat of one may partake of the other. Therefore let two cooked dishes suffice for all the brothers: and, if it is possible to obtain apples or growing vegetables, a third may be added. One full pound of bread shall suffice for a day, whether there be one refection, or a breakfast and a supper. But if they are going to have supper, the third part of that same pound shall be reserved by the cellarer, to be given back to those who are about to sup. But if, perchance, some greater labour shall have been performed, it shall be in the will and power of the abbot, if it is expedient, to increase anything; surfeiting above all things being guarded against, so that indigestion may never seize a monk: for nothing is so contrary to every Christian as surfeiting, as our Lord says: "Take heed to yourselves, lest your hearts be overcharged with surfeiting." But to younger boys the same quantity shall not be served, but less than that to the older ones; moderation being observed in all things. But the eating of the flesh of quadrupeds shall be abstained from altogether by every one, excepting alone the weak and the sick.

Concerning the Amount of Drink. Each one has his own gift from God, the one in this way, the other in that. Therefore it is with some hesitation that the amount of daily sustenance for others is fixed by us. Nevertheless, in view of the weakness of the infirm we believe that a hemina [just less than half a liter] of wine a day is enough for each one. Those moreover to whom God gives the ability of bearing abstinence shall know that they will have their own reward. But the prior shall judge if either the needs of the place, or labour or the heat of summer, requires more; considering in all things lest satiety or drunkenness creep in. Indeed we read that wine is not suitable for monks at all. But because, in our day, it is not possible to persuade the monks of this, let us agree at least as to the fact that we should not drink till we are sated, but sparingly. For wine can make even the wise to go astray. Where, moreover, the necessities of the place are such that the amount written above can not be found—but much less or nothing at all—those who live there shall bless God and shall not murmur. And we admonish them to this above all: that they be without murmuring. . . .

Concerning the Daily Manual Labour. Idleness is the enemy of the soul. And therefore, at fixed times, the brothers ought to be occupied in manual labour; and again, at fixed times, in sacred reading. . . . There shall certainly be appointed one or two elders, who shall go round the monastery at the hours in which the brothers are engaged in reading, and see to it that no troublesome brother chance to be found who is open to idleness and trifling, and is not intent on his reading; being not only of no use to himself, but also stirring up others.

After reading this selection and the previous one, consider these questions:

1. How, according to Knowles, did the role of the monastery change from the early to the High Middle Ages?
2. What was the Rule of St. Benedict?
3. What were main values encouraged by the Rule?

CHAPTER 8
Feudal Power and Feudal Society

The Middle Ages in the West developed new forms of political power and legal authority—ones that both differed from those of antiquity and, even though connected to our own, differed from those of modern times. In the Greek polis and the Roman *res publica* (republic), politics was public, open to all citizens (although, of course, citizenship itself was highly restricted). All citizens stood equal before the law. With their intense political activities, these city-states were, as we have seen, incorporated into the larger political units of the Hellenistic kingdoms of the eastern Mediterranean and the Roman Empire. Even then, however, a sense of the universal nature of the legal system continued; and, in the various cities of the Roman Empire, a sense of duties owed to the local commune survived. In the Middle Ages this sense of a common political space and of a universal law code dissolved. For various reasons, political power and legal authority came to be defined in very different ways. Strange as it seems, notions of private power and private laws came to prevail. In theory, men and women of the Middle Ages continued to think of authority descending from the emperor or a king and ultimately from God, through middling lords to knights, with the least power at the bottom. This is the famous "pyramid" theory of medieval monarchy. In practice, however, power became a highly local concern, with little overall organization, regularity, or hierarchy. Medieval Europe appeared as a crazy quilt, consisting of a great variety of local practices, customs, and laws. Only as these various centers of local power were collected into larger and larger units can we begin to speak of the formation of the great feudal monarchies of the High Middle Ages.

In the general sense in which we employ it today, the term *feudalism* did not come into use until the seventeenth century. But modern historians have found it a helpful term in describing the effective employment of social, political, and legal power in medieval Europe. What is feudalism? As larger royal or imperial structures increasingly failed to provide effective military protection, ensure undisrupted trade, and mete out justice, local lords built castles, set up markets, collected revenues, and generally kept the peace. The confusion of public and private political, legal, and military powers on the part of local magnates provided the foundations of feudalism. These magnates themselves formed part of a military caste. Other individuals became dependent on them, becoming their vassals in exchange for some type of service. In its fully worked out form, feudalism became intertwined with the granting of a manor. In a structure historians call manorialism, this included two main aspects: (1) linking the status of a vassal to the management of the land; and (2) bringing the local peasant population into the condition of serfdom, that is denying them of their freedom by tying them to the village and manor.

Vassalage comes from the Celtic word *vassal* or "servant," and means a set of obligations to a lord (Latin *dominus;* French, *seigneur*). It can be traced back to the Carolingian monarchy of the seventh and eighth centuries. The Carolingian empire survived about a century after the death of Charlemagne (ca. 742–814). The combination of vassalage with land tenure seems to have developed in the forms we know it only in the ninth and tenth centuries. The new invasions of the Vikings from the north, the Muslims from the south, and the Magyars from the east, which overwhelmed the remnants of the Carolingian empire, gave rise to the need for more effective military power on a very local level. In other words, while ultimate authority came from the distant king or emperor, actual power devolved to the local level. Gradually, what must have originally been a very informal set of relationships of mutual aid between lord and vassal became defined in a highly legalistic and ritualistic manner called fealty. The following selection of documents indicates how vassalage evolved from mere contractual (and even cash) obligations under the Carolingians, becoming tied to the use and management of landholdings (manors). The original practice of sheltering one's vassals was not always satisfactory, if only because housing and feeding a vassal and his family became rather cumbersome. Eventually lords started granting estates to their vassals for the purposes of providing them both with subsistence and with enough land and peasant labor to free them to train for war.

SELECTION 1:

The Origins of Feudalism

In his book Feudal Society, *French historian Marc Bloch describes the basic features of feudalism.*

To be the 'man' of another man: in the vocabulary of feudalism, no combination of words was more widely used or more comprehensive in meaning. In both the Romance and the Germanic tongues it was used to express personal dependence *per se* and applied to persons of all social classes regardless of the precise legal nature of the bond. The count was the 'man' of the king, as the serf was the 'man' of his manorial lord. Sometimes even in the same text, within the space of a few lines, radically different social stations were thus evoked. An instance of this, dating from the end of the eleventh century, is a petition of Norman nuns, complaining that their 'men'—that is to say their peasants—were forced by a great baron to work at the castles of his 'men', meaning the knights who were his vassals. The ambiguity disturbed no one, because, in spite of the gulf between the orders of society, the emphasis was on the fundamental element in common: the subordination of one individual to another.

If, however, the principle of this human nexus permeated the whole life of society, the forms which it assumed were none the less very diverse—with sometimes almost imperceptible transitions, from the highest to the humblest. Moreover there were many variations from country to country. It will be useful if we take as a guiding thread one of the most significant of these relationships of dependence, the tie of vassalage; studying it first in the most highly 'feudalized' zone of Europe, namely, the heart of the former Carolingian Empire, northern France, the German Rhineland and Swabia; and endeavouring, before we embark on any inquiries into its origins, to describe the most striking features of the institution at the period of its greatest expansion, that is to say, from the tenth to the twelfth century.

Imagine two men face to face; one wishing to serve, the other willing or anxious to be served. The former puts his hands together and places them, thus joined, between the hands of the other

man—a plain symbol of submission, the significance of which was sometimes further emphasized by a kneeling posture. At the same time, the person proffering his hands utters a few words—a very short declaration—by which he acknowledges himself to be the 'man' of the person facing him. Then chief and subordinate kiss each other on the mouth, symbolizing accord and friendship. Such were the gestures—very simple ones, eminently fitted to make an impression on minds so sensitive to visible things—which served to cement one of the strongest social bonds known in the feudal era. Described or mentioned in the texts a hundred times, reproduced on seals, miniatures, bas-reliefs, the ceremony was called 'homage' (in German, *Mannschaft*). The superior party, whose position was created by this act, was described by no other term than the very general one of 'lord'. Similarly, the subordinate was often simply called the 'man' of this lord; or sometimes, more precisely, his 'man of mouth and hands' (*homme de bouche et de mains*). But more specialized words were also employed, such as 'vassal' or, till the beginning of the twelfth century at least, 'commended man' (*commendé*).

In this form the rite bore no Christian imprint. Such an omission, probably explained by the remote Germanic origins of the symbolism, in due course ceased to be acceptable to a society which had come to regard a promise as scarcely valid unless God were guarantor. Homage itself, so far as its form was concerned, was never modified. But, apparently from the Carolingian period, a second rite—an essentially religious one—was superimposed on it; laying his hand on the Gospels or on relics, the new vassal swore to be faithful to his master. This was called fealty, *foi* in French (in German *Treue*, and, formerly, *Hulde*). . . .

The tie thus formed lasted, in theory, as long as the two lives which it bound together, but as soon as one or other of these was terminated by death it was automatically dissolved. We shall see that in practice vassalage very soon became, in most cases, hereditary; but this *de facto* situation allowed the legal rule to remain intact to the end. It mattered little that the son of the deceased vassal usually performed this homage to the lord who had accepted his father's, or that the heir of the previ-

From *Feudal Society*, vol. I: *The Growth of Ties of Dependence*, by Marc Bloch, translated by L.A. Manyon, (London: Routledge & Kegan Paul, 1967). Translation copyright © 1961, 1962 by Routledge & Kegan Paul. Reprinted by permission of the University of Chicago Press.

ous lord almost invariably received the homage of his father's vassals: the ceremony had none the less to be repeated with every change of the individual persons concerned. Similarly, homage could not be offered or accepted by proxy; the examples to the contrary all date from a very late period, when the significance of the old forms was already almost lost. In France, so far as it applied to the king, this privilege was legalized only under Charles VII and even then not without many misgivings. The social bond seemed to be truly inseparable from the almost physical contact which the formal act created between the two men. . . .

To seek a protector, or to find satisfaction in being one—these things are common to all ages. But we seldom find them giving rise to new legal institutions save in civilizations where the rest of the social framework is giving way. Such was the case in Gaul after the collapse of the Roman Empire.

Consider, for example, the society of the Merovingian period. Neither the State nor the family any longer provided adequate protection. The village community was barely strong enough to maintain order within its own boundaries; the urban community scarcely existed. Everywhere, the weak man felt the need to be sheltered by someone more powerful. The powerful man, in his turn, could not maintain his prestige or his fortune or even ensure his own safety except by securing for himself, by persuasion or coercion, the support of subordinates bound to his service. On the one hand, there was the urgent quest for a protector; on the other, there were usurpations of authority, often by violent means. And as notions of weakness and strength are always relative, in many cases the same man occupied a dual rôle—as a dependent of a more powerful man and a protector of humbler ones. Thus there began to be built up a vast system of personal relationships whose intersecting threads ran from one level of the social structure to another.

In yielding thus to the necessities of the moment these generations of men had no conscious desire to create new social forms, nor were they aware of doing so. Instinctively each strove to turn to account the resources provided by the existing social structure and if, unconsciously,

something new was eventually created, it was in the process of trying to adapt the old. Moreover, the society that emerged from the invasions had inherited a strange medley of institutions and practices in which the traditions of the Germans were intermingled with the legacy of Rome, and with that of the peoples whom Rome had conquered without ever completely effacing their native customs. . . .

Among the lowly people who sought a protector, the most unfortunate became simply slaves, thereby binding their descendants as well as themselves. Many others, however, even among the most humble, were anxious to maintain their status as free men; and the persons who received their allegiance had as a rule little reason to oppose such a wish. For in this age when personal ties had not yet strangled the institutions of government, to enjoy what was called 'freedom' meant essentially to belong by undisputed right to the people ruled by the Merovingian kings—to the *populus Francorum*, as contemporaries called it, lumping together under the same name the conquerors and the conquered. As a result, the two terms 'free' and 'frank' came to be regarded as synonymous and continued to be so regarded through the ages. To be surrounded with dependents who enjoyed the judicial and military privileges characteristic of free men was, for a chief, in many respects more advantageous than to command only a horde of slaves. . . .

The relationships of private dependence were not subject to the principle of the 'personality of laws', since they were still on the fringe of all legal systems. The fact that they were not officially controlled rendered them all the more capable of being adapted to an infinite variety of circumstances. The king himself, in his capacity as leader of his people, owed his support to all his subjects without discrimination and was entitled in turn to their allegiance as confirmed by the universal oath of free men; nevertheless he granted to a certain number of them his personal *maimbour* [protection]. A wrong done to persons thus placed 'within his word' was regarded as a offence against the king himself and was in consequence treated with exceptional severity. Within this rather ill-assorted group there arose a more restricted and more distinguished body of royal retainers who were called the *leudes* of the prince, that is to say his 'men'; in the anarchy of later Merovingian times they more than once controlled both king and state. As in Rome, a little earlier, the young man of good family who wished to get on in the world 'entrusted' himself to a powerful man—if his future had not already in his childhood been assured in this way by a farsighted father. In spite of the prohibitions of councils, many ecclesiastics of every rank did not scruple to seek the protection of laymen. But it was apparently in the lower strata of society that the relationships of subordination were most widely diffused as well as most exacting. The only formula of 'commendation' that we possess shows us a poor devil who only accepts a master because 'he lacks the wherewithal to feed and clothe himself'. There was no distinction of words, however, and no difference—at least no very clear one—in conception between these diverse aspects of dependence, despite all differences of social status.

Whatever the status of the person who commended himself, he seems almost invariably to have taken an oath to his master. Was it also customary for him to make a formal act of submission? We do not know with any certainty. The official legal systems, which are concerned only with the old institutions regulating the affairs of the people and the family, are silent on this point. As to the agreements themselves, they were hardly ever put in writing, which alone provides definite evidence. From the second half of the eighth century, however, the documents begin to mention the ceremony of the joined hands. The very first example shown to us is a case where the persons involved are of the highest rank, the protégé being a foreign prince, the protector the king of the Franks; but we must not be deceived by this one-sidedness on the part of those who compiled the records. The ceremony did not seem worth describing unless, being associated with matters of high policy, it was one of the features of an interview between rulers; in the normal course of life it was regarded as a commonplace event and so was passed over in silence. Undoubtedly the ceremony had been in use for a considerable time before it thus suddenly appeared in the texts. The similarity of the custom among the Franks, the Anglo-Saxons and the Scandinavians attests its Germanic origin. But the symbolism was too obvious for it not to be readily adopted by the whole population. In England and among the Scandinavians we find it being used indiscriminately to express very different forms of subordination— that of the slave to the master, that of the free companion to the warrior chieftain. Everything points to the conclusion that this was also the case for a long time in Frankish Gaul. The gesture served to conclude protective contracts of various kinds; sometimes performed, sometimes omitted, it did not seem indispensable to any of them. An institution requires a terminology without too much ambiguity and a relatively stable ritual; but in the Merovingian world personal relationships remained on the level of customary procedure.

SELECTION 2:

Homage and Fealty

As Marc Bloch points out, the actual process of becoming a vassal, becoming someone's "man" or "liege man," assumed a quasi-religious ceremony known as homage and fealty. The following description of such a ceremony involves the count of Flanders and takes place in 1127. Note *how the clasping of hands of the vassal and the clasping of the lord's hands around them symbolizes the basis of the relation in protection.*

I, Thiebault, count palatine of Troyes, make known to those present and to come that I have given in fee to Jocelyn d'Avalon and his heirs the manor which is called Gillencourt, which is of the castellanerie of La Ferte sur Aube; and whatever the same Jocelyn shall be able to acquire in the same manor I have granted to him and his heirs in augmentation of that fief I have granted, moreover, to him that in no free manor of mine will I retain men who are of this gift. The same Jocelyn,

From *Chronicle of the Death of Charles the Good*, by Galbert de Bruges, in *Translations and Reprints from the Original Sources of European History*, translated by E.P. Cheyney (Philadelphia: University of Pennsylvania Press, 1898).

moreover, on account of this has become my liege man, saving however, his allegiance to Gerard d'Arcy, and to the lord duke of Burgundy, and to Peter, count of Auxerre. Done at Chouaude, by my own witness, in the year of the Incarnation of our Lord 1200 in the month of January. Given by the hand of Walter, my chancellor; note of Milo.

After reading this selection and the previous one, consider these questions:
1. What is feudalism?
2. What was the foundation of the feudal relationship?
3. What were the obligations on each side of this relationship?

SELECTION 3:
Manorialism

Originating as a military obligation, the feudal bond evolved to include a much more extensive set of relations. In general, this meant for both lord and vassal keeping the peace in the local area. As there was no public power to speak of, public uses of power merged with private ones. Holding a fief, in other words, carried the responsibilities of policing and rendering justice. Local lords and certain vassals actually held court.

The manor of the fief did not just become a means of exchange (rather than cash, which was generally in short supply), it also constituted the basic social and economic structure of the medieval world in the West. It was basically a large self-sufficient farm consisting of a rural population grouped in a village or several hamlets. Part of the manor, the demesne, was land reserved for the exclusive use of the lord of the manor, and this is where he lived with his family and several of his knights. The other inhabitants of the manor were tenants, either serfs tied to the land or free peasants. On their own, tenants worked all the nondemesne lands. They were also responsible for work on the demesne in the form of compulsory service. When landlords consolidated their power over their manors, they collected not only dues and services but also fees for the use of their flour mills, bakeries, and breweries. Some lords even claimed wider powers:

collecting taxes, hearing legal cases, levying fines, and organizing men for defense.

Contemporary French historian Georges Duby describes the economic organization of the medieval manor.

A demesne bore the same appearance as a *manse* [the dwelling of a householder], for it was after all the *manse* of the master, *mansus indominicatus*. But it was an outsize *manse,* because it corresponded to a specially numerous, productive and demanding 'household' or *familia.* Even so, its structure was no different from that of other *manses*. At the centre was an enclosure, the courtyard, the space surrounded by a solid palisade, enclosing as well as the orchard and kitchen garden a collection of buildings which amounted to a hamlet. Here is a description of Annapes, which belonged to the king. Around a well-built stone palace containing three halls on the ground floor and eleven rooms upstairs stood a cluster of wooden buildings, a cowhouse, three stables, kitchen, bakehouse and 17 huts to shelter the servants and store the food. As for the *appendicia*, attached to the central plot, there were extensive stretches of arable and meadow, as many vineyards as possible, and finally huge tracts of waste. The farm of Somain, near Annapes, had attached to it fields measuring 625 acres, meadow measuring 110 acres and 1,970 acres of woods and pasture. Other 'farms' were not always so well provided for; the one belonging to the abbey of St Pierre-du-Mont-Blandin at Ghent possessed less than 250 acres.

However, generally speaking, the *mansus indominicatus* was equal in size to several dozen peasant *manses* held as tenancies. And the picture most frequently given by the evidence is of a number of tenanted *manses* supporting the one farmed by the master. The area of arable possessed by the tenanted *manses* varied very greatly in size, as we have seen, but was always less than the quantity of land which theoretically corresponded to the physical capacity of a peasant family. Those holdings called 'free' were on the average endowed with attached fields larger in extent than the 'servile' holdings—but the status of the *manse* was not always the same as the personal status of its tenant.

The primary function of the great demesnes was to allow a few men to live in idleness, abundance and the exercise of power. They maintained a narrow circle of the magnates in a magnificent way of life. In a society still primitive, and at a time when food supplies were limited, the 'man of power' showed himself first of all as the man who could always eat as much as he wished. He was also open handed, the man who provided others with food, and the yardstick of his prestige was the number of men whom he fed, and the size of his 'household'. Around the great lay and religious leaders congregated vast retinues of relatives, friends, people receiving patronage (the latter were known officially at the court of Charlemagne as *les nourris*), guests welcomed with liberality who would spread tales of the greatness of a house, and a host of servants, amongst whom would be found those artists in metal, woodcarving and weaving who could fashion weapons, jewellery and ornaments, and thereby enhance the luxurious setting appropriate to the exalted rank of the ruler. This way of life assumed housekeeping on a gigantic scale; barns and cellars filled to overflowing; well-tended and fruitful gardens, trellises and vineyards; the cultivation of fields of almost limitless extent to provide sufficient grain in spite of low yields; and lastly the existence of enormous forests and wastes to harbour game and give pasture to the riding and warhorses which were the mark of the aristocrat. The springs of wealth had to be inexhaustible. It was the privilege of the noble at all times to avoid any appearance of shortage. He had to be prodigal in the midst of famine, but, as harvests fluctuated from year to year, his steward, anxious never to find himself in short supply, naturally tried to increase output, especially of corn.

From *Rural Economy and Country Life in the Medieval West*, by Georges Duby (Columbia: University of South Carolina Press, 1968). Reprinted by permission of the publisher.

It is important, however, not to attribute an incipient profit motive to the anxiety of masters and their agents to develop their resources and enlarge their revenues. They had no wish to accumulate goods as such: their desire was merely, without anxiety for the morrow, to have something always in hand to provide for the 'family' and if need be to increase the number of their dependants. In those days personal devotion and service was a virtue upon which great store was set. Our sources mostly reveal the principles of estate management laid down by the heads of religious houses and these 'intellectuals' were very probably more conscious of the need to provide for the future. Their main preoccupation, however, was to specify the exact extent of their requirements in terms of agricultural output. This certainly appears to have been the object of the 'statutes' compiled by Abbot Adalard for the monastery of Corbie; they specified in minute detail the quality of bread, the weight of the loaves, the provenance of the flour from which they were to be made, how many different recipients there were and what the ration of each was to be. An exact knowledge of what was required thus preceded and regulated the apportionment of supplies from different demesnes according to their capacity to produce. The tours of the surveyors and the preparation of inventories were intended to improve this apportionment as well as to find out whether extra brothers could be supported and more alms given away, thus increasing the number of mouths which would have to be fed. Behind the long-term plans which were concerned with consumption rather than production lay the fact that the *villa* was the provider and must not be found wanting in the hour of need. . . .

In return for their endowment the peasant 'households' owed to the 'household' of their master various dues the nature of which was usually the same for each category of *manses* on the *villa* and also on other *villae* belonging to the same landowner. There were to begin with the various dues which had to be taken to the lord's hall on certain days of the year. The amounts were fixed, a few pieces of money, some chickens, eggs, one or two small animals such as sheep or pigs. These payments can be taken either as payments for the use of the woods and wastes of the lord, or as taxes of public origin. Some of them were the relics of the charges formerly imposed on peasants for supplies to the royal armies. It was the duty of the landlord to collect these, and in time he appropriated them for himself. These different dues were never heavy and the profit of the recipient was minimal. Their impact on the economy of the *villa* cannot have affected the real struggle for existence, the toil connected with garnering the main food supply, but was more a marginal matter of backyard poultry and small surplus items of diet. They formed only a superficial charge on the tenants' own farm production; and to the lord, as well, these odd amounts of food and small sums of money were trifling matters which contributed little if anything to his standard of living.

On the other hand the labour services imposed on the holdings were the essential economic link between them and the demesne and formed the very nexus of the demesne system. The manpower available on each satellite farm unit was, as we have seen, greater than that required to cultivate its fields. And this surplus manpower had to go to the demesne. It might take the form of periodic deliveries of objects upon which labour had been expended: thus, each *manse* might have to prepare a load of firewood, or a certain number of stakes, beams or planks, or perhaps some of those simple tools which could be constructed by any unskilled person. On servile holdings the women would weave cloth for the demesne. But the main tasks were agricultural, and they took three distinct but often interconnected forms.

1. The *manse* could in the first place be charged with a definite task. It could be responsible, for instance, for erecting in springtime a certain length of temporary fencing to protect the crops and the hay. More usually it was given the responsibility for an entire season's cultivation of a given plot of land, the *ansange*, taken from the demesne arable; activities which began with preliminary ploughing and continued right until storing of the grain in the lord's barn. In this way, every year some parcels of the demesne arable which needed cultivating were temporarily detached from the rest and were joined to the *ap-*

pendicia of the peasant *manses*. They rounded off the latter and absorbed the underemployed productive effort of the tenant population.

2. Other obligations were more exacting, since they left the workers less freedom. To perform them they were periodically taken away from the family group and put to join a team of workers on the lands attached to the demesne. These demands—the *corvées* in the real sense of the term, since the word means 'demand' or 'requisition'—only affected one labour unit in each *manse,* a worker either by hand or with a draught animal, i.e. a man or a plough team. If a *manse* was occupied by several families, or if the tenants themselves owned servants, as was fairly frequent, the service would be much lightened. Sometimes the *manse* owed a fixed number of days either at certain seasons, or else each week, and sometimes the man subject to the *corvée* assisted in a definite task until it was completed. In certain cases it was really manual labour (*manoperae*), for the man in question would come in the morning to the lord's hall to join the farm servants and await his orders whilst his implements and plough team were left behind at the *manse*. Another kind of forced labour was specially assigned to certain tasks. The work of the women from the servile *manses* in the demesne workshops was of such a kind, and so were the errands and cartage requiring the use of cart and draught animals, which were usually the responsibility of the better-equipped, so-called 'free' *manses*.

3. Tasks referred to in the inventories as 'nights' were the third kind of work which might be required. These placed the tenant at the service of the lord for several days at a stretch without the certainty of returning home each evening. This enabled him to be employed at a distance or to be sent away on a mission, and it is clear that these obligations of an indeterminate nature provided the demesne with a reserve of immediately available and reliable labour in cases of unforeseen need.

These different tasks were often combined. But for the free *manse* they were usually lighter, more limited, and of less degrading nature. The free *manses* were generally occupied by peasants of free status, whose ancestors had often been in-dependent, but who, because they were poor or weak, had allowed their lands to become part of the economic system of the *villa* in exchange for help and protection. But even where rural migration, mixed marriages and the alienation of land had obliterated the connection between the 'freedom' of the tenancy and the free status of the tenants, the holdings were of sufficient size to support the larger domestic animals. To be able to provide oxen or a horse, and thus to take part in ploughing, cartage and contacts with the outside world, was probably their most valuable contribution to the demesne activities; they could supply ploughmen, drivers and horsemen, rather than unskilled labourers. On the other hand, it is easy to believe that when landlords created servile *manses* to house some of their domestic serfs in order to be rid of responsibility for their maintenance and to let them bring up their own children, they did not for one moment relax their right to command obedience or to use them at their will. They had to do manual labour because they did not usually possess draught animals. It was they who guarded the headquarters of the demesne at night, did the laundry, dipped and sheared sheep, while their wives and daughters worked in the demesne workshops. Servile *manses* were also burdened with the weekly labour services of undefined nature. In Germania they had usually to put a man at the disposal of the lord for three days a week; or in other words each *manse* had to provide one half-time servant throughout the year. This explains their smaller allocation of arable land than that of the free *manses*. Their holders were forced to work away from home for longer and could thus devote less time to their own farms, but on the other hand, when performing forced labour in the demesne they ate in the refectory, and their consumption of food at home was accordingly reduced.

Since the profit to be derived from a tenancy did not correspond to the services which it owed, the tenancy was not exactly a wage. The letting out of the *manses* ought primarily to be thought of as a way of relieving the demesne management of the necessity to provide the servants with board and lodging. The demesne could in this way have an abundant source of labour at its disposal. It has been calculated that the 800 dependent families of the abbey of San Giulia of Brescia at the beginning of the tenth century owed service to their masters amounting to 60,000 working days. The lord, here as elsewhere, wanted to dip into a bottomless well, to be permanently able to command instant service in the event of unforeseen need. But in normal times it is unlikely that all the labour services owing were actually called upon.

This then was the manorial system. The surplus productive effort of the peasant families was appropriated by the lord, to whose rule they were subject, for the purpose of farming his lands. But since human labour could by itself produce so little, this surplus was also limited. And because of this, the demesne needed a large number of satellite *manses*.

After reading this selection, consider these questions:
1. How were medieval manors organized?
2. What was the demesne?
3. What was the *manse?*

SELECTION 4:

Peasant Families in the Middle Ages

I*n her book* The Ties That Bound, *modern social historian Barbara A. Hanawalt explores the nature of medieval peasant families in England. Because of the limited number of primary sources, she concentrates on the organization of these families in the late Middle Ages, during the fourteenth and fifteenth centuries.*

The fourteenth and fifteenth centuries were traumatic ones for the English peasantry. Each generation faced new threats to life and livelihood. In the first quarter of the fourteenth century famine brought starvation to poor peasants and belt tightening to rich. Disease was ever present following the first wave of the Black Death in 1348 through the late fifteenth century. In addition to natural disasters, royal tax collectors and recruiters came to collect money, carry off goods, and impress peasant lads into service. Even if some of the peasants thrived despite adverse conditions or because reduced population presented new economic opportunities, the possibility of death was very close, taking life before the rewards of hard work could be enjoyed or killing heirs who would have profited from the fruits of their parents' labors. Radical changes threatened the institutions of English society, eventually resulting in the demise of serfdom in the fifteenth century. But what happened to that basic institution of peasant society, the family? . . .

The peasant family remained much the same throughout these two centuries of cataclysmic changes and, moreover, . . . the family was able to maintain its basic structure because it was a remarkably flexible institution, permitting the pursuit of a variety of options while retaining the integrity of the unit. The family was the basic economic unit for working the land, producing and socializing the younger generation, and finally passing on wealth from one generation to another. Even a sweep of plague through a community did not destroy these familial capacities. People remarried if they lost a spouse, and relatives came to claim a family holding left vacant. Constant regroupings of families occurred to compensate for losses. Using a range of economic strategies, the peasant family continued to function effectively and often expanded its wealth and options as new economic opportunities opened up in the fifteenth century.

Economic necessity alone, however, did not hold families together or keep people continually regrouping into conjugal units. Traditional role structures for men, women, and children made people more comfortable within a family structure. Folklore and long custom ascribed various functions to youths, to married couples, and to children. Thus village fertility festivals were the province of single youths, but married men held village offices and married women officiated at births. Cultural roles for family members reinforced those that biology had imposed on humans. Children must be nurtured, the sexual drives are strongest in youth, and the need for food and shelter forces mature men and women into economic activities to provide for themselves and their offspring.

While family remained a stable institution during the fifteenth century, the community changed, as did the relation of family to it. In the fourteenth century the peasant community was a fairly close-knit social and political group. Their mutual reliance and emphasis on self-regulation did not mean that the community members always got along with one another, but rather that they used institutions such as village bylaws, manorial courts, and even royal courts to regulate disputes, punish offenders, and enforce contracts and debts. By the fifteenth century the traumas of the previous century began to erode these institutions of village regulation, and neighbor became estranged from neighbor.

My assertion that family was the basic unit of peasant society, and that peasant communities, not family structures, changed, requires elaboration. A few rudimentary definitions and some background description of late medieval social and economic conditions are in order.

As other historians of medieval families have noted, contemporary language was deficient in describing the institution on which we have lavished so much study. *Familia* was a Latin word used in the Middle Ages, as it had been earlier, to describe the households of lords or ecclesiastical establishments and included the master, his immediate kin, servants, and other household residents. In the fourteenth century it would not have applied to a peasant with his wife and children. Nor was the aristocratic concept of "house" as a lineage used among peasantry. Instead, from Anglo-Saxon times the more specific terms for the roles in the family were used. The husband was the holder of a house, the wife (his woman) and his children completed his immediate circle at the hearth. In late medieval records intrafamilial relations continued to be specified as in "Matilda wife of William" or "John son of Richard." Manorial court records speak of "William and his wife Matilda surrendering land to the lord and taking it back for themselves and the heirs of their body." Such references to family served the peasants' linguistic needs as effectively as the more abstract category of "family" does for us today.

The household units . . . tended to be nuclear or conjugal families. Peasants showed a strong preference for having only a conjugal family in a household. As we shall see in the first section on the material environment, one reason that this preference was so feasible in practice was that the peasants' wattle and daub housing was cheap to construct. Old people could often have a dower cottage rather than living in the family residence, and even the propertyless and children inheriting only minimal wealth could at least have a hovel of their own. . . .

One must be careful not to present too rosy a picture of life in the fifteenth century, however, for the plague revisited about every generation and there were a number of other diseases that were new and deadly. Furthermore, a new social structure was developing in the countryside that eventually eroded some of the good features of the old communities. The social stratification within the rural population became much greater than it was in the early fourteenth century. . . .

In defining peasant families and discussing their fortunes during this brief review of economic and social conditions in the countryside, it is apparent that peasants had a range of economic options open to them. The flexibility of the peasant household economy permitted it to adapt to the radically different conditions of the two centuries under study. One of the major goals of this study has been to create a flexible model of peasant household economy that takes into con-

sideration the sex roles in the household, age of members, social status, and economic options.

After reading this selection, consider these questions:

1. How does Hanawalt describe the structure of peasant families in the late Middle Ages?
2. Did the organization of the peasant family change over the course of the fourteenth and fifteenth centuries?
3. What held these families together, according to Hanawalt?

SELECTION 5:

Fulk Nerra, Count of Anjou

Once the vast areas of lands of central and western Europe were organized into manors and brought under the military, political, and social control of feudalism, there gradually developed a competition among local magnates for control over larger and larger sections of surrounding territory. The tenth, eleventh, and twelfth centuries saw continuous warfare among these lords, generally resulting in the establishment of a single dominant family. In the process, former lords became the vassals of greater ones. Although this was less the case in such places as the south of France, in the north various princes arose who controlled a large number of castles and whose power extended over large geographical areas. The winners in these contests eventually were confirmed in their power by the king or emperor, possessing various noble titles. Such is the case with Fulk Nerra, count of Anjou (987–1040), who, through various contests with rival counts, eventually controlled a wide area from Blois to Nantes along the Loire River. In the following selection, noted historian R.W. Southern describes this process of consolidation by the counts of Anjou in central France.

Politically, the great question in the tenth century, outside Germany, was how far the disintegra-

From *The Making of the Middle Ages*, by R.W. Southern (New Haven, CT: Yale University Press, 1953). Reprinted by permission of Yale University Press.

tion of authority would go. The immediate cause of the disintegration was lack of loyalty, and with lack of loyalty to persons went a decay and confusion of the ideas for which the persons stood. It was a time when claims of allegiance and duty, however well founded in law or in history, counted for nothing when they went beyond the bounds of effective personal power. It was easy for the Count of Anjou to throw off his obligations to the King of France. Would it prove equally possible for the lord of Loches or of any of the castles of the Loire to throw off the authority of the Count of Anjou? How far would the process go? The answer depended partly on the range of those small bodies of armoured, mounted soldiers who were growing up round the strong points of government. Partly it depended on the extent of the sacrifices people would be prepared to make for peace and security. It was no accident that after the confusion of the tenth century the strongest governmental units appeared where there was least in the way of marsh, mountain or forest to separate one community from another—in the open plains where the competition for power was most intense, and where the need for organization was consequently most keenly felt. But even in the most favourable geographical conditions, man's technical equipment was so primitive that this helplessness before Nature—which added to his misery in one way—saved him from the misery of organized tyranny. There was a mercifully large gap between the will to rule and the power to do so, and it may be that bad roads and an intractable soil contributed more to the fashioning of familiar liberties than any other factor at this time.

Perhaps more simply than anywhere else in Europe, the shaping of a new political order may be seen in the valley of the river Loire. There was here so clean a sweep of ancient institutions, title deeds and boundaries, that the emergence of new forms of loyalty and authority was facilitated. Elsewhere the same processes are to be observed, men have the same objects in view, but they work towards them less directly and less swiftly. We shall observe the ambitions, and the restraints imposed on the wills, of some of the most powerful personalities of their time, in studying the emergence of one of the strongest new political units of the eleventh century in the Loire valley.

The County of Anjou. The history of this county from the late tenth to the mid-twelfth century provides a rich portrait gallery of the makers of a medieval "state". Like other families, the counts took a great interest in their past; they were proud of it, and in the course of years they left a large

collection of documents, which illuminate their history. Towards the end of the eleventh century, there was a historically minded Count, Fulk Rechin, who set himself to record the traditions of the family and his own recollections of his predecessors. Looking back from the eminence which the family had attained in his time, he could dimly perceive the origins of their good fortune in the career of an ancestor two hundred years earlier. Nothing was clearly reported about this ancestor except that his name was Ingelgarius, nor was much known about his descendants for nearly another hundred years; but the later panegyrists of the family were able to fill this gap by proclaiming that Ingelgarius was descended from an ancient Romano-British family of high rank. No amount of research or invention could discover how the family had lived in the intervening period since the fall of Rome, but it was concluded that "the matter is unimportant for we often read that senators have lived on the land and emperors have been snatched from the plough". This classical background was a twelfth-century addition to the history of the family—it reveals the romantic prejudices of that period—but in essentials the historians of the family were right. They saw that the effective origins of the family were to be sought in the later years of the ninth century—a time when, as one of them remarked, "the men in established positions relied on the merits of their ancestors and not on their own", and allowed themselves to be elbowed out of the way by new men pushing their way to the front by superior energy and military effectiveness.

The family of Ingelgarius were among these new men. War made them conspicuous, grants of land established their position, marriage consolidated it, and the acquisition of ancient titles of honour cloaked their usurpations. Ingelgarius gained the first foothold in the valley of the Loire, but it was his son Fulk the Red—with a name and physical characteristic which kept reappearing in his descendants—who made the family a power to be reckoned with in the neighbourhood: marriage added to his possessions, force held them together, and the comital rights (for what they were worth), which had previously been shared, were now acquired outright. . . .

By 987 the family was ready to emerge from its legendary and epic age on to the stage of history. At this moment there appeared one of those powerful figures, who combined all the qualities and ferocity of his race and consolidated the achievements of the last four generations: Fulk Nerra, the Black, Count of Anjou from 987 to 1040. We cannot do better than look at him through the eyes of his grandson, Count Fulk Rechin. This is what he records of Fulk Nerra:

1. He built thirteen castles, which he can name, and many more besides.

2. He won two pitched battles, against his neighbours to East and West.

3. He built two abbeys, one at Angers and the other near Loches, the great outpost of his power in the South East.

4. He went twice to Jerusalem (this is an understatement: it is almost certain that he went three times); and he died on his way home during his last journey.

Each one of these items, properly considered, stamps him as a man of note: taken together they convey a vivid impression of a pioneer in the art of feudal government. In the first place, the castles: they were the guarantee of the stability of the régime. Fulk was a pioneer in the building of stone keeps, and one formidable example of his handiwork still survives at Langeais. The inexpugnable fortresses solved at once the problem of defence and of government—they made loyalty easy. The battles were more speculative—brilliant gambles based on the solid capital of defensive positions. It was a time when he who committed himself to open battle, committed his fortune to the winds. But the reward of successful enterprise was great, as befitted the uncertainty of the outcome; and the battle of Conquereuil in 992 against the Count of Brittany was one of the foundations of Angevin [Anjou] greatness.

We pass to the expressions of Fulk Nerra's religious zeal. He and his contemporary Duke of Normandy were the greatest of the pilgrims who set on foot the movement to Jerusalem. In them the alternation of headlong violence with abrupt acts of remorse and atonement, which charac-

terises the early feudal age, has its full play. Perhaps more than in anything else, the nature of the man is revealed in the documents which recount his religious benefactions. They breathe a vigorous and autocratic spirit, unencumbered by any feeling after intangible things, yet accessible to a sense of guilt and stirred by a sense of littleness before the miraculous disturbances of nature. These documents deal with stark facts:

> I give them (says Fulk's charter to Beaulieu) the blood, the thieves and all evil deeds, of whatsoever kind they are (that is to say, jurisdiction over, and the profits arising from the punishment of, murderers, thieves and other criminals), between the rivulet *de Concere* and the oak of St. Hilary, and between the vegetable garden and the elm on which men are hanged. And wheresoever, on my land, the abbot does battle for anything, if his champion is beaten, he shall go free and pay no fine to my reeve or any official.

So far as Fulk speaks to us at all, he speaks to us in words like these. Yet, when all is said, we are very far from understanding a man like Fulk Nerra. It is only occasionally that we are allowed to see behind the façade of ruthlessness and activity to the not overconfident humanity which guided arm and hand. It takes some extraordinary event to reveal these men in their more domestic moods. They must often have sat with their wives at the upper windows of their newly built castles, but it is not until a meteor falls into the garden below that we have a picture of Fulk's formidable son Geoffrey Martel and his wife Agnes . . . racing down to the spot where it fell and vowing to found an abbey dedicated to the Holy Trinity, in memory of the three glowing fragments which had flashed before their awestruck eyes. It was in the face of the miraculous that they became most human. When the Duke of Aquitaine heard that a rain of blood had fallen in his duchy, he did not reflect that he was hostile to the royal pretensions—he humbly wrote and asked the king if he had any learned men who could explain the event. And their answers were such as to make any man pause in a career of wrong-doing. But, on the whole, the secular leaders of the early eleventh century must be judged by what they did, and not by what they thought or intended. Judged by this standard Fulk Nerra is the founder of the greatness of the County of Anjou.

His life-time brings us to an age of serious, expansive wars waged by well-organized and strongly fortified territorial lords. The confused warfare, haphazard battles and obscure acts of force of the first hundred years of the family's history had turned scattered and precarious rights into a complex, but geographically compact and militarily impregnable association, dependent on the Count. The process was directed by an instinctive feeling for strategic advantage, which perhaps lends to the history of these years an appearance of consistency greater than in fact it possessed. The methods were not refined, but they were practised with a consistency of purpose which inspires a certain respect. The swallowing of an important strong point might be preceded by many years of steady encroachment. It was necessary, first, to get established at some point within the territory to be threatened—an operation carried out by a careful marriage, a purchase which the documents represent as a gift, or an act of force or fraud. Then a castle was built as a base of operations. After that, watchfulness: a minority, the chance offered by the enemy's engagement elsewhere, or a lucky battle, might complete the circle. The town of Tours, for instance, was not swallowed until 1044, but in a sense the whole history of the family was a preparation for this event: the good relations with the church of the city seem to go back to the founder of the dynasty; the encircling of the town by a ring of cas-tles at Langeais, Montbazon, Montrichard and Montboyau had been begun by Fulk Nerra fifty years before the final victory. How much was design and how much a kind of inspired opportunism it would be useless to enquire. Once started, the process went on as relentlessly as the operations of the Stock Exchange.

But by the middle of the eleventh century, easy progress by these familiar methods was no longer possible. The weak had been made dependent, the strongholds of intruding neighbours had been taken and, by the same token, distant claims of the Counts outside their own territory had been abandoned. To the west stood Brittany, to the east Blois, to the north—across the still debatable land of Maine—Normandy, to the south Poitou. They faced each other as equals. Although the armed peace was often broken, the chief interest of the next hundred and fifty years lies in the emergence of stable political institutions and the elaboration of a new system of law. The swashbuckling days were over, and the régimes which had emerged began to clothe themselves in habits of respectability. Up to this point, St. Augustine's dictum that secular governments are nothing but large-scale robbery seemed to be abundantly justified by the facts: but slowly something more complex, more sensitive to the positive merits of organized society, seemed to be required. Government became something more than a system of exactions from a conquered countryside, and there developed a routine for the peaceful exploitation of resources and for the administering of justice.

SELECTION 6:

The Magna Carta

*S*imilar *processes were at work at the top of the feudal pyramid. Both political power and social relations were redefined as monarchs were able to make large landowners—namely counts and dukes—into their vassals.*

Those monarchs achieved success if they could become the leading feudal magnate in a world made up of hundreds of competing feudal lords. The kings of France and especially of England were able to unite vast areas of land under their control. Their power was still not direct, linking subjects directly to monarch; rather, the feudal structure meant that power still functioned through various levels. Political and legal authority continued to be private and individual, not public and universal.

Monarchs did not simply accrue military, political, and legal power. Although the English monarch Henry II (reigned 1154–1189)—one of the great kings of the Middle Ages—successfully exercised power over his nobles, his sons were less successful. After Henry's son Richard the Lion-hearted died in 1199, another son, John, became king of England (reigned 1199–1216). Through the exigencies brought on by an extended period of conflict with the French king, John forced his vassals to pay ever-increasing amounts of scutage (taxes in lieu of military service) and in other ways impinged on what were considered the rights of his nobles. Defeated in 1214 in France, John immediately faced an uprising by his nobles against his high-handed practices. After a period of conflict between them, the nobles finally succeeded in making John recognize their feudal rights. The document they made him sign is the famous Magna Carta or "great charter" of 1215, which is excerpted in the following selection. It has come to be seen as a major step in defining the basic rights of all English men and women, but it arose simply as a way of protecting the customary liberties of the barons against growing monarchical encroachments.

1. In the first place we have granted to God, and by this our present charter confirmed for us and our heirs for ever that the English church shall be free, and shall have her rights entire, and her liberties inviolate; and we will that it be thus observed; which is apparent from this that the freedom of elections, which is reckoned most important and very essential to the English church, we, of our pure and unconstrained will, did grant, and did by our charter confirm and did obtain the ratification of the same from our lord, Pope Innocent III, before the quarrel arose between us and our barons: and this we will observe, and our will is that it be observed in good faith by our heirs for ever. We have also granted to all freemen of our kingdom, for us and our heirs for ever, all the underwritten liberties, to be had and held by them and their heirs, of us and our heirs for ever. . . .

From the *Magna Carta* as found in *Source Problems in English History*, edited by Albert Beebe White and Wallace Notestein (New York: Harper & Bros., 1915).

13. And the city of London shall have all its ancient liberties and free customs, as well by land as by water; furthermore, we decree and grant that all other cities, boroughs, towns, and ports shall have all their liberties and free customs.

14. And for obtaining the common counsel of the kingdom and the assessing of an aid . . . or of a scutage, we will cause to be summoned the archbishops, bishops, abbots, earls, and greater barons, severally by our letters; and we will moreover cause to be summoned generally, through our sheriffs and bailiffs, all others who hold of us in chief, for a fixed date, namely, after the expiry of at least forty days, and at a fixed place; and in all letters of such summons we will specify the reason of the summons. And when the summons has thus been made, the business shall proceed on the day appointed, according to the counsel of such as are present, although not all who were summoned have come.

15. We will not for the future grant to any one license to take an aid from his own free tenants, except to ransom his body, to make his eldest son

a knight, and once to marry his eldest daughter; and on each of these occasions there shall be levied only a reasonable aid.

16. No one shall be distrained for performance of greater service for a knight's fee, or for any other free tenement, than is due therefrom.

17. Common pleas shall not follow our court, but shall be held in some fixed place.

18. Inquests of novel disseisin [dispossession], of mort d'ancester, and of darrein presentment, shall not be held elsewhere than in their own county courts and that in manner following,— We, or, if we should be out of the realm, our chief justiciar, will send two justiciars through every county four times a year, who shall, along with four knights of the county chosen by the county, hold the said assize in the county court, on the day and in the place of meeting of that court.

19. And if any of the said assizes cannot be taken on the day of the county court, let there remain of the knights and freeholders, who were present at the county court on that day, as many as may be required for the efficient making of judgments, according as the business be more or less.

20. A freeman shall not be amerced for a slight offense, except in accordance with the degree of the offense; and for a grave offense he shall be amerced in accordance with the gravity of the offense, yet saving always his "contenement"; and a merchant in the same way, saving his "merchandise"; and a villein shall be amerced in the same way, saving his "wainage"—if they have fallen into our mercy: and none of the aforesaid amercements shall be imposed except by the oath of honest men of the neighborhood.

21. Earls and barons shall not be amerced except through their peers, and only in accordance with the degree of the offense.

22. A clerk shall not be amerced in respect of his lay holding except after the manner of the others aforesaid; further, he shall not be amerced in accordance with the extent of his ecclesiastical benefice.

23. No village or individual shall be compelled to make bridges at river-banks, except those who from of old were legally bound to do so.

24. No sheriff, constable, coroners, or others of our bailiffs, shall hold pleas of our Crown.

25. All counties, hundreds, wapentakes, and trithings (except our demesne manors) shall remain at old rents, and without any additional payment.

26. If any one holding of us a lay fief shall die, and our sheriff or bailiff shall exhibit our letters patent of summons for a debt which the deceased owed to us, it shall be lawful for our sheriff or bailiff to attach and catalogue chattels of the deceased, found upon the lay fief, to the value of that debt, at the sight of law-worthy men, provided always that nothing whatever be thence removed until the debt which is evident shall be fully paid to us; and the residue shall be left to the executors to fulfil the will of the deceased; and if there be nothing due from him to us, all the chattels shall go to the deceased, saving to his wife and children their reasonable shares.

27. If any free man shall die intestate, his chattels shall be distributed by the hands of his nearest kinsfolk and friends, under supervision of the church, saving to every one the debts which the deceased owed to him.

28. No constable or other bailiff of ours shall take corn or other provisions from any one without immediately tendering money therefor, unless he can have postponement thereof by permission of the seller.

29. No constable shall compel any knight to give money in lieu of castle-guard, when he is willing to perform it in his own person, or (if he cannot do it from any reasonable cause) then by another responsible man. Further, if we have led or sent him upon military service, he shall be relieved from guard in proportion to the time during which he has been on service because of us.

30. No sheriff or bailiff of ours, or other person, shall take the horses or carts of any free man for transport duty, against the will of the said free man.

31. Neither we nor our bailiffs shall take, for our castles or for any other work of ours, wood which is not ours, against the will of the owner of that wood.

32. We will not retain beyond one year and one day, the lands of those who have been convicted of felony, and the lands shall thereafter be handed over to the lords of the fiefs.

After reading this selection and the previous one, consider these questions:

1. How were various territories consolidated under the rule of single individuals and families in the early Middle Ages?

2. What were the main features of the large feudal monarchies of England and France?

3. What were the main concerns of the feudal barons of England who demanded the signing of the Magna Carta?

CHAPTER 9
New Beginnings: The Rise of the Towns

Within this predominately rural world of early feudalism and manorialism, towns continued to exist. As we have seen, they were for the most part the remnants of the once thriving towns that dotted Roman Italy, Spain, Gaul, Britain, and Germany. As early as the fourth century, these towns were already in decline; St. Ambrose even spoke of the "decayed cities" of Italy. From the fifth to the tenth centuries, what remained of these ancient towns were only the vestiges of the town centers, now more often than not the diocesan seat of a bishop. These bishops looked after the political, legal, and even military needs of the townfolk and the people of the surrounding countryside. By the eleventh and twelfth centuries, however, urban civilization was reviving in the West. Towns throughout central and northern Italy and northeastern Spain (Aragón) began to develop as the result of the renewal of Mediterranean trade with the Muslim east and south. In the interior of Europe as well, centers of political power (Paris and London) and towns on the coast (Bordeaux and Bristol) began to grow in population and expand their commercial enterprises. New towns also emerged along trade routes stretching along both the north-south axis and the east-west axis of Europe. By the High Middle Ages, places like Troyes in eastern France and Nuremberg in southern Germany had become thriving cities, largely because they formed hubs of international trade and travel.

This European "urban revolution" was largely the result of the reestablishment of trade throughout the continent and between Europe and the Near East. The international trade in Eastern goods, especially in spices brought to the Mediterranean coast by Muslim traders, was the acme of commercial activity of the Middle Ages. Within Europe, trade developed in shoes and cloth, iron goods, and grains. Small towns as well as large cities served local markets as the surpluses from the surrounding agricultural communities were brought to town and exchanged for money or commodities. There were, in other words, many levels of trade in medieval Europe; in each case the origins lay in local manufacture and local commerce. What distinguished these towns from those of the ancient world was that they were first and foremost the place of production. Goods needed for everyday use were produced within the towns and either exchanged there or transported to other towns.

With all this innovation, the ways in which these towns organized themselves perpetuated what might be called the core principle of medieval society—the effective organization of small-scale communal efforts. Privileged groups (called corporations), and not individuals, were characteristic of the towns, as well as of their smaller units just as they were of manorialism, feudalism, monasticism, and the medieval church.

SELECTION 1:

The Rebirth of Commercial Activity

One of the rare accounts of the life of an early medieval merchant is the Life of St. Godric *by Reginald of Durham. It tells the story of a very primitive level of commercial activity. Godric (ca. 1065–1170) was an English "chapman" (small-time traveling salesman), merchant, and ultimately saint (the reason why his life was recorded). He made his living by trading on land and sea. After two pilgrimages to Jerusalem, his "monkish heart beneath his layman's clothes" took hold of him, and he settled down as a hermit at Finchale, near Durham in northern England.*

This holy man's father was named Ailward, and his mother Edwenna; both of slender rank and wealth, but abundant in righteousness and virtue. They were born in Norfolk, and had long lived in the township called Walpole. . . . When the boy had passed his childish years quietly at home; then, as he began to grow to manhood, he began to follow more prudent ways of life, and to learn carefully and persistently the teachings of worldly forethought. Wherefore he chose not to follow the life of a husbandman, but rather to study, learn and exercise the rudiment of more subtle concep-

tions. For this reason, aspiring to the merchant's trade, he began to follow the chapman's way of life, first learning how to gain in small bargains and things of insignificant price; and thence, while yet a youth, his mind advanced little by little to buy and sell and gain from things of greater expense. For, in his beginnings, he was wont to wander with small wares around the villages and farmsteads of his own neighborhood; but, in process of time, he gradually associated himself by compact with city merchants. Hence, within a brief space of time, the youth who had trudged for many weary hours from village to village, from farm to farm, did so profit by his increase of age and wisdom as to travel with associates of his own age through towns and boroughs, fortresses and cities, to fairs and to all the various booths of

From "Life of St. Godric," by Reginald of Durham, in *Social Life in Britain from the Conquest to the Reformation*, edited by G.G. Coulton (Cambridge: Cambridge University Press, 1918).

the market-place, in pursuit of his public chaffer. He went along the high-way, neither puffed up by the good testimony of his conscience nor downcast in the nobler part of his soul by the reproach of poverty. . . .

Yet in all things he walked with simplicity; and, in so far as he yet knew how, it was ever his pleasure to follow in the footsteps of the truth. For, having learned the Lord's Prayer and the Creed from his very cradle, he oftentimes turned them over in his mind, even as he went alone on his longer journeys; and, in so far as the truth was revealed to his mind, he clung thereunto most devoutly in all his thoughts concerning God. At first, he lived as a chapman for four years in Lincolnshire, going on foot and carrying the smallest wares; then he travelled abroad, first to St Andrews in Scotland and then for the first time to Rome. On his return, having formed a familiar friendship with certain other young men who were eager for merchandise, he began to launch upon holder courses, and to coast frequently by sea to the foreign lands that lay around him. Thus, sailing often to and fro between Scotland and Britain, he traded in many divers wares and, amid these occupations, learned much worldly wisdom. . . . He fell into many perils of the sea, yet by God's mercy he was never wrecked; for He who had upheld St Peter as he walked upon the waves, by that same strong right arm kept this His chosen vessel from all misfortune amid these perils. Thus, having learned by frequent experience his wretchedness amid such dangers, he began to worship certain of the Saints with more ardent zeal, venerating and calling upon their shrines, and giving himself up by wholehearted service to those holy names. In such invocations his prayers were oftentimes answered by prompt consolation; some of which prayers he learned from his fellows with whom he shared these frequent perils; others he collected from faithful hearsay; others again from the custom of the place, for he saw and visited such holy places with frequent assiduity. Thus aspiring ever higher and higher, and yearning upward with his whole heart, at length his great labours and cares bore much fruit of worldly gain. For he laboured not only as a merchant but also as a shipman . . .

to Denmark and Flanders and Scotland; in all which lands he found certain rare, and therefore more precious, wares, which he carried to other parts wherein he knew them to be least familiar, and coveted by the inhabitants beyond the price of gold itself; wherefore he exchanged these wares for others coveted by men of other lands; and thus he chaffered most freely and assiduously. Hence he made great profit in all his bargains, and gathered much wealth in the sweat of his brow; for he sold dear in one place the wares which he had bought elsewhere at a small price.

Then he purchased the half of a merchant-ship with certain of his partners in the trade; and again by his prudence he bought the fourth part of another ship. At length, by his skill in navigation, wherein he excelled all his fellows, he earned promotion to the post of steersman. . . .

And now he had lived sixteen years as a merchant, and began to think of spending on charity, to God's honour and service, the goods which he had so laboriously acquired. He therefore took the cross as a pilgrim to Jerusalem, and, having visited the Holy Sepulchre, came back to England by way of St James [of Compostella]. Not long afterwards he became steward to a certain rich man of his own country, with the care of his whole house and household. But certain of the younger household were men of iniquity, who stole their neighbours' cattle and thus held luxurious feasts, whereat Godric, in his ignorance, was sometimes present. Afterwards, discovering the truth, he rebuked and admonished them to cease; but they made no account of his warnings; wherefore he concealed not their iniquity, but disclosed it to the lord of the household, who, however, slighted his advice.

Wherefore he begged to be dismissed and went on a pilgrimage, first to St Gilles and thence to Rome the abode of the Apostles, that thus he might knowingly pay the penalty for those misdeeds wherein he had ignorantly partaken. I have often seen him, even in his old age, weeping for this unknowing transgression. . . .

Godric . . . abode but a brief while at home; for he was now already firmly purposed to give himself entirely to God's service. Wherefore, that he might follow Christ the more freely, he sold all his possessions and distributed them among the poor. Then, telling his parents of this purpose and receiving their blessing, he went forth to no certain abode, but whithersoever the Lord should deign to lead him; for above all things he coveted the life of a hermit.

SELECTION 2:

The Revitalization of the Towns

In their book The Medieval Town, *historians John H. Mundy and Peter Riesenberg describe the decline of urban civilization in the late Roman Empire and then the slow rise of towns in Europe in the succeeding centuries. As security increased in the eleventh and twelfth centuries, commercial activities increased and towns became the centers of production. Internally, towns developed a number of self-regulating institutions.*

The administrative functions of the town . . . underwent simplification. Having first experienced town life along the Roman military frontier, the German kings combined civil and military administration under counts appointed to govern each old Roman *civitas*, or city. This served to continue the town as administrative capital of the area about its walls. On the other hand, it reduced the revenue that went to town purposes and diminished the already weakened electoral autonomy of late Roman times. Even the attempt of Charlemagne to insist that townsmen elect their *scabini* or assessor-judges and notaries did little more for the moment than underline the decline of old institutions. The town also continued to lose direct control of the countryside. Town counts were obliged to treat rural areas as quasi-independent and to separate the rural courts of the hundreds or the vicarages from that in the town.

Furthermore, the bishops began to play an increasing role in town administration. Elected by clergy and people of the town alone, they soon assumed an effective presidency. While their power was sometimes only informal, it was often recognized by a grant of comital grade or of immunity from the ordinary royal administration. It thus came about that the bishop and his lay and clerical court were the true heirs of the civil as against the military tradition of Roman urbanism. As the system of registering documents in town archives before the town fathers and notaries slowly collapsed, the clergy began to assume these functions also. Even in Italy, most ninth century scribes were clerks. In the north, the church monopolized the documentation of property right. Although the church provided continuity with the classic past, the secular urban culture of Rome had all but disappeared.

In spite of atrophy, several progressive trends may be seen in town life during this long period. The decline was not consistent and there were even several brief periods of growth. During much of the sixth and seventh centuries and again during the late eighth and early ninth, Frankish success and maintenance of the peace encouraged towns to grow a little. By the latter ninth century, Cologne boasted six churches, other than its cathedral: three were of Roman origin, two Merovingian, and one Carolingian. While this statistic shows increase, it also indicates that each period of growth was less significant than

From *The Medieval Town*, by John H. Mundy and Peter Riesenberg (Princeton, NJ: Van Nostrand, 1958).

the one before. When the Scandinavians overran it in 882, Trier was a small settlement huddled in a corner of the Roman walled enclosure. . . .

Unfortunately for the west, the future was not so bright as Charlemagne's reign seemed to promise. Aided by the forgetfulness of peaceful years, the separatism that was part of the Roman inheritance moved provinces, the clergy and magnates, to minimize royal power. The new west again began to split up. Scandinavians, Saracens, Hungarians, and even Slavs profited from this disintegration to raid and desolate Europe during the ninth and tenth centuries. There was need in their attacks: the Moslems sought slaves and the Norse ironware and weapons. The past militarism of the Franks, moreover, had educated their enemies. The vigorous Magyars had replaced the enslaved Avars in Hungary. Seeking gold and slaves, they raided as far as Rheims and Nîmes. From 826, also, the entry of Frankish Christianity into the Scandinavian north emphasized the power of the Christian king and thus dispossessed the old pagan sacred nobilities. These now led a Norse emigration against Latin Europe. . . .

Although there are evidences as early as the ninth century for Italy, the Latin west generally began to grow again during the tenth century. From that time, Europe rose, slowly at first and then more rapidly in the eleventh and twelfth centuries. The most obvious evidence is the growth of population, of the area under tillage, and of towns. So impressive was the increase in human fecundity that it itself has been described as the reason for Europe's upswing.

Dependent upon psychological and practical factors, however, population increase cannot be used to explain itself. Historians have therefore looked elsewhere for the cause of Europe's advance. Henri Pirenne underlined the importance of outside stimuli. The Norse brought Byzantine gold and other commodities into the Baltic and North Sea, for example, thereby enlivening industry and trade in Flanders, England, and Germany. More consequent was the rise of Italian maritime traffic with the eastern Mediterranean at the time of Byzantine greatness in the ninth and tenth centuries. Venetians and Amalfitans sold slaves to Islam and brought back Byzantine luxuries to Europe. . . .

While useful, therefore, the theory of external stimulus does not suffice to explain the rise of European commerce. Other reasons for this phenomenon must be sought in Europe's internal development. Historians have often lamented the decentralizing or feudalizing of civil and military power that marked this age. But there were advantages to this process. The downward passage of political power filled Europe with fortified centers of local resistance. Marches such as Catalonia and Flanders were designed for defense. But it was not so much the fortifications themselves as it was the reinvigoration of western community and cultural solidarity. The developing institution of vassalage linked together the military aristocracy. More, the devolution of political and social command engendered a community sense that bound the inhabitants of the seignory or larger castellany to their lord, their chief in war and peace. By the eleventh century, Europe possessed an interlocking system of defense in depth.

A capacity to defend oneself establishes a sort of peace, but is insufficient in itself. Within each society, individuals seek their advantage beyond the frontiers or, if repressed, at the cost of community harmony. A healthy society builds agencies to capitalize and direct outward this lively aggressiveness. Capitalization requires an assembly of goods, money, and technical personnel that a decentralized economy lacks. Seignors and towns had land or basic techniques but they lacked means of mobilization. The eleventh century counts of Flanders, for example, stimulated town and country alike by building fortified bourgs and by draining marshes. But the scope of their efforts was purely regional.

The church, however, had a broader reach than any secular prince. In the towns, the bishops aided princes to foster a simplified version of late Roman economic regulation, reminding men of the services they owed the community. Although rarely effectively prohibited, usury was frowned upon, thereby steering investors away from the immediate profits of luxury and consumer credit into more basic enterprise. In short, a provident and traditional police protected the first growth of

Europe's economy. But the church had a still more positive role to play. While the secular clergy was essentially local or regional, Europe-wide monastic orders arose from the tenth century. Primarily agrarian, these orders were able to mobilize ample resources for great purposes. Throughout the eleventh and twelfth centuries, the monks invested in land mortgages. Capital was dear in those early days, but land was plentiful and barely settled. But the primary activity of the clergy was not, nor could ever be, lending money. The monks usually worked in partnership with secular or ecclesiastical lords to develop lands and capitalize exploitations. These partnerships had implications that transcend economics. They were instrumental in creating the feudal seignory or castellany. . . .

It was in this circumstance that the Latin town rose again. The earliest signs of the new age of urban history were in the ninth and particularly the tenth centuries. First touched were the areas that profited from outside stimulus: Venice and southern Italy, and, to a lesser degree, the northern coasts of the German empire. The first evidences of growth seem petty and occasional; they were efforts to rehabilitate, not really to expand. The real expansion began during the eleventh and twelfth centuries. At that time, the weight of town growth moved from the frontiers toward the center. Southern Italian commerce played second fiddle to that of North Italy by the end of the eleventh century. Towns in Flanders and Picardy moved ahead of the seaports of the North and Baltic seas.

By the twelfth century, the central axis of European commerce had been established. It ran from Flanders through the Champagne and Rhineland, down the Rhone valley to Liguria and Lombardy. Thence the Pisans, Genoese, and Venetians sailed to the eastern Mediterranean. By the end of the thirteenth century, expanding western commerce had filled all France and most of Spain with towns and trade routes. A direct sea route from the Mediterranean to Flanders was created. The northern and eastern German plains bloomed during the fourteenth century, and new towns multiplied east of the Elbe river. At the same time, Baltic and North sea commerce reached its apogee under the direction of the German Hanse, or league of northern towns.

As commerce and industry multiplied, the towns themselves grew larger. At their peak in the early fourteenth century, however, the largest western cities rarely boasted a population of 100,000. Milan and Venice were among the few towns that surpassed this number. By far the greatest northern town, Paris had about 80,000 souls. Naturally enough, urbanism developed more in some than in other areas. After Lombardy, the second greatest urban area was Flanders. Her great towns averaged from twenty to forty thousand souls. Languedoc may be cited as a region of modest town: Toulouse probably attained 25,000, Beziers 14,000, Carcassonne 10,000. A relatively backward area, England, had only one great town: London, with about 40,000 inhabitants.

As is evident, parts of Europe were more developed than others. Flanders and North Italy were predominantly urban. This statement, however, must be put in context. During the middle ages, indeed, until the industrial revolution, Europe was essentially agrarian. But, with this in mind, it is certain that the economic relationship of areas of strong town life to those of weak explains a great deal of the medieval epoch. The Plantagenet empire sometimes seems to be almost an appendage to the great cloth manufacturing towns of Flanders. Bordeaux and Poitou supplied wine and grain and England exported wool to this urban market. The importance of this commerce for the relations of the kings of France and of England is obvious. French control over Flanders would have been decisive not only for England's trade. It would also have weakened the English king's independence from his barons. In 1297, the barons claimed that the royal tax on exported wool equaled a fifth part of the value of the whole land of England. . . .

To conclude our general observations on the rise of towns, the most consequential achievement of the medieval period was the development of northern Europe. This marked a great step in the migration of civilization and its urban form from the Mediterranean. Before this time, urbanism had initially been associated with large rivers, as in the "hydraulic" societies of Egypt and Mesopotamia. Classic Greece and Rome extended this civilization along the coasts and savannahs of the *Mare Nostrum*. The middle ages spread it to the inland areas of a continent. The development of a continental civilization based upon the extensive northern plain was the great advantage that enabled Europe to conquer the world in modern times.

SELECTION 3:

The Craft Guilds

Modern historian Norman Zacour draws an even sharper picture of the relationship between production and the development of the guilds.

Before the rapid commercial expansion of the twelfth century the limited demand for services and manufactures of local lords and church establishments was usually satisfied by the servants of the manor, some of whom specialized in one of a few basic crafts. But the expansion of population and growth of commerce led to an increased need for and supply of all kinds of goods, not only foodstuffs but manufactured articles as well. For many the days were gone when the simple needs of everyday agricultural life could be met by home or manorial handicraft—when one made and repaired one's own farming tools, coarse clothing, and the thatched roof over one's head. The addition of a merchant population living in towns that were not economically self-sufficient produced a growing number of artisans and specialists in food processing, cloth making, building and construction work, the manufacture of household articles and implements for storage and transportation, and a host of other services and goods. The larger markets of the medieval town stimulated specialization of economic function; more and more people found that they could meet their wants more satisfactorily by, in effect, selling a special skill, be it woodworking or leather making, and buying what they needed from others better equipped to provide it.

The nature of industrial development and organization was often determined by whether its products entered into local or international trade. Commodities for local consumption were usually provided by petty artisans working in small shops with relatively little capital investment. These small producers, when there were enough of them in any given occupation, organized themselves in associations called craft gilds, which sought to regulate the employment of skilled workers and apprentices, control the supplies and therefore the prices of the raw materials of their trade, standardize workmanship, maintain retail prices for their products, and promote piety and fellowship among their members. Such craft gilds became important only from the thirteenth century on. They were never important, however, in very small communities or in towns given over for the most part to international commerce, such as seaports, or to a single great industry, such as the textile towns of Flanders, where manufacturing was carried on primarily for export. It was in the medium-sized towns, those not dominated by any single industry and in which industrial production was carried on mostly for local consumption, that craft gilds were to be found in large numbers. Here the demand was large and

From *An Introduction to Medieval Institutions*, 2nd ed., by Norman Zacour. Copyright © 1976 by Bedford/St. Martin's Press, Inc. Reprinted with permission from Bedford/St. Martin's Press, Inc.

stable enough to maintain sufficient numbers of individuals in any given trade to make the formation of a gild useful and profitable to them.

While the coming together of artisans in a given craft allowed for the promotion of their common interests, it did not in itself alter traditional patterns of production and sale. Industry remained essentially an individual or family operation. The small shop, employing one or two journeymen and apprentices and selling directly to the consumer over the counter, remained the backbone of town industry throughout the Middle Ages. The techniques of a trade were handed down from master to apprentice with little opportunity for innovations. The market, being local and stable, exerted no pressure to produce in large quantities.

Craft gilds, where they were strong enough, frequently tried to control the supply of the raw materials of their craft and to maintain within the town a monopoly control over the trade in which they were engaged. In these efforts they were rarely completely successful. Local nongildsmen, neighboring villagers, and other outsiders frequently enjoyed some limited rights to penetrate the town market. Gilds enjoyed a virtual monopoly of raw materials and retail sales only when the sources of supply were limited and adequate substitutes unavailable, as in the case of gold- and silversmiths and a few other trades. Where, however, supplies of the necessary raw material were usually abundant (wool, for instance), or where the commodity was such that substitutes for it might be found, the gilds were usually far less monopolistic. It was the same with foodstuffs, since the community at large tended to ensure that its welfare would not depend wholly on the monopoly of a gild.

To allay hostility among the townspeople, gilds were forced to adopt regulations for the standards of workmanship within their respective trades. In some crafts, especially those dealing with foodstuffs, gildsmen were frequently under strong suspicion of benefiting from fluctuations in prices—of taking advantage of the fact that they dealt in the necessities of life. The perennial problem of inadequate and irregular food supplies occasioned by poor transportation, poor storage facilities, and recurring local famine frequently produced violent price fluctuations; the gilds were often suspected of creating these fluctuations or at least of exaggerating them for their own profit. Therefore, even though gilds usually sought to raise prices, or at least keep them from falling, town suspicions ensured that their success was not great.

Another area of gild concern was the supply of skilled labor, which was controlled through an apprenticeship system. The gilds fixed the number of apprentices that a member could use in his shop, their age, the length and nature of their training, and their upbringing. The gilds were frequently accused of abusing the system by limiting unduly the number of apprentices used, but such limitations, when they occurred, were often dictated by considerations other than the desire to keep the number of their members down—death, runaways, the intimate nature of the family workshop and the difficulty of absorbing more than a very few apprentices, the tendency of wealthier gildsmen to take more than their share, and, before the fourteenth century, the continual shortage of labor.

The protective devices of craft gilds could not be maintained if the craftsmen had to depend on sources of material and markets beyond their control. This explains the general hostility of local gildsmen to interregional trade, their distrust of the international merchant, and their constant attempts to regulate the supplies and costs of raw materials coming from outside the town and the volume and prices of finished products. Further, the gild, in its many regulations, sought an ideal equality among members by reducing competition among them to a minimum. The obsession with equality had the effect of imposing a very conservative attitude toward change. Gildsmen tended to resist improvements that, requiring capital outlay, would have given advantages to the richer members and reduced the others to the status of employees. There was a good deal of opposition to the merging of different gilds in mutually supporting crafts, which might have led to innovations and increased production. There was resistance to bulk purchases by gilds, which might have reduced costs. Gilds adopted many internal regulations to reduce competition, concerning the hours of work, prices charged, and the amount of labor that each master could hire.

But despite all this, equality remained an elusive ideal, and over a period of time large disparities appeared. While towns grew, the gilds grew with them. But by the end of the thirteenth century the great economic expansion was over; and in many towns the gilds, through various devices, closed their ranks to newcomers, frequently converted gild membership into a hereditary privilege, and took on all the airs of an aristocracy. Economic disparity between gildsmen grew too; some waxed rich, and therefore important, while others struggled on in marginal businesses or slid into the ranks of wage earners.

In the medium-sized towns where trade organization reflected the different occupations of the townsmen, the old merchant gild, that early association of those engaged in trade, frequently withered away. But in those few areas dominated by a single great industry, the merchant gild remained strong, controlling the exchange of the product concerned and dominating the craft gilds whose members were often no better than wage earners. Since all or nearly all industrial production depended not on local but on distant markets, the merchant remained of first importance—and the gild of which he was a member, an institution of great power.

This was typical of Flanders, where by the eleventh century a growing population could no longer support itself on the land. This in part explains why so many from this region were to be found in such far-flung enterprises as the crusades, large emigrations to the east, and the rapid growth of towns, to which many flocked in large numbers. It was an area in which old social forms broke down more rapidly than elsewhere, where economic insecurity became chronic. Flanders had been an area of cloth production in the early Middle Ages. The Viking raids of the ninth century, far from disrupting cloth manufacture, may even have encouraged it, for the settlement of the Northmen on both sides of the English Channel created new demands and facilitated the exchange of cloth over wider areas. By the twelfth century Flemish merchants were selling woolen cloth in Italy or to Italian merchants who ventured north of the Alps, and the cloth of Flanders soon came to be an important staple not only in northern Europe but in the east-west Mediterranean trade as well. Its wide popularity was a measure of its relative excellence.

Flanders soon outstripped its local sources of raw wool, which then bad to be imported, and of course it had to sell its finished product on a world market. Therefore the merchant who had contacts abroad and sufficient access to capital and credit came to control the first and the last crucial stages: the purchase of raw materials (wool, dye, potash, and other materials used in the processing of cloth) imported from England, France, Spain, the Baltic countries, and even the Near East through the Italians, and the disposal of the finished cloth in all these regions, frequently through the operation of the great fairs of Flanders and Champagne. Many of the intermediate operations in the manufacture of cloth were performed in the homes of the craftsmen—cleaning, carding, spinning, and weaving. Often the work was done by women, and the tools for the most part were simple and inexpensive, although weaving called for large looms. Dyeing and finishing demanded considerable skill and expensive tools. The very nature of woolen manufacture dictated an organization quite unlike that to be seen where individual crafts controlled all phases of production from the acquisition of raw material to the final retail sale. It was a capitalist industry in fact. The artisans here did not, could not, deal with the consumer directly. Furthermore, the combination of so many processes required some central direction, which was supplied by the capitalist, that is to say, the merchant with capital who bought the materials, put them out to different crafts for different operations, and marketed the finished product. Sometimes he might actually invest in and thus control directly some of the intermediate steps, with his own dye house, fulling vats, looms, and frames. In these establishments there could be no pretense of craft independence; the workers were direct employees. But even when the merchant put out work to independent craftsmen, the latter, although owning their own tools, came to be by the very nature of the industry completely dependent for their welfare on the operations of the merchant.

Control of the cloth industry by the merchant gild was extremely effective, and dealings in raw materials and finished products were carefully reserved to its members. This control was exercised through the town corporations, in which the merchants were most influential. The towns legislated for all aspects of the industry, especially techniques of production, standards of size, weight, and quality, hours of labor, and wages. As a result, the social and economic cleavage between workers and merchants grew. This was not critical in good times, but it was disastrous in bad. The cloth industry, dependent ultimately on international sources and markets, was peculiarly sensitive to international affairs. The growth of a native cloth industry in Italy in the thirteenth century, the decline of the international fairs of northern France, the development of cloth making in England, which consumed much of the best raw wool, the political rivalry between England and France with Flanders caught in between, the taxation of wool by French and English kings as an economic weapon against each other—all these produced serious disruptions in Flanders' woolen industry and exacerbated the tension between workers and merchants.

The conditions of workers in those Italian cities where cloth making was important were no different. Again, control by the entrepreneur led to suppression of a working class that, dependent upon fluctuations of the international market, often suffered unemployment and bad pay with little hope of obtaining that political power which they hoped could be used to better their lot. The *Arte della Lana*, the great gild of woolen cloth dealers in Florence, not only controlled all aspects of the industry but itself participated as a corporation in the manufacture of woolen cloth, investing funds in, and emerging as the dominant partner if not the outright owner of, many of the craft shops engaged in the operations of the industry. In these the craftsmen were out and out wage earners. Heaven help anyone who tried to organize the workers. In 1345 one Ciuto Brandini, "a man of low condition and evil reputation," tried to organize the carders, combers, and other laborers in the woolen cloth industry in Florence, holding meetings and collecting fees to strengthen his "wicked organization," and was executed for his trouble.

After reading this selection and the previous ones, consider these questions:

1. What does the *Life of St. Godric* tell us about economic life in the early Middle Ages?
2. Why did towns develop in medieval Europe?
3. What is a craft guild, and how did it function?

SELECTION 4:

Guild Regulations

Trade and merchant guilds developed from confraternities for religious devotion, convivial feasting, charitable activities, and craft regulations. As these guilds grew in size and numbers, they increasingly drew up detailed statutes and rules to protect themselves and control the activities of their members. Guild regulations determined working hours, fixed prices, and set standards for materials and production. The following document was drawn up in 1231 by the cloth manufacturers of the German town of Stendal.

John and Otto, by the grace of God, margraves of Brandenburg. . . . We make known . . . that we . . . desiring to provide properly for our city of Stendal, have changed, and do change, for the better, the laws of the gild brethren, and of those who are called cloth-cutters, so that they might have the same laws in this craft as their gild brethren the garment cutters in Magdeburg have been accustomed to observe in the past.

These are the laws:

1. No one shall presume to cut cloth, except he be of our craft; those who break this rule will amend to the gild with three talents.

2. Thrice a year there ought to be a meeting of the brethren, and whoever does not come to it will amend according to justice.

3. Whoever wishes to enter the fraternity whose father was a brother and cut cloth will come with his friends to the meeting of the brethren, and if he conduct himself honestly, he will be able to join the gild at the first request on payment of five solidi, and he will give six denarii to the master. And if he be dishonest and should not conduct himself well, he should be put off until the second or third meeting. But any of our citizens who wish to enter the gild, if he be an honest man, and worthy, will give a talent to the brethren on entry into the gild, and will present a solidus to the master. But if a guest who is an honest man should decide to join our fraternity, he will give thirty solidi to the gild on his entry, and eighteen denarii to the master.

4. But in the time of the fairs, that is of the annual fair, any guest, even if he be not of the craft, will be able to cut cloth during the whole fair.

5. If any of our burgesses holding office wish to enter the crafts he will abjure his office, and, on entrance to the gild, will present one mark of gold freely to the brethren, and to the master eighteen denarii.

6. If any brother has been accustomed to prepare cloth in his house and is wont to cut or sell it at the wish of others, he will either cease or have no part in his fraternity.

7. Whatever two parts of the brethren have decreed to do the third part ought to consent to do; but if that third be unwilling, each will amend with three solidi, and will pay them at the next meeting.

8. Every year a master and four other good men who shall preside over the affairs of the gild will be faithfully chosen.

9. Moreover whoever goes contrary to these decrees and is unwilling to obey the master and brethren according to justice, his contumacy ought to be referred to the judgment of his superior.

From *A Source Book for Medieval Economic History*, by Roy C. Cave and Herbert H. Coulson (Milwaukee: Bruce, 1936).

SELECTION 5:

The Guild Merchant

Not only craftsmen but also merchants formed such guilds. Guild merchants, as were often called, held a trading monopoly within a chartered town. The following selection from the Ordinances of the Guild Merchant of Southampton, England, dates from the fourteenth century, but many of its first eleven statutes are derived from earlier versions dating from the twelfth century.

1. In the first place, there shall be elected from the gild merchant, and established, an alderman, a steward, a chaplain, four skevins, and an usher. And it is to be known that whosoever shall be alderman shall receive from each one entering into the gild fourpence; the steward, twopence; the chaplain, twopence; and the usher, one penny. And the gild shall meet twice a year: that is to say, on the Sunday next after St. John the Baptist's day, and on the Sunday next after St. Mary's day.

2. And when the gild shall be sitting no one of the gild is to bring in any stranger, except when required by the alderman or steward. And the alderman shall have a sergeant to serve before him, the steward another sergeant, and the chaplain shall have his clerk.

3. And when the gild shall sit, the alderman is to have, each night, so long as the gild sits, two gallons of wine and two candles, and the steward the same; and the four skevins and the chaplain, each of them one gallon of wine and one candle, and the usher one gallon of wine.

4. And when the gild shall sit, the lepers of La Madeleine shall have of the alms of the gild, two sesters [approximately eight gallons] of ale, and the sick of God's House and of St. Julian shall have two sesters of ale. And the Friars Minors shall have two sesters of ale and one sester of wine. And four sesters of ale shall be given to the poor wherever the gild shall meet.

5. And when the gild is sitting, no one who is of the gild shall go outside the town for any business, without the permission of the steward. And if any does so, let him be fined two shillings, and pay them.

6. And when the gild sits, and any gildsman is outside of the city so that he does not know when it will happen, he shall have a gallon of wine, if his servants come to get it. And if a gildsman is ill and is in the city, wine shall be sent to him, two loaves of bread and a gallon of wine and a dish from the kitchen; and two approved men of the gild shall go to visit him and look after his condition.

7. And when a gildsman dies, all those who are of the gild and are in the city shall attend the service of the dead, and the gildsmen shall bear the body and bring it to the place of burial. And whoever will not do this shall pay according to his oath, two pence, to be given to the poor. And those of the ward where the dead man shall be ought to find a man to watch over the body the night that the dead shall lie in his house. And so long as the service of the dead shall last, that is to say the vigil and the mass, there ought to burn four candles of the gild, each candle of two pounds weight or more, until the body is buried. And these four candles shall remain in the keeping of the steward of the gild.

8. The steward ought to keep the rolls and treasures of the gild under the seal of the alderman of the gild.

9. And when a gildsman dies, his eldest son or his next heir shall have the seat of his father, or of his uncle, if his father was not a gildsman, and of no other one; and he shall give nothing for his seat. No husband can have a seat in the gild by right of his wife, nor demand a seat by right of his wife's ancestors. . . .

19. And no one of the city of Southampton shall buy anything to sell again in the same city, unless he is of the gild merchant or of the franchise. And if anyone shall do so and is convicted of it, all which he has so bought shall be forfeited to the king; and no one shall be quit of custom unless he proves that he is in the gild or in the franchise, and this from year to year.

20. And no one shall buy honey, fat, salt herrings, or any kind of oil, or millstones, or fresh hides, or any kind of fresh skins, unless he is a gildsman: nor keep a tavern for wine, nor sell cloth at retail, except in market or fair days; nor keep grain in his granary beyond five quarters, to sell at retail, if he is not a gildsman; and whoever shall do this and be convicted, shall forfeit all to the king. . . .

22. If any gildsman falls into poverty and has not the wherewithal to live, and is not able to work or to provide for himself, he shall have one mark from the gild to relieve his condition—when the gild shall sit. No one of the gild nor of the franchise shall avow another's goods for his

From John Davies, *A History of Southampton* (London: Hamilton, Adams, 1883).

by which the custom of the city shall be injured. And if any one does so and is convicted, he shall lose the gild and the franchise; and the merchandise so avowed shall be forfeited to the king.

23. And no private man nor stranger shall bargain for or buy any kind of merchandise coming into the city before a burgess of the gild merchant, so long as the gildsman is present and wishes to bargain for and buy this merchandise; and if anyone does so and is convicted, that which he buys shall be forfeited to the king. . . .

35. The common chest shall be in the house of the chief alderman or of the steward, and the three keys of it shall be lodged with three discreet men of the aforesaid twelve sworn men, or with three of the skevins, who shall loyally take care of the common seal, and the charters and of the treasure of the town, and the standards, and other muniments of the town; and no letter shall be sealed with the common seal, nor any charter taken out of the common-chest but in the presence of six or twelve sworn men, and of the alderman or steward; and nobody shall sell by any kind of measure or weight that is not sealed, under forfeiture of two shillings. . . .

63. No one shall go out to meet a ship bringing wine or other merchandise coming to the town, in order to buy anything, before the ship be arrived and come to anchor for unlading; and if any one does so and is convicted, the merchandise which he shall have bought shall be forfeited to the king.

After reading this selection and the previous one, consider these questions:

1. What was a guild, and what were its functions?
2. What did the statutes of the guild regulate?
3. What role did guild merchants play in the emergence of towns?

SELECTION 6:

The Revolt of the Towns

Within the feudally dominated world of the early Middle Ages, the new towns had no legal or political definition. For the most part, they emerged on lands ruled by the local feudal magnates. The twelfth and thirteenth centuries witnessed many attempts by these towns to break away from their lords' political dominance and tax burdens to establish legal and political authority. The ultimate goal of many of these towns was to appeal beyond the local magnates to their overlord and even to the king to obtain a charter, granting them rights to self-rule. These attempts took a number of forms from the creation of towns by feudal lords themselves (who were interested in making money), to petitioning counts, bishops, and kings, to simply declaring themselves independent communes of freely associated townspeople. Sometimes, when these peaceful means failed, violence ensued. The following account of the revolt of the French town of Laon in 1115 is a good example of this all-important process of urban self-definition. It was written by the eminent churchman and writer Guibert of Nogent, who had grown up in Laon.

Now after some time when he [Bishop of Laon] had set out for England to extract money from the English king, whom he had served, and who had formerly been his friend, the Archdeacons Walter and Guy, with the nobles of the city, devised the following plan: Of old time such ill-fate had settled upon that city that neither God nor any lord was feared therein, but according to each man's power and lust the state involved in rapine and murder. For to begin with the source of the plague, whenever it happened that the king came there, he who ought to have exacted respect for himself with royal severity, was himself first shamefully fined on his own property. When his horses were led to the water morning or evening, his grooms were beaten and the horses carried off. It was known that the very clergy were held in such contempt, that neither their persons nor their goods were spared, as it is written, "Like as the people, so the priest." But what shall I say about the baser people? No one of the countrymen came into the city, no one except under the safest conduct approached it, who was not thrown into prison and held to ransom, or was not, as opportunity served, drawn without cause into a lawsuit. As an example let me adduce one practice, which occurring amongst barbarians or Scythians, men having no code of laws, would be regarded as most iniquitous. When on the Saturday the country populace from different parts came there to buy and sell, the town folk carried round as for sale, beans, barley or any kind of corn in cup and platter or other kind of measure in the market-place, and when they had offered them for sale to the countrymen seeking such things, the latter having settled the price promised to buy. "Follow me," said the seller, "to my house that you may there see the rest of the corn which I am selling you, and when you have seen it, may take it away." He followed, but when he came to the bin, the honest seller having raised and held up the lid, would say, "Bend your head and shoulders over the bin, that you may see that the bulk does not

differ from the sample which I shewed you in the market-place." And when the buyer getting up on the pediment of the bin leaned his belly over it, the worthy seller standing behind lifted up his feet and pushed the unwary man into the bin, and having put the lid down on him as he fell, kept him in safe prison until he ransomed himself. Such and like things were done in the city. No one was safe going out at night. There remained for him nothing but plunder, capture or murder.

The clergy with the archdeacons considering this, and the nobles catching at pretexts for exacting money from the people, offer them through agents the choice of making composition by paying a sum to cover them. Now Commune is a new and a bad name of an arrangement for all the poorest classes to pay their usual due of servitude to their lords once only in the year, and to make good any breach of the laws they have committed by the payment fixed by law, and to be entirely free from all other exactions usually imposed on serfs. The people seizing on this opportunity for freeing themselves gathered huge sums of money to fill the gaping mouths of so many greedy men. And they, pleased with the shower poured upon them, took oaths binding themselves in the matter.

A pledge of mutual aid had been thus exchanged by the clergy and nobles with the people, when the Bishop returned with much wealth from England and being moved to anger against those responsible for this innovation, for a long time kept away from the city. . . .

Saying therefore that he was moved with relentless wrath against those who had taken that oath and the principals in the transaction, in the end his loud-sounding words were suddenly quieted by the offer of a great heap of silver and gold. Therefore he swore that he would maintain the rights of the Commune according to the terms duly drawn up at Noyon and Saint-Quintin. The King too was induced by a bribe from the people to confirm the same by oath. O my God, who could say how many disputes arose when the gifts of the people were accepted, how many after oath had been sworn to reverse what they had agreed to, whilst they sought to bring back the serfs who had been freed from the oppression of their yoke, to their former state. At least there

From *The Autobiography of Guibert, Abbot of Nogent-sous-Coucy*, translated by C.C. Swinton Bland (London: Routledge, 1925).

was implacable hate by the Bishop and nobles against the citizens. . . . Whenever one of the people entered a court of law, where he was dependent not on the justice of God, but on his ability to please his judges, if I may say so, he was drained of his substance to the last penny. . . .

Having therefore summoned the nobles and certain of the clergy on the last day of Lent in the holy days of the Passion of our Lord . . . [the Bishop] determined to urge the annulment of the Commune, to which he had sworn, and had by bribes induced the King to swear, and the day before the Passover, that is to say, on the day of the Lord's Supper, he summoned the King to this pious duty and instructed the King and all his people to break their oaths. . . .

The compact of the Commune being broken, such rage, such amazement seized the citizens that all the officials abandoned their duties and the stalls of the craftsmen and cobblers were closed and nothing was exposed for sale by the innkeepers and hucksters, who expected to have nothing left when the lords began plundering. For at once the property of all was calculated by the Bishop and nobles, and whatever any man was known to have given to arrange the Commune, so much was demanded of him to procure its annulment. . . . All the efforts of the prelate and the nobles in these days were reserved for fleecing their inferiors. But those inferiors were no longer moved by mere anger, but goaded into a murderous lust for the death of the Bishop and his accomplices and bound themselves by oath to effect their purpose. Now they say that four hundred took the oath. . . .

The next day, that is, the fifth in Easter week, after midday, as . . . [the Bishop] was engaged in business with Archdeacon Walter about the getting of money, behold there arose a disorderly noise throughout the city, men shouting "Commune" and again through the middle of the chapel of the Blessed Mary through that door by which the murderers of Gerard had come and gone, there citizens now entered the Bishop's court with swords, battle-axes, bows and hatchets, and carrying clubs and spears, a very great company. As soon as this sudden attack was discovered, the nobles rallied from all sides to the Bishop, having sworn to give him aid against such an onset, if it should occur. In this rally Guinimon, the chatelain, an aged nobleman of handsome presence and guiltless character, armed only with shield and spear, ran out through the church and as he entered the Bishop's ball, was the first to fall, struck on the back of the head with a battle-axe by a certain Rainbert, who was his fellow-citizen. . . .

Next the outrageous mob attacking the Bishop and howling before the walls of his palace, he with some who were succouring him fought them off by hurling of stones and shooting of arrows. For he now, as at all times, shewed great spirit as a fighter; but because he had wrongly and in vain taken up another sword, by the sword he perished. Therefore being unable to stand against the reckless assaults of the people, he put on the clothes of one of his servants and flying to the vaults of the church hid himself in a cask, shut up in which with the head fastened on by a faithful follower he thought himself safely hidden. And as they ran hither and thither demanding where, not the Bishop, but the hangdog, was, they seized one of his pages, but through his faithfulness could not get what they wanted. Laying hands on another, they learn from the traitor's nod where to look for him. Entering the vaults, therefore, and searching everywhere, at last they found him. . . .

And as he piteously implored them, ready to take oath that he would henceforth cease to be their Bishop, that he would give them unlimited riches, that he would leave the country, and as they with hardened hearts jeered at him, one named Bernard lifting his battle-axe brutally dashed out the brains of that sacred, though sinner's, head, and he slipping between the bands of those who held him, was dead before he reached the ground stricken by another thwart blow under the eye-sockets and across the middle of the nose.

SELECTION 7:

The Self-Government of the Towns

*E*ventually Laon appealed to King Louis VI for a charter. The town now had the right to govern and tax itself (and therefore to control its own future economic development), while the monarch found in the towns both a source of tax money and a political ally in their contests with their own feudal nobility. The incorporation of towns as independent entities within the rural economy and feudal organization of medieval Europe marked a significant new development. This development would ultimately see the rise of new lifestyles, values, and opportunities for the men and women of medieval Europe. The following account of the urban privileges granted by King Louis VII (the successor of Louis VI) in the 1155 charter for the town of Lorris, in northern France, is typical of such relations.

1. Every one who has a house in the parish of Lorris shall pay as cens [rent] sixpence only for his house, and for each acre of land that he possesses in the parish.

2. No inhabitant of the parish of Lorris shall be required to pay a toll or any other tax on his provisions; and let him not be made to pay measurage fee on the grain which he has raised by his own labor.

3. No burgher shall go on an expedition, on foot or on horseback, from which he cannot return the same day to his home if he desires.

4. No burgher shall pay toll on the road to Etampes, to Orleans, to Milly (which is in the Gatinais), or to Melun.

5. No one who has property in the parish of Lorris shall forfeit it for any offense whatsoever, unless the offense shall have been committed against us or any of our hotes.

6. No person while on his way to the fairs and markets of Lorris, or returning, shall be arrested

From *A Source Book of Medieval History*, edited by Frederic Austin Ogg (New York: American Book Co., 1907).

or disturbed, unless he shall have committed an offense on the same day. . . .

9. No one, neither we nor any other, shall exact from the burghers of Lorris any tallage, tax, or subsidy. . . .

12. If a man shall have had a quarrel with another, but without breaking into a fortified house, and if the parties shall have reached an agreement without bringing a suit before the provost, no fine shall be due to us or our provost on account of the affair. . . .

15. No inhabitant of Lorris is to render us the obligation of corvee, except twice a year, when our wine is to be carried to Orleans, and not elsewhere.

16. No one shall be detained in prison if he can furnish surety that he will present himself for judgment.

17. Any burgher who wishes to sell his property shall have the privilege of doing so; and, having received the price of the sale, he shall have the right to go from the town freely and without molestation, if he so desires, unless he has committed some offense in it.

18. Any one who shall dwell a year and a day in the parish of Lorris, without any claim having

pursued him there, and without having refused to lay his case before us or our provost, shall abide there freely and without molestation. . . .

35. We ordain that every time there shall be a change of provosts in the town the new provost shall take an oath faithfully to observe these regulations; and the same thing shall be done by new sergeants every time that they are installed.

After reading the selection and the previous one, consider these questions:

1. What does the revolt of Laon in 1115 tell us about the rise of the towns?
2. What rights were granted to a town by a charter?
3. What role did the monarchy play in the rise of the towns?

CHAPTER 10
The Making of a Christian Civilization

The Middle Ages in Europe, as we have seen, transformed institutions and forms of religious and philosophical thought of the ancient world into a distinct set of values and a unique civilization. Even though limited to western and central sections of the continent, Europe was united under a single church hierarchy and increasingly organized within the larger kingdoms of England, France, and Spain or under the Holy Roman Empire. Beneath this unity and organization, there remained a Europe of great diversity and local customs. The Middle Ages thus presents a picture of a world that was at once united in basic values and beliefs yet varied in its modes of thought and lifestyles. It could be highly rationalistic, as in Scholastic theology, while it could also seem rather crude and gullible in its acceptance of miracles and the power of saints' relics. The age emphasized the communal nature of religion (the church guided Christians as a unified society) and of social and economic activities (through town government and guild organizations). But the age also witnessed the development of more individualized forms of faith in mysticism and personal piety and a growing emphasis on individual initiative and even individual rights in social and economic activities. Values and even lifestyles were also often sharply divided among the clergy, the nobility, the burghers of the towns and cities, and the peasantry of the countryside; yet across the boundaries of these functionally defined groups was a sense of belonging to a common Christian civilization.

This civilization was, of course, Christian in a general sense but medieval Christian in a specific sense. In other words, from a common Christian set of ideals inherited from the ancient world and shaped in the last centuries of the Roman Empire, there emerged in the early Middle Ages a distinctive set of Christian values and Christian rituals that were the product both of historical development and of the constant interchange between the great varieties of peoples and the immense diversities of customs that was Europe in the Middle Ages. Within this great multiplicity, the Roman church provided both unity and leadership. Legitimate uses of power, from the emperor of the Holy Roman Empire to the monarchs of France and England, from the elected leaders of the cities and towns to the members of the guilds and other corporate forms, rested on Christian notions of rule and social organization.

From one important perspective, the history of the church in the High Middle Ages (eleventh through late thirteenth centuries) is a success story. From a period marked by a withdrawal from the world (represented by early monasticism) and only the beginning of the organization of the spiritual authority of the papacy in the sixth and seventh centuries, the church succeeded in Christianizing and bringing under the control of Rome territories from Scandinavia to Sicily, from Portugal to Poland. The church rose to become the center of a vast array of monasteries spread throughout northern and southern Europe and the head of an international organization of ecclesiastical government, which, at its base, was represented by the "secular clergy"—those who are out in the world as parish priests, as opposed to the "regular clergy" in the monasteries.

This notion of the spiritual power of the church should not be dismissed as an empty claim. Although the empire in the eleventh century and the great feudal monarchies in the twelfth and thirteenth centuries would challenge the often extravagant claims to authority of the church (especially under the papacy of Gregory VII, Innocent III, and Boniface VIII), still these powers recognized that the ultimate source of all legitimate authority derived from God and that the major purpose of their rule was to guard Christian society and protect it against heretics. In a world that recognized divine guidance and the importance of the church in the salvation of the individual, the spiritual power of the papacy and clergy could not be easily dismissed. Through the sacramental system, individuals within the world received divine grace. Withdrawal of the sacraments by the clergy could thus be a powerful force. In the more extreme forms of excommunication of individuals or the placement of entire kingdoms under interdict, the church withdrew of its spiritual protection. This meant a denial of both the means of salvation in the next world and the source of all legitimate exercise of power in this world. From the eleventh through the thirteenth centuries especially, the church fully exercised its powers and successfully contended with both emperors and kings in the name of the superiority of spiritual power over all forms of secular authority.

Christianization can also be measured on the individual level. As the Middle Ages progressed, the sharp divide between monastic withdrawal as the only true form of Christian existence and all other types of life became more blurred. Individuals, from warriors who increasingly saw themselves as Christian knights to those in the towns and cities who sought to live a fully Christian life in this world, came to define themselves in specifically religious terms. Knights who once were simply crude warriors increasingly defined themselves in terms of Christian values and legitimated their military and political powers in terms of protecting Christian society. The Crusades, both as a Christian military mission and the ideal of chivalry—the highest model of Christian knighthood—contributed to this development. Even in the towns, we find the increasingly significant role played by the various mendicant orders and the identification of various craft and commercial guilds with the Christian activities of helping widows and orphans and providing for the poor.

In addition to new cultural forms, there developed under the auspices of the church new approaches to theology. Among the highly symbolic modes of interpreting Scripture (dating at least from the time of St. Augustine and confirmed by Pope Gregory I), there developed new, rational approaches to theology. Even before the texts of Aristotle were completely known in the West or united to theological thought, a number of thinkers, especially Peter Abelard, devised a more logical approach to interpreting Scripture and the writing of the church fathers. With the growing demands for the teaching of theology, as well as for a more general need for an educated clergy, there arose in the Europe of the High Middle Ages a set of universities that, in addition to theology, taught law, medicine, and philosophy.

Perhaps the most interesting developments occurred in various forms of lay piety. The high-medieval church provided new ways of giving expression to popular forms of religious experience. In such institutionalized forms as the feast of Corpus Christi (celebrating the Host) and especially the cult of the Virgin (based on the growing importance of the mother of God in defining a more personal form of worship and a reconceptualization of the church itself as mother), the church found new ways of tying itself to the larger lay society.

SELECTION 1:

The Church Within the World

This "success story" of the church must be qualified. As the secular world became increasingly Christian, Christianity became increasingly secular. This is witnessed not only with the emerging role of the secular clergy (as opposed to the regular clergy) ministering to individuals outside the monasteries but also in the ways in which the church on various levels of its organization became more tightly intertwined with the political, social, and economic life of medieval Europe. This latter phenomenon is clearly seen in the ways in which the church, both in its ecclesiastical structure and in its monastic organization, became tied to the ownership of vast landholdings and therefore bound to the feudal system. In The Medieval World View, *historians William R. Cook and Ronald B. Herzman describe the church's increasing involvement with economic and political power and the corrupting influence such involvement exerted on both individual members of the clergy and the ecclesiastical organization as a whole. They then point to the beginning of reform, emanating from the monastery of Cluny in France.*

Since the Church had come to control a great deal of land and since land was the chief source of wealth and warriors, lay rulers often sought and obtained control over bishoprics and even abbacies, either to bestow on trustworthy persons—usually relatives—or to sell to the highest bidder. Furthermore, parish priests were often semiliterate at best, usually serfs or peasant farmers; many were married and passed on the job to their sons. Monasteries to some extent became dumping grounds for younger sons of the landed aristocracy, many of whom were lax in their observance of the Rule of St. Benedict. These problems had their beginnings as early as the Merovingian period but intensified following the collapse of central authority after the death of Charlemagne.

In addition to all of this, the papacy suffered. It is certainly arguable that the tenth and first half of the eleventh centuries were the bleakest times in the history of the papacy. Potential for corruption came with the development of papal temporal power in central Italy, which was accelerated with the Donation of Pepin [which gave the pope sovereignty over Ravenna]. Leo III was expelled from Rome but restored by Charlemagne. With the demise of the Holy Roman Empire, however, there was no longer a temporal power to rescue the papacy from local, essentially political squabbles. By 900, the papacy had become the plaything of Italian nobles. The depths to which the papacy had sunk can be symbolized by the example of Pope Formosus. When he died in 896, a member of the family opposed to his political policies was elected pope and convened a synod that exhumed Formosus's body, put him on trial, and convicted him of usurping the papal office. His body was stripped of the papal garments; the

From *The Medieval World View: An Introduction,* by William R. Cook and Ronald B. Herzman. Copyright © 1983 by Oxford University Press, Inc. Used by permission of Oxford University Press, Inc.

fingers on the right hand, used in giving the benediction, were broken; and his body was thrown into the Tiber. Clearly, the sacred and the secular, temporal and spiritual power, were thoroughly mixed and confused; from the parishes and monasteries to the great prelates and the papacy, the Church was in need of a reform.

A harbinger of a later general reform movement in the Church and the beginning of important monastic reform was the foundation of the Burgundian monastery of Cluny in 910. The most important part of its foundation charter declared that the monastery was to be completely free of lay control and even from local episcopal jurisdiction. Cluny was placed directly under papal control. In essence, this was a declaration of complete independence since the bishops of Rome at this time cared little about exercising control over a monastery far away. The monks of Cluny were not exactly like Benedict's on Monte Cassino four hundred years earlier. Their observance was based on the reforms of Benedict of Aniane in the ninth century, and included elaborate liturgical development, the use of splendid works of art, and virtually no manual labor. The Cluniacs had lay brothers or serfs to do manual labor while the monks spent as much as seven hours a day singing the monastic offices. Its independence from lay control and its way of observing the Rule of St. Benedict struck a responsive chord in monasteries throughout Western Europe. Even in the century of its foundation, Cluny established daughter houses and sent its monks to monasteries desiring the Cluniac reform. Although there really was no official Cluniac Order, the Cluniac form of monasticism spread to all parts of Latin Christendom. A key reason for the spread of Cluniac monasticism was the fact that from 948 to 1109, Cluny had only three abbots, all holy men with administrative skills. The best known of these was Hugh the Great, abbot from 1049 to 1109. It was he who oversaw perhaps a thousand monasteries that had adopted at least some of the elements of the Cluniac reform. The most trusted man in Europe, he was often called upon to try to establish peace between the papacy and the Empire; it was Hugh who began the building of the great Romanesque church at Cluny. For four hundred years the abbey church at Cluny was the largest church in Christendom; even after the building of the new St. Peter's in Rome in the sixteenth century, it remained second biggest until its destruction during the French Revolution. The buildings, habits, and works of art that existed at Cluny set it apart from the simplicity originally intended by Benedict at Monte Cassino.

In the second half of the eleventh century came the reform of the papacy and its re-emergence as an important political as well as ecclesiastical institution throughout Europe. The year 1046 was one of particular scandal in Rome. The papacy was sold by Benedict IX to a sincere reformer named Gregory VI; then Benedict reclaimed it. To add to the confusion and degradation, a rival Roman faction had its own candidate. Thus there were three claimants to the throne of Peter. The concerned Holy Roman Emperor Henry III called a synod that deposed all three, and Henry appointed a new pope. This pope and the one who succeeded him quickly died in suspicious circumstances; but Henry's third appointment, Leo IX (r.1049–54), initiated a great papal reform that is called by the general name of the Gregorian Reform, after Leo's most famous successor in the reform tradition, Gregory VII (r.1073–85). Leo recognized as the great evil of his day the encroachment of the secular on the sacred. He sought to prohibit clerical marriage, perceived as the reversal of religious and lay functions and thus a symbol of the general problem. However, the chief ill that he tried to cure was the practice of simony—the buying and selling of Church offices. The elimination of simony became the chief concern of Leo's pontificate both because of its intrinsic seriousness and because it epitomized the Church's corruption. Leo brought men to Rome to help in the reform movement and gave them the title of cardinal. These included several Cluniac monks, Hildebrand—the future Gregory VII—the irascible and coldly intellectual Humbert, and the ascetic Peter Damian. Leo was faced with the problem of enforcing his reform decrees throughout Christendom. He wrote letters, appointed legates (men given his authority in a specific geographical area or in a specific matter), held synods, and traveled with an impressive entourage to literally show Europe the reformed papacy. His activity at the dedication of the new Monastery of St. Remigius at Reims illustrates his method. After processing through the city with the relics of its patron, Saint Remigius, he demanded that all bishops take an oath in the presence of the relics that they did not buy their office. Several refused, one was deposed on the spot, and the archbishop of Reims himself was ordered to appear later in Rome. Leo meant business. . . .

A series of reformers in the tradition of Leo succeeded him on the papal throne. In 1059 Nicholas II issued a decree establishing a procedure for papal election by the cardinals; although this was altered somewhat about a hundred years later by Alexander III, it is still the basis for papal election. The purpose of this decree was to keep the election of the pope out of the hands of lay persons, including the Holy Roman Emperor; since it was a Holy Roman Emperor who appointed the first reform pope, there is a certain irony here.

The election of Cardinal Hildebrand in 1073 as Gregory VII brought to the throne of St. Peter the most experienced man in the curia. His pontificate is pivotal in understanding the subsequent history of medieval Europe. . . .

Within two years of his accession to the papal throne, Gregory was in open conflict with the Holy Roman Emperor-elect Henry IV. The specific issue was lay investiture—the practice of a layperson, such as the Holy Roman Emperor, investing a bishop with the *spiritual* symbols of his office. Henry knew that to control his empire in fact as well as theory he needed loyal bishops, for they controlled vast amounts of territory, the means for providing him with an army. The only way to ensure the bishops' loyalty was to have complete control over their selection and investiture. This was obviously in clear opposition to the principles of the papal reform movement to which Gregory was heir. The conflict that broke out in 1075 after Henry invested the bishop of Milan was for more than who was to hand over a ring and staff to a bishop; it was a struggle for the leadership of Latin Christendom. Gregory died in exile in 1085, but Henry faced rebellion even within his own family and died in the midst of a struggle against a major coalition of opposition in 1106.

In the year 1122, the issue of lay investiture was settled by compromise in the Concordat of Worms. Bishops were to be elected only by clergy, but an imperial representative could be present at the election. Investiture of the spiritual symbols of office was to be performed by other bishops but only after investiture of the temporal symbols was performed by the emperor or his representative. However, the larger question of the leadership of Christian society was far from being decided. The Empire was severely weakened, both in theory and practice. Bishops could no longer be selected solely by the emperor, and the bitter struggle between popes and emperors destroyed the Church's support of the Empire. Furthermore, the theory of theocratic kingship, an important buttress of the emperor's position that was developed in the Carolingian period, was swept away by the sharp distinctions between priesthood and kingship made by advocates of the papal position.

SELECTION 2:
Medieval Civilization as a "World Revolution"

A noted historian of medieval Europe, Norman F. Cantor describes the reforms of the twelfth century as a "world revolution," comparable to those fundamental changes of the Reformation of the sixteenth century and the Enlightenment of the eighteenth.

The eight decades from the middle of the eleventh century to the end of the third decade of the twelfth constitute one of the great turning points in European history. It was one of those periods during which vitally important changes in all aspects of life occur simultaneously and with such great rapidity that no contemporary could foresee the far-reaching consequences of many of them.

From "The Gregorian World Revolution," in *The Civilization of the Middle Ages*, by Norman F. Cantor. Copyright © 1963, 1968, 1974, 1993 by Norman F. Cantor. Reprinted by permission of HarperCollins Publishers, Inc.

Such a period of fundamental and, at the same time, rapid change was the age of the Gregorian reform and the investiture controversy that the Gregorian reform precipitated. The Gregorian reform gets its name from Pope Gregory VII (1073–1085), the most visible leader of the reform movement. The term *investiture controversy* is derived from the crucial issue of whether kings and other great lords had the right to invest bishops and abbots with the symbols of their office, that is, whether laymen had the right to appoint church officials. The period from 1050 to 1130 was the period of enormous commercial expansion, of the well-known rise of urban communities, of the first expression of political influence by the new burgher class. It was an age in which the first really successful medieval monarchy was created in Anglo-Norman England on the basis of the feudal institutions and administrative methods and personnel created by the energetic and far-seeing Norman dukes. It was an age in which the long separation of the new western European civilization from the life of the Mediterranean world came to an end. This isolation, in existence since the eighth century, was now replaced by the political and economic penetration of the western European peoples into the Mediterranean basin to the detriment of the Moslems and Byzantines, who had long ruled the Mediterranean lands and controlled Mediterranean trade without a challenge from the north. It was an age of tremendous intellectual vitality that witnessed the most important contributions to the Latin Christian theology since Augustine and the slow transformation of some of the cathedral schools of northern France and the municipal schools of northern Italy into the universities of the following centuries. It was an age of great vitality in legal thought, in which Roman law came to be carefully studied for the first time since the German invasion of the fifth century, and great strides were made in the codification of the canon law.

But as in the eras of fundamental change in modern history, these achievements must be accorded second place by the historian in favor of an ideological struggle. Out of a far-reaching controversy on the nature of the right order to be established in the world the pattern of civilization of the following centuries was to emerge. The period from 1050 to 1130 was dominated by an attempt at world revolution that influenced in highly effective ways the other aspects of social change. It seems, in retrospect, that it was almost necessary for a revolutionary onslaught to shake the order of the early Middle Ages to its foundations, so that the new political, economic, and intellectual forces could be given the opportunity to develop in the face of the old institutions and ideas.

It has been characteristic of the history of the West that its destiny has been shaped by world revolutions in which previous tendencies culminated and from which new ideas and systems emerged. A world revolution is a widespread and thoroughgoing revolution in worldview, the emergence of a new ideology that rejects the results of several centuries of development organized into the prevailing system and calls for a new right order in the world. The investiture controversy, which the Gregorian reform engendered, constitutes the first of the great world revolutions of western history, and its course follows the same pattern as the well-known revolutions of modern times.

Each world revolution has begun with some just complaint about moral wrongs in the prevailing political, social, or religious system. In the investiture controversy the leaders of the revolution, who have been called the Gregorian reformers, complained about the domination of the church by laymen and the involvement of the church in feudal obligations. This system had led to severe abuses, especially that of simony, which came to be defined in its most general sense as the interference of laymen with the right ordering of church offices and sacraments. In their condemnation of simony as heresy, the Gregorians had a perfectly valid complaint.

It has been characteristic of all the world revolutions, however, that while each has begun by complaining about abuses in the prevailing world order, the ultimate aim of the revolutionary ideologists has been not the reform of the prevailing system but its abolition and replacement by a new order. In the case of the investiture controversy, the complete freedom of the church from control by the state, the negation of the sacramental character of kingship, and the domination of the papacy over secular rulers constituted the ideal new order.

As in all other world revolutions, the ideology of the Gregorians called forth violent opposition from both vested interests and sincere theoretical defenders of the old order. After many acrimonious disputes and a flood of propaganda literature, bitter and protracted warfare resulted. The polarization of educated society into revolutionary and conservative left a large group of uncommitted moderates, including some of the best minds of the age, who could see right and wrong on both sides.

As in all other world revolutions, the ideologists of the investiture controversy were only partially successful in creating the new order. They succeeded in destroying the old system, but the new world was not the revolutionary utopia. Rather, it was a reconstruction of the political and religious system that took into account both old and new elements and left room for the human limitations of greed and power. The church gained a large measure of freedom from secular control, and there was a noticeable improvement in the moral and intellectual level of the clergy. But the church itself, from the time of the investiture controversy, became more and more interested in secular affairs, and so the papacy of the High Middle Ages competed successfully for wealth and power with kings and emperors. The church itself became a great superstate that was governed by the papal administration.

As in all other world revolutions, the ideologists during the investiture controversy were themselves united only upon the most immediate and more limited aims of the revolution. As the revolution proceeded, the Gregorians divided into a moderate and a radical wing, each led by eminent cardinals. The radicals were headed by Humbert and Hildebrand, the moderates by Peter Damiani. As in the modern world revolutions, the radicals were in control of the Gregorian reform movement, a period that was long enough to destroy the old order. But as the conservatives and moderates of various complexions at last perceived the real aim of the radicals and their reckless disregard for consequences, the radicals lost their leadership and were unable to realize their utopian ideals.

As in the modern world revolutions, the radicals lost their leadership not to the moderates of their own group, whom they had earlier swept aside, but to the politicians, the practical statesmen who called a halt to the revolution and tried to reconstruct from the shattered pieces of the old system and the achievements of the revolution a new and workable synthesis that would again make progress possible. This tendency is already evident during the pontificate of Urban II in the last decade of the eleventh century, and it became dominant in the papacy during the 1120s.

Like all world revolutions, the investiture controversy never reached a final and complete solution. New ideas in a new generation made former issues less meaningful, and the men of the new generation turned to other interests and new problems. In the 1130s many educated churchmen could not understand why popes and kings should have quarreled over lay investiture only two or three decades before.

The age of the investiture controversy may rightly be regarded as the turning point in medieval civilization. It was the fulfillment of the early Middle Ages, because in it the acceptance of the Christian religion by the Germanic peoples reached a final and decisive stage. On the other hand, the pattern of the religious and political system of the High Middle Ages emerged out of the events and ideas of the investiture controversy.

The Gregorians revolted against the medieval equilibrium and hence against many things that eleventh-century Cluny and its allies represented What, then, were the origin and cause of the Gregorian reform movement that brought about the decisive turning point in medieval history?

The Gregorian reform movement was the logical outcome, but by no means the inevitable and absolutely necessary outcome, of the early medieval equilibrium itself. As the church in the late tenth and eleventh centuries penetrated more and more into the world, imposing its ideals on the lay society, it began to face the dangerous possibility of losing its distinctive identity and hence its leadership in western society. For as the lay piety steadily increased throughout western Europe, the special qualities of the clergy stood out less clearly. No longer did a devout attitude toward dogma and ritual and the veneration of the saints and their relics suffice to distinguish the outlook of ecclesiastic and layman. By the middle of the eleventh century it was apparent that lay piety had in many cases attained the level of religious devotion hitherto exhibited only by the more conscientious among the clergy. Cardinal Peter Damiani, whose writings so frequently served as a sort of barometric indicator of eleventh-century attitudes, observed that every faithful Christian was a microcosm of the whole church: "Each of the faithful seems to be, as it were, a lesser church." If the Holy Spirit raised some of the faithful to the ministry of ecclesiastical dignity, Damiani asserted, it was to be expected that these ministers of God would reveal their special divine gifts by a superior form of religious life. Above all, the monks, who had professed the most perfect religious life, should at least act as the militia of Christ.

The great increase in lay piety created a new problem for the church, and its own traditional hierocratic doctrine, reflected in Damiani's statement, made the problem particularly urgent. The power of the priesthood and the papacy had been built upon the principle that "him to whom more is given, from him more will be demanded." Previously there was no doubt that more in the way of the spirit was demanded from the clergy; hence the justification of sacerdotal powers in the popular mind. Now doubts were arising on this issue. To many eleventh-century churchmen it seemed that only a greatly improved morality and heightened religious fervor among the clergy could continue to justify the exclusive powers of the sacerdotium. Otherwise the ecclesia would be absorbed into the thoroughly Christianized mundus, and the clergy would lose its distinctive position in society.

By the middle of the eleventh century churchmen everywhere in western Europe were encountering this new, critical problem. They knew that kings such as Henry III of Germany and Edward the Confessor were monks in worldly garb, always eager to lead the procession in a translation of holy relics. They found many nobles who took seriously the Peace of God, who endowed monasteries and cathedrals, undertook arduous pilgrimages, and hoped to be accorded the privilege of dying enshrouded in the monastic habit. Even the scurvy bourgeois gave glimpses of falling in with this new tendency, with their support of municipal churches and their devotion to religious festivals. Such laymen would expect a clergy to be still as morally superior to themselves as it was in the old days when society was savage and heathen, save in the most nominal sense. The hold of the church over lay society, the universal respect that the monks especially received from laymen, could be maintained only by a greatly enhanced piety and morality among the monks themselves.

SELECTION 3:

The Clarification of Doctrine

The success of these reforms can be measured not only in the strengthening of the ecclesiastical structure of the church but also in the greater articulation of Christian doctrine and values. The Lateran Council, organized by Pope Innocent III in 1215, in many ways marked the high point of the medieval church. It clarified the sacramental system and gave new definition to the role of the secular clergy within the daily life of individual Christians. Therefore, it tied Christian values more closely to the lives of individuals through clear conception of each sacrament. The council also dealt with a number of abuses by the clergy, including ignorance of Scripture, simony, and pluralism (the holding of more than one benefice).

CANON 11

Summary. In every cathedral church and other churches also that have sufficient means, a master is to be appointed to instruct gratis the clerics and poor students. The metropolitan church ought to have a theologian who shall teach the clergy whatever pertains to the cura animarum (i.e. care of souls).

Text. Since there are some who, on account of the lack of necessary means, are unable to acquire an education or to meet opportunities for perfecting themselves, the Third Lateran Council in a salutary decree provided that in every cathedral church a suitable benefice be assigned to a master who shall instruct gratis the clerics of that church and other poor students, by means of which benefice the material needs of the master might be relieved and to the students a way opened to knowledge. But, since in many churches this is not observed, we, confirming the aforesaid decree, add that, not only in every cathedral church but also in other churches where means are sufficient, a competent master be appointed by the prelate with his chapter, or elected by the greater and more discerning part of the chapter, who shall instruct gratis and to the best of his ability the clerics of those and other churches in the art of grammar and in other branches of knowledge. In addition to a master, let the metropolitan church have also a theologian, who shall instruct the priests and others in the Sacred Scriptures and in those things especially that pertain to the cura animarum. To each master let there be assigned by the chapter the revenue of one benefice, and to the theologian let as much be given by the metropolitan; not that they thereby become canons, but they shall enjoy the revenue only so long as they hold the office of instructor. If the metropolitan church cannot support two masters, then it shall provide for the theologian in the aforesaid manner, but for the one teaching grammar, let it see to it that a sufficiency is provided by another church of its city or diocese. . . .

From *Disciplinary Decrees of the General Councils: Text, Translation, and Commentary*, by J.J. Schroeder (St. Louis: Herder, 1937).

CANON 15

Summary. Clerics, who after being warned do not abstain from drunkenness, shall be suspended from their office and benefice.

Text. All clerics shall carefully abstain from drunkenness. Wherefore, let them accommodate the wine to themselves, and themselves to the wine. Nor shall anyone be encouraged to drink, for drunkenness banishes reason and incites to lust. We decree, therefore, that that abuse be absolutely abolished by which in some localities the drinkers bind themselves suo modo to an equal portion of drink and he in their judgment is the hero of the day who out drinks the others. Should anyone be culpable in this matter, unless he heeds the warning of the superior and makes suitable satisfaction, let him be suspended from his benefice or office. . . .

CANON 16

Summary. Clerics are not to engage in secular pursuits, attend unbecoming exhibitions, visit taverns, or play games of chance. Their clothing must be in keeping with their dignity.

Text. Clerics shall not hold secular offices or engage in secular and, above all, dishonest pursuits. They shall not attend the performances of mimics and buffoons, or theatrical representations. They shall not visit taverns except in case of necessity, namely, when on a journey. They are forbidden to play games of chance or be present at them. They must have a becoming crown and tonsure and apply themselves diligently to the study of the divine offices and other useful subjects. Their garments must be worn clasped at the top and neither too short nor too long. They are not to use red or green garments or curiously sewed together gloves, or beak-shaped shoes or gilded bridles, saddles, pectoral ornaments (for horses), spurs, or anything else indicative of superfluity. At the divine office in the church they are not to wear cappas with long sleeves, and priests and dignitaries may not wear them elsewhere except in case of danger when circumstances should require a change of outer garments. Buckles may under no condition be worn, nor sashes having ornaments of gold or silver, nor rings, unless it be in keeping with the dignity of their office. All bishops must use in public and in the church outer garments made of linen, except those who are monks, in which case they must wear the habit of their order; in public they must not appear with open mantles, but these must be clasped either on the back of the neck or on the bosom. . . .

CANON 21

Summary. Everyone who has attained the age of reason is bound to confess his sins at least once a year to his own parish pastor with his permission to another, and to receive the Eucharist at least at Easter. A priest who reveals a sin confided to him in confession is to be deposed and relegated to a monastery for the remainder of his life.

Text. All the faithful of both sexes shall after they have reached the age of discretion faithfully confess all their sins at least once a year to their own (parish) priest and perform to the best of their ability the penance imposed, receiving reverently at least at Easter the sacrament of the Eucharist, unless perchance at the advice of their own priest they may for a good reason abstain for a time from its reception; otherwise they shall be cut off from the Church (excommunicated) during life and deprived of Christian burial in death. Wherefore, let this salutary decree be published frequently in the churches, that no one may find in the plea of ignorance a shadow of excuse. But if anyone for a good reason should wish to confess his sins to another priest, let him first seek and obtain permission from his own (parish) priest, since otherwise he (the other priest) cannot loose or bind him. Let the priest be discreet and cautious that he may pour wine and oil into the wounds of the one injured after the manner of a skilful physician, carefully inquiring into the circumstances of the sinner and the sin, from the nature of which he may understand what kind of advice to give and what remedy to apply, making use of different experiments to heal the sick one. But let him exercise the greatest precaution that he does not in any degree by word, sign, or any other manner make known the sinner, but should he need more prudent counsel, let him seek it cautiously without any mention of the person. He who dares to reveal a sin confided to him in the tribunal of penance, we decree that he be not only deposed from the sacerdotal

office but also relegated to a monastery of strict observance to do penance for the remainder of his life. . . .

CANON 29

Summary. Anyone having a benefice with the cura animarum annexed, if he accepts another, shall lose the first; and if he attempts to retain it, he shall lose the other also. After the reception of the second benefice, the first may be freely conferred on another. If he to whom that collation belongs should delay beyond six months, then it shall devolve on another and the form shall indemnify the church for the losses incurred during the vacancy.

Text. With much foresight it was prohibited in the Lateran Council that no one should, contrary to the sacred canons, accept several ecclesiastical dignities or several parochial churches; otherwise the one receiving should lose what he received, and the one who bestowed be deprived of the right of collation. But since, on account of the boldness and avarice of some, the aforesaid statute has thus far produced little or no fruit, we, wishing to meet the situation more clearly and emphatically, declare in the present decree that whoever shall accept a benefice to which is annexed the cura animarum after having previously obtained such a benefice, shall ipso jure be deprived of this (the first one); and if perchance he should attempt to retain it, let him be deprived of the other one also. He to whom the collation of the first benefice belongs may freely confer it, after the incumbent has accepted a second, on anyone whom he may deem worthy; should he delay to do so beyond a period of six months, then in accordance with the decree of the Lateran Council, let not only its collation devolve on another, but also let him be compelled to indemnify the church in question from his own resources equal to the amount of the revenues drawn from it during its vacancy. The same we decree is to be observed in regard to dignities (personatus), adding, that no one may presume to have several dignities in the same church, even though they have not the cura animarum annexed. Only in the case of eminent and learned persons who are to be honored with major benefices, can the Apostolic See, if need be, grant a dispensation.

After reading this selection and the previous ones, consider these questions:

1. What were the main concerns of the Lateran Council of 1215?

2. Why was the church in need of reform?

3. What, according to Norman Cantor, is the historical significance of these reforms?

SELECTION 4:

The Origins of Scholasticism

Another major development of the High Middle Ages was the creation of the university. Originating as "cloister schools" in order to train the clergy, they quickly developed into centers of learning not only in theology and philosophy but also in medicine and law. The medieval universities laid the foundations of modern universities in the West. The origins of the medieval university were closely tied to the development of Scholastic theology. The origins of this theology are found in what historians have generally referred to as "the renaissance of the twelfth century"—a new sense of the power of human reason to understand both nature and faith.

This new power of reason is nowhere better exemplified than in the thought of the French philosopher and theologian Peter Abelard (1079–1142). Abelard pointed out the contradiction in the various writing of the fathers of the church and devised a new way of approaching these contradictions and of understanding faith as a whole. Although others had pointed to the contradictions among scriptural passages, the writing of the church fathers, and the various decisions of the papacy, Abelard celebrated these discrepancies, asserting that doubts led to inquiries and inquiries led to ultimate truth. In such important matters for the faith as the nature of the Trinity, he applied what he called "human and logical reasons," claiming that "words were useless if the intelligence could not follow them, [and] that nothing could be believed unless it was first understood." Perhaps his most influential work was the textbook Sic et Non (Yes and No), *written in 1122–1123. In it Abelard covered 156 questions—among them such issues as "That God is one and the contrary" and "That all are permitted to marry and the contrary"—in order to, as he writes, excite "young readers to the maximum of effort in inquiring into the truth."*

There are many seeming contradictions and even obscurities in the innumerable writings of the church fathers. Our respect for their authority should not stand in the way of an effort on our part to come at the truth. The obscurity and con-

From *Sic et Non* (*Yes and No*), by Peter Abelard, in *Readings in European History*, vol. 1, edited by James Harvey Robinson (Boston: Ginn, 1904).

tradictions in ancient writings may be explained upon many grounds, and may be discussed without impugning the good faith and insight of the fathers. A writer may use different terms to mean the same thing, in order to avoid a monotonous repetition of the same word. Common, vague words may be employed in order that the common people may understand; and sometimes a writer sacrifices perfect accuracy in the interest of a clear general statement. Poetical, figurative language is often obscure and vague.

Not infrequently apocryphal works are attributed to the saints. Then, even the best authors often introduce the erroneous views of others and leave the reader to distinguish between the true and the false. Sometimes, as Augustine confesses in his own case, the fathers ventured to rely upon the opinions of others.

Doubtless the fathers might err; even Peter, the prince of the apostles, fell into error: what wonder that the saints do not always show themselves inspired? The fathers did not themselves believe that they, or their companions, were always right. Augustine found himself mistaken in some cases and did not hesitate to retract his errors. He warns his admirers not to look upon his letters as they would upon the Scriptures, but to accept only those things which, upon examination, they find to be true.

All writings belonging to this class are to be read with full freedom to criticize, and with no obligation to accept unquestioningly; otherwise the way would be blocked to all discussion, and posterity be deprived of the excellent intellectual exercise of debating difficult questions of language and presentation. But an explicit exception must be made in the case of the Old and New Testaments. In the Scriptures, when anything strikes us as absurd, we may not say that the writer erred, but that the scribe made a blunder in copying the manuscripts, or that there is an error in interpretation, or that the passage is not understood. The fathers make a very careful distinction between the Scriptures and later works. They advocate a discriminating, not to say suspicious, use of the writings of their own contemporaries.

In view of these considerations, I have ventured to bring together various dicta [sayings] of the holy fathers, as they came to mind, and to formulate certain questions which were suggested by the seeming contradictions in the statements. These questions ought to serve to excite tender readers to a zealous inquiry into truth and so sharpen their wits. The master key of knowledge is, indeed, a persistent and frequent questioning. Aristotle, the most clear-sighted of all the philosophers, was desirous above all things else to arouse this questioning spirit, for in his *Categories* he exhorts a student as follows: "It may well be difficult to reach a positive conclusion in these matters unless they be frequently discussed. It is by no means fruitless to be doubtful on particular points." By doubting we come to examine, and by examining we reach the truth.

SELECTION 5:
The Rejection of Rational Theology

Peter Abelard's rational approach to faith did not go unchallenged. One of the leading theologians of the age, St. Bernard of Clairvaux (ca. 1090–1153), saw the dangers in such an approach. He claimed that Abelard was "presumptuously prepared to give a reason for everything, even of those things which are above reason." In a letter from 1140, St. Bernard points out some of these problems.

Master Peter Abelard is a monk without a rule, a prelate without responsibility. . . . He speaks iniquity openly. He corrupts the integrity of the faith and the chastity of the Church. He oversteps the landmarks placed by our Fathers in discussing and writing about faith, the sacraments, and the Holy Trinity; he changes each thing according to his pleasure, adding to it or taking from it. In his books and in his works he shows himself to be a fabricator of falsehood, a coiner of perverse dogmas, proving himself a heretic not so much by his error as by his obstinate defence of error. He is a man who does not know his limitations, making void the virtue of the cross by the cleverness of his words. Nothing in heaven or on earth is hidden from him, except himself. . . . He has defiled the Church; he has infected with his own blight the minds of simple people. He tries to explore with his reason what the devout mind grasps at once with a vigorous faith. Faith believes, it does not dispute. But this man, apparently holding God suspect, will not believe anything until he has first examined it with his reason. When the Prophet says, "Unless you believe, you shall not understand," this man decries willing faith as levity, misusing that testimony of Solomon: "He that is hasty to believe is light of head." Let him therefore blame the Blessed Virgin Mary for quickly believing the angel when he announced to her that she should conceive and bring forth a son. Let him also blame him who, while on the verge of death, believed those words of One who was also dying: "This day thou shalt be with me in Paradise."

From *The Letters of St. Bernard of Clairvaux*, translated by Bruno Scott James (Chicago: Regnery, 1953).

SELECTION 6:

The Summa Theologiae

Although allegorical readings of Scripture and symbolic understanding of the faith as a whole continued, Peter Abelard's rational approach to reading texts and to questions of belief in general continued. In many ways, this approach found its highest expression in the compilation of the great summae *of faith produced in the twelfth and thirteenth centuries. The most famous of these was produced by St. Thomas Aquinas. Born to a noble Italian family in 1224 or 1225, he eventually joined the Dominican order and was sent to study theology in Paris, the site of Europe's leading university. In the 1240s the University of Paris was an exciting place as the newly obtained works of Aristotle challenged theologians to find common ground between the revealed truth of faith and the new sense of nature and logic presented in the works of the Greek philosopher. Thomas Aquinas dedicated the rest of his life to defining this common ground in his famous* Summa Theologiae, *which he wrote between 1266 and 1273.*

The Summa Theologiae *is a highly systematic work, divided into the major topics of theology (what Thomas Aquinas calls "questions") which are further subdivided into various challenges to a given position ("articles"). In the following selection taken from the opening sections of the* Summa, *St. Thomas Aquinas presents problems with the initial articles and concludes with a "responsio," which he considers the correct answer.*

Since a teacher of catholic truth should instruct not only the advanced but beginners as well—as St. Paul says, "Like babes in Christ I fed you milk and not meat" (I Cor. 3:1)—our intention in this work is to convey the content of the Christian religion in a way fit for the training of beginners. We have seen that novices in this study are greatly hindered by the various writings on the subject. They are hindered partly because of the multiplication of useless questions, articles and arguments in these writings; partly because the order in which essential material is delivered in these writings is determined, not by the nature of doctrine itself, but by the books on which the writings are commenting; and partly because frequent repetition has bred boredom and confusion in the minds of hearers.

Eager to avoid these and other pitfalls we shall now attempt to examine the content of sacred doctrine briefly and clearly, so far as the material allows, twisting in God's aid.

Question 1: Sacred doctrine, what it is and what it includes. In order to contain our investigation within limits, we must first investigate sacred doctrine itself, asking what it is and how far it extends. Ten questions must be asked.

1. Whether it is necessary

2. Whether it is a science

3. Whether it is one or many

4. Whether it is speculative or practical

5. How it compares with other sciences

6. Whether it is wisdom

7. What is its subject

8. Whether it is argumentative

9. Whether it should use metaphorical or symbolic language

10. Whether the sacred scripture containing this doctrine is to be interpreted according to several senses.

Article 1: Whether it is necessary to have another doctrine besides the philosophical disciplines. Let us proceed to the first point. It seems that there is no necessity for any doctrine beyond the philosophical disciplines. Man should not strive after that which is beyond his reason. As Ecclesiasticus says, "Do not be curious about what is above you" (Ecclus. 3:22). The things which can be investigated by reason are sufficiently covered in the philosophical disciplines, however. Thus it seems superfluous to have some doctrine beyond the philosophical disciplines.

Furthermore, any doctrine can deal only with that which is; for nothing can be known except that which is true, and that which is true is identical with that which is. Yet everything other than signification, through which the things signified by the words signify something else in turn, is called the spiritual sense. It is based on the literal sense and presupposes it.

But on the contrary Paul says, "All divinely-inspired scripture is useful for teaching, arguing, correcting and instructing in justice" (II Tim. 3:16). Divinely-inspired scripture does not pertain to philosophical disciplines, however, for they are discovered by human reason. Thus it is useful to have another, divinely-inspired doctrine besides the philosophical disciplines.

Response. It must be said that, besides the philosophical disciplines which are investigated by human reason, another doctrine based on revelation was necessary for human well-being. Such is true, in the first place, because man is or-

From *Summa Theologiae*, by Thomas Aquinas, translated by David Burr, from the on-line *Medieval Source Book*, at http://www.fordham.edu/halsall/source/aquinas1.html. Reprinted by permission of David Burr.

dered by God to a certain end which exceeds the grasp of reason. As Isaiah says, "Eye has not seen, God, without you, what you have prepared for those who love you" (Isa. 64:4). The end must be fore known to man, however, since he must order his intentions and actions to that end. Thus it was necessary to human well-being that certain things exceeding human reason be made known to man through divine revelation.

Even in the case of those things which can be investigated by human reason, it was necessary for man to be instructed by divine revelation. The truth concerning God, if left to human reason alone, would have appeared only to a few, and only after a long search, and even then mixed with many errors; yet all of man's well-being, which is in God, depends on knowledge of this truth. Thus, in order that this well-being should become known to men more commonly and more securely, it was necessary that they be instructed by divine revelation.

Thus it was necessary that, besides the philosophical doctrines which can be investigated by reason, there be a sacred doctrine known through revelation.

To the first argument, therefore, it must be said that, although what is above human knowledge should not be investigated by reason, once revealed by God it should be accepted through faith. Thus it is added in the same chapter of Ecclesiasticus, "Many things above human understanding are shown to you" (Ecclus. 3:25). Sacred doctrine consists of these things.

To the second argument it must be said that there are diverse sciences because things can be known in various ways. For example, the astronomer and the natural philosopher both demonstrate the same conclusion, such as that the world is round; yet the astronomer does so through mathematics, while the natural philosopher does so in a way that takes matter into account. Thus there is no reason why those things treated by the philosophical disciplines through natural reason should not also be treated by another science insofar as they are known by the light of divine revelation. Thus the theology which pertains to sacred doctrine differs from that theology which is a part of philosophy.

After reading this selection and the previous ones, consider these questions:

1. What were the origins of Scholastic theology?
2. How did St. Thomas Aquinas attempt to reconcile faith and reason?
3. How would a theologian like St. Bernard have reacted to the fully developed scholastic theology of St. Thomas?

SELECTION 7:

The Rise of the Mendicant Orders

Monasticism also experienced new growth and development in the High Middle Ages. New or newly organized orders, such as the Cistercian order of monks that arose from within the original Benedictine organization, were characteristic of the new vitality of monasticism of the era. The late twelfth and early thirteenth centuries also witnessed a further development and transformation of the relation of the clergy to the lay public.

If the early Middle Ages found the Christian ideal in the life of the good monk who renounced this world, and the High Middle Ages found in the secular clergy and the church hierarchy that it represented a new attitude toward the world and its worth within something called a Christian civilization, the High and late Middle Ages witnessed a further progression in the church's involvement with the world. The last decades of the 1100s saw new forms of ministry arise that were neither enclosed within the walls of a monastery nor tied directly to the secular arm of the church. These were the mendicant orders. Originally developing outside the authority of the church, each of these movements eventually were confirmed as orders within the structure of the church itself. In these new orders, individuals placed themselves under a rule but they remained in the world, ministering to the Christian needs of the growing lay community. These orders included the Dominicans and Carmelites, but the most popular, both in terms of individuals who wanted to join and in terms of the acceptance by the lay community, were the Franciscans.

Both Franciscans and Dominicans insisted on preaching and poverty, defining their mission in terms of ministering to the growing numbers of individuals from all social classes within the towns and cities of Europe. In this sense, the new mendicant orders filled a definite need within the world of the High and late Middle Ages. They and their message were overwhelmingly popular and laypeople readily accepted their new approach to preaching and their simple lifestyles. By 1277 there were 414 Dominican houses, and in the early fourteenth century more than 1,400 Franciscan houses were founded throughout the continent.

St. Francis, the founder of the Franciscan order, died on October 3, 1226. Just before his death, he dictated what has come to be called his Testament, *in which he once again stated the meaning of his teaching and the purposes of his order. Although Francis, as can been seen in this document, wanted a simple form of organization, the enormous popularity of his teaching and the subsequent rapid growth of his order necessitated, soon after his death, a more complex form of organization and a more liberal interpretation of its basic principles.*

This is how the Lord gave me, brother Francis, the power to do penance. When I was in sin the sight of lepers was too bitter for me. And the Lord himself led me among them, and I pitied and helped them. And when I left them I discovered that what had seemed bitter to me was changed into sweetness in my soul and body. And shortly afterward I rose and left the world.

And the Lord gave me such faith in churches

From *Testament*, by Francis of Assisi, translated by David Burr, from the on-line *Medieval Source Book*, at http://www.fordham.edu/halsall/source/stfran-test.html. Reprinted by permission of David Burr.

that I prayed simply, saying, "I adore you, Lord Jesus Christ, with all your churches throughout the world, and we bless you because you redeemed the world through your holy cross. Later God gave me and still gives me such faith in priests who live according to the form of the Holy Roman Church that even if they persecuted me I would still run back to them, because of their position. And if I had all the wisdom of Solomon and came upon some poor little priests in their parishes, I would preach there only if they wished me to do so. And I want to fear, love and honor these and all others as my lords. And I do not even want to think about there being any sin in them, because I see the Son of God in them and they are my lords. And I do this because in this world I physically see the most high Son of God only in his most holy body and blood, which they receive and they alone administer to others. And I want this holy mystery to be honored above all things, venerated, and kept in costly containers. Whenever I find his holy names or words in improper places I pick them up and ask that they be collected and stored in a proper place. And we ought to honor and venerate all theologians and those who administer the holy divine word, for they administer to us spirit and life.

And when God gave me brothers, no one showed me what I should do, but the Most high revealed to me that I should live according to the form of the holy gospel. I had it written in few words and simply, and the lord pope confirmed it for me. And those who came to receive life gave all that they had to the poor and were content with one tunic patched inside and out, with a cord and trousers. And we did not wish to have more.

We who were clerics said the office like other clerics, and the laymen said the "Our Father," and we gladly stayed in churches. And we were ignorant and subject to all. And I worked with my hands, and want to do so still. And I definitely want all the other brothers to work at some honest job. Those who don't know how should learn, not because they want to receive wages but as an example and to avoid idleness. And when our wages are withheld from us, let us return to the Lord's table, begging alms from door to door. The Lord revealed what greeting we should use: "The Lord give you peace."

The brothers must be careful not to accept any churches, poor dwellings, or anything else constructed for them unless these buildings reflect the holy poverty promised by us in the rule. We should always live in these places as strangers and pilgrims. I firmly command all the brothers, by the obedience they owe me, that wherever they are they should not dare to ask either directly or through an intermediary for any letter from the Roman court to secure a church or any other place, to protect their preaching, or to prevent persecution of their bodies; but wherever they are not received, they should flee into another land

and do penance with God's blessing.

And I firmly wish to obey the minister general of this brotherhood, and any other guardian the minister should want to give me. And I want to be such a captive in his hands that I cannot go anywhere or do anything without his desire and command, because he is my lord. And although I am simple and ill, I always want to have a cleric who can perform the office for me, as the rule states. And all the other brothers are thus bound to obey their guardians and perform the office according to the rule. And whenever some are found who do not wish to perform the office according to the rule and want to change it, or who are not Catholic in their beliefs, then all the brothers wherever they may be are bound by obedience to turn such people over to the custodian nearest the place where they found them. The custodian in turn is bound by obedience to guard him strongly like a man in chains, day and night, so that he cannot possibly escape from his hands until he personally places him in the hands of his minister. And the minister is bound by obedience to place him in the care of brothers who will guard him night and day like a man in chains until they turn him over to our lord bishop of Ostia, who is the lord protector and corrector of the whole brotherhood.

And the brothers must not say, "This is another rule," for it is a recollection, admonition, exhortation and my testament which I, poor brother Francis, make for you my brothers, so that we may observe the rule we have promised to God in a more Catholic manner. And the general minister and all other ministers and custodians are bound by obedience not to add or subtract from these words. And they must always have this writing with them in addition to the rule. And in all chapter meetings held by them, when they read the rule, they must also read these words.

And I firmly forbid my brothers, both clerics and laymen, to place glosses on the rule or say, "This is what it means." But just as the Lord gave me the power to compose and write both the rule and these words simply and purely, so you must understand them simply and without gloss and observe them by holy action until the end.

And whoever observes them will be filled in

heaven with a blessing of the most high Father and on earth he will be filled with the blessing of his beloved Son, with the Holy Spirit the Comforter and all the powers of heaven and all the saints. And, I, brother Francis, your servant insofar as I can be, internally and externally confirm for you this holy blessing.

After reading this selection, consider these questions:

1. What does St. Francis see as the model for his life?
2. What does St. Francis understand as the relationship of his order to the church?
3. How does St. Francis describe the current problems faced by his order?

SELECTION 8:

The Feast of Corpus Christi

One response to this sense of sin and insecurity was the development of the new cults and new forms of religious ritual in the High and late Middle Ages. One of the most interesting of these (and one that illustrates the texture of religious life in the late medieval period) is the feast of Corpus Christi. As historian Miri Rubin points out, this feast crystallized around the central symbol of medieval civilization, the Eucharist.

The eucharist, it is true, was an important symbol in early Christianity, but it was refigured in the eleventh and twelfth centuries to create a new structure of relations, thus modifying the symbolic order, and the social relations and political claims which could be attached to it. In this new order we witness the raising of a fragile, white, wheaten little disc to amazing prominence, and fallible, sometimes ill-lettered, men to the status of mediator between Christians and the supernatural. The eucharist emerged as a unifying symbol for a complex world, as a symbol unburdened by local voices and regional associations. Its language differed from that associated with pilgrimage sites and the cult of saints; thus it was one which provided a framework for interaction and communication between disparate interests

and identities. It linked together identities already locally bound in the emerging quasi-national units which were more closely in touch in the increasingly more cosmopolitan world which the eleventh and twelfth centuries heralded. Within the developing parochial net cast over Europe in these centuries the eucharist was reckoned to be equally efficacious in Vienna or Valladolid, viewed or received by woman or man, at cathedral altar or village chancel: it mediated grace and supernatural power in rituals independent of contingent boundaries of political variation. Thus, it possessed universal meaning.

Sacramental mediation was not the only metaphor for expressing the world, but it was one which highlighted a stage in the narrative of Christian medieval culture. Tensions inherent in the scriptural tales themselves, the versions of the synoptic gospels and in the Pauline epistles, were resolved in the eucharist in the creation of a symbol which bound the essential narratives of incarnation, crucifixion, and the legacy of redemption. It was this-

From *Corpus Christi: The Eucharist in Late Medieval Culture,* by Miri Rubin. Copyright © Cambridge University Press 1991. Reprinted with the permission of Cambridge University Press.

worldly in emphasising that channels of regeneration and salvation were available and attainable, renewable and never exhaustible. It possessed little of the eschatological pull which informed the cultural worlds of late antiquity, or of the early modern era, but was geared towards the present, was fulfilled here and now, offering powerful and tangible rewards to the living in the present, as well as to their relatives, the dead. The eucharist provided an axis around which worlds revolved; in it were bound order and hierarchy, inducements towards conformity and promises of reward in health, prosperity, tranquillity. Our task has been to trace and interpret the workings of this world of meaning, its construction and use by some and by others, its implications, threats and promises.

So in the orthodox teaching, in vernacular preaching, in story and tale, in magic as in civic ceremonial, the eucharist was used and reused, determined and applied. Those who possessed power and authority could articulate the symbol through their own positions most forcefully. They did so by inducing moods, designing rituals, commissioning works of art, in drama, by exerting authority and charisma, and thus influencing directions in eucharistic readings, creating hegemonic symbolic idioms around themselves. The power exercised in the networks of social relations is always realised through symbolic formations which tend to attach themselves to the holy. A variety of local and universal, individual and collective, lay and sacerdotal claims came to reside in the eucharist; and they were sometimes fleeting and private and at other times public, sometimes bespeaking a single perception, and other times densely inscribed in ways which *overdetermined* the symbol. It thus became linked to partly compatible, but also varying and vying claims which militated against the smooth, lofty, universal, equally shared and accessible pristine nature which had made it so powerful at the outset. This gave it the power to encompass divergent notions about authority, the supernatural, virtue and legitimacy. In its use, however, it was interpreted through a process which entailed the filling up of gaps and spaces for evasion and ambiguity; we have here the aging of a symbol. . . .

In our interpretive venture we are not obliged to assign a causal necessity between symbol and its meanings, its referents. Artifacts do not possess inherent stable meanings since they are always constructed in the context of their use, their apprehension. Yet symbols have the power to suggest, so what do we make of the wheaten bread, the wine, the eating, the body of the eucharist as they emerge packed with associations into new powerful symbolic configurations, as they become apt metaphors which reordered the sacred and the profane, the natural and the supernatural? Why did a ritual of mediation, the symbol of the supernatural upon earth, the source of virtue and salvation, come to reside in the bread and the wine? This can only be interpreted, contextualised—never explained. And it must be seen as a product of an on-going process of *bricolage*, that is, of the creative combinations of existing texts and symbols to produce new meanings leading to different types of action. This is the essence of cultural formation. The structure of relations between symbols creates their meaning and thus very old symbols can appear in different contexts with differing meanings. . . .

The late medieval language of religion posited certain dispositions of power as both natural and necessary, and thus created, by association, an ideology which suggested that this was so. The church, royalty, urban elites, the gentry, used the language of religion in a variety of idioms hinged on central symbols. Conversely, the boldly stated symbolic order also generated change through processes of creative extrapolation, comparison, analogy and extension. Religion has manifested itself here as a mythopoeic field, as creative in the intense metaphorisation that it necessitates to effect the signification of the holy from the very mundane and material, of life and death, of the passing and the eternal. And religion's universal claims do, none the less, leave space for personal dispositions and notions, for *action* in the use of language itself, in the formulation of a single utterance of it. The creative processes of acting through language bring together materials into structures of relations which recreate their very meaning. . . .

It is, therefore, of special interest to attempt and understand the compelling power of a symbol related so closely to the image of the body, because the body seems so natural, so inclusive and familiar to all, and yet at a closer glance, it is burdened with layers of expectation and interpretation in medieval culture. In early Christianity the mortified body was a site for glorious triumph over the world and human frailty; the body rose from it pulled by eschatological powers which made bearable and meaningful the sufferings of the flesh. . . . In medieval culture representations of the body sometimes powerfully assimilated it into moments of agonising sacrificial torment within the language of religion, occasions on which it was made most human, suffering, passing, feminine, tormented, vulnerable. At such moments frailty and humanity were celebrated, and thus expressed a pact between the supernatural and the natural, earthly and heavenly, the godly and the human. It was a symbol of many reconciliations.

The body is always a complex image, and eating the body is a particularly disturbing one especially that of eating a sacrificed body, sometimes in the form of a child's body. The juxtaposition of simplest natural act, of eating, with the holiest and most taboo-ridden of nourishments, the human body, associates acts and symbols which in any other contexts would be abhorrent and unutterable. Cannibalism is never absent from any society, either in the form of threats, or in rumours and tales about such transgression in cases of extreme need and hunger. But in the eucharist God's body was said to be eaten, blood, flesh and all, as a matter of course. Heretics homed in on the horror of it, just as Christians had once accused pagans of cannibalistic excesses, and as ritual murder accusations imputed the sacrifice and eating of a child to the Jews. It is probably best to go no further into psychological speculation on the meaning of all this. We know too little about the inner workings of minds to be able to assess the impact of invocation of the taboo of eating human flesh, the fears and desires related to it. But what we can assert is that by combining the most holy with the most aberrant/abhorrent, the routine workings of sacramental power—an image of the fulness of life-giving, which dwells in the image of utmost transgression—a very powerful symbol was created, as awesome as it was promising. In the elaboration of perfectly orthodox tales of eucharistic miracles in which flesh stuck in believers' throats, in which a child appeared in a host poised for the priest's consumption, transgression of taboo was sanctioned in limited areas. This area of the symbolic gave the occasion for playing with things dangerous, and going away from them unscathed.

There are, of course, issues . . . such as a comparison between the Byzantine cultural world and that of Western Europe. The sacred was highly mystified in Byzantine ritual; it was not parcelled and pinpointed but rather unfolded in a *déroulement*, in a whole drama of liturgical interaction which never settled for a particular climax. The varieties of Byzantine eucharistic sentiment only partially overlapped with those that developed in the West from the twelfth century. Whereas in the East the mass remained a very solemn unfolding of sacerdotal mystery, part of which was not only hidden by the priest's body, as in the West, but took place behind a screen, in the West forms of parcelling and allocation, sharing and consumption of the holy were developing and the attendant procedures and routines spelt out.

SELECTION 9:

Personal Piety

Religious experiences were not always controlled by the church, as the experience of St. Francis indicates. His attempts to imitate the life of

Christ and the growth of a large following was eventually accepted by the official church. Others, however, in the High and late Middle Ages also had personal experiences of God that were not so readily accepted by the church; the established forms of religion were not always adequate for many who sought a more intense and more personal religious experience. One of the most popular writers was an uneducated woman named Margery Kempe. In what has come to be known as The Book of Margery Kempe, *she describes her life and her visions of Jesus Christ.*

She desired many times that her head might be smitten off with an axe upon a block for the love of our Lord Jesu. Then said our Lord Jesu in her mind: "I thank thee, daughter, that thou wouldest die for My love; for as often as thou thinkest so, thou shalt have the same meed in heaven, as if thou suffredest the same death, and yet there shall no man slay thee.

"I assure thee in thy mind, if it were possible for Me to suffer pain again, as I have done before, Me were lever to suffer as much pain as ever I did for thy soul alone, rather than thou shouldest depart from Me everlastingly.

"Daughter, thou mayst no better please God, than to think continually in His love."

Then she asked our Lord Jesu Christ, how she should best love Him. And our Lord said: "Have mind of thy wickedness, and think on My goodness.

"Daughter, if thou wear the habergeon or the hair, fasting bread and water, and if thou saidest every day a thousand Pater Nosters, thou shalt not please Me so well as thou dost when thou art in silence, and suffrest Me to speak in thy soul.

"Daughter, for to bid many beads, it is good to them that can not better do, and yet it is not perfect. But it is a good way toward perfection. For I tell thee, daughter, they that be great fasters, and great doers of penance, they would that it should be holden the best life. And they that give them unto many devotions, they would have that the best life. And those that give much almesse, they would that it were holden the best life. And I have often told thee, daughter, that thinking, weeping, and high contemplation is the best life in earth, and thou shalt have more merit in heaven for one year thinking in thy mind than for an hundred year of praying with thy mouth; and yet thou wilt not believe Me, for thou wilt bid many beads.

"Daughter, if thou knew how sweet thy love is to Me, thou wouldest never do other thing but love Me with all thine heart.

"Daughter, if thou wilt be high with Me in heaven, keep Me alway in thy mind as much as thou mayst, and forget not Me at thy meat; but think alway that I sit in thine heart and know every thought that is therein, both good and bad.

"Daughter, I have suffered many pains for thy love; therefore thou hast great cause to love Me right well, for I have bought thy love full dear."

"Dear Lord," she said, "I pray Thee, let me never have other joy in earth, but mourning and weeping for Thy love; for me thinketh, Lord, though I were in hell, if I might weep there and mourn for Thy love as I do here, hell should not noye [annoy] me, but it should be a manner of heaven. For Thy love putteth away all manner of dread of our ghostly enemy; for I had lever be there, as long as Thou wouldest, and please Thee, than to be in this world and displease Thee; therefore, good Lord, as Thou wilt, so may it be."

She had great wonder that our Lord would become man, and suffer so grievous pains, for her that was so unkind a creature to Him. And then, with great weeping, she asked our Lord Jesu how she might best please Him; and He answered to her soul, saying: "Daughter, have mind of thy wickedness, and think on My goodness." Then she prayed many times and often these words: "Lord, for Thy great goodness, have mercy on my great wickedness, as certainly as I was never so wicked as Thou art good, nor never may be though I would; for Thou art so good, that Thou mayst no

From *Treatise of Contemplation*, by Margery Kempe, translation on the Christian Classics Ethereal Library (CCEL) at http://www.ccel.org/g/gardner/cell/cell16.htm.

202 WESTERN CIVILIZATION, VOLUME I

better be; and, therefore, it is great wonder that ever any man should be departed from Thee without end." When she saw the Crucifix, or if she saw a man had a wound, or a beast, or if a man beat a child before her, or smote a horse or another beast with a whip, if she might see it or hear it, she thought she saw our Lord beaten or wounded, like as she saw in the man or in the beast.

The more she increased in love and in devotion, the more she increased in sorrow and contrition, in lowliness and meekness, and in holy dread of our Lord Jesu, and in knowledge of her own frailty. So that if she saw any creature be punished or sharply chastised, she would think that she had been more worthy to be chastised than that creature was, for her unkindness against God. Then would she weep for her own sin, and for compassion of that creature.

Our Lord said to her: "In nothing that thou dost or sayest, daughter, thou mayst no better please God than believe that He loveth thee. For, if it were possible that I might weep with thee, I would weep with thee for the compassion that I have of thee."

Our merciful Lord Jesu Christ drew this creature unto His love, and to the mind of His passion, that she might not endure to behold a leper, or another sick man, specially if he had any wounds appearing on him. So she wept as if she had seen our Lord Jesu with His wounds bleeding; and so she did, in the sight of the soul; for, through the beholding of the sick man, her mind was all ravished in to our Lord Jesu, that she had great mourning and sorrowing that she might not kiss the leper when she met them in the way, for the love of our Lord: which was all contrary to her disposition in the years of her youth and prosperity, for then she abhorred them most.

Our Lord said: "Daughter, thou hast desired in thy mind to have many priests in the town of Lynn, that might sing and read night and day for to serve Me, worship Me, and praise Me, and thank Me for the goodness that I have done to thee in earth; and therefore, daughter, I promise thee that thou shalt have meed and reward in heaven for the good wills and good desires, as if thou haddest done them in deed.

"Daughter, thou shalt have as great meed and as great reward with Me in heaven, for thy good service and thy good deeds that thou hast done in thy mind, as if thou haddest done the same with thy bodily wits withoutforth.

"And, daughter, I thank thee for the charity that thou hast to all lecherous men and women; for thou prayest for them and weepest for them many a tear, desiring that I should deliver them out of sin, and be as gracious to them as I was to Mary Magdalene, that they might have as much grace to love Me as Mary Magdalene had; and with this condition thou wouldest that everich [everyone] of them should have twenty pounds a year to love and praise Me; and, daughter, this great charity which thou hast to them in thy prayer pleaseth Me right well. And, daughter, also I thank thee for the charity which thou hast in thy prayer, when thou prayest for all Jews and Saracens, and all heathen people that they should come to Christian faith, that My name might be magnified in them. Furthermore, daughter, I thank thee for the general charity that thou hast to all people that be now in this world, and to all those that are to come unto the world's end; that thou wouldest be hacked as small as flesh to the pot for their love, so that I would by thy death save them all from damnation, if it pleased Me. And, therefore, daughter, for all these good wills and desires, thou shalt have full meed and reward in heaven, believe it right well and doubt never a deal."

She said: "Good Lord, I would be laid naked upon an hurdle for Thy love, all men to wonder on me and to cast filth and dirt on me, and be drawn from town to town every day my life time, if Thou were pleased thereby, and no man's soul hindered. Thy will be fulfilled and not mine."

"Daughter," He said, "as oftentimes as thou sayest or thinkest: *Worshipped be all the holy places in Jerusalem, where Christ suffered bitter pain and passion in:* thou shalt have the same pardon as if thou were there with thy bodily presence, both to thyself and to all those that thou wilt give to.

"The same pardon that was granted thee aforetime, it was confirmed on Saint Nicholas day, that is to say, playne [plenary] remission; and it is not only granted to thee, but also to all those that believe, and to all those that shall believe unto the world's end, that God loveth thee, and shall thank God for thee. If they will forsake their sin, and be in full will no more to turn again thereto, but be sorry and heavy for that they have done, and will do due penance therefore, they shall have the same pardon that is granted to thyself; and that is all the pardon that is in Jerusalem, as was granted thee when thou were at Rafnys."

That day that she suffered no tribulation for our Lord's sake, she was not merry nor glad, as that day when she suffered tribulation.

Our Lord Jesu said unto her: "Patience is more worth than miracles doing. Daughter, it is more pleasure to Me that thou suffer despites, scorns, shames, reproofs, wrongs, and diseases, than if thine head were stricken off three times a day every day in seven year."

"Lord," she said, "for Thy great pain have mercy on my little pain."

When she was in great trouble, our Lord said: "Daughter, I must needs comfort thee, for now thou hast the right way to heaven. By this way came I and all My disciples; for now thou shalt know the better what sorrow and shame I suffered for thy love, and thou shalt have the more compassion when thou thinkest on My passion."

"O my dear worthy Lord," said she, "these graces Thou shouldest shew to religious men and to priests."

Our Lord said to her again: "Nay, nay, daughter, for that I love best that they love not, and that is shames, reproofs, scorns, and despites of the people; and therefore they shall not have this grace; for, daughter, he that dreadeth the shames of this world may not perfectly love God."

After reading this selection and the previous one, consider these questions:
1. What is the feast of Corpus Christi?
2. According to Miri Rubin, what is the meaning of the feast of Corpus Christi?
3. How does Margery Kempe define Christian piety?

CHAPTER 11
The Harvest of the Middle Ages

As with the supposed end of antiquity and the Fall of the Roman Empire, the notion of the "end" of the Middle Ages or even of the "senility" of medieval civilization is problematic. These "endings" mark less an event that can be clearly dated and described through reference to obvious facts than periods of major transformation within the civilization that are open to various interpretations. As such they raise questions of what within the civilization is transferred to succeeding centuries and what is not. But even this formulation is a bit too simplistic, since the problem of transference is itself not an event but a process. Systems of land ownership, for instance, with the modes of communal agriculture, manorialism, and serfdom, developed through the centuries of the early and High Middle Ages and continued in western Europe until the seventeenth and eighteenth centuries (and in central and eastern Europe until the nineteenth and even twentieth centuries). Town life, with its notions of guild organization and communal rights, also continued to develop along lines originally laid out in the eleventh and twelfth centuries until the abolition of guild regulations and the rise of new industrial towns in modern times. Medieval concepts of government as well, based on feudal bonds of loyalty, though greatly altered in the sixteenth and seventeenth centuries, were not greatly altered and redefined until they were radically redefined in the eighteenth and nineteenth centuries. The same is true of the university. Although they grew out of their original religious forms and began to serve wider and more secular aims, they continued in their basic medieval forms and organization.

What did change in the late Middle Ages? Why do some historians still speak of the "end" of medieval civilization? These questions will not be fully answered in this chapter. Rather, they will form the basis of unit 3 of this volume, in which we consider the problem of what constitutes early modern Europe. In this chapter, we will begin to see how several historians look at medieval civilization in the fourteenth and fifteenth centuries.

A number of historians have emphasized how there was a greater concentration of power in the hands of the secular monarchies in these centuries. As power accrued to the center, earlier feudal notions of shared power between king and nobles were challenged. There also was a sharp decline in the spiritual leadership of the Roman Catholic Church and its faltering hierarchical organization. The decline in the power of the church seems to have reached a climactic moment in what is called "the Babylonian Captivity of the Church." For over a century, from the early fourteenth into the early fifteenth centuries, the French king not only determined the appointments of the popes but also transferred the papal court from Rome to the town of Avignon in southern France. On the heels of this move, there developed what is called "the Great Schism" of the church, in which two or sometimes three claimants vied for the papal throne. What has also fascinated historians is that knighthood itself seems to have become transformed in these centuries. While there was a clear move to redefine the position and function of warriors in Christian terms in the High Middle Ages (and the Crusades mark an important turning point in this process), the final centuries of medieval Europe saw the development of new and extravagant forms of knighthood. At least in its ideal form, knighthood became defined in terms of a code of chivalry and even merged with notions of romantic love.

SELECTION 1:

Chivalry Defined

Ramón Lull (ca. 1235–1315) gave one of the clearest definitions of chivalry. Himself the son of a famous soldier on the island of Majorca in the western Mediterranean, Lull served in the court of King James II of Aragon before experiencing a vision of the crucified Christ. He subsequently devoted his life to the conversion of the Saracens, traveling several times to Africa. In pursuance of this goal, Lull also set up a college in Majorca to teach monks the Arabic language. He wrote widely on many topics, including what became known as Lullian logic. Lull was stoned to death by Arabs in 1315. The following selection is drawn from the thirteenth-century Book of the Order of Chivalry.

It is to the praise and glory of God, Lord and Sovereign of all heavenly and earthly things that I begin this treatise concerning the order of chivalry so as to show that in the same way as God, the almighty Prince, rules the seven planets

From The Book of the Order of Chivalry, by Ramón Lull, edited by Alfred T.P. Byles, translated by Graham Pendreigh (London: Early English Text Society, 1926).

traversing the heavens and has power and dominion in government, as well as regulating earthly bodies, so kings, princes and lords should have authority and command over knights. Similarly these knights ought to have power and domination over those of middle standing.

Regarding the Office of the Knight

This office is the origin and end of the chivalric order: if any knight does not put his office to good use, he is acting contrary to the order and purpose of chivalry and is accordingly not truly a knight, even if he has that title. Such a knight is baser than a smith or a carpenter who undertakes the requirements of his particular trade, having learned what is involved in the craft. It is the duty of the knight to preserve and defend the Holy Catholic faith, by which God the Father sent His Son into the world to take upon human flesh in the glorious Virgin, our Lady and Saint, Mary. . . . As our Lord God has chosen the clergy to safeguard the Holy Catholic faith by means of Scripture and reason against heretics and infidels, He has similarly appointed knights to defeat those heretics continually striving to destroy the church. God holds the knights as friends, honored both in this world and the next, when they uphold the faith by which we look to our salvation. . . . There are many who hold offices bestowed upon them in this world by God, by which He might be served and revered, but the most honorable are the offices of clergy and knights.

Chivalry is so noble that each knight should govern a sizable region or territory, but because there are so many knights that there is not enough land to indicate that one person is paramount. The Emperor ought to be a knight and the Commander of the knights, but as he cannot rule directly over all the knights himself, he has to have kings, themselves knights, beneath him to assist in upholding chivalry. In their turn, kings must have authority over dukes, earls, counts and other nobility. Below the barons are the knights themselves. . . .

It is the duty of the knight to obey and defend his temporal lord, since a king or noble cannot command his retinue without some help. If anyone acts contrary to the will of a prince, knights are obligated to come to the aid of their lord. . . .

A perverse knight who would rather aid rebels depose his lord from his rightful position, does not conduct himself as a knight.

Justice must be upheld by knights. . . . Knights should joust on horseback and participate in tournaments; they should hold an open table; they should hunt stags, boars and other wild animals because in doing so they exercise their martial prowess, so as to maintain chivalry. . . . As all these activities are essential to the nature of the knight, so justice, humility, strength, hope, swiftness and all other virtues are integral to the soul of the knight. If he engages in all the outward aspects of the order and lacks the inner virtues, he is an enemy of the order.

It is the duty of the knight to maintain the land, as it is because of the dread with which the peasants view knights that they work and cultivate the soil. On account of this fear of the power of the knight, they also fear the king and other nobles from whom the authority of the knight proceeds.

It is the duty of the knight to defend women, and widows and orphans as well as those men unable to defend themselves on account of physical infirmities. As both custom and reason dictate that the strongest aid the weak, who in turn should be able to rely upon the mighty, the order of chivalry is just since it possesses honor and power, helping those of less honor and power than the knight.

The office requires both a castle and a horse so that the knight may maintain the highways and defend peasants. In addition, knights should have authority in the towns in order to administer justice to all and to gather together craftsmen whose skills are essential for the preservation of daily life among the populace.

How Is a Squire Admitted to the Order of Chivalry?

When entering the order, a squire must make confession and then receive chivalry with the intent that he will serve God, a glorious calling. If cleansed of his sin, he should receive his Savior. The conferral of knighthood is appropriate on some important feast day, such as Christmas, Easter, Whitsuntide or any other solemn day, because many people are likely to come together on account of the festivities where the ceremony is to be performed. On this occasion, prayers of adoration and supplication should be made to God, asking that the squire be given grace to live in accordance with the order of chivalry. The squire must fast on the vigil of the feast in honor of the saint whose day it is, and during the night he must attend church to pray and to hear preaching of the Scriptures. . . . On the morning following the feast, the squire must attend a solemn Mass, and approaching the altar of the priest, the representative of God, the honor due to the Almighty, vowing to keep chivalric honor with all his power. On the same day, a sermon recounting the twelve articles of the Holy Catholic faith, the Ten Commandments, the seven sacraments and other tenets is to be delivered. . . .

The squire then must kneel before the altar and raise both his bodily and spiritual eyes, as well as his hands, toward heaven. The knight will make the sign of chastity, justice and charity upon him with his sword and then kissing the squire, offer his hand so that the squire will remember what he has received and promised, the great obligation to which he now is bound, and be mindful of the honor that has come upon him through the order of chivalry.

When the spiritual knight, namely the priest, and the temporal knight have performed these re-quirements for making this new knight, he in turn must ride through the town presenting himself to all, so that they will be aware and see that knighthood has been conferred upon him.

Regarding the Importance of the Arms of the Knight

As the vestments of a priest performing the Mass are indicative of his office, there is some similarity between the priesthood and knighthood. Chivalry dictates that all aspects of knighthood ought to designate the nobility of the order. The knight is presented with a sword made in the form of a cross signifying that our Lord God overcame the death of the human lineage on that cross on which he was condemned for the sinfulness of our first father Adam. So, the knight must overwhelm and defeat the enemies of the cross with his sword. As it is the object of chivalry to maintain justice, the sword is sharpened on both edges to denote that it is by this sword that the knight preserves both the chivalric code and justice. A spear, which is both straight and evenly balanced, is also given to the knight to symbolize truth and that truth precedes falseness. The iron head of the spear signifies the strength which truth has over falsity, and, the pennon signifies that truth manifests faith to all, having no fear of falsehood or treachery.

SELECTION 2:

Chivalry in Practice

Historian Arno Borst places Ramón Lull's conception of chivalry within a larger context. He claims that there were several competing ways to define Christian knighthood, one of which clearly emphasizes the forms of romantic love the knight offered to his lady.

From *Medieval Worlds: Barbarians, Heretics, and Artists in the Middle Ages*, by Arno Borst, translated by Eric Hansen (Chicago: University of Chicago Press, 1992). English translation © Polity Press 1992. Reprinted by permission of the publisher.

All the more astonishing, then, is the change, developing in the lower nobility, that spread chivalry throughout all Europe, initially in France of the late eleventh century and proceeding through all of Germany and as far as Portugal, Sweden and Hungary. Hot-headed warriors everywhere were disciplined and organized thanks to growing large-scale principalities, to the awe of sacral monarchial anointment and to church reforms that regulated aristocratic feuds under the Peace of God. It became rare for knights to fight against plundering strangers; now they were summoned to the crusade against the heathens of the Orient. A new adventure! One knight was so excited about it he exclaimed: 'Even if I were in paradise, I would come down again to fight the Muslims!' In foreign countries, the lords learned service, largely because they had begun thinking of themselves as an international community and had learned to pay attention to the opinions of their peers. Since around 1100, they had been calling themselves by names that had similar origins in all languages: *chevaliers*, *Ritter*, *cavalieri*, *caballeros*, knights, and considering themselves as an order with specific initiation rites, a code of honour and the ideals of aristocratic power and cavalry service.

Just whom the new men's club was meant to serve, however, was never really clear. At least three chivalric prototypes were propagated by clerics, singers and poets in the twelfth and thirteenth centuries, but these were hardly compatible with each other, nor with real life. The first of these prototypes was the Christ-like knight, God's warrior, the strong serving the weak. His job was to help the church, priests, widows, orphans, sick, pilgrims, animals and possibly even heathens. His selfless service was meant to overcome the disorder of the world and spread justice; his ascetic discipline was meant to elevate his earthly life and guarantee an eternal one. In 1159, the English cleric John of Salisbury wrote in his *Policraticus:* 'What purpose does ordained knighthood serve? To protect the church, to battle against disloyalty, to honour the office of the priesthood, to put an end to injustice towards the poor, to bring peace to the land, to let his own blood be spilled for his brothers, and, if necessary, to give up his own life.' Part of this ideal was personified in the crusades and the orders of knighthood, but mostly it remained theory. One

has only to compare John of Salisbury's catalogue of virtues with the catalogue of vices of which the French Cistercian monk, Alan of Lille, accused the nobility in his handbook of sermons from around 1200:

> In our day, knights have become predators and robbers; they no longer serve in war but in plunder, and under the cloak of chivalry they practise the cruelty of highwaymen. They battle not against enemies, but rage against the poor; those whom they should defend with the shield of their protection, they persecute with the sword of their wildness.

Though this severe complaint may be exaggerated in part, it shows what the chronicles confirm: the chivalric community was not filled with monastic devotion.

The second prototype, that of the gallant knight, was more loved than that of the Christ-like one. This knight was to serve his 'gracious lady', and might go so far, at times, as to address her as such: she was usually the wife of another man. He was to court her with elegant songs and do battle to increase her glory. It was the stubborn hope for love reciprocated in secret, an unresolved tension meant to elevate the lover. Should the coveted lady refuse, discipline and manners must force the man to maintain his self-control. The reality of love became a game of the seductive moment, an 'if' suspended in the air, and the slightest glance was practically fulfilment. An example, taken from French poetry, is the Breton *Lai de l'Ombre* from around 1200. The knight stands beside a well with his beloved lady, and gives her, as a token of his love, a golden ring. She refuses it. Seeing her reflection in the water of the well, he says: 'Then I will give this ring to my beautiful mistress, whom I love most next to you.' 'Who is that?' asks the lady with growing jealousy. 'Your shadow,' says the knight, and casts the ring into the well. Such noble prodigality characterizes many nobles of the time. Most of them, however, appear closer to its opposite, the image of greed; this image is not absent from poetry either. In the Spanish *Cantar de mio Cid*, composed around 1140, the two distinguished *infantes* of Carrión solicit the hands of the Cid's two daughters only in the hope of getting hold of the Cid's rich war spoils. As soon as they have the dowry, they drag their wives into a forest, rape them, beat them half dead and leave them lying there. . . . Gallantry, though certainly desired, was often rejected on grounds of bare necessity. For nobles not firstborn, the hunt for a rich heiress was the search for a basis of survival, and this battle for existence was not always polite. The prototype was even less effective with the older knights, who were more settled in their ways and already had wives and estates. Not every honourable family father was ready, like the knight [and thirteenth-century poet] Ulrich of Lichtenstein, to sip his beloved's bath water or chop off his own finger for love. A minnesinger was once mocked by his audience, who told him that instead of a juicy roast as payment for his entertainment, he should get what he had been in raptures about: flowers and the twittering of birds, with a little water. And [German minnesinger] Wolfram von Eschenbach said plainly that the true concern of a man was battle service, not minstrelsy. It was a simple fact of life that a community of knighthood could not be based on gallantry.

Wolfram belonged to the propagators of the third chivalric prototype, that of the courtly knight. This knight . . . performed purposeless tasks in enchanted forests, not for his own profit, but for the good of King Arthur's chivalric round table. Splendidly surrounded by fine weapons, robes and horses, the courtly knight would further the standards of his group: love and honour. He should be neither too gallant nor too devout; he would seek the extreme situations of chance in order to gain chivalric character. God and man would drive this knight into unprecedented dangers all alone; not until he had survived them with impeccable dignity would the courtly community accept him into their circle. Again, an example from poetry, this time German, from *Iwein* of Hartmann von Aue. In the enchanted forest of Breziljan, a knight encounters a terrifying giant surrounded by wild animals. But the monster remains peaceful. The knight calls out challengingly that he seeks adventure, namely a battle with someone, at which the forest giant shakes his head and says what any of us might have said: that he has never heard of anyone who strove for

hardship and did not prefer to live comfortably. He sends the knight deeper into the enchanted forest; perhaps he will find adventure there. In the French original, from which Hartmann adapted his epic poem, the *Yvain* of Chrétien de Troyes, the knight introduces himself by saying: 'I am, as you can see, a knight, who looks for what he cannot find; already I have searched long, but have found nothing.' One could not admit more clearly that this prototype followed unrealistic goals, far from the real world. The nobility of the twelfth and thirteenth century actually greeted hardship only when it appeared a means for gaining a more comfortable future at the expense of their fellow men and competitors.

All three literary prototypes were unrealistic for the knight of the twelfth and thirteenth centuries. In France, many knights had to live down in the villages, working behind the plough, letting rust slowly devour their armour. In Wolfram's Frankish castle, not even mice had enough to eat; another German poet lamented that knights never talked about Parsifal [the heroic knight from Wolfram's poem], but only about crops and milch cows. They had no time to fight dragons and sorceresses in the wilderness, and they had no chance of choosing between service to God, to the lady or to the court. Not even [the German poet] Walther von der Vogelweide had good advice to offer on how to place the three prototypes into one shrine, how to unite them in the hearts of men. Yet nearly everyone learned something from these ideals: they respected the church, courted the women and hurried to court. We should not underestimate the self-declarations of such chivalric prototypes; they encouraged moral and mannered behaviour. Yet, ideally, could they have been more than aesthetic norms, pretty gestures, exchangeable pretexts? This question must be tested on an actual case, on the behaviour of a knight in the face of danger, and for this we need not the poets, but the chroniclers. . . .

None the less, the lords and burghers, the champions of the Later Middle Ages, loved imitating chivalric lifestyles. From about 1344, the English King Edward III had been seized by a desire to reconstruct at Windsor Castle the legendary Round Table of King Arthur; 300 years before Don Quixote, errant knights actually wandered through the forests of Spain. Through all this, it becomes clear that chivalric lifestyles were being conveyed not by literary models, but by social attitudes; those who no longer understood their roles confused the ideal with the real, they flattered themselves with fine gestures that meant nothing. Crusade vows, for example, were a part of good chivalrous manners up to the late fifteenth century; but ever since the death of Louis IX (St Louis) in 1270, no army or knightly host ever made their vows good. Christian rulers in the Later Middle Ages arranged dozens of knightly jousts among themselves in order to resolve political conflicts; not a single one of these duels ever took place. The aims and means of combat had changed; only the label of knighthood remained.

Now, six-year-old sons of princes were being dubbed knights, as well as financiers and royal scholarly advisers. Orders of knights existed only to serve the courtly pageantry of the lords, the Burgundian Order of the Golden Fleece, for example, the English Order of the Garter, or a certain Catalan order that accepted only women as members, yet called itself the 'Order of the Axe'. These playful fraternities were no longer an essential part of life; they developed quickly into our modern orders, which are nothing more than factories turning out badges of honour. The 'chevalier' became the 'cavalier', the 'squire' became the 'page' on smooth parquet floors. Courtly festivals were moved from fortresses to palaces, from the open air into the halls, from day to night, and the common people stayed outside. The dances turned to ballets, the tournament to a masquerade ball or to a contest between professional wrestlers, where points were counted to determine the winner. The old knights, on the other hand, went to the courts as officers or officials or to the city as patricians or merchants. Those who could not join in the march of time drew closer together in their aristocracy and farther away from everything else, an exclusive birth rank with no social function but that of maintaining their own dignity. Except for a few true robber barons, they all knew precisely what behaviour was fitting; but the formal label could hardly hide the isolation of their lives. The game had lost its earnestness and its participants. Before the decisive battle with the English at Crécy in 1346, the French King Philip VI sent out a scout team of four knights to reconnoitre the English position. When they returned, impatiently anticipated and bearing the message on which the French strategy depended, they put on a show of politeness; each insisted on modestly remaining silent, no one wanted to make his report before the others. This was the same attitude for which [crusader] Eberhard von Siverey had given his life 100 years earlier [as a vassal of Jeande Joinville]; only this time it no longer served common interests, but only damaged them. The duo of chivalrous service and chivalrous play, one dependent upon the other, had split up long before [German painter and engraver Albrecht] Dürer began portraying the purely idealistic knight.

After reading this selection and the previous one, consider these questions:

1. How does Ramón Lull define the main features of chivalry?
2. What was the relationship between the knight and God?
3. What were the various orders of chivalry and what was their purpose in the High and late Middle Ages?

SELECTION 3:

Romantic Love

Well-known comparative mythologist Joseph Campbell argues that the development of romantic love in the late Middle Ages marked one of the most distinctive components of Western (as opposed to Eastern) civilization. Romantic love defined a new relationship between men and women. Love was no longer just a form of sexual gratification, and marriage was no longer just a property arrangement or a form of alliance between families. In this selection, Campbell emphasizes the spiritualization of love and the changed values that medieval notions of romance brought about. He also sees in the literary expressions of romantic love, as well as in the Arthurian romances as a whole, a greater emphasis on the importance of the individual and his striving to achieve goals. Compared to the models of Greek aretē, Roman virtue, and Christian asceticism—all of which were universal and thus impersonal in their formulations—this move to find more individually specific forms of giving worth to human life indicated a clear break from earlier traditions. For Campbell, the ideals associated with romantic love and individualized values did not come to an end with the close of the Middle Ages; they are still foundational to the modern West.

In the following selection, Campbell interprets the main actions of Wolfram von Eschenbach's great medieval poem, Parzival. *Campbell begins his interpretation with the setting out of the young and untried knight, Parzival.*

[The Knight Parzival] rides off. Again the reins are slack on the neck of the horse, and that evening he pulls up at a lake. Out in the lake there's a boat, and in it are two men fishing, and one of them has peacock feathers in his bonnet. This is the Grail King, who is, in this story, symbolic of the whole problem of the Waste Land. The Grail King did not earn his position, he inherited it. When he was a beautiful young man, one fine day he rode out of the palace with the war cry *"Amors!"*

That's all right for a nice young man, but it's not the proper intention of the keeper of the Grail, a symbol of the highest spiritual fulfill-

ment. . . . As he was riding out, he came to a forest. Out of the forest came riding a pagan knight from the Holy Land near the place of the Holy Sepulcher. The two knights placed their lances and rode at each other. The Grail King's lance killed the pagan knight, and the pagan knight's lance castrated the king and broke the tip of the lance remaining in the wound.

What is Wolfram telling us? He is telling us that the spiritual ideal of the Middle Ages, which distinguished supernatural from natural grace, has castrated Europe. The natural grace—the movement of the horse—is not allowed, is not what dictates life. What dictates life is supernatural grace, this notion of some spiritual thing that comes by way of the cardinals of the church telling you what's good and what's bad. Nature has been killed in Europe. The energy of nature—this is Wolfram's lesson, and he says it—

From pages 254–60 of *Transformations of Myth Through Time*, by Joseph Campbell. Copyright © 1990 by Mythology Ltd. Reprinted by permission of HarperCollins Publishers, Inc., and of the Joseph Campbell Foundation (www.jcf.org).

has been killed. The death of that pagan knight symbolizes it, and the spiritual impotence of the Grail King is the consequence.

The Grail King, in terrific pain, rode back to the court. When the lance tip was withdrawn from his wound, on it was the word *Grail*. The meaning of this is: the natural tendency of nature is to the spirit, whereas he—the lord of the spirit—had rejected nature. The Waste Land. How is the Waste Land going to be cured? The answer is by the spontaneous act of a noble heart, whose impulse is not of ego but of love—and love in the sense not of sexual love, but of compassion. That's the Grail problem.

Parzival, on the shore, says, "Look, it's getting late, is there someplace around here where a person can spend the night?" The king himself says, "Around the corner you'll see a castle; give a call, they'll let the drawbridge down. If you can get there, and don't get lost—a lot of people get lost here—I'll see you tonight. I'll be your host." It all works out. He arrives at the castle and is received with great expectation.

Now, the interesting thing about enchantment is that the people who are enchanted know how the enchantment is to be lifted, but they can't lift it. The one who is to lift the enchantment does not know how it is to be lifted, but by his spontaneous act he does the thing that has to be done. So these people know that a knight will come and through the proper act lift the enchantment. They think, "Here he is, this beautiful boy."

That evening there is an enormous festival in the great hall—symbolically rendered, beautifully, by Wolfram—and in the course of it, the king is brought in on a litter. He can neither stand nor sit nor lie. T.S. Eliot takes that line right out of Wolfram von Eschenbach and uses it in [his 1922 poem] *The Waste Land:* "Here one can neither sit nor stand nor lie down." And Parzival—here's the key now, this is the crisis of the story—is filled with compassion and is moved to ask, "What ails you, uncle?" But immediately he thinks, "A knight does not ask questions." And so, in the name of his social image, he continues the Waste Land principle of acting according to the way you've been told to act instead of the way of the spontaneity of your noble nature.

The adventure fails. The king is very cordial, polite. Everyone knows what has happened, but Parzival doesn't. The king, as the host, gives his guest a present, a sword. It is a sword which is going to break at a critical moment, just as he broke at a critical moment. He's ushered to his room, put sweetly to bed, and when he gets up in the morning, there isn't a soul in the castle, the place is completely quiet. He looks out the window; there's his horse, with his lance and shield. He doesn't know what's happened. He goes down, gets on the horse, and as he rides across the drawbridge, it is lifted just a little too soon and clips the horse's heels. A voice shouts at him, "Go on, you goose!". . .

Parzival spends the next five years trying to get back to that castle. He rides around not knowing where he is, what he's doing, people cursing him. [King] Arthur's court, meanwhile, has gone to find this great guy. So one fine morning in early winter, he's riding on his horse looking for the castle. He can't find it. Although it's right where it was and he's right where it was, it's not visible to him. He sees red blood and black feathers on the white snow where a falcon has attacked a goose. It reminds him of [his wife] Condwiramurs, her red lips, her white skin, her black hair. He's fascinated, in a love trance.

Meanwhile, Arthur's court arrives, with their pavilions and tents. A young page sees in the distance this knight sitting on his horse just gazing at the snow. He rousts the court, and Sir Segramors, an eager young knight, dashes into Arthur's tent, snatches the covers off Arthur and Guinevere—there they are stark naked—and pleads to be the first to ride against the unknown knight. Laughing, they consent, and he rides out against the entranced Parzival, whose horse—this marvelous horse—simply turns so that Parzival's lance sends Segramors flying. So they send Sir Keie, the lout of Arthur's group, who also gets thrown, and ends up with a broken arm and leg. Then they send Sir Gawain, who goes out unarmed. Now Gawain's around thirty-six or so. He's been around. He's known as the lady's knight. He sees Parzival in absorbed arrest and says to himself, "This is a love trance." So he flings his big yellow scarf so that it falls over the sign on the snow. Parzival's trance is broken, they have a courteous conversation, and Gawain invites him to Arthur's court.

So he brings Parzival to Arthur's court. The court welcomes him delightedly, and they set up a picnic. On a flowery field they spread a great big circular cloth of Orient silk, and all sit around it—knight, lady, knight, lady—and await the adventure that must precede their meal. And then, on the horizon, they see a tall, sort of pinkish mule, and riding on the mule is a lady, with a face like a boar and hands that are about as beautiful as those of a monkey, and she has a very fashionable hat from London hanging down in back. This is the Grail messenger. She rides directly to Arthur and says, "You are disgraced forever, receiving into your court this foul monster here." And then she goes to Parzival and says, "Despite the beauty of your face you are more ugly than I." Then she tells what he did and says, "God's curse is on you." Turning to the company, she says, "I have another adventure to suggest. There is a castle with four hundred knights and four hundred ladies that's under enchantment. Who will go on that?"

Several knights take up that adventure, and when Gawain is leaving, he says to the shamed Parzival, "I commit you to God's graces." Parzival says, "I hate God. I have nothing to do with God. I thought I was serving God. I thought doing as I had been told was the sacred thing to do. And look what he's done to me. I'm through with God." Then Parzival leaves and goes off on his quest.

On his quest he comes to a hermitage, and the hermit says, "Come in and have dinner." When he sits down, the hermit says, "Let's say grace." Parzival says, "I don't say grace. I hate God." The hermit, whose name is Trevrizent, says, "You hate God? Who's crazy here? God returns manyfold what you give to him. Give him love, and you will have his love. Give him hate, and you will have his hate." This is an interesting thought, that the relation to God is a function of you. Parzival tells him of his adventure and says, "I'm going to go back to that castle." Trevrizent says, "You can't. The adventure must be done spontaneously, the first time; you can't go back to it." Parzival says, "I'm going to do it." He rides off.

Well, the story goes on and on and on and on, and finally Gawain has rescued the four hundred knights and the four hundred ladies and has, meanwhile, fallen in love. Now, this is a guy who has been with one lady after another and, finally, he is taken. He's riding up a hill one day, when he sees this woman seated with her horse nearby, and he is smitten. He gets off his horse and says, "I'm your man." "Oh," she says, "don't be silly. I don't take things like that." He says, "Well, take 'em or not, I'm your man." She says, "I'll give you a hard time." He says, "You'll only be injuring your own property." And she does give him a hard time—it's a wild story—but Gawain's commitment is steadfast.

The high virtue in all of this is loyalty: in love, loyalty; in marriage, loyalty. This is the high, high virtue of this knightly affair. Well, finally, Gawain solves all the problems for this really mad woman, and they're to be married. So Arthur's court and the four hundred men and four hundred women from the castle that Gawain has disenchanted are assembled for his great marriage, when a solitary knight approaches across the plain. Gawain and the stranger ride at each other and unhorse each other and then find who is who and so forth. The interloper, of course, is Parzival, and so an invitation goes out to him: "We're having a wonderful time here at the marriage of Sir Gawain, be with us." Well, as Wolfram says, "There was love and joy in the pavilions."

But when Parzival sees all this going on, he can't stay there because his own heart is loyal to Condwiramurs, and so out of love for her, he leaves the greatest party the Middle Ages has ever seen and goes riding away. As he's riding, out of the dark forest comes a pagan knight riding toward him—it's the repetition of the old story. The two knights ride at each other, unhorse each other, go at each other with swords, and Parzival's sword breaks on the helmet of the pagan knight, who throws his own sword away and says, "I don't fight a man without weapons. Let's sit down." They sit down and take off their helmets. The pagan knight is black and white. He's Feirefiz, Parzival's brother. So they begin talking about their father.

Parzival then says, "Well, there's a great party

down the way, perhaps you'd enjoy it." So they go back to the party, and Wolfram says the ladies were particularly enchanted by the grace of Feirefiz, probably because of his interesting complexion.

There then appears on the horizon a tall, pink mule, and on it is the lady with the stylish London hat and the face of a boar, and she rides up to Parzival and says, "Come to the Grail castle. Through your loyalty you have achieved the adventure. And bring your friend." Now this is something. Very few Christians could come to the Grail castle, and here the Grail messenger invites a pagan, a Muslim. What counts is your spiritual stature, not whether you were baptized or whether you were circumcised.

So the two come to the castle where the ceremonial adventure takes place. The Grail Maiden comes in. Now it's interesting to recall that the clergy of that period were such an immoral bunch that Pope Innocent III himself called them a sty of pigs. Saint Augustine had implicitly condoned their immorality back in the fifth century, when he responded to the Donatists' heretical declaration that sacraments administered by immoral clergymen don't work, by saying, "No, the sacrament is incorruptible and it doesn't matter." So the clergy's morality didn't matter, and the result was what they had in the twelfth and thirteenth centuries.

The Grail castle, however, is not a church, and the Grail is carried by the Grail Maiden, who is a virgin. She really *is* a virgin. These are people who are what they are said to be, not inauthentic at all. Well, the Grail Maiden is a beautiful girl, and this Muslim has an eye for the girls, and soon people notice that he can't see the Grail, all he can see is the girl. So they begin to murmur and think, Well, he should be baptized. The first time I came to this part of the story I thought, Now, Wolfram, don't, don't, don't let me down. And he didn't.

An old priest comes in with an empty baptismal font made of ruby, and Wolfram says it's an old priest who has converted and baptized

many a heathen. The baptismal font is tipped toward the Grail and fills with Grail water. Now, the name of the Grail is *Lapis exilis,** and that's the name of the philosopher's stone. With this Grail water, then, the pagan is being baptized, when he says, "What's this, what's going on here? What are you people doing?" They say, "We're turning you into a Christian." He says, "What does that mean?" They say, "That means you give up your God and you accept our God." He says, "Is your God her God?" They say, "Yes." He says, "I'm a Christian."

So there he is, baptized, and then, not only does he see the Grail, but there appears on the Grail an inscription.

> If any member of this community should, by the grace of God, become the ruler of an alien people, let him see to it that they are given their rights.

This is the first time, I think, in the history of civilization that such a thought was expressed. The Magna Carta was written 1215 in England, but that was the barons asking for their rights from the king. Here is the idea of the king ruling, not in his name, but in the name of his people. So we have in Wolfram marriage for love, love confirmed through loyalty in marriage, and the king ruling for the people. Big stuff, and in the early thirteenth century.

Then Parzival asks the king, "What ails you?" Immediately, the king is healed, and Parzival himself becomes the Grail King, the guardian of the highest spiritual values—compassion and loyalty. And then his lovely wife arrives, now with two little boys—one of them is Lohengrin—and there's a beautiful scene of reunion.

And finally, Trevrizent—the hermit who had said "You can't do it" when Parzival had said "I am going back to that castle"—says to Parzival, "You, through your tenacity of purpose have changed God's law." That's big talk. The god within us is the one that gives the laws and can change the laws. And it is within us.

---

*Lapis exilis is one of several names for the Grail, all of which are corruptions of an unknown Latin phrase.

SELECTION 4:

Parzival

In the previous selection Joseph Campbell specifically drew attention to German poet Wolfram von Eschenbach's great poem Parzival. Parzival *is one of a number of accounts of the Grail legend. The Grail was the cup that Jesus drank from at the Last Supper. In addition to its historical importance, it was also the cup that originated the sacrament of the Eucharist. Although lost, its recovery became the quest—at least in literature—of a group of knights known as the Grail Knights. The quest itself required singleness of purpose and purity of soul, and the Grail legend exemplified a model of the ideal knight. The following selection is taken from book 9 of* Parzival, *in which the powers of the Grail are identified and its relationship to Anfortas, the fisher king, is defined.*

"**W**ell I know," said his host, "that many brave knights dwell with the Grail at Munsalvaesche. Always when they ride out, as they often do, it is to seek adventure. They do so for their sins, these templars, whether their reward be defeat or victory. A valiant host lives there, and I will tell you how they are sustained. They live from a stone of purest kind. If you do not know it, it shall here be named to you. It is called *lapsit exillis*.* By the power of that stone the phoenix burns to ashes, but the ashes give him life again. Thus does the phoenix molt and change its plumage, which afterward is bright and shining and as lovely as before. There never was a human so ill but that, if he one day sees that stone, he cannot die within the week that follows. And in looks he will not fade. His appearance will stay the same, be it maid or man, as on the day he saw the stone, the same as when the best years of his life began, and though he should see the stone for two hundred years, it will never change, save that

*Lapis exillis is one of several names for the Grail, all of which are corruptions of an unknown Latin phrase.

From *Parzival*, by Wolfram von Eschenbach, translated by Helen M. Mustard and Charles E. Passage. Copyright © 1961 by Helen M. Mustard and Charles E. Passage. Reprinted by permission of Vintage Books, a division of Random House, Inc.

his hair might perhaps turn grey. Such power does the stone give a man that flesh and bones are at once made young again. The stone is also called the Grail. . . ."

Then Parzival spoke and said, "If knighthood with shield and spear can win renown in this life and Paradise for the soul as well—for knighthood I have always striven. I fought wherever I found a battle, and in such way that my armed hand had highest honor within its reach. If God is a good judge of fighting, He should summon me by name to the Grail so that they may come to know me. My hand shall not fail me there in battle."

"But there," said his devout host, "a humble will would have to guard you against pride. Your youth could all too easily tempt you to violate the virtue of moderation. Pride has always sunk and fallen." So said the hermit, and tears welled up in his eyes as he thought of the things which he was about to tell.

Then he said, "Sir, a king was there who was called and is still called Anfortas. You, and I too, poor though I be, should never cease to feel compassion for his grief of heart, which pride gave him as reward. His youth and power brought grief to all around him, and his desire for love beyond all restraint and bounds.

"Such ways are not fitting for the Grail. There

both knight and squire must guard themselves against incontinence. Humility has conquered their pride. A noble brotherhood dwells there, who with valiant strength have warded off the people of all lands so that the Grail is unknown save to those who have been called by name to Munsalvaesche to the Grail's company. Only one came there unbidden. That was a foolish man who took sin away with him, since he said not a word to the king about the distress he could see in him. I make no reproach to anyone, but he will have sin to atone for in not inquiring about his host's affliction. He was so heavily stricken with suffering that never was such great anguish known. . . ."

[Then the hermit said,] "When Frimutel, my father, lost his life, they chose his eldest son to succeed him as king and Lord of the Grail and the Grail's company. That was my brother Anfortas, who was worthy of crown and power. We were still small. Then my brother reached the age when his beard began to grow—the time when Love wages battle with youth. Here Love does not act quite honorably, one must say, for she presses her friend so hard. But if any Lord of the Grail craves a love other than the writing on the Grail allows him, he will suffer distress and grievous misery.

"My lord and brother chose for himself a lady, of virtue, so he thought. Who she was does not matter. In her service he fought as one from whom cowardice has fled. Many a shield's rim was riddled for her by his good hand. With his adventures the sweet and valiant man won such fame that never in all the lands where chivalry held sway could any one question that his was the greatest of all. *Amor* was his battle cry. But that cry is not quite appropriate for a spirit of humility.

"One day the king rode out alone—and sorely did his people rue it—in search of adventure, rejoicing in Love's assistance. Love's desire compelled him to it. With a poisoned spear he was wounded so in the jousting, your sweet uncle, that he never again was healed, pierced through the testicles.

"It was a heathen who fought him in that joust, born in Ethnise, where from Paradise the Tigris flows. This heathen was sure that his valor would win the Grail. Its name was engraved on his spear, and only for the sake of the Grail's power did he seek knightly deeds far off, roaming over sea and land. In this battle our joy was lost to us.

"Your uncle's fighting was deserving of praise; with the iron spearhead in his body he rode away. When that gallant young man came home to his people, great indeed was their grief. The heathen lay dead where he had left him. Let us make lament for him too—but sparingly.

"When the king returned to us so pale and all his strength ebbed away, a physician probed the wound until he found the iron spearhead and a splinter of the reed shaft, and removed them. I fell on my knees and prayed. I made a vow to God Almighty that nevermore would I practice knighthood if only He, for the sake of His own great name, would help my brother from that distress. And I renounced flesh also, and wine and bread, and all things that have blood in them, and swore nevermore to desire them. That caused fresh sorrow for the people, dear nephew—and I am speaking the truth—when I parted with my sword. They said, 'Who shall be the guardian now of the mystery of the Grail?' Bright eyes were weeping there.

"Straightway, hoping for God's help, they carried the king to the Grail. When the king beheld the Grail, that brought him further anguish, since now he could not die. Death was not permitted him, seeing I had dedicated myself to a life of poverty, and the lordship of that noble race hung upon such weak strength.

"The king's wound had festered, and we found no help in all the books of medicine we read. All cures that are known for aspis, ecidemon, ehcontius and lisis, jecis and meatris—these harmful snakes all bear a burning poison—and all that are known for the stings of other venomous serpents, all the herbs wise physicians have found in their study of the art of healing—but let me be brief—none of these could help. God himself denied us their aid.

"We sought help from the Geon and the Fison, the Euphrates and the Tigris, the four streams flowing out of Paradise, and to Paradise we came so near, where its sweet fragrance has still not faded away, to see if perhaps there might come drifting some herb that would take our sorrow from us. It was labor lost. Our grieving began afresh.

"Still we kept on trying various things. We obtained the very bough which the Sibyl had told [the Greek hero] Aeneas would protect him from Hell's pain and from the smoke of the Phlegethon and from the other rivers flowing there. Long did we search till we found that healing bough, thinking perhaps the dreadful spear, which was destroying our joy, might itself have been poisoned and tempered in the fire of hell. But that proved not to be so.

"There is a bird called the pelican. When it has young, it loves them beyond all measure. Its loyal love impels it to bite its own breast and let the blood run into the beaks of the young ones. It dies in that very hour. We secured the blood of this bird, to try if its loyal love would help us too, and we rubbed it as best we could on the wound. That did not help us.

"There is a beast called the unicorn, which is so attracted by the purity of virgins that it falls asleep in their laps. We took a portion of this animal's heart to heal the king's pain. And we took the garnet from the same animal's forehead where it grows beneath the horn. We rubbed the edge of the wound and even inserted the stone into the wound, which seemed to be full of venom. This was painful to us and to the king.

"Then we got an herb called trachonte. Of this herb we hear it said that when a dragon is slain, it springs up from the blood. This herb is inclined to have the characteristics of air [being dry and hot]. Perhaps the [zodiacal] Scorpion's orbit in the sky would help us too in the time before the planets turn backward in their course and the change of the moon begins—this was when the wound pained most. But even this herb's high and noble origin was of no avail.

"We fell on our knees in prayer before the Grail. All at once we saw written upon it that a knight should come, and if from him a question came, our sorrow would be ended, but if anyone, child or maid or man, should prompt him in any way to the question, his question would not help, but the wound would remain as before and pain more violently. The writing said, 'Have you understood? Any prompting from you can do great harm. If he does not ask the first night, the power of his question will vanish. But if at the right time his question is asked, he shall be king of the realm and an end shall be made of your sorrow by the Hand of the Highest. Then Anfortas shall be healed, but he shall no longer be king.'"

After reading this selection and the previous one, consider these questions:

1. What is the main significance of medieval romance, according to Campbell?
2. What is the Grail and its significance?
3. Who is the fisher king and what is his significance?

SELECTION 5:

Medieval Modes of Perception

Whereas Arno Borst and Joseph Campbell see the lines of continuity between certain medieval values and our own, historian William J. Brandt emphasizes that, while certain values and institutions survived, the over-arching set of "perceptions" of the world that we know as medieval did not. He begins by underscoring how men and women of the Middle Ages "experienced" their forms of existence.

What we primarily mean by "medieval" is a kind of shape that experience assumed for men living at a particular time—or rather, we refer to one of two possible shapes to be found in the literature of the period. I would assume, although this study has not attempted to argue it, that many medieval artifacts besides those specifically considered in the text reflect these ways of seeing. Surely medieval art and architecture do.

For the clerk, meaningful experience assumed a kind of triadal shape; it presented itself as a pre-existent norm, an intrusive interruption to that norm, and some sort of conclusion or readjustment. The active element in that shape, the interruption, was generated by attributes and not by objects, human or nonhuman. These attributes were necessarily attached to bodies, but they were not expressive of them. The experienced world of the clerk was a world of discrete and (at least ideally) self-contained actions arising in bodies, but separate from them.

The world of the clerk consequently differed from the modern world in two important respects. In the first place, it was nontemporal, as least as time is perceived today. Our modern feeling for time is a function of our feeling for process; time is the measure of continuous change. The discrete and self-contained character of action as perceived by the medieval clerk meant that the world could not be perceived as process. Secondly, the peculiar relationship between attributes and the objects in which they inhered meant that the objects—including human objects—were in the Middle Ages as unapproachable as prime matter.

The world of the aristocrat was unrelated to the world of the clerk. His was a world of values; experience was not to be investigated but to be appreciated. As a consequence, his perception of action was narrative in character. But this narrative was, by modern standards, thin, because it was not directed toward understanding. Furthermore, the public character of aristocratic values meant that

From *The Shape of Medieval History: Studies in Modes of Perception*, by William J. Brandt (New York: Schocken Books, 1973). Copyright © 1966 by Yale University. Reprinted by permission of Yale University Press.

good was ultimately to be located in one's posture. The aristocratic world of the Middle Ages was a universe of stances. As a consequence, it no more permitted the perception of human individuality, as it has been understood since the Renaissance, than did the clerical world. . . .

On the other hand, these modes of perception as described are generalizations, which cannot, by the nature of things, prohibit exception. To ignore medieval modes of perception in evaluating a particular individual is one hazard, but another is to assume that when we have some clue about the mind of another period we can assert that every individual in that period was completely representative. If this were the case, men would still be thinking the thoughts of cave men. Men of exceptional vitality and intelligence can always think new thoughts. When two intellectual worlds exist simultaneously, as was the case in the Middle Ages, men may even learn to think in new ways, since each one may constitute, for the gifted individual, a criticism and correction of the other. John of Salisbury, Simon de Montfort, and Geoffrey Chaucer—these men bear an ambiguous relationship to their own time. Surely others did.

But a conclusion much more important emerges from this study. In the Middle Ages, modes of perception mediating experience were not innate; they were learned. Once learned, they were remarkably tenacious. They existed side by side for at least three hundred years (and probably much longer) without seriously modifying each other.

Furthermore, these modes of perception, viewed separately, were remarkably coherent. The clerk did not have one way of seeing nature and another way of perceiving men; both were perceived in the same way. And one is impressed, over and over, by the congruence with which action and objects were perceived. What I have called modes of perception in the Middle Ages were not different kinds of spectacles put on for one occasion or another. There was one pair of spectacles for all occasions. As a consequence, while the clerk and the aristocrat perceived experience differently, the experience of each was both coherent and self-consistent.

It appears that one can legitimately presume, at least for the purposes of investigation, that the relationship of modern man to his experience is no different. We too perceive experience by means of categories, and once learned, these categories become inclusive. This human situation, in its modern dress, seems to me to offer a most exciting challenge to the intellectual historian. He is in no better position than anyone else to speak of ultimate reality; he, too, approaches reality through the mediation of his perceptual categories. But there is at least the possibility that he can make conscious his a priori modes of perception. He cannot solve the problems, but he can, perhaps, move the discussion to a level at which real solutions may be possible. He can move the modern dialogues, between scientist and human-

ist, between the political left and right, and perhaps even between the different philosophical schools, to the presuppositions which at present inhibit communication.

After reading this selection, consider these questions:
1. What does Brandt mean by medieval perception?
2. What were the chief characteristics of the medieval form of perception?
3. How does the modern form of perception differ from the medieval one?

SELECTION 6:

The Two Cities

In his twelfth-century history The Two Cities, *the great German ecclesiastic bishop Otto of Freising (ca.1114–1158) tells the history of the world up to his own times. The following prologues from the first and eighth books indicates something of what William J. Brandt means by the specifically medieval forms of perception. Although men and women of the Middle Ages were aware of the world around them, they understand events and processes within a framework markedly different from our own. The meaning of historical events, as with the meaning of life on earth as a whole, was interpreted in relation to the eternal symbols of the revealed truths of faith.*

Prologue of the First Book. In pondering long and often in my heart upon the changes and vicissitudes of temporal affairs and their varied and irregular issues, even as I hold that a wise man ought by no means to cleave to the things of time, so I find that it is by the faculty of reason alone that one must escape and find release from them. For it is the part of a wise man not to be whirled

about after the manner of a revolving wheel, but through the stability of his powers to be firmly fashioned as a thing foursquare. Accordingly, since things are changeable and can never be at rest, what man in his right mind will deny that the wise man ought, as I have said, to depart from them to that city which stays at rest and abides to all eternity? This is the City of God, the heavenly Jerusalem, for which the children of God sigh while they are set in this land of sojourn, oppressed by the turmoil of the things of time as if they were oppressed by the Babylonian captivity. For, inasmuch as there are two cities—the one of

From *The Two Cities: A Chronicle of Universal History to the Year 1146 A.D.*, by Otto, Bishop of Freising, translated by Charles Christopher Mierow, edited by Austin P. Evans and Charles Knapp. (New York: Columbia University Press, 1928).

time, the other of eternity; the one of the earth, earthy, the other of heaven, heavenly; the one of the devil, the other of Christ—ecclesiastical writers have declared that the former is Babylon, the latter Jerusalem.

But, whereas many of the Gentiles have written much regarding one of these cities, to hand down to posterity the great exploits of men of old (the many evidences of their merits, as they fancied), they have yet left to us the task of setting forth what, in the judgment of our writers, is rather the tale of human miseries. There are extant in this field the famous works of Pompeius Trogus, Justin, Cornelius [*i.e.,* Tacitus], Varro, Eusebius, Jerome, Orosius, Jordanes [all scholars from the first century B.C. through the sixth century A.D.], and a great many others of our number, as well as of their array, whom it would take too long to enumerate; in those writings the discerning reader will be able to find not so much histories as pitiful tragedies made up of mortal woes. We believe that this has come to pass by what is surely a wise and proper dispensation of the Creator, in order that, whereas men in their folly desire to cleave to earthly and transitory things, they may be frightened away from them by their own vicissitudes, if by nothing else, so as to be directed by the wretchedness of this fleeting life from the creature to a knowledge of the Creator. But we, set down as it were at the end of time, do not so much read of the miseries of mortals in the books of the writers named above as find them for ourselves in consequence of the experiences of our own time. For, to pass over other things, the empire of the Romans, which in Daniel is compared to iron on account of its sole lordship—monarchy, the Greeks call it—over the whole world, a world subdued by war, has in consequence of so many fluctuations and changes, particularly in our day, become, instead of the noblest and the foremost, almost the last. So that, in the words of the poet, scarcely

"a shadow of its mighty name remains."

For being transferred from the City [Rome] to the Greeks [the Byzantine Empire], from the Greeks to the Franks, from the Franks to the Lombards, from the Lombards again to the German Franks,

that empire not only became decrepit and senile through lapse of time, but also, like a once smooth pebble that has been rolled this way and that by the waters, contracted many a stain and developed many a defect. The world's misery is exhibited, therefore, even in the case of the chief power in the world, and Rome's fall foreshadows the dissolution of the whole structure. . . .

Since, then, the changeable nature of the world is proved by this and like evidence, I thought it necessary, my dear brother Isingrim [a monk who was promoted in 1145 to be Abbot of the monastery of Ottenbeuren in Swabia], in response to your request, to compose a history whereby through God's favor I might display the miseries of the citizens of Babylon and also the glory of the kingdom of Christ to which the citizens of Jerusalem are to look forward with hope, and of which they are to have a foretaste even in this life. I have undertaken therefore to bring down as far as our own time, according to the ability that God has given me, the record of the conflicts and miseries of the one city, Babylon; and furthermore, not to be silent concerning our hopes regarding that other city, so far as I can gather hints from the Scriptures, but to make mention also of its citizens who are now sojourning in the worldly city. In this work I follow most of all those illustrious lights of the Church, Augustine and [the fifth-century A.D. Spanish priest Paulus] Orosius, and have planned to draw from their fountains what is pertinent to my theme and my purpose. The one of these has discoursed most keenly and eloquently [Augustine] on the origin and the progress of the glorious City of God and its ordained limits, setting forth how it has ever spread among the citizens of the world, and showing which of its citizens or princes stood forth preëminent in the various epochs of the princes or citizens of the world. The other [Orosius], in answer to those who, uttering vain babblings, preferred the former times to Christian times, has composed a very valuable history of the fluctuations and wretched issues of human greatness, the wars and the hazards of wars, and the shifting of thrones, from the foundation of the world down to his own time. Following in their steps I have undertaken to speak of the Two

Cities in such a way that we shall not lose the thread of history, that the devout reader may observe what is to be avoided in mundane affairs by reason of the countless miseries wrought by their unstable character, and that the studious and painstaking investigator may find a record of past happenings free from all obscurity. . . .

The Eighth Book. It remains now to tell in this eighth book about the third state, namely, how the one City is to attain to the highest blessedness, the other to fail and to descend to the utmost misery, when the most righteous Judge shall, at the last judgment, examine and shall decide the case of each city. Because, as Solomon says, before destruction the heart is constantly exalted, before honor is constantly humbled, I think it appropriate to tell by way of preface what humiliation precedes this glory of His City, what transient exaltation under Antichrist goes before this downfall of the evil city—insofar as it is pos-

sible to reach conclusions from the authoritative books. For thus after the dense darkness of the persecutions the eternal day of eternal peace will appear the more delightful, and after the approving smile of this world the grievous storm of punishments and the eternal night will appear the more terrible, inasmuch as the hope of that glory makes present troubles light, the fear of that doom detracts from this temporal pleasure (if there be any such) because it is fleeting.

After reading this selection, consider these questions:
1. What, according to Otto, are the two cities?
2. What was the relationship between the two cities?
3. What was the meaning of history for Otto?

SELECTION 7:
The Harvest of the Middle Ages

Finally, the early twentieth-century Dutch historian Johan Huizinga offers what is perhaps the most enduring of interpretations of the last two centuries of the Middle Ages. In the ninth chapter of his famous overview of the period, The Autumn of the Middle Ages, *Huizinga both describes the rich harvest of medieval civilizations in this period and explains the reasons for its decline. For Huizinga, both of these phenomena are related. They are the result of the medieval mental habit of interpreting the world through a highly developed set of symbols, which at once opened the world as a fully meaningful place and limited the ways in which it could be understood. From within this symbolic network, a point was reached, according to Huizinga, in which this symbolic structure became highly articulated and overly complicated and finally collapsed of its own weight.*

Religious emotions always tended to transform themselves into lively images. The mentality of the time believed it had come to understand a mystery once it had placed it before its eyes. Therefore, this need to worship the inexpressible through visible signs resulted in the constant creation of new images. . . .

There was no great truth of which the medieval mind was more certain than those words from the Corinthians, "Videmus nunc per speculum in aenigmate, tunc autem facie ad faciem" ("For now we see through a glass darkly; but then face to face"). They never forgot that everything would be absurd if it exhausted its meaning in its immediate function and form of manifestation, and that all things extend in an important way into the world beyond. That insight is still familiar to us as an inarticulate feeling in those moments when the sound of rain on leaves or the light of a lamp on a table penetrates momentarily into a deeper level of perception than that serving practical thought and action. It may surface in the form of a sickening obsession to the effect that all things seem to be pregnant with a threatening personal intent or with an enigma that we must solve but cannot. It may also, more frequently, fill us with that calm and strengthening certainty that our own life shares in the mysterious meaning of the world. The more that feeling condenses into awe of the One from which all things flow, the more readily it will move from the clear certainty of isolated moments to a lasting, ever present feeling or even to an articulated conviction. "By cultivating the continuous sense of our connection with the power that made things as they are, we are tempered more towardly for their reception. The outward face of nature need not alter, but the expressions of meaning in it alter. It was dead and is alive again. It is like the difference between looking on a person without love, or upon the same person with love. . . . When we see all things in God, and refer all things to him, we read in common matters superior expressions of meaning."

From The Autumn of the Middle Ages, by Johan Huizinga, translated by Rodney J. Payton and Ulrich Mammitzsch (Chicago: University of Chicago Press, 1996). Copyright © 1996 by The University of Chicago. Reprinted by permission of the publisher.

This is the emotional foundation from which symbolism arises. In God, nothing empty or meaningless exists. . . . As soon as the idea of God was conceptualized, everything originating in Him and finding meaning in Him also crystalized into thoughts articulated in words. And thus comes into being that noble and lofty idea of the world as a great symbolic nexus—a cathedral of ideas, the highest rhythmic and polyphonic expression of all that can be thought. . . .

Viewed from the standpoint of causal thinking, symbolism represents an intellectual shortcut. Thought attempts to find the connection between things, not by tracing the hidden turns of their causal ties, but rather by suddenly jumping over these causal connections. The connection is not a link between cause and effect, but one of meaning and purpose. The conviction that such a link exists may come into existence whenever two things share an essential quality that relates to something of general value. Or, in other words, any association on the basis of any identity may be directly transformed into an awareness of an essential and mystic connection. . . .

White and red roses bloom among thorns. The medieval mind immediately sees in this fact symbolic significance: virgins and martyrs shine in glory among those who persecute them. How is this postulate of identity achieved? By virtue of the identity of the qualities: beauty, tenderness, purity. The blood red tint of the roses is also that of the virgin and the martyr. But this connectedness is only truly meaningful and full of mystic significance if the linkage, the quality, the essence between the two constituents of the particular symbolism are shared by each of them. In other words, where red and white are regarded not as mere labels for physical differences on a quantitative basis, but as real entities, as realities themselves. . . .

The waning Middle Ages display this entire world of thought in its last flourishing. The world was perfectly pictured through that all encompassing symbolism, and the individual symbols turned into petrified flowers. From the time of antiquity, symbolism had a tendency to become purely mechanical. Once established as a principle of thought, symbolism arises not only from poetic imagination and enthusiasm, but attaches itself to the intellectual function like a parasitic plant and degenerates into pure habit and a disease of thought. Whole perspectives of symbolic contact arise, particularly when the symbolic contact comes from a mere correspondence in number. Symbolizing becomes simply the use of arithmetical tables. The twelve months are supposed to signify the twelve apostles, the four seasons the Evangelists, and the entire year is then bound to mean Christ.

Conglomerates of systems based on the number seven take shape. The Seven Cardinal Virtues correspond to the seven requests of the Lord's Prayer, the Seven Gifts of the Holy Spirit, the Seven Praises of Bliss, and the Seven Penitential Psalms. These, in turn are related to the Seven Moments of the Passion and the Seven Sacraments. Every individual unit of the sevens corresponds again as contrast or cure for the Seven Cardinal Sins, which are represented by seven animals that are followed by seven diseases. For a true healer of souls and moralist such as [fifteenth century theologian Jean de] Gerson, from whom the above examples are taken, the practical ethical value of the symbolic relations predominates. For a visionary such as [fifteenth century mystic] Alain de la Roche, it is the aesthetic element in the relationship that is most important. He has to establish a system depending on the numbers ten and fifteen because the prayer cycle of the Brotherhood of the Rosary, which commanded his zealous support, comprises 150 aves interrupted by fifteen paters. The fifteen paters are the fifteen moments of the Passion, the 150 aves are the Psalms. But they mean much more. Multiplying the eleven heavenly spheres plus the four elements by the ten categories: *substantia, qualitas, quantitas,* etc. yields the 150 *habitudines naturales;* the same *habitudines naturales* one obtains by multiplying the Ten Commandments by the fifteen virtues. The three theological, the four cardinal, the seven capital virtues amount to fourteen, "restant duae: religio et poenitentia," which means that there is one too many, but Temperantia, the Cardinal Virtue, corresponds to Abstinentia, the Capital Virtue, which means that fifteen are left. Each of these

virtues is a queen who has her bridal bed in one of the segments of the Lord's Prayer. Each of the words of the ave means one of the Fifteen Perfections of Mary and at the same time a precious stone on the *rupis angelica* which is Mary herself; every word drives away a sin or the animal symbolizing it. They are also branches of a tree laden with fruit in which all the saints are sitting, and the steps of a stair. For example, the word ave signifies Mary's innocence and a diamond. It drives away pride, which, in turn, is symbolized by a lion. The word Mary means her wisdom and a carbuncle; it drives away envy, symbolized by a black dog. In his vision, Alain sees the disgusting figures of the sin-symbolizing animals and the shining colors of the precious stones. The stones' miraculous powers, long famous, give rise, in turn, to new symbolic associations. The sardonyx is black, red, and white just as Mary was black in her humility, red in her pain, and white in her glory and mercy. Used as a seal, wax will not stick to this stone. This signifies the virtue of honorability, it drives away unchastity and causes people to be honorable and chaste. The pearl is the word *gratia* and also Mary's own mercy. It is generated inside a seashell from a heavenly dew. . . . Mary herself is this shell; in this instance the symbolism is slightly shifted because one would expect that Mary would be the pearl if one were to follow the pattern of the other precious stones. The kaleidoscopic nature of symbolism is also strikingly expressed here: the words "created from heavenly dew" also call to mind, albeit not made explicit, the other trope of the virgin birth, the fleece on which Gideon prayed that the holy sign might descend.

The symbolizing mode of thought had been almost entirely spent. Finding symbols and allegories had become mere play, a superficial fantasizing on a simple association of ideas. A symbol retains an emotional value only by virtue of the holiness of the thing it symbolizes; as soon as symbolizing shifts from the purely religious realm to one exclusively moral, its hopeless degeneration is exposed. [French poet Jean] Froissart, in an elaborate poem "Le orloge amoureus," manages to connect all the qualities of love to the different parts of a clockwork. [The fifteenth-century chroniclers Georges] Chastellain and [Jean] Molinet compete in political symbolism. In the three estates the characteristic qualities of Mary are represented; the seven Electors of the Holy Roman Empire, three spiritual and four secular, represent the three Theological and the four Cardinal Virtues; the five cities, St. Omer, Aire, Lille, Douai, and Valenciennes, that remained loyal to Burgundy in 1477 become the Five Wise Virgins. Actually, this is a reverse symbolism; the lower does not point to the higher, but rather the higher to the lower, since, in the mind of the inventor, the earthly things that he intends to glorify with some heavenly ornamentation are foremost. The *Donatus moralisatus seu per allegoriam traductus*, occasionally ascribed to Gerson, blended Latin grammar with theological symbolism: the noun is man, pronouns show that he is a sinner.

UNIT 3

Early Modern Europe

CONTENTS

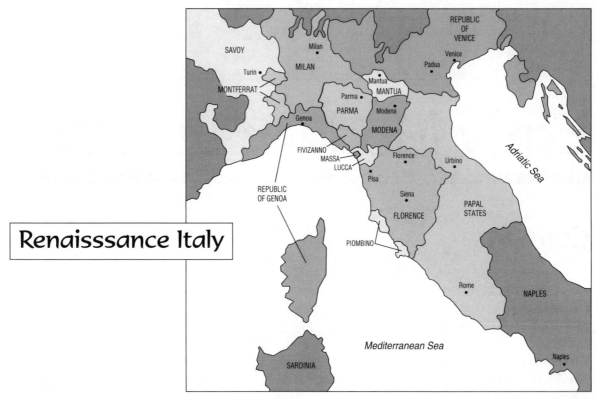

Renaisssance Italy

Established religion of Ireland is Anglican, but the majority of the population remained Roman Catholic.

Legend:
- ▲ Anglican
- ○ Roman Catholic
- + Calvinist
- ★ Lutheran
- Greek Orthodox
- □ Anabaptist
- ⊙ Islamic

Religious Divisions in Europe About 1600

CHAPTER 12
The Diversity of Early Modern Europe

As with all the other supposed epochs in the history of Western civilization—the "end" of antiquity and the "beginning" of the Middle Ages, for instance—there is less of a clear break and the beginning of something entirely new and more of an opening of new directions of movement and a process of transformation and building on what had gone before. Unlike the beginning of the medieval period, however, the transformation to the modern period in the history of the West did not involve the salvaging of what was left of a once great civilization and otherwise meeting as best as it could the conditions of an increasingly violent and barbarous world. While one main strand of modernity will develop from yet another retrieval of the classical heritage, which we associate with the Renaissance and humanism, modernity cannot simply be understood in terms of this recovery of ancient models. Neither can modernity, even in its early form of the fifteenth, sixteenth, and seventeenth centuries, be comprehended in terms of a redefinition of the Christian faith, which is associated with the Protestant Reformation and with the reforms of the Catholic Church that are known as the Counter Reformation. These various "movements"—so important to the ways in which Europeans came to find meaning in their individual and collective lives and to the social and political forms they eventually developed—themselves responded to a whole series of trends and transformations that Europe was experiencing in these centuries. Unlike the early Middle Ages, Europe of the fifteenth and sixteenth centuries was a rapidly developing and expanding civilization, a civilization outgrowing various inherited medieval institutions, values, and forms of thought.

To stress the fact that a number of the central institutions of the Middle Ages were in decline does not mean either that they ceased to exist or that they failed to function. The growing impotence of the Holy Roman Empire brought about not a total collapse but the transference of its imperial political, legal, and military institutions. And the great monarchies of England, France, and Spain continued to thrive into the early modern period. In different ways, and to various degrees, they transformed themselves into modern political forms.

Even the medieval church, after suffering from the domination of the French monarchy, the relocation to Avignon, the Great Schism, and an attempt to redefine the church in terms of the rule of its bishops (the conciliar movement of the fifteenth century), transformed itself into the Renaissance church and then into the Tridentine church (redefined by the Council of Trent) of the modern period. The vitality of Europe is perhaps best illustrated by the fact that its economy and society were able to recover from the devastating impact of the Black Death, which killed perhaps 30 percent of the population.

SELECTION 1:

Carnival and Popular Culture

The more popular forms of European culture, which emerged and developed in the High and late Middle Ages, only continued to thrive in the early modern period. Although originating in the rural areas where the vast bulk of the population still resided, these cultural forms became fully articulated within the popular culture of the various cities and towns of Europe. Early modern Europe united both high and popular culture and offered a brightly hued tapestry of rich and diverse social groupings and cultural modes. All levels of society had their own cultural activities and modes of expression, but there were also common forms of cultural expression in saints' days, feasts, and festivals. And there was Carnival—celebrated on the beginning of the new year or the start of Lent—which became an occasion both for general celebration and for "playing with" (if not challenging) the social and clerical hierarchies that dominated life in early modern Europe. Carnival evolved as a major form of celebration in the many European towns and cities of the fourteenth, fifteenth, and sixteenth centuries. In Carnival in Romans *(in France), historian Emmanuel Le Roy Ladurie analyzes the role of Carnival during the sixteenth century.*

I will define the insertion of Carnival-Lent into the Christian calendar: The essence of Lent and the primordial concept of Carnival is burying one's pagan life, having one last pagan debauchery before embarking on the ascetic rigors of lenten season. This would result in spiritual and baptismal rebirth at Easter. In short, the strict facts of the rites of Carnival were a logical prelude, an introductory antithesis to Lenten fasting and preaching. In Romans, as elsewhere, these festivities had been inserted into the Christian, more specifically the Catholic cycle of the year. (The Protestants who abolished Lenten fasting were thus obliged by necessity to get rid of the preliminary feasting as well. They made a spirited attempt throughout the sixteenth century to destroy all traces of this Eden of inequity.) Car-

From *Le Carnaval du Romans*, by Emmanuel Le Roy Ladurie (Paris: Editions Gallimard, 1979). English translation by Benjamin Sax © 2000 by Greenhaven Press, Inc.

nival in the "papal" system was situated in the unrolling of the long calendar that ran from All Saints' Day to Advent and Christmas, then Carnival, Lent, Easter, and St. John's Day (Midsummer Day). The episode in Romans of 1580 did not contradict this conception. St. Blaise and the Holy Spirit were honored. And the rich men's Mass was celebrated on lundi gras [fat Monday], with a few folk embellishments. In Paris as well one sees the organized religious yet lewd Mardi Gras [fat Tuesday] processions organized by the League [strident Catholics during the religious wars of the sixteenth century]; the people forced parish priests to take part in them.

The problem is this: Carnival's pre-Lenten yet anti-Lent functions made it antithetic to the ascetic values of Christianity. Lent exalts abstention from food and sex, celebrates virtuous behavior. It was a time of peace, the Truce of God. Carnival, on the other hand, emphasized sins of the flesh, gluttony, and lubricity. It glorified feasting (the price list of foodstuffs, the "kingdom" banquets, "the apotheosis of proteins") and enjoyment and triumph of sexuality (the maximum number of annual weddings and conceptions; dances; election of kings and queens [of Carnival]; latent threats of rape and kidnapping against patrician ladies). It displayed finally the activities of war, real or imagined (the poor people's sword dance, the elite's military parade). In this sense Carnival approached a system of pre-Christian or non-Christian reality (in other words folk or rustic, even pagan values). Insofar as its aim was to "bury pagan ways," it directly reproduced parts of the ancient winter festivities which had been adopted into the church along with the common folk as the countryside was converted during the first millennium, a period of prodigious cultural grafting. Among such pagan rites, the Saturnalian role reversals, the Lupercalian animal masquerades and floggings, the donkey ride, and so forth, were prominent. But Christianity is after all a religion based on the concept of sin. It is not unusual, then, that it was able to digest these pagan rites so thoroughly, and that it had fully assimilated the peccant joys of Carnival, if only to banish them when Lent arrived.

These religious views are pertinent, but they do not describe Carnival's existential content (sea-sonal, agricultural) or the class (or clan) struggle it incorporated. For Carnival festivities were not only cyclical and annual . . . or pagan plus Christian; they also had to do with the changing of seasons. They were specifically connected to the approach of the end of winter, a crucial moment for a society which was still semi-agricultural and thus close to nature. In this change of seasons the reigning character was the Candlemas bear; it was in this disguise that Paumier [the leader of the popular uprising in Romans in 1579–1580] briefly occupied a consul's seat in Romans's town hall. In Dauphin as in Savoy, the bear announced (or did not announce) the end of the cold season. On February 2 it came out of the den where it had been hibernating and looked at the sky. If it were cloudy, superstition maintained, the bear would decree winter was over. But if the sky were blue the cold would continue for forty more days, and the bear would lumber back into its den to sleep for a few more weeks. . . .

Lent-Carnival was not only to give time a push, move forward the end of winter. It also dispensed fertility, for women and couples, crops, the community. It was at once symbolizer and purger of the various ills and sins which might affect the human body and soul, the social group, and the crops. This supported the structures of Catholic belief: Carnival embodied unbridled pleasure, the joys of life and the dance, the pagan sins (gourmandizing, luxury, and so on) which would be excrementally eliminated by Lent. In early February 1580 Romans's St. Blaise's Day dancers mimed the winter farm work of flailing, raking, and sweeping the threshing-floor. Even more specific was the role of the children carrying brandons (flaming wooden torches) during the mid-February massacre in Romans; their function (symbolically) was to exterminate parasites preying on fruit trees and cereal crops. These young torchbearers simultaneously warded off Paumier's men, the enemies of social order, and the moles or fieldmice attacking apples or grain. Well into the seventeenth century the old-style Carnival in France, from February 2 until the beginning of Lent, was packed with such propitiatory practices. Many of them were found in Dauphin, for instance crêpes and blessed candles for Candlemas; the ringing of bells (more bells!) on February 5; a halt to spinning; aspersion with *andouille* (chitterling) broth; the burial of *carême-prenant* (the Provençal Carnival effigy); *brandons* and *fassenotes*. The purpose of all this was that people hoped not to lack a good supply of money during the year; to keep safe from lightning and evil spells of every sort; to chase way witches on the night of St. Agnes, to prevent foxes from eating the chickens, mice from chewing up yarn; to make their Lenten fasting easier; guard the crops from fieldmice, tares, blight; assure good yields from gardens and make onions grow big; help find brides and grooms for the young men and women of the village. The idea of Carnival and more generally winter festivities as fertility rites, has been developed in detail by several anthropologists and historians . . . who contend that the macabre animal masks (bears, etc.) worn by a community's young people during the festivities in fact represented demons and dead souls. It was commonly believed that the dead moved among the living and could influence the next growing season for good or bad through the ice of the cold season. It was thus essential that everyone give a gift to these masked youths, so that the spirits they represented would guarantee a good year

and good health to all. After this, these infernal creatures would conveniently disappear. Dead souls, as we have seen, were also included among the masked revelers . . . during Romans' Candlemas celebration. In 1580 they demanded their fair share of the urban wealth, amid a macabre din of bells. It is obvious, however, that this notion does not necessarily imply that the people were resorting to long-defunct pagan practices. Medieval Catholicism admitted the people's firm belief in ghosts, devils, and their intervention in everyday affairs. . . .

Carnival, then, was agricultural, biological. But it was socially useful as well. The two are inseparable (just as the Maypole expressed an indissoluble bond between political power, phallic fertility, abundance of plant life).

After reading this selection and the previous one, consider these questions:

1. How does Le Roy Ladurie describe the role of Carnival in early modern European society?
2. What, according to Le Roy Ladurie, was the meaning of Carnival?
3. What were the origins of Carnival?

SELECTION 2:

Rabelais and Popular Culture

In Carnival in Romans, *Emmanuel Le Roy Ladurie describes how the Carnival of 1580 led to a revolt against city authorities in the French town of Romans. He then analyzes the various cultural, social, and political reasons why such forms of popular culture were restricted and sometimes abolished in the course of the late sixteenth and early seventeenth centuries. For Le Roy Ladurie, there arose in the cities and towns of Europe the need for greater regularity, greater control, and more official restrictions on the lives of urban citizens. Local political (and also increasingly nonlocal secular and religious) authorities intervened to outlaw such popular forms of entertainment. This is as true of Catholic France and the other Catholic states as it was of Protestant England, Germany, and Scandinavia. Although cer-*

tain forms of carnival and popular festivals survive in altered forms into the nineteenth and even twentieth centuries, they are more restricted and offer less of an opportunity to challenge the social and political powers that be.

The renowned twentieth-century Russian literary theorist Mikhail Bakhtin has uncovered a number of ways in which these forms of early modern popular culture lay behind and continued to generate various forms of literature. In Rabelais and His World, *Bakhtin interprets the writings of French friar François Rabelais against the background of a reconstruction of the entire world of European popular culture. For him, the central form of this culture was the notion of the "carnivalesque." Bakhtin sees in carnival not just a form of celebration or a way of "letting off steam" but an entire world view, with notions of nature, the relation of power, and the "real" organization of society.*

The selection opens with a discussion of a late medieval popular drama before turning to a more detailed discussion of Rabelais's great work, Gargantua and Pantagruel. *Gargantua and Pantagruel are the two main characters of the novel. They are giants.*

Our starting point will be a brief analysis of the French comic drama "The Play in the Bower" (*Jeu de la Feuillée*) of the troubadour Adam de la Halle from Arras. This drama was written in 1262. . . . The first comic play, it presents a feast of carnival type, using this theme and all the privileges implied by it: the right to emerge from the routine of life, the right to be free from all that is official and consecrated. The theme is treated simply, but directly. It is typically carnivalesque from beginning to end.

The "Play in the Bower" has scarcely any footlights, one might say, to separate it from real life. The performance was given in Arras and the action is also set in Arras, the author's hometown. The characters are the author himself (the young troubadour), his father Maître Henri, and other citizens of Arras who appear under their real names. The topic of the play is Adam's intention to leave Arras and his wife to study in Paris. This episode actually took place in the troubadour's life. However, there is a fantastic element interwoven with the many features of real life. The play was performed on the first of May, which was the time of the fair and of a popular festival,

From *Rabelais and His World,* by Mikhail Bakhtin, translated by Helene Iswolsky (Cambridge, MA: MIT Press, 1968). Copyright © 1968 by The Massachusetts Institute of Technology. Reprinted by permission of the publisher.

and the drama's entire action is coordinated with these events.

"The Play in the Bower" is divided into three parts. The first part could be defined as carnivalesque and biographical, the second part as carnivalesque and fantastic, and the last part as a carnivalesque banquet.

In the first part of this play the personal family affairs of the author, Adam, are presented with utmost freedom and familiarity. There follows a no less frank presentation of the other citizens of Arras, in which their private lives and their boudoir secrets are disclosed.

The play starts with Adam appearing in a scholastic gown (this is a masquerade, since he is not yet a student). He declares that he is leaving his wife, Marie, to go to Paris and improve his education. He intends to place his wife under his father's care. He tells how much Marie attracted him before their marriage. This leads to a detailed, very frank and free enumeration of her charms. Enter the father, Maître Henri. Asked by Adam to give him some money, the father says that he is unable to do so, being old and sick. The physician diagnoses the father's disease as "avarice" and names several other townfolk afflicted with this disease. Then the physician is consulted by a prostitute (Dame Douce). Apropos of this consultation the play offers a "survey" of the boudoir life of Arras and names other young women of shady reputation. During this medical dialogue, urine figures as the determining factor of human character and destiny.

The images of the physician and of the diseases and vices are treated here in the carnivalesque spirit. Enter a monk collecting a donation for St. Acarius, who cures madness and folly. Some people wish to be helped by this saint. Enter a madman accompanied by his father. The role of the madman, as well as the theme of insanity and folly in general, is important in the play. The madman freely criticizes a decree of Pope Alexander IV which reduces the privileges of scholastics (among them those of Maître Henri). Thus ends the first part of the play. The free talk and obscenities of these scenes are usually interpreted by scholars as the "coarseness of the times." Actually, this coarseness has a system and a style of its own. They represent the grotesque aspect of the world with which we are already familiar.

The boundaries between the play and life are intentionally erased. Life itself is on stage.

The second part with its fantastic theme starts after the monk, symbolizing the official Church and the official truth, falls asleep near a bower which forms the main section of the stage. A table is set in the bower, awaiting the visit of three fairies who are allowed to appear only on the eve of May Day and only when the official world is absent. Before their entrance "Harlequin's army" marches by with a jingle of bells. Enter King Harlequin's messenger, a comic devil. Then the three fairies enter. The next scene presents the fairies' supper in the bower, their conversation among themselves and with King Harlequin's messenger. His name is Croquesots, "fool-eater." The fairies predict the future, good or evil, and some of it concerns the author, Adam.

They spin the "wheel of fortune." At the end of the supper Dame Douce enters. Fairies protect prostitutes, who also reign supreme on May Day eve with its license and revelry. Dame Douce and the fairies represent the unofficial world, which that night is granted full liberty and impunity.

The last part, a carnivalesque banquet, takes place before sunrise in a tavern where the participants in the May Day festivities and the charac-

ters of the play are assembled. All drink, laugh, sing, and roll dice. They play for the monk who has fallen asleep once more. The host of the tavern takes the monk's reliquary and parodies his curing of fools; his antics provoke loud laughter. At the end of this scene the madman breaks into the tavern. But at that moment dawn breaks and church bells begin to ring. May Night with its freedoms is over. Upon the monk's invitation the guests betake themselves to church.

Such are the main elements of the first French drama. . . .

Let us stress first of all the close relation of the play to May Day. It springs, up to its minutest detail, from this feast's theme and atmosphere, which determine its form and character as well as its content. The authority of the official realm of Church and state is suspended, with all its norms and values. The world is permitted to emerge from its routine. The end of festive freedom is clearly heralded by the ringing of the morning church bells; while earlier in the play the bells of the marching harlequins begin to tinkle as soon as the monk has made his exit. The banquet theme plays an essential role in the play, with feasting in the bower and in the tavern. Let us also stress the theme of dice; not only are dice a common form of recreation but they are also intimately linked with the feast. Games are extra-official and are governed by rules contrary to the current laws of life. Further, the suspension of the Church's exclusive power brings back the uncrowned pagan gods: marching harlequins, the messenger Croquesots, and the fairies directing the dance of the prostitutes. The theme of Dame Douce merits our special attention. On May Day eve prostitutes enjoy special privileges and even authority; in our play Dame Douce prepares to settle accounts with her enemies. Finally, an important element in the play is represented by the wheel of fortune and the predictions and curses of the fairies. The feast looks into the future, and this future acquires not only a utopian character but also the primitive archaic form of prophecies, curses, and blessings (which initially concerned the future harvest, the increase of cattle, etc.). The theme of the relics is also characteristic, related as it is to the dismemberment of the body. A typical role is played by the physician and the attribute of his profession: urine. The theme of madness and folly is very important. Something like the market place *cri*, but addressed to fools, is introduced into the play and determines in part its atmosphere. The feast grants a right to folly.

Folly is, of course, deeply ambivalent. It has the negative element of debasement and destruction (the only vestige now is the use of "fool" as a pejorative) and the positive element of renewal and truth. Folly is the opposite of wisdom—inverted wisdom, inverted truth. It is the other side, the lower stratum of official laws and conventions, derived from them. Folly is a form of gay festive wisdom, free from all laws and restrictions, as well as from preoccupations and serious-ness. Let us recall the apology of the fifteenth-century "feast of fools.". . . The defenders of this feast understood it as a gay and free expression of "our second nature" in which gay folly was opposed to "piousness and fear of God." Thus the champions of the festival considered it a "once-a-year" liberation, not only from routine but also from the religious outlook. It permitted the people to see the world with "foolish eyes," and this right belonged not to the "feast of fools" alone but to every feast in its popular marketplace aspect.

This is why the theme of folly and the image of the incurable fool are so important in the festive atmosphere of the "Bower." The play ends with the fool appearing just before the church bells start ringing.

SELECTION 3:

Gargantua and Pantagruel

Mikhail Bakhtin points to the diverse and complex forms of popular culture in the writings of François Rabelais. Rabelais was both a Dominican friar and a highly educated physician, and thus a member of a small elite in sixteenth-century France. But he picked up and employed for his own purposes these popular forms throughout his most famous work, Gargantua and Pantagruel. The following selection indicates both the work's famous "Rabelaisian" humor and the playfulness with which he approached the life of individuals and the types of education of his age. The following selection comes from chapter 21 ("Gargantua's Studies, and His Way of Life, According to His Philosophical Teachers").

He with all his heart submitted his study to the discretion of Ponocrates; who for the beginning appointed that he should do as he was accustomed, to the end he might understand by what meanes, in so long time, his old Masters had made him so sottish and ignorant. He disposed therefore of his time in such fashion, that ordinarily he did awake betwixt eight and nine a clock, whether it was day or not, (for so had his ancient governours ordained,) alledging that which David saith *Vanum est vobis ante lucem surgere* [It does you no good to wake before day begins]. Then did he tumble and tosse, wag his legs, and wallow in the bed sometime, the better to stirre up, and rouse his vital spirits, and apparelled himself according to the season: but willingly he would weare a great long gown of thick

From *Gargantua and Pantagruel*, by François Rabelais, translated by Sir Thomas Urquhart and Peter Le Motteux (London: David Nutt, 1900).

freeze, furred with fox-skins. Afterwards he combed his head with an [philosopher Jacob] Alman combe, which is the foure fingers and the thumb; for his Praeceptor [teacher] said, that to comb himself otherwayes, to wash and make himself neat, was to lose time in this world. Then he dung'd, pist, spued, belched, cracked, yawned, spitted, coughed, yexed, sneezed and snotted himself like an Arch-deacon; and, to suppresse the dew and bad aire, went to breakfast, having some good fried tripes, faire rashers on the coales, excellent gamons of bacon, store of fine minced meat, and a great deal of sippet brewis, made up of the fat of the beef-pot, laid upon bread, cheese, and chop't parsley strewed together. Ponocrates chewed him, that he ought not to eat so soon after rising out of his bed, unlesse he had performed some exercise beforehand: Gargantua answered, What! have not I sufficiently well exercised my self? I have wallowed and rolled my self six or seven turns in my bed, before I rose: is not that enough? Pope Alexander did so, by the advice of a Jew his physician, and lived till his dying day in despite of his enemies. My first Masters have used me to it, saying that to breakfast made a good memory, and therefore they drank first. I am very well after it, and dine but the better: and Master Tubal, (who was the first Licentiat at Paris,) told me, that it was not enough to run apace, but to set forth betimes; so doth not the total welfare of our humanity depend upon perpetual drinking in a rible rable, like ducks, but on drinking early in the morning: *unde versus*,

To rise betimes is no good houre,
To drink betimes is better sure.

After that he had throughly broke his fast, he went to Church, and they carried to him in a great basket, a huge impantoufled or thick-covered breviary, weighing what in grease, clasps, parchment and cover, little more or lesse then eleven hundred and six pounds. There he heard six and twenty or thirty Masses: This while, to the same

place came his orison-mutterer impaletocked, or lap't up about the chin, like a tufted whoop, and his breath pretty well antidoted with store of the vine-tree-sirrup: with him he mumbled all his Kiriels, and dunsical breborions, which he so curiously thumbed and fingered, that there fell not so much as one graine [rosary bead] to the ground; as he went from the Church, they brought him upon a Dray [cart] drawn with oxen, a confused heap of Patenotres and Aves of Sante Claude [carved-wood rosaries], every one of them being of the bignesse of a hat-block; and thus walking through the cloysters, galleries or garden, he said more in turning them over, then sixteen Hermites [hermits] would have done. Then did he study some paltry half-houre with his eyes fixed upon his book. . . . Pissing then a full Urinal, he sate down at table; and because he was naturally flegmatick [calm], he began his meale with some dozens of gammons [hams], dried neats tongues, hard rowes of mullet, called Botargos, Andouilles or sauciges, and such other forerunners of wine; in the mean while, foure of his folks did cast into his mouth one after another continually mustard by whole shovels full. Immediately after that, he drank a horrible draught of white-wine for the ease of his kidneys. When that was done, he ate according to the season meat agreeable to his appetite, and then left off eating when his belly began to strout, and was like to crack for fulnesse; as for his drinking, he had in that neither end nor rule; for he was wont to say, that the limits and bounds of drinking were, when the cork of the shoes of him that drinketh swelleth up half a foot high.

After reading this selection and the previous one, consider these questions:
1. What does Bakhtin mean by the term *carnivalesque*?
2. What were the functions of Carnival?
3. What were some of the carnivalesque qualities in the writings of Rabelais?

SELECTION 4:

Festive Comedy

Such popular forms of culture are also seen within forms of drama. Like Carnival, the feast of Corpus Christi became the occasion for the development of late medieval forms of popular culture. Especially in England, there developed a series of plays, the so-called miracle plays, associated with the religious feast. Both in direct and indirect ways, Elizabethan drama, including the plays of William Shakespeare, developed out of these popular forms of entertainment. Shakespearean scholar C.L. Barber points out these lines of continuity between medieval popular forms and Shakespearean use of them. What Barber refers to as "Shakespeare's festive comedies" include such plays as As You Like It, Twelfth Night, Love's Labour's Lost, *and* Much Ado About Nothing.

Come, woo me, woo me! for now I am in a holiday humour, and like enough to consent. [*As You Like It*, act 4, scene 1]

Such holiday humor is often abetted by directly staging pastimes, dances, songs, masques, plays extempore, etc. But the fundamental method is to shape the loose narrative so that "events" put its persons in the position of festive celebrants: if they do not seek holiday it happens to them. A tyrant duke forces Rosalind into disguise; but her mock wooing with Orlando amounts to a Disguising, with carnival freedom from the decorum of her identity and her sex. The misrule of Sir Toby is represented as personal idiosyncrasy, but it follows the pattern of the Twelfth Night occasion; the flyting match of Benedict and Beatrice, while appropriate to their special characters, suggests the customs of Easter Smacks and Hocktide abuse between the sexes. Much of the poetry and wit, however it may be occasioned by events, works in the economy of the whole play to promote the effect of a merry occasion where Nature reigns. . . .

The two gestures [invocation and abuse] were

still practiced in the "folly" of Elizabethan Maygame, harvest-home, or winter revel: invocation, for example, in the manifold spring garlanding customs, "gathering for Robin Hood"; abuse, in the customary license to flout and fleer at what on other days commanded respect. The same double way of achieving [comedic] release appears in Shakespeare's festive plays. There the poetry about the pleasures of nature and the naturalness of pleasure serves to evoke beneficent natural impulses; and much of the wit, mocking the good housewife Fortune from her wheel, acts to free the spirit as does the ritual abuse of hostile spirits. A saturnalian attitude, assumed by a clear-cut gesture toward liberty, brings mirth, an accession of wanton vitality. In the terms of Freud's analysis of wit, the energy normally occupied in maintaining inhibition is freed for celebration. The holidays in actual observance were built around the enjoyment of the vital pleasure of moments when nature and society are hospitable to life. In the summer, there was love in out-of-door idleness; in the winter, within-door warmth and food and drink. But the celebrants also got something for nothing from festive liberty—the vitality normally locked up in awe and respect. . . . Shakespeare's gay comedy is like Aristophanes' because its expression of life is shaped by the form of feeling of such saturnalian occasions as these. The traditional Christian culture within which such holidays were celebrated in the Renaissance of course gave a very different emphasis and perspective to Shakespeare's art. . . .

The *clarification* achieved by the festive comedies is concomitant to the release they dramatize: a heightened awareness of the relation between man and "nature"—the nature celebrated on holiday. The process of translating festive experience into drama involved extending the sort of awareness traditionally associated with holiday, and also becoming conscious of holiday itself in a new way. The plays present a mockery of what is unnatural which gives scope and point to the sort of scoffs and jests shouted by dancers in the churchyard or in "the quaint mazes in the wanton green." And they include another, complementary mockery of what is merely natural, a humor which puts holiday in perspective with life as a whole.

The butts in the festive plays consistently exhibit their unnaturalness by being kill-joys. On an occasion "full of warm blood, of mirth," they are too preoccupied with perverse satisfactions like pride or greed to "let the world slip" and join the dance. Satirical comedy tends to deal with relations between social classes and aberrations in movements between them. Saturnalian comedy is satiric only incidentally; its clarification comes with movement between poles of restraint and release in everybody's experience. Figures like Malvolio [in *Twelfth Night*] and Shylock [in *The Merchant of Venice*] embody the sort of kill-joy qualities. . . . Craven or inadequate people appear, by virtue of the festive orientation, as would-be revellers, comically inadequate to hear the chimes at midnight. Pleasure thus becomes the touchstone for judgment of what bars it or is incapable of it. And though in Shakespeare the judgment is usually responsible—valid we feel for everyday as well as holiday—it is the whirligig of impulse that tries the characters. Behind the laughter at the butts there is always a sense of solidarity about pleasure, a communion embracing the merrymakers in the play and the audience, who have gone on holiday in going to a comedy.

While perverse hostility to pleasure is a subject for aggressive festive abuse, highflown idealism is mocked too, by a benevolent ridicule which sees it as a not unnatural attempt to be more than natural. It is unfortunate that Shakespeare's gay plays have come to be known as "the romantic comedies," for they almost always establish a humorous perspective about the vein of hyperbole they borrow from Renaissance romances. Wishful absolutes about love's finality, cultivated without reserve in conventional Arcadia, are made fun of by suggesting that love is not a matter of life and death, but of springtime, the only pretty ring time. The lover's conviction that he will love "for ever and a day" is seen as an illusion born of heady feeling, a symptom of the festive moment:

> Say 'a day' without the 'ever.' No, no, Orlando! Men are April when they woo, December when they wed. Maids are May when they are maids, but the sky changes when they are wives. [*As You Like It*, act 4, scene 1]

This sort of clarification about love, a recognition of the seasons, of nature's part in man, need not qualify the intensity of feeling in the festive comedies: Rosalind when she says these lines is riding the full tide of her passionate gaiety. Where the conventional romances tried to express intensity by elaborating hyperbole according to a pretty, pseudo-theological system, the comedies express the power of love as a compelling rhythm in man and nature. So the term "romantic comedies" is misleading. Shakespeare, to be sure, does not always transform his romantic plot materials. In the Claudio-Hero business in *Much Ado*, for example, the borrowed plot involved negative behavior on the basis of romantic absolutes which was not changed to carry festive feeling. Normally, however, as in *Twelfth Night*, he radically alters the emphasis when he employs romantic materials. Events which in his source control the mood, and are drawn out to exhibit extremity of devotion, producing now pathos, now anxiety, now sentiment, are felt on his stage, in the rhythm of stage time, as incidents controlled by a prevailing mood of revel. What was sentimental extremity becomes impulsive extravagance. And judgment, not committed to systematic wishful distortion, can observe with Touchstone how

> We that are true lovers run into strange capers; but as all is mortal in nature, so is all nature in love mortal in folly. [*As You Like It*, act 2, scene 4]

To turn on passionate experience and identify it with the holiday moment, as Rosalind does in insisting that the sky will change, puts the moment in perspective with life as a whole. Holiday, for the Elizabethan sensibility, implied a contrast with "everyday," when "brightness falls from the air." Occasions like May day and the Winter Revels, with their cult of natural vitality, were maintained within a civilization whose daily view of life focused on the mortality implicit in vitality. The tolerant disillusion of Anglican or Catholic culture allowed nature to have its day. But the release of that one day was understood to be a temporary license, a "misrule" which implied rule, so that the acceptance of nature was qualified. Holiday affirmations in praise of folly were limited by the underlying assumption that the natural in man is only one part of him, the part that will fade.

"How that a life was but a flower" [*As You Like It*, act 5, scene 3] was a two-sided theme: it was usually a gesture preceding "And therefore take the present time"; but it could also lead to the recognition that

> so, from hour to hour, we ripe and ripe,
> And then, from hour to hour, we rot and
> rot. [*As You Like It*, act 2, scene 7]

The second emphasis was implicit in the first; which attitude toward nature predominated depended, not on alternative "philosophies," but on where you were within a rhythm. And because the rhythm is recognized in the comedies, sentimental falsification is not necessary in expressing the ripening moment. It is indeed the present mirth and laughter of the festive plays—the immediate experience they give of nature's beneficence—which reconciles feeling, without recourse to sentimentality or cynicism, to the clarification conveyed about nature's limitations. . . .

In creating Falstaff, Shakespeare fused the clown's part with that of a festive celebrant, a Lord of Misrule, and worked out the saturnalian implications of both traditions more drastically and more complexly than anywhere else. If in the idyllic plays the humorous perspective can be described as looking past the reigning festive moment to the work-a-day world beyond, in *1 Henry IV*, the relation of comic and serious action can be described by saying that holiday is balanced against everyday and the doomsday of battle. . . .

The sort of interpretation I have proposed in outline here does not center on the way the comedies imitate characteristics of actual men and manners; but this neglect of the social observation in the plays does not imply that the way they handle social materials is unimportant. Comedy is not, obviously enough, the same thing as ritual; if it were, it would not perform its function. To express the underlying rhythm his comedy had in common with holiday, Shakespeare did not simply stage mummings; he found in the social life of his time the stuff for "a kind of history." We can see in the Saint George plays how cryptic and arbitrary action derived from ritual becomes when it is merely a fossil remnant. In a self-conscious culture, the heritage of cult is kept alive by art which makes it relevant as a mode of perception and expression. The artist gives the ritual pattern aesthetic actuality by discovering expressions of it in the fragmentary and incomplete gestures of daily life. He fulfills these gestures by making them moments in the complete action which is the art form. The form finds meaning in life.

This process of translation from social into artistic form has great historical as well as literary interest. Shakespeare's theater was taking over on a professional and everyday basis functions which until his time had largely been performed by amateurs on holiday. And he wrote at a moment when the educated part of society was modifying a ceremonial, ritualistic conception of human life to create a historical, psychological conception. His drama, indeed, was an important agency in this transformation: it provided a "theater" where the failures of ceremony could be looked at in a place apart and understood as history; it provided new ways of representing relations between language and action so as to express personality. In making drama out of rituals of state, Shakespeare makes clear their meaning as social and psychological conflict, as history. So too with the rituals of pleasure, of misrule, as against rule: his come-dy presents holiday magic as imagination, games as expressive gestures. At high moments it brings into focus, as part of the play, the significance of the saturnalian form itself as a paradoxical human need, problem and resource.

SELECTION 5:

Shakespeare's Henry IV

The following selection from Shakespeare's Henry IV, Part I *illustrates C.L. Barber's point. Jack Falstaff is directly identified as "old father Antic," one of the names of the lord of misrule, who was elected at carnival time to oversee the festivities. This "lord" was clearly an inverted form of the established authority, as Falstaff is to Henry IV.*

FALSTAFF Now, Hal, what time of day is it, lad?

PRINCE Thou art so fat-witted with drinking of old sack,[1] and unbuttoning thee after supper, and sleeping upon benches after noon, that thou hast forgotten[2] to demand that truly which thou wouldst truly know. What a devil[3] hast thou to do with the time of the day? Unless hours were cups of sack, and minutes capons, and clocks[4] the tongues of bawds, and dials the signs of leaping houses,[5] and the blessed sun himself a fair hot wench in flame-colored taffeta,[6] I see no reason why thou shouldst be so superfluous[7] to demand the time of the day.

FALSTAFF Indeed, you[8] come near me now, Hal, for we that take purses go by[9] the moon and the seven stars,[10] and not by Phoebus, "he, that wandering knight so fair."[11] And I prithee, sweet wag, when thou art king, as, God save Thy Grace[12]—Majesty I should say, for grace thou wilt have none—

PRINCE What, none?

FALSTAFF No, by my troth,[13] not so much as will serve to be prologue[14] to an egg and butter.

PRINCE Well, how then? Come, roundly,[15] roundly.

FALSTAFF Marry,[16] then, sweet wag,[17] when thou art king, let not us that are squires of the night's body be called thieves of the day's beauty.[18] Let us be Diana's foresters,[19] gentlemen of the shade, minions[20] of the moon; and let men say we be men of good government,[21] being governed, as the sea is, by our noble and chaste mistress the moon, under whose countenance[22] we steal.[23]

PRINCE Thou sayest well, and it holds well[24] too, for the fortune of us that are the moon's men doth ebb and flow like the sea, being governed, as the sea is, by the moon. As, for proof, now: a purse of gold most resolutely snatched on Monday night and most dissolutely spent on Tuesday morning, got with swearing "Lay by"[25] and spent with crying "Bring in,"[26] now in as low an ebb as the foot of the ladder[27] and by and by in as high a flow as the ridge[28] of the gallows.

FALSTAFF By the Lord, thou sayst true, lad. And is not my hostess of the tavern a most sweet wench?

PRINCE As the honey of Hybla,[29] my old lad of the castle.[30] And is not a buff jerkin[31] a most sweet robe of durance?[32]

From *William Shakespeare: "Henry IV, Part I,"* edited by David Bevington. Copyright © 1988 by David Bevington (introduction and notes). Used by permission of Bantam Books, a division of Random House, Inc.

FALSTAFF How now, how now, mad wag, what, in thy quips and thy quiddities?[33] What a plague have I to do with a buff jerkin?

PRINCE Why, what a pox[34] have I to do with my hostess of the tavern?

FALSTAFF Well, thou hast called her to a reckoning[35] many a time and oft.

PRINCE Did I ever call for thee to pay thy part?

FALSTAFF No, I'll give thee thy due, thou hast paid all there.

PRINCE Yea, and elsewhere, so far as my coin would stretch, and where it would not I have used my credit.

FALSTAFF Yea, and so used it that, were it not here apparent that thou art heir apparent—But I prithee, sweet wag, shall there be gallows standing in England when thou art king? And resolution[36] thus fubbed[37] as it is with the rusty curb of old Father Antic[38] the law? Do not thou, when thou art king, hang a thief.

PRINCE No, thou shalt.

FALSTAFF Shall I? O rare! By the Lord, I'll be a brave[39] judge.

PRINCE Thou judgest false already. I mean, thou shalt have the hanging of the thieves,[40] and so become a rare[41] hangman.

FALSTAFF Well, Hal, well; and in some sort it jumps with my humor[42] as well as waiting in the court,[43] I can tell you.

PRINCE For obtaining of suits?[44]

FALSTAFF Yea, for obtaining of suits, whereof the hangman hath no lean wardrobe. 'Sblood,[45] I am as melancholy as a gib cat[46] or a lugged bear.[47]

PRINCE Or an old lion, or a lover's lute.

FALSTAFF Yea, or the drone of a Lincolnshire bagpipe.

PRINCE What sayest thou to a hare,[48] or the melancholy of Moorditch?[49]

FALSTAFF Thou hast the most unsavory similes, and art indeed the most comparative,[50] rascalliest, sweet young prince. But, Hal, I prithee, trouble me no more with vanity.[51] I would to God thou and I knew where a commodity[52] of good names[53] were to be bought. An old lord of the Council rated[54] me the other day in the street about you, sir, but I marked him not; and yet he talked very wisely, but I regarded him not; and yet he talked wisely, and in the street too.

PRINCE Thou didst well, for wisdom[55] cries out in the streets and no man regards it.

FALSTAFF O, thou hast damnable iteration,[56] and art indeed able to corrupt a saint. Thou hast done much harm upon me, Hal, God forgive thee for it! Before I knew thee, Hal, I knew nothing;[57] and now am I, if a man should speak truly, little better than one of the wicked. I must give over this life, and I will give it over. By the Lord, an[58] I do not I am a villain. I'll be damned for never a king's son in Christendom.

PRINCE Where shall we take a purse tomorrow, Jack?

FALSTAFF Zounds,[59] where thou wilt, lad, I'll make one.[60] An I do not, call me villain and baffle[61] me.

PRINCE I see a good amendment of life in thee—from praying to purse taking.

FALSTAFF Why, Hal, 'tis my vocation, Hal. 'Tis no sin for a man to labor in his vocation.

Enter Poins.

Poins! Now shall we know if Gadshill[62] have set a match.[63] O, if men were to be saved by merit,[64] what hole in hell were hot enough for him? This is the most omnipotent[65] villain that ever cried "Stand!" to a true[66] man.

PRINCE Good morrow, Ned.

POINS Good morrow, sweet Hal. What says Monsieur Remorse? What says Sir John Sack and Sugar Jack? How agrees the devil and thee about thy soul that thou soldest him on Good Friday last for a cup of Madeira and a cold capon's leg?

PRINCE Sir John stands[67] to his word; the devil shall have his bargain, for he was never yet a breaker of proverbs. He will give the devil his due.

POINS Then art thou damned for keeping thy word with the devil.

PRINCE Else[68] he had been damned for cozening[69] the devil.

POINS But, my lads, my lads, tomorrow morning, by four o'clock early, at Gad's Hill,[70] there are pilgrims going to Canterbury with rich offerings and traders riding to London with fat purses. I have vizards[71] for you all; you have horses for yourselves. Gadshill lies[72] tonight in Rochester. I have bespoke[73] supper tomorrow night in Eastcheap. We may do it as secure as sleep. If you will go, I will stuff your purses full of crowns; if you will not, tarry at home and be hanged.

FALSTAFF Hear ye, Yedward,[74] if I tarry at home and go not, I'll hang you[75] for going.

POINS You will, chops?[76]

FALSTAFF Hal, wilt thou make one?

PRINCE Who, I rob? I a thief? Not I, by my faith.

FALSTAFF There's neither honesty, manhood, nor good fellowship in thee, nor thou cam'st not of the blood royal, if thou darest not stand for ten shillings.[77]

PRINCE Well then, once in my days I'll be a madcap.

FALSTAFF Why, that's well said.

PRINCE Well, come what will, I'll tarry at home.

FALSTAFF By the Lord, I'll be a traitor then, when thou art king.

PRINCE I care not.

POINS Sir John, I prithee leave the Prince and me alone. I will lay him down such reasons for this adventure that he shall go.

FALSTAFF Well, God give thee the spirit of persuasion and him the ears of profiting, that what thou speakest may move and what he hears may be believed, that the true prince may, for recreation's sake, prove a false thief; for the poor abuses of the time want countenance.[78] Farewell. You shall find me in Eastcheap.

PRINCE Farewell, thou latter spring! Farewell, All-hallown summer![79] [*Exit Falstaff.*]

After reading this selection and the previous one, consider these questions:

1. How did late medieval forms of drama relate to popular culture?
2. What does Barber mean by the term *festive comedy*?
3. What features of Shakespeare's plays expressed this notion of festive comedy?

Notes

1. **sack** a Spanish white wine 2. **forgotten** forgotten how 3. **a devil** in the devil 4. **dials** clocks 5. **leaping houses** houses of prostitution 6. **taffeta** (Commonly worn by prostitutes.) 7. **superfluous** (1) unnecessarily concerned (2) self-indulgent 8. **you . . . now** i.e., you've scored a point on me 9. **go by** (1) travel by the light of (2) tell time by 10. **the seven stars** the Pleiades 11. **Phoebus . . . fair** (Phoebus, god of the sun, is here equated with the wandering knight of a ballad or popular romance.) 12. **Grace** royal highness (with pun on spiritual *grace* and also on the *grace* or blessing before a meal) 13. **troth** faith 14. **prologue . . . butter** i.e., grace before a brief meal 15. **roundly** i.e., out with it 16. **Marry** indeed. (Literally, "by the Virgin Mary.") 17. **wag** joker 18. **let . . . beauty** i.e., let not us who are attendants on the goddess of night, members of her household, be blamed for stealing daylight by sleeping in the daytime 19. **Diana's foresters** (An elegant name for thieves by night; Diana is goddess of the moon and the hunt.) 20. **minions** favorites 21. **government** (1) conduct (2) commonwealth 22. **countenance** (1) face (2) patronage, approval 23. **steal** (1) move stealthily (2) rob 24. **it holds well** the comparison is apt 25. **Lay by** (A cry of highwaymen, like "Hands up!") 26. **Bring in** (An order given to a waiter in a tavern.) 27. **ladder** (1) pier ladder (2) gallows ladder 28. **ridge** crossbar 29. **Hybla** (A town, famed for its honey, in Sicily near Syracuse.) 30. **old . . . castle** (1) a roisterer (2) the name, Sir John Oldcastle, borne by Falstaff in the earlier version of the Henry IV plays 31. **buff jerkin** a leather jacket worn by officers of the law 32. **durance** (1) imprisonment (2) durability, durable cloth 33. **quiddities** subtleties of speech 34. **pox** syphilis (Here, *what a pox* is used as an expletive, like "what the devil.") 35. **reckoning** settlement of the bill (with bawdy suggestion) 36. **resolution** courage (of a highwayman) 37. **fubbed** cheated 38. **Antic** buffoon 39. **brave** excellent 40. **have . . . thieves** (1) be in charge of hanging thieves (or protecting them from hanging) (2) hang like other thieves 41. **rare** (1) rarely used (2) excellent 42. **jumps . . . humor** suits my temperament 43. **waiting in the court** being in attendance at the royal court 44. **suits** petitions (But Falstaff uses the word to mean suits of clothes; clothes belonging to an executed man were given to the executioner.) 45. **'Sblood** by his (Christ's) blood 46. **gib cat** tomcat 47. **lugged bear** bear led by a chain and baited by dogs 48. **hare** (A proverbially melancholy animal.) 49. **Moorditch** (A foul ditch draining Moorfields, outside London walls.) 50. **comparative** given to abusive comparisons 51. **vanity** worldliness 52. **commodity** supply 53. **names** reputations 54. **rated** chastised 55. **wisdom . . . it** (An allusion to Proverbs 1:20–24.) 56. **iteration** repetition (of biblical texts, with a neat twist) 57. **nothing** i.e., no evil 58. **an** if 59. **Zounds** by his (Christ's) wounds 60. **make one** be one of the party 61. **baffle** publicly disgrace 62. **Gadshill** (The name of one of the highwaymen.) 63. **set a match** arranged a robbery 64. **by merit** i.e., according to their deservings rather than by God's grace 65. **omnipotent** i.e., unparalleled, utter 66. **true** honest 67. **stands to** keeps 68. **Else** otherwise 69. **cozening** cheating 70. **Gad's Hill** (Location near Rochester on the road from London to Canterbury; one of the highwaymen is called Gadshill.) 71. **vizards** masks 72. **lies** lodges 73. **bespoke** ordered 74. **Yedward** (Nickname for Edward, Poins's first name.) 75. **hang you** have you hanged 76. **chops** i.e., fat jaws or cheeks 77. **stand . . . shillings** (1) stand up and fight for money (2) be worth 10 shillings, the value of the *royal*, the gold coin alluded to in *blood royal* 78. **want countenance** lack encouragement and protection (from men of rank) 79. **All-hallown summer** (Cf. "Indian summer"; Falstaff's summer or *latter spring*, i.e., his youth, has lasted to All Saints' Day, November 1.)

SELECTION 6:
The Civilizing Process

At the time when popular forms of culture were ascending, there also arose a countermove, which was not directly related to the power structure of church and state. The impact of humanism and of the notion of a "higher" and more refined type of life was also spreading throughout Europe. From this time onward, historians perceive a widening split between high forms of civilization and the culture of the great majority of the population. Education—even the particular type of education favored by the humanists—was not the only reason for this division. Even uneducated nobles and wealthy members of towns and cities increasingly wanted to observe a type of social intercourse and refined manners that would set them apart. In a pioneering study of these new attitudes, sociologist Norbert Elias describes the attitudes behind the rise of manners in the sixteenth century. Elias explains the introduction of manners in terms of what he calls "the civilizing process." He begins with a definition of civilité, *or civility.*

The decisive antithesis expressing the self-image of the West during the Middle Ages is that between Christianity and paganism or, more exactly, between correct, Roman-Latin Christianity, on the one hand, and paganism and heresy, including Greek and Eastern Christianity, on the other.

In the name of the Cross, and later in that of civilization, Western society wages, during the Middle Ages, its wars of colonization and expansion. And for all its secularization, the watchword "civilization" always retains an echo of Latin Christendom and the knightly-feudal crusade. The memory that chivalry and the Roman-Latin faith bear witness to a particular stage of Western society, a stage which all the major Western peoples have passed through, has certainly not disappeared.

The concept of *civilité* acquired its meaning for Western society at a time when chivalrous society and the unity of the Catholic church were disintegrating. It is the incarnation of a society

which, as a specific stage in the formation of Western manners or "civilization," was no less important than the feudal society before it. The concept of *civilité*, too, is an expression and symbol of a social formation embracing the most diverse nationalities, in which, as in the Church, a common language is spoken, first Italian and then increasingly French. These languages take over the function earlier performed by Latin. They manifest the unity of Europe, and at the same time the new social formation which forms its backbone, court society. The situation, the self-image, and the characteristics of this society find expression in the concept of *civilité*.

The concept of *civilité* received the specific stamp and function under discussion here in the second quarter of the sixteenth century. Its individual starting point can be exactly determined. It owes the specific meaning adopted by society to a short treatise by Erasmus of Rotterdam, *De civilitate morum puerilium* (On civility in children), which appeared in 1530. This work clearly treated a theme that was ripe for discussion. It immediately achieved an enormous circulation, going through edition after edition. Even within

From *The History of Manners*, vol. 1, by Norbert Elias, translated by Edmund Jephcott (New York: Pantheon, 1982). Copyright © 1978 Urizen Books. Reprinted by permission of Blackwell Publishers.

Erasmus's lifetime—that is, in the first six years after its publication—it was reprinted more than thirty times. In all, more than 130 editions may be counted, 13 of them as late as the eighteenth century. The multitude of translations, imitations, and sequels is almost without limit. Two years after the publication of the treatise the first English translation appeared. In 1534 it was published in catechism form, and at this time it was already being introduced as a schoolbook for the education of boys. German and Czech translations followed. In 1537, 1559, 1569, and 1613 it appeared in French, newly translated each time.

As early as the sixteenth century a particular French type face was given the name *civilité*, after a French work by Mathurin Cordier which combined doctrines from Erasmus's treatise with those of another humanist, Johannes Sulpicius. And a whole genre of books, directly or indirectly influenced by Erasmus's treatise, appeared under the title *Civilité* or *Civilité puérile*; these were printed up to the end of the eighteenth century in this *civilité* type.

Here, as so often in the history of words, and as was to happen later in the evolution of the concept *civilité* into *civilisation,* an individual was the instigator. By his treatise, Erasmus gave new sharpness and impetus to the long-established and commonplace word *civilitas*. Wittingly or not, he obviously expressed in it something that met a social need of the time. The concept *civilitas* was henceforth fixed in the consciousness of people with the special sense it received from his treatise. And corresponding words were developed in the various popular languages: the French *civilité*, the English "*civility*," the Italian *civiltà*, and the German *Zivilität*, which, admittedly, was never so widely adopted as the corresponding words in the other great cultures.

The more or less sudden emergence of words within languages nearly always points to changes in the lives of people themselves, particularly when the new concepts are destined to become as central and long-lived as these.

Erasmus himself may not have attributed any particular importance to his short treatise *De civilitate morum puerilium* within his total *oeuvre*. He says in the introduction that the art of forming young people involves various disciplines, but that the *civilitas morum* is only one of them, and he does not deny that it is *crassissima philosophiae pars* (the grossest part of philosophy). This treatise has its special importance less as an individual phenomenon or work than as a symptom of change, an embodiment of social processes. Above all, it is the resonance, the elevation of the title word to a central expression of the self-interpretation of European society, which draws our attention to this treatise.

What is the treatise about? Its theme must explain to us for what purpose and in what sense the new concept was needed. It must contain indications of the social changes and processes which made the word fashionable.

Erasmus's book is about something very simple: the behavior of people in society—above all, but not solely, "outward bodily propriety." It is dedicated to a noble boy, a prince's son, and written for the instruction of boys. It contains simple thoughts delivered with great seriousness, yet at the same time with much mockery and irony, in clear, polished language and with enviable precision. It can be said that none of its successors ever equaled this treatise in force, clarity, and personal character. Looking more closely, one perceives beyond it a world and a pattern of life which in many respects, to be sure, are close to our own, yet in others still quite remote; the treatise points to attitudes that we have lost, that some among us would perhaps call "barbaric" or "uncivilized." It speaks of many things that have in the meantime become unspeakable, and of many others that are now taken for granted.

Erasmus speaks, for example, of the way people look. Though his comments are meant as instruction, they also bear witness to the direct and lively observation of people of which he was capable. "Sint oculi placidi, verecundi, compositi," he says, "non torvi, quod est truculentiae . . . non vagi ac volubiles, quod est insaniae, non limi quod est suspiciosorum et insidias molentium. . . ." This can only with difficulty be translated without an appreciable alteration of tone: a wide-eyed look is a sign of stupidity, staring a sign of inertia; the looks of those prone to anger are too sharp; too lively and eloquent those of the immodest; if your look shows a calm mind and a respectful amiability, that is best. Not by chance do the ancients say: the seat of the soul is in the eyes. "Animi sedem esse in oculis."

Bodily carriage, gestures, dress, facial expressions—this "outward" behavior with which the treatise concerns itself is the expression of the inner, the whole man. Erasmus knows this and on occasion states it explicitly: "Although this outward bodily propriety proceeds from a well-composed mind, nevertheless we sometimes find that, for want of instruction, such grace is lacking in excellent and learned men."

There should be no snot on the nostrils, he says somewhat later. A peasant wipes his nose on his cap and coat, a sausage maker on his arm and elbow. It does not show much more propriety to use one's hand and then wipe it on one's clothing. It is more decent to take up the snot in a cloth, preferably while turning away. If when blowing the nose with two fingers somethings falls to the ground, it must be immediately trodden away with the foot. The same applies to spittle.

With the same infinite care and matter-of-factness with which these things are said—the mere mention of which shocks the "civilized" man of a later stage with a different affective molding—we are told how one ought to sit or greet. Gestures are described that have become strange to us, e.g., standing on one leg. And we might reflect that many of the bizarre movements of walkers and dancers that we see in medieval paintings or statues not only represent the "manner" of the painter or sculptor but also preserve actual gestures and movements that have grown strange to us, embodiments of a different mental and emotional structure.

The more one immerses oneself in the little treatise, the clearer becomes this picture of a society with modes of behavior in some respects related to ours, and in many ways remote. We see people seated at table: "A dextris sit poculum, et cultellus escarius rite purgatus, ad laevam panis," says Erasmus. The goblet and the well-cleaned knife on the right, on the left the bread. That is how the table is laid. Most people carry a knife, hence the precept to keep it clean. Forks scarcely exist, or at most for taking meat from the dish.

Knives and spoons are very often used communally. There is not always a special implement for everyone: if you are offered something liquid, says Erasmus, taste it and return the spoon after you have wiped it.

When dishes of meat are brought in, usually everyone cuts himself a piece, takes it in his hand, and puts it on his plate if there are plates, otherwise on a thick slice of bread. The expression quadra used by Erasmus can clearly mean either a metal plate or a slice of bread.

"Quidam ubi vix bene considerint mox manus in epulas conjiciunt." Some put their hands into the dishes when they are scarcely seated, says Erasmus. Wolves or gluttons do that. Do not be the first to take from a dish that is brought in. Leave dipping your fingers into the broth to the peasants. Do not poke around in the dish but take the first piece that presents itself. And just as it shows a want of forbearance to search the whole dish with one's hand—"in omnes patinae plagas manum mittere"—neither is it very polite to turn the dish round so that a better piece comes to you. What you cannot take with your hands, take on your quadra. If someone passes you a piece of cake or pastry with a spoon, either take it with your quadra or take the spoon offered to you, put the food on the quadra, and return the spoon.

As has been mentioned, plates too are uncommon. Paintings of table scenes from this or earlier times always offer the same spectacle, unfamiliar to us, that is indicated by Erasmus's treatise. The table is sometimes covered with rich cloths, sometimes not, but always there is little on it: drinking vessels, saltcellar, knives, spoons, that is all. Sometimes we see the slices of bread, the quadrae, that in French are called tranchoir or tailloir. Everyone, from the king and queen to the peasant and his wife, eats with the hands. In the upper class there are more refined forms of this. One ought to wash one's hands before a meal, says Erasmus. But there is as yet no soap for this purpose. Usually the guest holds out his hands, and a page pours water over them. The water is sometimes slightly scented with chamomile or rosemary. In good society one does not put both hands into the dish. It is most refined to use only three fingers of the hand. This is one of the marks of distinction between the upper and lower classes.

The fingers become greasy. "Digitos unctos vel ore praelingere vel ad tunicam extergere . . . incivile est," says Erasmus. It is not polite to lick them or wipe them on one's coat. Often you offer others your glass, or all drink from a communal tankard. Erasmus admonishes: "Wipe your mouth beforehand." You may want to offer someone you like some of the meat you are eating. "Refrain from that," says Erasmus, "it is not very decorous to offer something half-eaten to another." And he says further: "To dip bread you have bitten into the sauce is to behave like a peasant, and it shows little elegance to remove chewed food from the mouth and put it back on the *quadra*. If you cannot swallow a piece of food, turn round discreetly and throw it somewhere."

Then he says again: "It is good if conversation interrupts the meal from time to time. Some people eat and drink without stopping, not because they are hungry or thirsty, but because they can control their movements in no other way. They have to scratch their heads, poke their teeth, gesticulate with their hands, or play with a knife, or they can't help coughing, snorting, and spitting. All this really comes from a rustic embarrassment and looks like a form of madness."

But it is also necessary, and possible, for Erasmus to say: Do not expose without necessity "the parts to which Nature has attached modesty." Some prescribe, he says, that boys should "retain the wind by compressing the belly." But you can contract an illness that way. And in another place: "Reprimere sonitum, quern natura fert, ineptorum est, qui plus tribuunt civilitati, quam saluti" (Fools who value civility more than health repress natural sounds.) Do not be afraid of vomiting if you must; "for it is not vomiting but holding the vomit in your throat that is foul."

With great care Erasmus marks out in his treatise the whole range of human conduct, the chief situations of social and convivial life. He speaks with the same matter-of-factness of the most elementary as of the subtlest questions of human intercourse. In the first chapter he treats "the seemly and unseemly condition of the whole body," in the second "bodily culture," in the third "manners at holy places," in the fourth banquets, in the fifth

meetings, in the sixth amusement, and in the seventh the bedchamber. This is the range of questions in the discussion of which Erasmus gave new impetus to the concept of *civilitas*.

Not always is our consciousness able to recall this other stage of our own history without hesitation. The unconcerned frankness with which Erasmus and his time could discuss all areas of human conduct is lost to us. Much of what he says oversteps our threshold of delicacy.

But precisely this is one of the problems to be considered here. In tracing the transformation of the concepts by which different societies have tried to express themselves, in following back the concept of civilization to its ancestor *civilité*, one finds oneself suddenly on the track of the civilizing process itself, of the actual change in behavior that took place in the West. That it is embarrassing for us to speak or even hear of much that Erasmus discusses is one of the symptoms of this civilizing process. The greater or lesser discomfort we feel toward people who discuss or mention their bodily functions more openly, who conceal and restrain these functions less than we do, is one of the dominant feelings expressed in the judgment "barbaric" or "uncivilized." Such, then, is the nature of "barbarism and its discontents" or, in more precise and less evaluative terms, the discontent with the different structure of affects, the different standard of repugnance which is still to be found today in many societies which we term "uncivilized," the standard of repugnance which preceded our own and is its precondition. The question arises as to how and why Western society actually moved from one standard to the other, how it was "civilized." In considering this process of civilization, we cannot avoid arousing feelings of discomfort and embarrassment. It is valuable to be aware of them. It is necessary, at least while considering this process, to attempt to suspend all the feelings of embarrassment and superiority, all the value judgments and criticism associated with the concepts "civilization" or "uncivilized." Our kind of behavior has grown out of that which we call uncivilized. But these concepts grasp the actual change too statically and coarsely. In reality, our terms "civilized" and "uncivilized" do not constitute an antithesis of the kind that exists between "good" and "bad," but represent stages in a development which, moreover, is still continuing. It might well happen that our stage of civilization, our behavior, will arouse in our descendants feelings of embarrassment similar to those we sometimes feel concerning the behavior of our ancestors. Social behavior and the expression of emotions passed from a form and a standard which was not a beginning, which could not in any absolute and undifferentiated sense be designated "uncivilized," to our own, which we denote by the word "civilized." And to understand the latter we must go back in time to that from which it emerged. The "civilization" which we are accustomed to regard as a possession that comes to us apparently ready-made, without our asking how we actually came to possess it, is a process or part of a process in which we are ourselves involved. Every particular characteristic that we attribute to it—machinery, scientific discovery, forms of state, or whatever else—bears witness to a particular structure of human relations, to a particular social structure, and to the corresponding forms of behavior. The question remains whether the change in behavior, in the social process of the "civilization" of man, can be understood, at least in isolated phases and in its elementary features, with any degree of precision.

SELECTION 7:

Erasmus: On Manners

As Norbert Elias points out, the writings of the prolific humanist writer Erasmus of Rotterdam (1466–1536) were central to the spread of this new ideal of civilized behavior. These reforms were only a small part of a much wider campaign that Erasmus undertook in the first three decades of the sixteenth century. Along with a number of leading educators and civil servants (which included Sir Thomas More), Erasmus hoped to end the disruptive wars among Christian princes and to improve the moral and religious life of Christians in general. Through a great range of popular writings, religious tracts, and remarkable works of scholarship, he forged a combination of humanistic principles and ideals with a reformed notion of simple religious piety and good works. This program of Christian humanism looked to education as the means to achieve these goals. He saw the education of boys in particular as the means by which to attain a new notion of civility and a new way for individuals to understand themselves, their bodies, and their relationships with others. Since piety lay at the heart of this educational program, a new understanding of the individual's relationship to God lay at its core. In his 1530 treatise On Good Manners for Boys *Erasmus instructs his readers how to behave with others.*

From "On Good Manners," by Desiderius Erasmus, in *The Erasmus Reader*, edited by Erika Rummel (Toronto: University of Toronto Press, 1990). Copyright © 1990 University of Toronto Press. Reprinted by permission of the publisher.

Thus, for the well-ordered mind of a boy to be universally manifested—and it is most strongly manifested in the face—the eyes should be calm, respectful, and steady: not grim, which is a mark of truculence; not shameless, the hallmark of insolence; not darting and rolling, a feature of insanity; nor furtive, like those of suspects and plotters of treachery; nor gaping like those of idiots; nor should the eyes and eyelids be constantly blinking, a mark of the fickle; nor gaping as in astonishment—a characteristic observed in Socrates; not too narrowed, a sign of bad temper; nor bold and inquisitive, which indicates impertinence; but such as reflects a mind composed, respectful, and friendly. For it is no chance saying of the ancient sages that the seat of the soul is in the eyes. Old pictures tell us that it was once a mark of singular modesty to observe with eyes half-closed, just as among certain Spaniards to avoid looking at people is taken as a sign of politeness and friendship. In the same we learn from pictures that it was once the case that tightly closed lips were taken as evidence of honesty. But the naturally decorous is recognized as such by everyone. Nevertheless in these matters too it is occasionally appropriate for us to play the polypus and adapt ourselves to the customs of the region. There are certain manners of the eyes which nature bestows differently upon different men and which do not fall within our purview, save that ill-composed gesture often destroys the character and appearance not only of the eyes but of the whole body as well. On the other hand, well-composed gestures render what is naturally decorous even more attractive: if they do not remove defects, at least they disguise and minimize them. It is bad manners to look at someone with one eye open and one shut. For what else is this than to deprive oneself of an eye? Let us leave that gesture to tunnies and smiths. . . .

The nostrils should be free from any filthy collection of mucus, as this is disgusting (the philosopher Socrates was reproached for that failing too). It is boorish to wipe one's nose on one's cap or clothing; to do so on one's sleeve or forearm is for fishmongers, and it is not much better to wipe it with one's hand, if you then smear the discharge on your clothing. The polite way is to catch the matter from the nose in a handkerchief, and this should be done by turning away slightly if decent people are present. If, in clearing your nose with two fingers, some matter falls on the ground, it should be immediately ground under foot. It is bad manners to breathe noisily all the time, which is the sign of furious anger. It is even worse to make a habit of snorting like one possessed, although we must make allowance for heavy breathers who are afflicted with asthma. It is ridiculous to trumpet with one's nose; this is for horn-blowers and elephants. Twitching the nose is for scoffers and buffoons. If you must sneeze while others are present, it is polite to turn away. When the attack has subsided you should cross your face, then, raising your cap and acknowledging the blessings of those who have (or you assume to have) blessed you (for sneezing, like yawning, completely mocks one's sense of hearing), beg pardon or give thanks. One should be scrupulous in blessing another when he sneezes. If older people are present and bless a high-ranking man or woman, the polite thing for a boy to do is to raise his cap. Again, to imitate or consciously repeat a sneeze—in effect to show off one's strength—is the sign of a fool. To suppress a sound which is brought on by nature is characteristic of silly people who set more store by 'good manners' than good health. . . .

If you should feel the urge to yawn and are unable to turn aside or withdraw, you should cover your mouth with a handkerchief or with the palm of the hand and then make the sign of the cross. To laugh at every word or deed is the sign of a fool; to laugh at none the sign of a blockhead. It is quite wrong to laugh at improper words or actions. Loud laughter and the immoderate mirth that shakes the whole body are unbecoming to any age but much more so to youth. The neighing sound that some people make when they laugh is also unseemly. And the person who opens his mouth wide in a rictus, with wrinkled cheeks and exposed teeth, is also impolite. This is a canine habit. The face should express mirth in such a way that it neither distorts the appearance of the mouth nor evinces a dissolute mind. Only fools use expressions like: 'I am dissolving with laughter,' 'I am bursting with laughter,' 'I am dying with laughter.' If something so funny should occur that it produces uncontrolled laughter of this sort, the face should be covered with a napkin or with the hand. To laugh when alone or for no obvious reason is put down to either stupidity or insanity. If, however, something of that sort happens, it is good manners to explain the reason for your laughter to others, or if you do not believe that a true reason should be offered, fabricate something lest someone suspect that he is being laughed at. It is not polite to grip the lower lip with the upper teeth, for this is a threatening gesture, as is biting the upper lip with the lower teeth. But it is simply silly to be repeatedly licking round the edges of the lips. Their pictures tell us that it was once a sign of politeness among the Germans to pucker the lips slightly and form them as for a kiss. It is foolish to poke the tongue out to mock someone. Turn away when spitting to avoid spitting on or spraying someone. If any disgusting matter is spat onto the ground, it should, as I have said, be ground under foot lest it nauseate someone. If that is impermissible, catch up the spittle with a cloth. Reswallowing spittle is uncouth as is the practice we observe in some people of spitting after every third word, not through need but through force of habit. Some have the distressing habit of coughing slightly while speaking, again, not through need but through habit. That is a gesture of liars and of those who deceitfully contrive their words when they speak. Some have the even more disagreeable habit of belching after every third word, a practice which if developed from the earliest years stays with one even in later life.

After reading this selection and the previous one, consider these questions:

1. What impact did humanism have on the world of popular culture?
2. How does Elias describe the origins and goals of manners?
3. According to Erasmus, how should a boy behave?

CHAPTER 13
The Renaissance: The Novelties of Rebirth

Even with the "setbacks" of the Black Death, the church schism, and continued warfare, Europe continued to evolve in the fourteenth and fifteenth centuries. More centralized types of government emerged within the great feudal monarchies of France and England as well as within the Holy Roman Empire. Late medieval towns established more sophisticated manufacturing and commercial practices, more complex forms of government, and new types of social and cultural organizations. Religious life, too, evolved, especially in terms of more individualized modes of religious experience, either through mysticism or in various types of lay piety. All of these developments, however, were still contained within the framework and the values set by the Christian civilization that had evolved in the High Middle Ages. Thus, these new forms were further articulations and refinements (often what appears to us overrefinement) of what the civilization had given them.

Beginning in the late fourteenth and early fifteenth century, within unfolding political, economic, social, and religious developments, there arose new ways to understand them, new languages to speak of them, and new ways to give meaning to them. These changes, in other words, did not so much break from the practical forms of the later Middle Ages as transform new ways of giving them direction. The most obvious changes first occurred in Italy. Loosened from the controls of the empire and church, and thus without the control of an overarching political and military structure, the social and cultural dominance of a royal court, or the direct control of religious and cultural life by the church and its hierarchy—there emerged in central and northern Italy a number of independent city-states that increasingly found new ways to organize political power, shape social organization in general, and define the good life. These new forms were most often expressed through a new understanding of ancient literature and of the worldly values that these writings exhibited. The so-called revival of antiquity, from which the term *Renaissance* ("rebirth") received its name, was not simply a matter of possessing or retrieving the lost texts of antiquity. Rather, newly recovered texts as well as those already known were read in new ways and were found to speak to the present situation in new ways. Although associated with the rebirth of ancient learning, what we call the Renaissance evolved more as a way of using this learning to reconceive of political and social life, to redefine the types and meaning of modern literature and the arts, and in general to reposition the individual's relationship to the world and to God. This complex process, however, was not a reinstitution of the language and forms of antiquity into the present; it involved a process of merging and transforming what had been developed from the Middle Ages into a new, more "worldly" form of existence. The term *worldly*, however, means not simply secularization but rather a reformulation of the notion and worth of lay society in relation to medieval notions of Christian contempt for the world.

SELECTION 1:

Jacob Burckhardt and the Italian Renaissance

No historian has been more influential in providing us with a definition of the Renaissance in Italy than Jacob Burckhardt. In his 1860 book Civilization of the Renaissance in Italy, *Burckhardt emphasizes that, although the revival of classical antiquity was all-pervasive, it alone does not suffice to define the Renaissance as a whole. Larger forces and more profound processes were at work. Although in the fifteenth and sixteenth centuries these forces were often spoken of and defined in terms of the models derived from antiquity, this revival neither caused nor fully circumscribed these forces and processes. For Burckhardt, these larger forces, changing at a basic level political structures and social organization, can most clearly be seen in the emergence of a new type of individual. By the notion of "the development of the individual," Burckhardt does not mean "individualism" as a political doctrine or an atomistic notion of human consciousness. Rather, Burckhardt stresses the ways in which individual human beings found the meaning and worth of existence within this world and in their actions within this world. A new image of the person, in other words, arose as individuals came to define themselves in ways unknown to the Middle Ages. No longer defining the meaning of actions in terms of their religious value, Renaissance men and women found new ways to give meaning to their lives. These ways were not necessarily anti-Christian or antireligious per se, but merely more worldly than their medieval counterparts.*

The formation of new personality types in the Renaissance broke from the Middle Ages in another sense. Whereas in early centuries individuals gave definition to themselves in terms of functional types—the warrior, the nun, the scholar, the merchant—individuals in the fourteenth and fifteenth centuries increasingly gave meaning to their lives in terms of more individually specific forms. The "Renaissance man," for Burckhardt, represented less a single personality model than it did a variety of ways in which individuals could define themselves. Some became specialists, as did Niccolò Machiavelli (1469–1527); others became "many-sided men," as with Filippo Brunelleschi (1377–1446); and still others evolved into that remarkable type, the "all-sided man," such as Leonardo da Vinci (1452–1519). The individual definitions are ultimately less important than the fact that a society arose and a culture formed in which such diversity was not only accepted but also encouraged. The revival of antiquity, the evolution of new social forms and new types of cultural expression, and even the ways in which the individual related to faith and morality, all depended on this new sense of the individual.

Burckhardt introduces this theme in the following selection. He begins by speaking of the contrast between the corporate forms of definitions, which, as we have seen, were dominant in the Middle Ages and indeed represented the creative force of the era, and this new sense of the single individual that gradually emerged in the course of the fourteenth and fifteenth centuries.

In the Middle Ages both sides of human consciousness—that which was turned within as that which was turned without—lay dreaming or half awake beneath a common veil. The veil was woven of faith, illusion, and childish prepossession, through which the world and history were seen clad in strange hues. Man was conscious of himself only as member of a race, people, party, family, or corporation—only through some general category. In Italy this veil first melted into air; an *objective* treatment and consideration of the State and of all the things of this world became possible. The *subjective* side at the same time asserted itself with corresponding emphasis; man became a spiritual *individual*, and recognized himself as such. In the same way the Greek had once distinguished himself from the barbarian, and the Arabian had felt himself an individual at a time when other Asiatics knew themselves only as members of a race. It will not be difficult to show that this result was owing, above all, to the political circumstances of Italy.

In far earlier times we can here and there detect a development of free personality which in Northern Europe either did not occur at all or could not display itself in the same manner. The band of audacious wrongdoers in the sixteenth century described to us by [the tenth-century historian] Luidprand, some of the contemporaries of Gregory VII, and a few of the opponents of the first Hohenstaufen [the German family that furnished sovereigns of Sicily], show us characters of this kind. But at the close of the thirteenth century Italy began to swarm with individuality; the charm laid upon human personality was dissolved, and a thousand figures meet us each in its own special shape and dress. Dante's great poem [*The Divine Comedy*] would have been impossible in any other country of Europe, if only for the reason that they all still lay under the spell of race. For Italy the august poet, through the wealth of individuality which he set forth, was the most national herald of his time. But this unfolding of the treasures of

From *The Civilization of the Renaissance in Italy*, vol. 1, by Jacob Burckhardt, translated by S.G.C. Middlemore (New York: Macmillan, 1904).

human nature in literature and art—this many-sided representation and criticism—will be discussed in separate chapters; here we have to deal only with the psychological fact itself. This fact appears in the most decisive and unmistakable form. The Italians of the fourteenth century knew little of false modesty or of hypocrisy in any shape; not one of them was afraid of singularity, of being and seeming unlike his neighbours. . . .

An acute and practised eye might be able to trace, step by step, the increase in the number of complete men during the fifteenth century. Whether they had before them as a conscious object the harmonious development of their spiritual and material existence is hard to say; but several of them attained it, so far as is consistent with the imperfection of all that is earthly. . . .

When this impulse to the highest individual development was combined with a powerful and varied nature, which had mastered all the elements of the culture of the age, then arose the "all-sided man"—l' *uomo universale*—who belonged to Italy alone. Men there were of encyclopaedic knowledge in many countries during the Middle Ages, for this knowledge was confined within narrow limits; and even in the twelfth century there were universal artists, but the problems of architecture were comparatively simple and uniform, and in sculpture and painting the matter was of more importance than the form. But in Italy at the time of the Renaissance we find artists who in every branch created new and perfect works, and who also made the greatest impression as men. Others, outside the arts they practised, were masters of a vast circle of spiritual interests. . . .

The fifteenth century is, above all, that of the many-sided men. There is no biography which does not, besides the chief work of its hero, speak of other pursuits all passing beyond the limits of dilettantism. The Florentine merchant and statesman was often learned in both the classical languages; the most famous humanists read the ethics and politics of Aristotle to him and his sons; even the daughters of the house were highly educated. It is in these circles that private education was first treated seriously. The humanist, on his side, was compelled to the most varied at-tainments, since his philological learning was not limited, as it now is, to the theoretical knowledge of classical antiquity, but had to serve the practical needs of daily life. While studying Pliny, he made collections of natural history; the geography of the ancients was his guide in treating of modern geography, their history was his pattern in writing contemporary chronicles, even when composed in Italian; he not only translated the comedies of [the early Roman playwright] Plautus, but acted as manager when they were put on the stage; every effective form of ancient literature down to the dialogues of [the Greek rhetorician] Lucian he did his best to imitate; and besides all this he acted as magistrate, secretary, and diplomatist—not always to his own advantage.

But among these many-sided men some who may truly be call "all-sided" tower above the rest. Before analysing the general phases of life and culture of this period we may here, on the threshold of the fifteenth century, consider for a moment the figure of one of these giants—Leon Battista Alberti (b. ? 1404, d. 1472). His biography, which is only a fragment, speaks of him but little as an artist, and makes no mention at all of his great significance in the history of architecture. We shall now see what he was apart from these special claims to distinction.

In all by which praise is won Leon Battista from his childhood excelled. Of his various gymnastic feats and exercises we read with astonishment how, with his feet together, he could spring over a man's head; how in the cathedral he threw a coin in the air till it was heard to ring against the distant roof; how the wildest horses trembled under him. In three things he desired to appear faultless to others, in walking, in riding, and in speaking. He learned music without a master, and yet his compositions were admired by professional judges. Under the pressure of poverty he studied both civil and canonical law for many years, till exhaustion brought on a severe illness. In his twenty-fourth year, finding his memory for words weakened, but his sense of facts unimpaired, he set to work at physics and mathematics. And all the while he acquired every sort of accomplishment and dexterity, cross-examining artists, scholars, and artisans of all descriptions, down to the cobblers, about the secrets and peculiarities of their craft. Painting and modelling he practised by the way, and especially excelled in admirable likenesses from memory. Great admiration was excited by his mysterious *camera obscura*, in which he showed at one time the stars and the moon rising over rocky hills, at another wide landscapes with mountains and gulfs receding into dim perspective, and with fleets advancing on the waters in shade or sunshine. And that which others created he welcomed joyfully, and held every human achievement which followed the laws of beauty for something almost divine. To all this must be added his literary works, first of all those on art, which are landmarks and authorities of the first order for the Renaissance of Form, especially in architecture; then his Latin prose writings—novels and other works—of which some have been taken for productions of antiquity; his elegies, eclogues, and humorous dinner-speeches. He also wrote an Italian treatise on domestic life in four books; various moral, philosophical, and historical works; and many speeches and poems, including a funeral oration on his dog. Notwithstanding his admiration for the Latin language, he wrote in Italian, and encouraged others to do the same; himself a disciple of Greek science, he maintained the doctrine that without Christianity the world would wander in a labyrinth of error. His serious and witty sayings were thought worth collecting, and specimens of them, many columns long, are quoted in

his biography. And all that he had and knew he imparted, as rich natures always do, without the least reserve, giving away his chief discoveries for nothing. But the deepest spring of his nature has yet to be spoken of—the sympathetic intensity with which he entered into the whole life around him. At the sight of noble trees and waving cornfields he shed tears; handsome and dignified old men he honoured as a "delight of nature," and could never look at them enough. Perfectly formed animals won his goodwill as being specially favoured by nature; and more than once, when he was ill, the sight of a beautiful landscape cured him. No wonder that those who saw him in this close and mysterious communion with the world ascribed to him the gift of prophecy. He was said to have foretold a bloody catastrophe in the [Italian princely] family of Este, the fate of Florence, and the death of the Popes years before they happened, and to be able to read into the countenances and the hearts of men. It need not be added that an iron will pervaded and sustained his whole personality; like all the great men of the Renaissance, he said, "Men can do all things if they will."

And Leonardo da Vinci was to Alberti as the finisher to the beginner, as the master to the *dilettante*. Would only that [the biographer of Italian artists Giorgio] Vasari's work were here supplemented by a description like that of Alberti! The colossal outlines of Leonardo's nature can never be more than dimly and distantly conceived.

SELECTION 2:
The Dignity of Man

In his interpretation of the Italian Renaissance, as well as with the organization of his The Civilization of the Renaissance in Italy, *Jacob Burckhardt found the central experience of the development of the individual and its highest expression in the Italian humanist Giovanni Pico della Mirandola's* Oration on the Dignity of Man. *Drawing on a rich variety of ancient sources—from classical antiquity, Christian mysticism, the revival of*

Hermetic wisdom, and the body of magical texts called the Jewish Kabal-ah, Pico (1463–1494) developed an image of the freely creative individ-ual—the microcosm—in relation to a loving and creating God—the macrocosm. No longer merely a creature of God, the individual found his definition as a creative being in the image of the creative God.

I have read in the records of the Arabians, rev-erend Fathers, that Abdala the Saracen, when questioned as to what on this stage of the world, as it were, could be seen most worthy of wonder, replied: "There is nothing to be seen more won-derful than man." In agreement with this opinion is the saying of Hermes Trismegistus: "A great miracle, [the Greek God] Asclepius, is man." But when I weighed the reason for these maxims, the many grounds for the excellence of human nature reported by many men failed to satisfy me—that man is the intermediary between creatures, the in-timate of the gods, the king of the lower beings, by the acuteness of his senses, by the discernment of his reason, and by the light of his intelligence the interpreter of nature, the interval between fixed eternity and fleeting time, and (as the Per-sians say) the bond, nay, rather, the marriage song of the world, on David's testimony but little lower than the angels. Admittedly great though these reasons be, they are not the principal grounds, that is, those which may rightfully claim for them-selves the privilege of the highest admiration. For why should we not admire more the angels them-selves and the blessed choirs of heaven? At last it seems to me I have come to understand why man is the most fortunate of creatures and consequent-ly worthy of all admiration and what precisely is that rank which is his lot in the universal chain of Being—a rank to be envied not only by brutes but even by the stars and by minds beyond this world. It is a matter past faith and a wondrous one. Why should it not be? For it is on this very account that man is rightly called and judged a great miracle and a wonderful creature indeed.

But hear, Fathers, exactly what this rank is and, as friendly auditors, conformably to your kindness, do me this favor. God the Father, the supreme Ar-chitect, had already built this cosmic home we be-hold, the most sacred temple of His godhead, by the laws of His mysterious wisdom. The region above the heavens He had adorned with Intelli-gences, the heavenly spheres He had quickened with eternal souls, and the excrementary and filthy parts of the lower world He had filled with a mul-titude of animals of every kind. But, when the work was finished, the Craftsman kept wishing that there were someone to ponder the plan of so great a work, to love its beauty, and to wonder at its vastness. Therefore, when everything was done (as Moses and Timaeus bear witness), He finally took thought concerning the creation of man. But there was not among His archetypes that from which He could fashion a new offspring, nor was there in His treasure-houses anything which He might bestow on His new son as an inheritance, nor was there in the seats of all the world a place where the latter might sit to contemplate the universe. All was now complete; all things had been assigned to the high-est, the middle, and the lowest orders. But in its final creation it was not the part of the Father's power to fail as though exhausted. It was not the part of His wisdom to waver in a needful matter through poverty of counsel. It was not the part of His kindly love that he who was to praise God's di-vine generosity in regard to others should be com-pelled to condemn it in regard to himself.

At last the best of artisans ordained that that creature to whom He had been able to give noth-ing proper to himself should have joint posses-sion of whatever had been peculiar to each of the different kinds of being. He therefore took man as a creature of indeterminate nature and, assign-ing him a place in the middle of the world, ad-dressed him thus: "Neither a fixed abode nor a form that is thine alone nor any function peculiar to thyself have we given thee, Adam, to the end that according to thy longing and according to thy judgment thou mayest have and possess what abode, what form, and what functions thou thyself shalt desire. The nature of all other beings is limited and constrained within the bounds of laws prescribed by Us. Thou, constrained by no limits, in accordance with thine own free will, in whose hand We have placed thee, shalt ordain for thyself the limits of thy nature. We have set thee at the world's center that thou mayest from thence more easily observe whatever is in the world. We have made thee neither of heaven nor of earth, neither mortal nor immortal, so that with freedom of choice and with honor, as though the maker and molder of thyself, thou mayest fashion thyself in whatever shape thou shalt prefer. Thou shalt have the power to degenerate into the lower forms of life, which are brutish. Thou shalt have the power, out of thy soul's judgment, to be reborn into the higher forms, which are divine."

O supreme generosity of God the Father, O highest and most marvelous felicity of man! To him it is granted to have whatever he chooses, to be whatever he wills.

SELECTION 3:
The Renaissance Family

Jacob Burckhardt's thesis has often been misunderstood. Medieval historians have pointed to the existence of strong individuals in the Middle Ages, and Burckhardt himself takes note of these strong individuals in The Civilization of the Renaissance in Italy. *He contends, however, that although there were instances of such individuals, what emerged in the Renaissance was a self-conscious striving for more individualized forms of existence. From this, new images of human beings came forth. This is new and not only indicated a new set of values but also a new set of social relations. Among historians of the Italian Renaissance, some point to the fact that the family—from which Burckhardt's individuals supposedly had to break away—remained a major social and political unit throughout the Renaissance period. Again, Burckhardt argues less that a clear-cut break from the more collective family allegiances of the Middle Ages occurred and more that a realignment took place among the family members as the image of themselves and the values they now prized shifted.*

The family did in fact remain the basic social unity of Renaissance Italy, more important for the individual than allegiance to church or state. Though based on ties of blood and marriage, the notion of the family included material possession, social status, and often political power. For these and other reasons, the family, along with its wealth, unity, and reputation, were highly valued throughout the Renaissance.

In the various ricordi, *or records, of the larger Florentine families, the head of the household chronicled financial transactions, marriages, and other major events within the family's history. These records clearly indicate the complexities and the continuing significance of the family throughout the Renaissance. The following selection from the* ricordi *of*

Gregorio Dati records his marriage arrangements during the late four-teenth and early fifteenth centuries

In the name of God and the Virgin Mary, of Blessed Michael the Archangel, of SS. John the Baptist and John the Evangelist, of SS. Peter and Paul, of the holy scholars, SS. Gregory and Jerome, and of St. Mary Magdalene and St. Elisabeth and all the blessed saints in heaven—may they ever intercede for us—I shall record here how I married my second wife, Isabetta, known as Betta, the daughter of Mari di Lorenzo Vilanuzzi and of Monna Veronica, daughter of Pagolo d'Arrigo Guglielmi, and I shall also record the promises which were made to me. May God and his Saints grant by their grace that they be kept.

On March 31, 1393, I was betrothed to her and on Easter Monday, April 7, I gave her a ring. On June 22, a Sunday, I became her husband in the name of God and good fortune. Her first cousins, Giovanni and Lionardo di Domenico Arrighi, promised that she should have a dowry of 900 gold florins and that, apart from the dowry, she should have the income from a farm in S. Fiore a Elsa which had been left her as a legacy by her mother, Monna Veronica. It was not stated at the time how much this amounted to but it was understood that she would receive the accounts. We arranged our match very simply indeed and with scarcely any discussion. God grant that nothing but good may come of it. On the 26th of that same June, I received a payment of 800 gold florins from the bank of Giacomino and Company. This was the dowry. I invested in the shop of Buonaccorso Berardi and his partners. At the same time I received the trousseau which my wife's cousins valued at 106 florins, in the light of which they deducted 6 florins from another account, leaving me the equivalent of 100 florins. But from what I heard from her, and what I saw myself, they had overestimated it by 30 florins or more. However, from politeness, I said nothing

about this. . . . Our Lord God was pleased to call to Himself the blessed soul of . . . Betta, on Monday, October 2 [1402] . . . and the next day, Tuesday, at three in the afternoon she was buried in our grave in S. Spirito. May God receive her soul in his glory. Amen. . . .

I record that on May 8, 1403, I was betrothed to Ginevra, daughter of Antonio di Piero Piuvichese Brancacci, in the church of S. Maria sopra Porta. The dowry was 1,000 florins: 700 in cash and 300 in a farm at Campi. On . . . May 20, we were married, but we held no festivities or wedding celebrations as we were in mourning for Manetto Dati [Gregorio's son], who had died the week before. God grant us a good life together. Ginevra had been married before for four years to Tommaso Brancacci, by whom she had an eight-month-old son. She is now in her twenty-first year.

After that [1411] it was God's will to recall to Himself the blessed soul of my wife Ginevra. She died in childbirth after lengthy suffering, which she bore with remarkable strength and patience. She was perfectly lucid at the time of her death, when she received all the sacraments: confession, communion, extreme unction, and a papal indulgence granting absolution for all her sins. . . . It comforted her greatly, and she returned her soul to her Creator on September 7. . . . On Friday the 8th she was honorably buried and on the 9th, masses were said for her soul.

Memo that on Tuesday, January 28, 1421, I made an agreement with Niccolò d'Andrea del Benino to take his niece Caterina for my lawful wife. She is the daughter of the late Dardano di Niccolò Guicciardini and of Monna Tita, Andrea del Benino's daughter. We were betrothed on the morning of Monday, February 3, the Eve of Carnival. I met Piero and Giovanni di Messer Luigi [Guicciardini] in the church of S. Maria sopra Porta, and Niccolò d'Andrea del Benino was our mediator. The dowry promised me was 600 florins, and the notary was Ser Niccolò di Ser Verdiano. I went to dine with her that evening in Piero's house and the Saturday after Easter. . . . I gave her the ring and then on Sunday evening,

From *Two Memoirs of Renaissance Florence*, edited by Gene Brucker, translated by Julia Martines (New York: Harper & Row, 1967). Reprinted by permission of Gene Brucker.

March 30, she came to live in our house simply and without ceremony.

After reading this selection and the previous ones, consider these questions:

1. How does Burckhardt define the new sense of the individual in the Renaissance?
2. How does this sense of the individual differ from earlier forms of individual definition?
3. How did the family continue to be a basic social and political unit during the Renaissance?

SELECTION 4:

The Origins of Renaissance Humanism

Within and alongside commitments to family, church, and state, there emerged new values in the Renaissance. This can be clearly seen in the new emphasis given to education and to an education of a very specific kind. The ways in which the reading of the authors of antiquity, especially Cicero, provided models of Latin style and also opened new attitudes toward a "this-worldly" existence can be seen in the writings of the first humanist, Francesco Petrarch (1304–1374). Especially in his Italian poems, he found more individual modes of expressing feeling than were known to the Middle Ages; likewise, he found a meaningful existence within his own immediate experience of life. Petrarch turned to the model of ancient literature both for his own literary endeavors and for his own sense of selfhood. In Petrarch, the ancient virtues of pride and fame again became worthy goals of human endeavor. Such adoration of ancient authors and values was never readily accepted. Especially in his mature years, Petrarch struggled with the questions of whether his poetry and the pride he took in it did not undermine and ultimately deny Christian virtues; pride and worldly fame still threatened the salvation of his soul. In an intimate and compelling account of these internal struggles, contained in a work entitled My Secret, *Petrarch speaks of his inner turmoil through a fictional debate with St. Augustine. The "Africa" mentioned in the dialogue refers to Petrarch's unfinished epic poem on Rome's conquest of Carthage—a poem clearly modeled after Virgil's* Aeneid.

From *Petrarch's Secret; or The Soul's Conflict with Passion*, translated by William H. Draper (London: Chatto & Windus, 1891).

S. AUGUSTINE. The desire of all good cannot exist without thrusting out every lower wish. You know how many different objects one longs for in life. All these you must first learn to count as nothing before you can rise to the desire for the chief good; which a man loves less when along with it he loves something else that does not minister to it.

PETRARCH. I recognise the thought.

S. AUGUSTINE. How many men are there who have extinguished all their passions, or, not to speak of extinguishing, tell me how many are there who have subdued their spirit to the control of Reason, and will dare to say, "I have no more in common with my body; all that once seemed so pleasing to me is become poor in my sight. I aspire now to joys of nobler nature"?

PETRARCH. Such men are rare indeed. And now I understand what those difficulties are with which you threatened me.

S. AUGUSTINE. When all these passions are extinguished, then, and not till then, will desire be full and free. For when the soul is uplifted on one side to heaven by its own nobility, and on the other dragged down to earth by the weight of the flesh and the seductions of the world, so that it both desires to rise and also to sink at one and the same time, then, drawn contrary ways, you find you arrive nowhither.

PETRARCH. What, then, would you say a man must do for his soul to break the fetters of the world, and mount up the perfect and entire to the realms above?

S. AUGUSTINE. What leads to this goal is, as I said in the first instance, the practice of meditation on death and the perpetual recollection of our mortal nature. . . .

S. AUGUSTINE. Do you remember with what delight you used to wander in the depth of the country? Sometimes, laying yourself down on a bed of turf, you would listen to the water of a brook murmuring over the stones; at another time, seated on some open hill, you would let your eye wander freely over the plain stretched at your feet; at others, again, you enjoyed a sweet slumber beneath the shady trees of some valley in the noontide heat, and revelled in the delicious silence. Never idle, in your soul you would ponder over some high meditation, with only the Muses for your friends—you were never less alone than when in their company, and then, like the old man in Virgil who reckoned himself

"As rich as kings, when, at the close of day,
Home to his cot he took his happy way,
And on his table spread his simple fare,
Fresh from the meadow without cost or care,"

you would come at sunset back to your humble roof; and, contented with your good things, did you not find yourself the richest and happiest of mortal men?

PETRARCH. Ah, well-a-day! I recall it all now, and the remembrance of that time makes me sigh with regret.

S. AUGUSTINE. Why—why do you speak of sighing? And who, pray, is the author of your woes? It is, indeed, your own spirit and none other which too long has not dared to follow the true law of its nature, and has thought itself a prisoner only because it would not break its chain. Even now it is dragging you along like a runaway horse, and unless you tighten the rein it will rush you to destruction. Ever since you grew tired of your leafy trees, of your simple way of life, and society of country people, egged on by cupidity, you have plunged once more into the midst of the tumultuous life of cities. I read in your face and speech what a happy and peaceful life you lived; for what miseries have you not endured since then? Too rebellious against the teachings of experience, you still hesitate! . . .

PETRARCH. Alas, alas, I am more wretched than I thought. Do you mean to tell me my soul is still bound by two chains of which I am unconscious?

S. AUGUSTINE. All the same they are plain enough to see; but, dazzled by their beauty, you think they are not fetters but treasures; and, to keep to the same figure, you are like some one who, with hands and feet fast bound in shackles of gold, should look at them with delight and not see at all that they are shackles. Yes, you yourself with blinded eyes keep looking at your bonds; but, oh strange delusion! you are charmed with the very chains that are dragging you to your death, and, what is most sad of all, you glory in them!

PETRARCH. What may these chains be of which you speak?

S. AUGUSTINE. Love and glory. . . .

S. AUGUSTINE. She [Laura] has detached your mind from the love of heavenly things and has inclined your heart to love the creature more than the Creator: and that one path alone leads, sooner than any other, to death.

PETRARCH. I pray you make no rash judgment. The love which I feel for her has most certainly led me to love God.

S. AUGUSTINE. But it has inverted the true order.

PETRARCH. How so?

S. AUGUSTINE. Because every creature should be dear to us because of our love for the Creator. But in your case, on the contrary, held captive by the charm of the creature, you have not loved the Creator as you ought. You have admired the Divine Artificer as though in all His works He had made nothing fairer than the object of your love, although in truth the beauty of the body should be reckoned last of all. . . .

PETRARCH. Well do I know that old story bandied about by the philosophers, how they declare that all the earth is but a tiny point, how the soul alone endures for infinite millions of years, how fame cannot fill either the earth or the soul, and other paltry pleas of this sort, by which they try to turn minds aside from the love of glory. But I beg you will produce some more solid arguments than these, if you know any; for experience has shown me that all this is more specious than convincing. I do not think to become as God, or to inhabit eternity, or embrace heaven and earth. Such glory as belongs to man is enough for me. That is all I sigh after. Mortal myself; it is but mortal blessings I desire.

S. AUGUSTINE. Oh, if that is what you truly mean, how wretched are you! If you have no desire for things immortal, if no regard for what is eternal, then you are indeed wholly of the earth earthy: then all is over for you; no hope at all is left. . . .

PETRARCH. I do not think my way of looking at it is so unreasonable as you imagine. My principle is that, as concerning the glory which we may hope for here below, it is right for us to seek while we are here below. One may expect to enjoy that other more radiant glory in heaven, when we shall

have there arrived, and when one will have no more care or wish for the glory of earth. Therefore, as I think, it is in the true order that mortal men should first care for mortal things; and that to things transitory things eternal should succeed; because to pass from those to these is to go forward in most certain accordance with what is ordained for us, although no way is open for us to pass back again from eternity to time.

S. AUGUSTINE. O man, little in yourself, and of little wisdom! Do you, then, dream that you shall enjoy every pleasure in heaven and earth, and everything will turn out fortunate and prosperous for you always and everywhere? But that delusion has betrayed thousands of men thousands of times, and has sunk into hell a countless host of souls. Thinking to have one foot on earth and one in heaven, they could neither stand here below nor mount on high. . . .

S. AUGUSTINE. Which foot you mean to hobble on, I do not know. You seem inclined to leave yourself derelict, rather than your books.

As for me, I shall do my duty, with what success depends on you; but at least I shall have satisfied my conscience. Throw to the winds these great loads of histories; the deeds of the Romans have been celebrated quite enough by others, and are known by their own fame. Get out of Africa and leave it to its possessors. You will add nothing to the glory of your Scipio or to your own. He can be exalted to no higher pinnacle, but you may bring down his reputation, and with it your own. Therefore leave all this on one side, and now at length take possession of yourself; and to come back to our starting-point, let me urge you to enter upon the meditation of your last end, which comes on step by step without your being aware. Tear off the veil; disperse the shadows; look only on that which is coming; with eyes and mind give all your attention there: let nought else distract you. Heaven, Earth, the Sea—these all suffer change. What can man, the frailest of all creatures, hope for?

SELECTION 5:
The Ideal Courtier

The values Petrarch drew from ancient literature were to be seen in the next two centuries as the foundations for a new definition of education and the place of education in the lives of individuals. As opposed to the professionally oriented education (in medicine or law) or the theologically dominated curriculum of the Middle Ages, the new humanist education spoke to the full development of the individual. Petrarch began this process through the recovery of ancient manuscripts; and, more importantly, in these manuscripts he found a new sense of Latin style and a new understanding of man's relationship to the world. In the course of the next century, this return to ancient models in literature and philosophy set a new standard for education (the studia humanitatis*) and created a new group of educated individuals, the humanists. Renaissance humanists pursued a wide array of activities, from recovering lost manuscripts to translating these texts and serving as civil servants in the governments of the republics or educated ornaments within the princely courts.*

Perhaps humanism received its clearest expression in the new types of education that evolved in the Italian Renaissance. The study of grammar and rhetoric was redefined and moral philosophy and history were added to the school curriculum. Petrus Paulus Vergerius (1370–1444) was one of the most influential of these humanist educators. He taught at Florence, Bologna, and Padua. Soon after 1400 he wrote a treatise on education that proved definitive for the new education. While admitting the importance of the medieval course of study of the trivium and quadrivium, and even of the traditional disciplines of medicine, law, and theology, Vergerius gave greater stress to the new "liberal studies" of history, moral philosophy, rhetoric, and literature.

The model of the educated human being became the dominant one, defining both who and how individuals behaved in society. Through their activities as educators and civil servants, the humanists were widely influential among the powerful and well-to-do of fifteenth-century Italy. The use of these ancient texts also inspired contemporary writers and artists to seek new kinds and new levels of creativity. Humanism influenced civic leaders, churchmen, and artists, but it also had an impact on the various princely courts of Italy.

Jacob Burckhardt finds in Baldassare Castiglione's Book of the Courtier *the fullest articulation of this new model of the cultivated individual in the service of a prince. Castiglione (1478–1529) himself served the dukes of Urbino.*

Without waiting any longer, signor Gaspar Pallavicino said: "So that our game may have the form prescribed and that we may not appear to esteem little that privilege of opposing which has been allowed us, I say that to me this nobility of birth does not seem so essential. And if I thought I was uttering anything not already known to us all, I would adduce many instances of persons born of the noblest blood who have been ridden by vices; and, on the contrary, many persons of humble birth who, through their virtue, have made their posterity illustrious. And if what you said just now is true, that there is in all things that hidden force of the first seed, then we should all be of the same condition through having the same source, nor would one man be more noble than another. But I believe that there are many other causes of the differences and the various degrees of elevation and lowliness among us. Among which causes I judge Fortune to be foremost; because we see her hold sway over all the things of this world and, as it seems, amuse herself often in uplifting to the skies whom she pleases and in burying in the depths those most worthy of being exalted.

"I quite agree with what you call the good fortune of those who are endowed at birth with all goodness of mind and body; but this is seen to happen with those of humble as well as with those of noble birth, because nature observes no such subtle distinctions as these. Nay, as I said, the greatest gifts of nature are often to be seen in persons of the humblest origin. Hence, since this nobility of birth is not gained either by talents or by force or skill, and is rather due to the merit of one's ancestors than to one's own, I deem it passing strange to hold that if the parents of our Courtier be of humble birth, all his good qualities are ruined, and that those other qualities which you have named would not suffice to bring him to the height of perfection; that is, talent, beauty of countenance, comeliness of person, and that grace which will make him at first sight lovable to all."

Then Count Ludovico replied: "I do not deny that the same virtues can rule in the lowborn as in the wellborn: but (in order not to repeat what we have said already, along with many further reasons which might be adduced in praise of noble birth, which is always honored by everyone, because it stands to reason that good should beget good), since it is our task to form a Courtier free of any defect whatsoever, and endowed with all that is praiseworthy, I deem it necessary to have him be of noble birth, not only for many other reasons, but also because of that public opinion which immediately sides with nobility. For, in the case of two courtiers who have not yet given any impression of themselves either through good or bad deeds, immediately when the one is known to be of gentle birth and the other not, the one who is lowborn will be held in far less esteem than the one who is of noble birth, and will need much time and effort in order to give to others that good impression of himself which the other will give in an instant and merely by being a gentleman. And everyone knows the importance of these impressions, for, to speak of ourselves, we have seen men come to this house who, though dull-witted and maladroit, had yet the reputation throughout Italy of being very great courtiers; and, even though they were at last discovered and known, still they fooled us for many days and maintained in our minds that opinion of themselves which they found already impressed thereon, even though their conduct was in keeping with their little worth. Others we have seen who at first enjoyed little esteem and who, in the end, achieved a great success.

"And there are various causes of such errors, one being the judgment of princes who, thinking to work miracles, sometimes decide to show favor to one who seems to them to deserve disfavor. And they too are often deceived; but, because they always have countless imitators, their favor engenders a great fame which on the whole our judgments will follow. And if we notice anything which seems contrary to the prevailing opinion, we suspect that we must be mistaken, and we continue to look for something hidden: because we think that such universal opinions must after all be founded on the truth and arise from reasonable causes. And also because our minds are quick to love and hate, as is seen in spectacles of combats and of games and in every sort of contest, where the spectators often side with one of the parties without any evident reason, showing the greatest desire that this one should win and the other should lose. Moreover, as for the general opinion concerning a man's qualities, it is good or ill repute that sways our minds at the outset to one of these two passions. Hence, it happens that, for the most part, we judge from love or hate. Consider, then, how important that first impression is, and how anyone who aspires to have the rank and name of good Courtier must strive from the beginning to make a good impression.

"But to come to some particulars: I hold that the principal and true profession of the Courtier must be that of arms; which I wish him to exercise with vigor; and let him be known among the others as bold, energetic, and faithful to whomever he serves. And the repute of these good qualities will be earned by exercising them in every time and place, inasmuch as one may not ever fail therein without great blame. And, just as among women the name of purity, once stained, is never restored, so the reputation of a gentleman whose profession is arms, if ever in the least way he sullies himself through cowardice or other disgrace, always remains defiled before the world and covered with ignominy. Therefore, the more our Courtier excels in this art, the more will he merit praise; although I do not deem it necessary that he have the perfect knowledge of things and other qualities that befit a commander, for since this would launch us on too great a sea, we shall be satisfied, as we have said, if he have complete loyalty and an undaunted spirit, and be always seen to have them. For oftentimes men are known for their courage in small things rather than in great. And often in important perils and where there are many witnesses, some men are found who, although their hearts sink within them, still, spurred on by fear of shame or by the company of those present, press forward with eyes shut, as it were, and do their duty, God knows how; and in things of little importance and when they think they can avoid the risk of danger, they are glad to play safe. But those men who, even when they think they will not be observed or seen or recog-

nized by anyone, show courage and are not careless of anything, however slight, for which they could be blamed, such have the quality of spirit we are seeking in our Courtier.

"However, we do not wish him to make a show of being so fierce that he is forever swaggering in his speech, declaring that he has wedded his cuirass, and glowering with such dour looks as we have often seen . . . ; for to such as these one may rightly say what in polite society a worthy lady jestingly said to a certain man (whom I do not now wish to name) whom she sought to honor by inviting him to dance, and who not only declined this but would not listen to music or take any part in the other entertainments offered him, but kept saying that such trifles were not his business. And when finally the lady said to him: 'What then is your business?' he answered with a scowl: 'Fighting.' Whereupon the lady replied at once: 'I should think it a good thing, now that you are not away at war or engaged in fighting, for you to have yourself greased all over and stowed away in a closet along with all your battle harness, so that you won't grow any rustier than you already are'; and so, amid much laughter from those present, she ridiculed him in his stupid presumption. Therefore, let the man we are seeking be exceedingly fierce, harsh, and always among the first, wherever the enemy is; and in every other place, humane, modest, reserved, avoiding ostentation above all things as well as that impudent praise of himself by which a man always arouses hatred and disgust in all who hear him."

Then signor Gasparo replied: "As for me, I have known few men excellent in anything whatsoever who did not praise themselves; and it seems to me that this can well be permitted them, because he who feels himself to be of some worth, and sees that his works are ignored, is indignant that his own worth should lie buried; and he must make it known to someone, in order not to be cheated of the honor that is the true reward of all virtuous toil. Thus, among the ancients, seldom does anyone of any worth refrain from praising himself. To be sure, those persons who are of no merit, and yet praise themselves, are insufferable; but we do not assume that our Courtier will be of that sort."

Then the Count said: "If you took notice, I blamed impudent and indiscriminate praise of one's self: and truly, as you say, one must not conceive a bad opinion of a worthy man who praises himself modestly; nay, one must take that as surer evidence than if it came from another's mouth. I do say that whoever does not fall into error in praising himself and does not cause annoyance or envy in the person who listens to him is indeed a discreet man and, besides the praises he gives himself, deserves praises from others; for that is a very difficult thing."

Then signor Gasparo said: "This you must teach us."

The Count answered: "Among the ancients there is no lack of those who have taught this; but, in my opinion, the whole art consists in saying things in such a way that they do not appear to be spoken to that end, but are so very apropos that one cannot help saying them; and to seem always to avoid praising one's self, yet do so; but not in the manner of those boasters who open their mouths and let their words come out haphazardly. As one of our friends the other day who, when he had had his thigh run through by a spear at Pisa, said that he thought a fly had stung him; and another who said that he did not keep a mirror in his room because when he was angry he became so fearful of countenance that if he were to see himself, be would frighten himself too much."

Everyone laughed at this, but messer Cesare Gonzaga added: "What are you laughing at? Do you not know that Alexander the Great, upon hearing that in the opinion of one philosopher there were countless other worlds, began to weep, and when asked why, replied: 'Because I have not yet conquered one'—as if he felt able to conquer them all? Does that not seem to you a greater boast than that of the fly sting?"

Then said the Count: "And Alexander was a greater man than the one who spoke so. But truly one has to excuse excellent men when they presume much of themselves, because anyone who has great things to accomplish must have the daring to do those things, and confidence in himself. And let him not be abject and base, but modest rather in his words, making it clear that he presumes less of himself than he accomplishes, pro-vided such presumption does not turn to rashness."

When the Count paused here briefly, messer Bernardo Bibbiena said, laughing: "I remember you said before that this Courtier of ours should be naturally endowed with beauty of countenance and person, and with a grace that would make him lovable. Now this grace and beauty of countenance I do believe that I have myself, wherefore it happens that so many ladies, as you know, are ardently in love with me; but, as to the beauty of my person, I am rather doubtful, and especially as to these legs of mine which in truth do not seem to me as well disposed as I could wish; as to my chest and the rest, I am quite well enough satisfied. Now do determine a little more in detail what this beauty of body should be, so that I can extricate myself from doubt and put my mind at ease."

After some laughter at this, the Count added: "Certainly such grace of countenance you can truly be said to have; nor will I adduce any other example in order to make clear what that grace is; because we do see beyond any doubt that your aspect is very agreeable and pleasant to all, although the features of it are not very delicate: it has something manly about it, and yet is full of grace. And this is a quality found in many different types of faces. I would have our Courtier's face be such, not so soft and feminine as many attempt to have who not only curl their hair and pluck their eyebrows, but preen themselves in all those ways that the most wanton and dissolute women in the world adopt; and in walking, in posture, and in every act, appear so tender and languid that their limbs seem to be on the verge of falling apart; and utter their words so limply that it seems they are about to expire on the spot; and the more they find themselves in the company of men of rank, the more they make a show of such manners. These, since nature did not make them women as they clearly wish to appear and be, should be treated not as good women, but as public harlots, and driven not only from the courts of great lords but from the society of all noble men.

"Then, coming to bodily frame, I say it is enough that it be neither extremely small nor big, because either of these conditions causes a certain contemptuous wonder, and men of either sort are gazed at in much the same way that we gaze at monstrous things. And yet, if one must sin in one or the other of these two extremes, it is less bad to be on the small side than to be excessively big; because men who are so huge of body are often not only obtuse of spirit, but are also unfit for every agile exercise, which is something I very much desire in the Courtier. And hence I would have him well built and shapely of limb, and would have him show strength and lightness and suppleness, and know all the bodily exercises that befit a warrior. And in this I judge it his first duty to know how to handle every kind of weapon, both on foot and on horse, and know the advantages of each kind; and be especially acquainted with those arms that are ordinarily used among gentlemen, because, apart from using them in war (where perhaps so many fine points are not necessary), there often arise differences between one gentleman and another, resulting in duels, and quite often those weapons are used which happen to be at hand. Hence, knowledge of them is a very safe thing. Nor am I one of those who say that skill is forgotten in the hour of need; for he who loses his skill at such times shows that out of fear he has already lost his heart and head."

After reading this selection and the previous one, consider these questions:

1. What conflict did Petrarch experience in his own life?
2. What values did the fictional Augustine express to Petrarch?
3. For Castiglione, what were the main characteristics of the model courtier?

SELECTION 6:

The New Statescraft

In addition to establishing a new understanding of the individual and providing new models for scholarship and education, the Renaissance also took what appears to be a more "objective" view of the world, compared to that of the Middle Ages. This can be seen by comparing the two eras' works of the plastic and literary arts, but it can also be observed in the differing ways that they understood the economic and especially the political forces of this world. No longer interpreting economic activities and political relations in terms of images derived from the Bible or symbols that found their meaning in levels of existence outside a worldly plane, men and women of the Renaissance began to see meaningful patterns of life in this world. In his histories and political commentaries, Niccolò Machiavelli (1469–1527) brought forth a new way of understanding political power and its operation. Although criticized for his supposedly immoral attitude, Machiavelli emphasized that one had to see power clearly for what it was and not just evaluate these things in moral terms. His most widely read work is The Prince *(1513), a work that distills both these observations and his own personal experiences in serving the city-state of Florence.*

Passing to the other qualities above referred to, I say that every Prince should desire to be accounted merciful and not cruel. Nevertheless, he should be on his guard against the abuse of this quality of mercy. . . .

A Prince should therefore disregard the reproach of being thought cruel where it enables him to keep his subjects united and obedient. For he who quells disorder by a very few signal examples will in the end be more merciful than he who from too great leniency permits things to take their course and so to result in rapine and bloodshed; for these hurt the whole State, whereas the severities of the Prince injure individuals only.

And for a new Prince, of all others, it is impossible to escape a name for cruelty, since new States are full of dangers. . . .

Nevertheless, the new Prince should not be too ready of belief, nor too easily set in motion; nor should he himself be the first to raise alarms; but should so temper prudence with kindliness that too great confidence in others shall not throw him off his guard, nor groundless distrust render him insupportable.

And here comes in the question whether it is better to be loved rather than feared, or feared rather than loved. It might perhaps be answered that we should wish to be both; but since love and fear can hardly exist together, if we must choose between them, it is far safer to be feared than loved. For of men it may generally be affirmed that they are thankless, fickle, false, studious to avoid danger, greedy of gain, devoted to you while you are able to confer benefits upon them, and ready, as I said before, while danger is distant, to shed their blood, and sacrifice their property, their lives, and their children for you; but in the hour of need they turn against you. The Prince, therefore, who without otherwise securing himself builds wholly on their professions is undone. For the friendships which we buy with a price, and do not gain by greatness and nobility of character, though they be fairly earned are not

made good, but fail us when we have occasion to use them.

Moreover, men are less careful how they offend him who makes himself loved than him who makes himself feared. For love is held by the tie of obligation, which, because men are a sorry breed, is broken on every whisper of private interest; but fear is bound by the apprehension of punishment which never relaxes its grasp.

Nevertheless a Prince should inspire fear in such a fashion that if he do not win love he may escape hate. For a man may very well be feared and yet not hated, and this will be the case so long as he does not meddle with the property or with the women of his citizens and subjects. And if constrained to put any to death, he should do so only when there is manifest cause or reasonable justification. But, above all, he must abstain from the property of others. For men will sooner forget the death of their father than the loss of their patrimony. Moreover, pretexts for confiscation are never to seek, and he who has once begun to live by rapine always finds reasons for taking what is not his; whereas reasons for shedding blood are fewer, and sooner exhausted.

But when a Prince is with his army, and has many soldiers under his command, he must needs disregard the reproach of cruelty, for without such a reputation in its Captain, no army can be held together or kept under any kind of control. Among other things remarkable in [the Carthaginian general] Hannibal this has been noted, that having a very great army, made up of men of many different nations and brought to fight in a foreign country, no dissension ever arose among the soldiers themselves, nor any mutiny against their leader, either in his good or in his evil fortunes. This we can only ascribe to the transcendent cruelty, which, joined with numberless great qualities, rendered him at once venerable and terrible in the eyes of his soldiers; for without this reputation for cruelty these other virtues would not have produced the like results.

Unreflecting writers, indeed, while they praise his achievements, have condemned the chief cause of them; but that his other merits would not by themselves have been so efficacious we may see from the case of [the Roman general] Scipio,

From *The Prince*, by Niccolò Machiavelli, translated by Ninian Hill Thomson, 2nd ed. (Oxford: Clarendon Press, 1897).

one of the greatest Captains, not of his own time only but of all times of which we have record, whose armies rose against him in Spain from no other cause than his too great leniency in allowing them a freedom inconsistent with military strictness. With which weakness [the Roman consul and army commander] Fabius Maximus taxed him in the Senate House, calling him the corrupter of the Roman soldiery. Again, when the Locrians were shamefully outraged by one of his lieutenants, he neither avenged them, nor punished the insolence of his officer; and this from the natural easiness of his disposition. So that it was said in the Senate by one who sought to excuse him, that there were many who knew better how to refrain from doing wrong themselves than how to correct the wrong-doing of others. This temper, however, must in time have marred the name and fame even of Scipio, had he continued in it, and retained his command. But living as he did under the control of the Senate, this hurtful quality was not merely disguised, but came to be regarded as a glory.

Returning to the question of being loved or feared, I sum up by saying, that since his being loved depends upon his subjects, while his being feared depends upon himself, a wise Prince should build on what is his own, and not on what rests with others. Only, as I have said, he must do his utmost to escape hatred.

After reading the selection, consider these questions:

1. What was new in Machiavelli's understanding of the power?
2. What was Machiavelli's method?
3. What values does Machiavelli promote in *The Prince*?

CHAPTER 14
The Age of Discovery: Europe and the World

The expansive nature of early modern Europe is perhaps most clearly indicated in the numerous overseas explorations that began in the fifteenth century. The "discovery" of a "new world" by Columbus puts into question both the notion of discovery (since Norsemen probably "found" the Western Hemisphere in the eleventh or twelfth century) and the notion of a new world (since North and South America were inhabited many thousands of years before Columbus and was "new" only from a European perspective). And yet, even with these qualifications, encountering the Americas—as well as gaining greater awareness of Africa and southern and eastern Asia—marked a new stage in Western concerns with the world outside Europe and in Westerners' self-awareness as Western and Christian. Contact with other civilizations initiated a number of reactions. From an initial sense of marvel and wonderment, there developed a sense of simple "otherness," which had to be accommodated into traditional European frames of reference. Civilizations that were considered to be on an equal or even higher level than that of Europe—Chinese civilization was the clearest case—had to be related to the Biblical story of creation. Civilizations considered lower—and here the Americas were the prime example—were considered by many to be pagans and therefore in need of conversion and (most likely) enslavement.

But gradually, over the course of the seventeenth and eighteenth centuries, alternative attitudes developed. No longer concerned primarily with positioning these other peoples within a medieval Christian framework, non-Western cultures were evaluated in terms of a more thoroughly secular spectrum ranging from savage to civilized. Supposedly this continuum formed the universal norm of developed reason and levels of technology. Only in the course of the nineteenth century did the idea occur to Europeans that other civilizations possessed values and understood the world in ways that were simply different and uniquely their own. Only then could the West come to understand itself as a culture among world cultures, which could only be comprehended by recording the history of its emergence.

SELECTION 1:

The Age of Discovery

What caused this interest in discovery and global exploration? J.H. Parry, the renowned historian of European exploration, relates this new interest to "the spirit of the Renaissance," which, by the late fifteenth century, was spreading from Italy to the rest of Europe.

Among the many and complex motives which impelled Europeans, and especially the peoples of the Iberian peninsula, to venture oversea in the fifteenth and sixteenth centuries, two were obvious, universal, and admitted: acquisitiveness and religious zeal. Many of the great explorers and conquerors proclaimed these two purposes in unequivocal terms. Vasco da Gama, on arrival at Calicut, explained to his reluctant Indian hosts that he had come in search of Christians and spices. Bernal Díaz, frankest of *conquistadores*, wrote that he and his like went to the Indies 'to serve God and His Majesty, to give light to those who were in darkness, and to grow rich, as all men desire to do.'

Land, and the labour of those who worked it, were the principal sources of wealth. The quickest, most obvious, and socially most attractive way of becoming rich was to seize, and to hold as a fief, land already occupied by a diligent and docile peasantry. Spanish knights and noblemen in particular had long been accustomed to this process, for which successful war against the Muslim states in Spain had offered occasion and excuse. In most parts of Europe, during the constant disorders of the fourteenth and early fifteenth centuries, such acquisitions of land had also often been made by means of private war. In the later fifteenth century, however, rulers were again becoming strong enough to discourage pri-

vate war; and even in Spain, the territory still open to acquisition by lawful force of arms was narrowly limited, and protected by its feudal relations with the Crown of Castile. Further opportunities were unlikely to arise unless the rulers of Granada denounced their vassalage, and so gave the Castilians occasion for a formal campaign of conquest. Even if that campaign were successful, kings and great noblemen would get the lion's share of the booty. For lesser men, the best chances of acquiring land by fighting for it lay outside Europe.

A second possibility was the seizure and exploitation of new land—land either unoccupied, or occupied by useless or intractable peoples who could be killed or driven away. New land could be colonized by adventurous farmers or by small owners of flocks and herds. Such men often wished to be their own masters, to avoid the increasingly irksome obligations imposed by feudal tenure and by the corporate privileges of transhumant graziers, particularly in Castile. This was a less attractive, but still promising alternative, which also could most readily be pursued outside Europe. Madeira and parts of the Canaries were occupied in this way in the fifteenth century, respectively by Portuguese and Spanish settlers, comparatively humble people, who borrowed capital from princely or noble promoters in return for relatively light obligations. The settlements were economically successful. They brought in revenue to the princes and noblemen—notably Prince Henry of Portugal—who financed them; and set a fashion for islands which lasted more than two hundred years. Ru-

From *The Age of Reconnaissance*, by J.H. Parry (Berkeley and Los Angeles: University of California Press, 1981). Copyright © 1981 by J.H. Parry. Reprinted by permission of Orion's Children's Books, London.

mours of further islands and mainlands to be discovered in the Atlantic all helped to encourage interest in this type of oversea adventure.

A less sure, and in most places socially less attractive way to wealth, was by investment in trade, especially long-distance trade. The most sought-after trades were in commodities of high value and small bulk, most of them either of eastern origin—spices, silk, ivory, precious stones and the like—or Mediterranean in origin but in demand in the East, such as coral and some high-quality textiles. These rich trades almost all passed through the Mediterranean and were conducted chiefly by the merchants of the Italian maritime cities, in particular Venetians and Genoese. Some Atlantic maritime peoples were already looking enviously at the rich trades. Portugal in particular possessed a long ocean seaboard, good harbours, a considerable fishing and seafaring population and a commercial class largely emancipated from feudal interference. Portuguese shippers were able and eager to graduate from an Atlantic coastal trade in wine, fish and salt, to more widespread and lucrative ventures in gold, spices and sugar. They had little hope of breaking into the Mediterranean trades, which were guarded by the Italian monopolists with formidable naval force; with unrivalled knowledge of the East derived from many generations of merchants and travellers; and with an assiduous diplomacy which reached across the ancient dividing line between Christendom and Islam. Merchant capitalists in Portugal and western Spain therefore had strong motives for seeking by sea alternative sources of gold, ivory and pepper; and according to information current in Morocco, such sources existed. It is highly likely that in undertaking West African voyages, the Portuguese were encouraged by information about the gold mines of the Guinea kingdoms, obtained through their conquest at Ceuta [in northern Morocco] and not available to the rest of Europe. At least, the voyages quickly demonstrated that sailing in the Tropics was easier and less dangerous than pessimists had supposed. If, as was hinted in some of the travel literature of the time, it were even possible to penetrate by sea to the oriental sources of silk and spice, that would provide a still stronger incentive for sea-borne exploration. . . .

All these economic considerations, these imaginative dreams of quick adventurous gain, were heavily reinforced by the promptings of religious zeal. The discoverers and *conquistadores* were devout men for the most part, whose devotion took forms at once orthodox and practical. Of the many possible forms of religious zeal, two in particular appealed to them, and to the rulers and investors who sent them out. One was the desire to convert—to appeal to the minds and hearts of individual unbelievers by preaching, reasoning, or force of example, by any means of persuasion short of force or threat, and so to bring unbelievers into the community of belief. The other was the more simple-minded desire to ensure by military and political means the safety and independence of one's own religious community and, better still, its predominance over others; to defend the believer against interference and attack; to kill, humiliate, or subdue the unbeliever. Of course, these two possible lines of action might be confused or combined. It might appear politic, for example, to subdue unbelievers in order to convert them. In general, however, two expressions of religious devotion in action were kept distinct in men's minds. The first called for intense effort, with little likelihood of immediate material gain. The second, the politico-military expression, provided an excuse for conquest and plunder on a grand scale. It was an aspect of religious zeal with which Europe had long been familiar, since for several centuries it had supplied one of the principal motives for the crusades.

The fifteenth-century voyages of discovery have often been described as a continuation of the crusades. Certainly the menacing proximity of Islam was always in the minds of fifteenth-century kings, especially in eastern and southern Europe. Nevertheless, those kings were realists enough, for the most part, to see that a crusade of the traditional pattern—a direct campaign against Muslim rulers in the eastern Mediterranean lands, with the object of capturing the Holy Places and establishing Christian principalities on the shores of the Levant—was no longer even a remote possibility. Crusades of this type in earlier centuries had been, in the long run, costly failures. . . .

With Renaissance literary conventions, Spaniards absorbed Renaissance attitudes of mind: the cult of the individual, the passion for personal reputation. This passion was vital in the mental make-up of the *conquistadores*, and goes far to explain their prickly pride, their dislike of discipline and regimentation, their insistence on being consulted about every decision. On the other hand, it also helps to explain their extravagant daring and their indifference to wounds and fatigue. They conducted themselves, and their chroniclers wrote, with the high seriousness of men conscious of taking part in great deeds; men who saw themselves not as imitators, but as rivals, of the heroes of antiquity and of romance. . . .

With a new attitude towards the individual, the Renaissance fostered a new attitude towards the State, also Italian in origin. A sensitive alertness, a studied, objective attention to the most effective and most elegant means of achieving desired ends, tended to supplant the older notion of the State as a network of fixed, traditional rights and duties, over which the monarch presided as a judge of disputes. It was becoming recognized that a government might use force, whether against subjects or against neighbouring princes, in pursuit of rational interests as well as in support of legal claims. Like many Italian rulers, Isabella of Castile owed her throne to a mixture of war and diplomacy. A masterful restoration of public order and discipline was one of her major achievements, and contributed greatly to the growth of authoritarian feeling in Castile. Machiavelli's principles of statecraft had no more successful exemplars than [kings] Ferdinand of Aragon and John II of Portugal. It is true that this more flexible attitude towards sovereignty and statecraft, this cult of governmental expediency, was restrained, particularly in Spain, by legalistic conservatism as well as by individual obstinacy. Nevertheless, it helped to prepare men's minds for the immense task of political and administrative improvisation which was to confront Spanish government in the New World.

After reading this selection, consider these questions:

1. According to Parry, why did Europeans explore the outside world?
2. What is the relationship between the Renaissance and the age of discovery?
3. What role did Queen Isabella of Spain play in the age of discovery?

SELECTION 2:

The Journals of Christopher Columbus

The account of Columbus's own experience of crossing the Atlantic and reaching what he believed to be islands off the coast of Japan is contained in the journal he kept of his first voyage in 1492. He began the journal entries with his commission from King Ferdinand and Queen Isabella. After the fall of the last Moorish stronghold on the Iberian peninsula, the monarchs were in the mood for greater conquests and the further Christianization of pagan and heathen populations.

Whereas, Most Christian, High, Excellent, and Powerful Princes, King and Queen of Spain and of the Islands of the Sea, our Sovereigns, this present year 1492, after your Highnesses had terminated the war with the Moors reigning in Europe, the same having been brought to an end in the great city of Granada, where on the second day of January, this present year, I saw the royal banners of your Highnesses planted by force of arms upon the towers of the Alhambra, which is the fortress of that city, and saw the Moorish king come out at the gate of the city and kiss the hands of your Highnesses, and of the Prince my Sovereign; and in the present month, in consequence of the information which I had given your Highnesses respecting the countries of India and of a Prince, called Great Can [Khan], which in our language signifies King of Kings, how, at many times he, and his predecessors had sent to Rome soliciting instructors who might teach him our holy faith, and the holy Father had never granted his request, whereby great numbers of people were lost, believing in idolatry and doctrines of perdition. Your Highnesses, as Catholic Christians, and princes who love and promote the holy Christian faith, and are enemies of the doctrine of Mahomet [Muhammed], and of all idolatry and heresy, determined to send me, Christopher Columbus, to the above-mentioned countries of India, to see the said princes, people, and territories, and to learn their disposition and the proper method of converting them to our holy faith; and furthermore directed that I should not proceed by land to the East, as is customary, but by a Westerly route, in which direction we have hitherto no certain evidence that any one has gone. So after having expelled the Jews from your dominions, your Highnesses, in the same month of January, ordered me to proceed with a sufficient armament to the said regions of India, and for that purpose granted me great favors, and ennobled me that thenceforth I might call myself Don, and be High Admiral of the Sea, and perpetual Viceroy and Governor in all the islands and continents which I might discover and acquire, or which may hereafter be discovered and acquired in the ocean; and that this dignity should be inherited by my eldest son, and thus descend from degree to degree forever. Hereupon I left the city of Granada, on Saturday, the twelfth day of May, 1492, and proceeded to Palos, a seaport, where I armed three vessels, very fit for such an enterprise, and having provided myself with abundance of stores and seamen, I set sail from the port, on Friday, the third of August, half an hour before sunrise, and steered for the Canary Islands of your Highnesses which are in the said ocean, thence to take my departure and proceed till I arrived at the Indies, and perform the embassy of your Highnesses to the Princes there, and discharge the orders given me. For this purpose I determined to keep an account of the voyage, and to write down punctually every thing we performed or saw from day to day, as will hereafter appear. Moreover, Sovereign Princes, besides describing every night the occurrences of the day, and every day those of the preceding night, I intend to draw up a nautical chart, which shall contain the several parts of the ocean and land in their proper situations; and also to compose a book to represent the whole by picture with latitudes and longitudes, on all which accounts it behooves me to abstain from my sleep, and make many trials in navigation, which things will demand much labor. . . .

Thursday, 11 October. Steered west-southwest; and encountered a heavier sea than they had met with before in the whole voyage. Saw pardelas and a green rush near the vessel. The crew of the Pinta saw a cane and a log; they also picked up a stick which appeared to have been carved with an iron tool, a piece of cane, a plant which grows on land, and a board. The crew of the Niña saw other signs of land, and a stalk loaded with rose berries. These signs encouraged them, and they all grew cheerful. Sailed this day till sunset, twenty-seven leagues.

After sunset steered their original course west and sailed twelve miles an hour till two hours after midnight, going ninety miles, which are twenty-two leagues and a half; and as the Pinta was the swiftest sailer, and kept ahead of the Ad-

From Christopher Columbus's journals, as found in the on-line *Medieval Source Book* at http://www.fordham.edu/halsall/source/columbus1.html.

miral, she discovered land and made the signals which had been ordered. The land was first seen by a sailor called Rodrigo de Triana, although the Admiral at ten o'clock that evening standing on the quarter-deck saw a light, but so small a body that he could not affirm it to be land; calling to Pero Gutierrez, groom of the King's wardrobe, he told him he saw a light, and bid him look that way, which he did and saw it; he did the same to Rodrigo Sanchez of Segovia, whom the King and Queen had sent with the squadron as comptroller, but he was unable to see it from his situation. The Admiral again perceived it once or twice, appearing like the light of a wax candle moving up and down, which some thought an indication of land. But the Admiral held it for certain that land was near; for which reason, after they had said the Salve which the seamen are accustomed to repeat and chant after their fashion, the Admiral directed them to keep a strict watch upon the forecastle and look out diligently for land, and to him who should first discover it he promised a silken jacket, besides the reward which the King and Queen had offered, which was an annuity of ten thousand maravedis. At two o'clock in the morning the land was discovered, at two leagues' distance; they took in sail and remained under the square-sail lying to till day, which was Friday, when they found themselves near a small island, one of the Lucayos, called in the Indian language Guanahani. Presently they described people, naked, and the Admiral landed in the boat, which was armed, along with Martín Alonzo Pinzón, and Vincent Yáñez his brother, captain of the Niña. The Admiral bore the royal standard, and the two captains each a banner of the Green Cross, which all the ships had carried; this contained the initials of the names of the King and Queen each side of the cross, and a crown over each letter. Arrived on shore, they saw trees very green, many streams of water, and diverse sorts of fruits. The Admiral called upon the two Captains, and the rest of the crew who landed, as also to Rodrigo de Escovedo notary of the fleet, and Rodrigo Sanchez, of Segovia, to bear witness that he before all others took possession (as in fact he did) of that island for the King and Queen his sovereigns, making the requisite declarations, which are more at large

set down here in writing. Numbers of the people of the island straightway collected together. Here follow the precise words of the Admiral: "As I saw that they were very friendly to us, and perceived that they could be much more easily converted to our holy faith by gentle means than by force, I presented them with some red caps, and strings of beads to wear upon the neck, and many other trifles of small value, wherewith they were much delighted, and became wonderfully attached to us. Afterwards they came swimming to the boats, bringing parrots, balls of cotton thread, javelins, and many other things which they exchanged for articles we gave them, such as glass beads, and hawk's bells; which trade was carried on with the utmost good will. But they seemed on the whole to me, to be a very poor people. They all go completely naked, even the women, though I saw but one girl. All whom I saw were young, not above thirty years of age, well made, with fine shapes and faces; their hair short, and coarse like that of a horse's tail, combed toward the forehead, except a small portion which they suffer to hang down behind, and never cut. Some paint themselves with black, which makes them appear like those of the Canaries, neither black nor white; others with white, others with red, and others with such colors as they can find. Some paint the face, and some the whole body; others only the eyes, and others the nose. Weapons they have none, nor are acquainted with them, for I showed them swords which they grasped by the blades, and cut themselves through ignorance. They have no iron, their javelins being without it, and nothing more than sticks, though some have fishbones or other things at the ends. They are all of a good size and stature, and handsomely formed. I saw some with scars of wounds upon their bodies, and demanded by signs the meaning of them; they answered me in the same way, that there came people from the other islands in the neighborhood who endeavored to make prisoners of them, and they defended themselves. I thought then, and still believe, that these were from the continent. It appears to me, that the people are ingenious, and would be good servants and I am of opinion that they would very readily become Christians, as they appear to have no religion.

They very quickly learn such words as are spoken to them. If it please our Lord, I intend at my return to carry home six of them to your Highnesses, that they may learn our language. I saw no beasts in the island, nor any sort of animals except parrots." These are the words of the Admiral.

Saturday, 13 October. "At daybreak great multitudes of men came to the shore, all young and of fine shapes, very handsome; their hair not curled but straight and coarse like horse-hair, and all with foreheads and heads much broader than any people I had hitherto seen; their eyes were large and very beautiful; they were not black, but the color of the inhabitants of the Canaries, which is a very natural circumstance, they being in the same latitude with the island of Ferro in the Canaries. They were straight-limbed without exception, and not with prominent bellies but handsomely shaped. They came to the ship in canoes, made of a single trunk of a tree, wrought in a wonderful manner considering the country; some of them large enough to contain forty or forty-five men, others of different sizes down to those fitted to hold but a single person. They rowed with an oar like a baker's peel, and wonderfully swift. If they happen to upset, they all jump into the sea, and swim till they have righted their canoe and emptied it with the calabashes they carry with them. They came loaded with balls of cotton, parrots, javelins, and other things too numerous to mention; these they exchanged for whatever we chose to give them. I was very attentive to them, and strove to learn if they had any gold. Seeing some of them with little bits of this metal hanging at their noses, I gathered from them by signs that by going southward or steering round the island in that direction, there would be found a king who possessed large vessels of gold, and in great quantities. I endeavored to procure them to lead the way thither, but found they were unacquainted with the route. I determined to stay here till the evening of the next day, and then sail for the southwest; for according to what I could learn from them, there was land at the south as well as at the southwest and northwest and those from the northwest came many times and fought with them and proceeded on to the southwest in search of gold and precious stones. This is a large and level island, with trees extremely flourishing, and streams of water; there is a large lake in the middle of the island, but no mountains: the whole is completely covered with verdure and delightful to behold. The natives are an inoffensive people, and so desirous to possess any thing they saw with us, that they kept swimming off to the ships with whatever they could find, and readily bartered for any article we saw fit to give them in return, even such as broken platters and fragments of glass. I saw in this manner sixteen balls of cotton thread which weighed above twenty-five pounds, given for three Portuguese ceutis. This traffic I forbade, and suffered no one to take their cotton from them, unless I should order it to be procured for your Highnesses, if proper quantities could be met with. It grows in this island, but from my short stay here I could not satisfy myself fully concerning it; the gold, also, which they wear in their noses, is found here, but not to lose time, I am determined to proceed onward and ascertain whether I can reach Cipango [Japan]. At night they all went on shore with their canoes.

SELECTION 3:

The Old World and the New

*I*n *an insightful essay, literary scholar Stephen Greenblatt directs attention to the language of early exploration and conquest. In the following* *selection, excerpted from his book* Marvelous Possessions: The Wonder of the New World, *Greenblatt analyzes what appears a strange mixture of humane attitudes and Christian missionary values, on the one hand, and an overwhelming greed and desire for conquest, on the other.*

Let us begin at the most famous of beginnings: As I know that you will be pleased at the great victory with which Our Lord has crowned my voyage, I write this to you, from which you will learn how in thirty-three days, I passed from the Canary Islands to the Indies with the fleet which the most illustrious king and queen, our sovereigns, gave to me. And there I found very many islands filled with people innumerable, and of them all I have taken possession for their highnesses, by proclamation made and with the royal standard unfurled, and no opposition was offered to me. To the first island which I found, I gave the name *San Salvador*, in remembrance of the Divine Majesty, Who has marvelously bestowed all this; the Indians call it 'Guanahani'. To the second, I gave the name *Isla de Santa María de Concepción*; to the third, *Fernandina*; to the fourth, *Isabella*; to the fifth, *Isla Juana*, and so to each one I gave a new name.

Thus begins Columbus's celebrated account, in a letter to Luis de Santangel, of his first voyage. The moment, of course, has become fixed in the popular imagination: the great adventurer on the beach, unfurling the royal standard and taking possession of the New World. Columbus's words are filled out by what we know to have followed: other voyages, widening discoveries, the dawning realization that classical geography was wrong and that a whole new hemisphere had been discovered, the violent encounter of civilizations, the missionary enterprise, mass enslavement and death, the immense project of colonization. . . .

For Columbus taking possession is principally the performance of a set of linguistic acts: de-claring, witnessing, recording. The acts are public and official: the admiral speaks as a representative of the king and queen, and his speech must be heard and understood by competent, named witnesses, witnesses who may subsequently be called upon to testify to the fact that the unfurling of the banner and the 'declarations that are required' took place as alleged. At issue is not only the crown's claim to sovereignty but Columbus's own status; after months of difficult negotiation, he had obtained, in the Capitulations of April 17, 1492, appointment as Admiral, Viceroy, and Governor-General over all islands and mainland 'which by his labor and industry shall be discovered or acquired.' He was also granted one-tenth of all the treasure and merchandise produced or obtained in these domains, free of all taxes. In a further, extraordinary concession, the crown agreed that Columbus's title and prerogatives would be enjoyed by his heirs and successors 'perpetually.' On October 12 then Columbus is not only the medium through which the crown could claim possession; he also enacts the ritual of possession on his own behalf and on behalf of his descendants.

And because Columbus's culture does not entirely trust verbal testimony, because its judicial procedures require written proofs, he makes certain to perform his speech acts in the presence of the fleet's recorder (for a fleet which had no priest had a recorder), hence ensuring that everything would be written down and consequently have a greater authority. The papers are carefully sealed, preserved, carried back across thousands of leagues of ocean to officials who in turn countersign and process them according to the procedural rules; the notarized documents are a token of the truth of the encounter and hence of the legality of the claim. Or rather they help to produce 'truth' and 'legality,' ensuring that the words Columbus speaks do not disappear as soon as their sounds fade, ensuring that the memory of the encounter is fixed, ensuring that there are not competing versions of what happened on the beach on October 12th. A priest may be said to facilitate a transaction with eternity, but an *escrivano* [fleet recorder] facilitates a transaction with a more immediately useful form of temporality, the institutional form secured by writing. . . .

It is odd: Columbus has just unilaterally taken possession of everything he sees on behalf of the king and queen of Spain; he declares moreover that 'as soon as I arrived in the Indies, in the first island which I found, I took by force some of them, in order that they might learn and give me information'. Yet this armed invader who seizes lands and people regards his own intentions as impeccably generous: 'at every point where I have been and have been able to have speech, I have given to them of all that I had, such as cloth and many other things, without receiving anything for it'. It is characteristic of Columbus's discourse that it yokes together actions, attitudes, or perceptions that would seem ethically incompatible, here seizing everything on the one hand and giving everything on the other. The two are clearly related in some way, but they do not directly impinge on one another, just as there is an unexpressed, unacknowledged relation between the fact that the natives do not understand his language and the fact that no one contradicts his proclamation. It would, I suppose, be possible to term this hypocrisy, but the term suggests a staging of moral attitudes that are not actually felt in the deep recesses of the heart, a theatrical self-consciousness, that seems to me quite alien to Columbus's ardent faith. I think rather that we are encountering an important aspect of Columbus's discursive economy, a characteristic rhetorical feature of what we may call his Christian imperialism.

This discursive economy brings opposites into the closest conjunction with one another and yet leaves the heart of their relation a mystery. Columbus takes absolute possession on behalf of the Spanish crown in order to make an absolute gift; he seeks earthly gain in order to serve a divine purpose; the Indians must lose everything in order to receive everything; the innocent natives will give away their gold for trash, but they will receive treasure far more precious than gold; the wicked natives (the 'cannibals') will be enslaved

in order to be freed from their own bestiality. . . .

From the first moments, the encounter with the New World mobilizes in Columbus cravings for power and status and wealth, cravings that sit in an uneasy relation to his Franciscan religiosity, his appetite to convert and save, his apocalyptic dreams. It would be a mistake to think of these simply as opposed desires—a spiritual side of Columbus at war with his carnal side—for the whole achievement of the discourse of Christian imperialism is to represent desires as *convertible* and in a constant process of exchange. Were these desires actually identical, Columbus would have no need to articulate all of the ways in which they are cross-coupled; were they actually opposed, he would not be able to exchange one for the other. The possibility of such an exchange, rooted perhaps in his experience of Italian merchant life, haunts his writing: 'Genoese, Venetians, and all who have pearls, precious stones, and other things of value, all carry them to the end of the world in order to exchange them, to turn [*convertir*] them into gold. Gold is most excellent. Gold constitutes treasure, and he who possesses it may do what he will in the world, and may so attain as to bring souls to Paradise'. In this rhapsodic moment, from his account of the fourth voyage, the conversion of commodities into gold slides liquidly into the conversion and hence salvation of souls. If it seems strange, we might recall that in the Spanish of the Middle Ages and Renaissance, the Crusade to the Holy Land was called not the *cruzada*—that word referred to the special papal concessions granted to the Spanish crown to fight against the infidel within its own territory—but rather the *empresa* or *negocio*, terms in which the mercantile and the religious are intertwined.

After reading this selection and the previous ones, consider these questions:

1. How did Columbus understand his voyages of discovery?
2. What values motivated Columbus?
3. What contradictions played themselves out in the language of exploration?

SELECTION 4:

The Idea of Conquest

In later voyages Columbus enslaved the indigenous population both for sale back in Spain and for working sugar plantations in Madeira. When the potential for material gain was realized by the Spanish monarchy, it asserted direct royal control over the Americas. By sending out officials and priests, it soon established a policy of economic exploitation and religious conversion. These policies did not go unchallenged; in fact, they incited a number of debates concerning the meaning and justification of such activities. In 1547 the Spanish theologian Juan Ginés de Sepúlveda penned a treatise to justify Spanish policies in the New World. Sepúlveda applied concepts derived from natural law (the universal form of reasoning derived from the Scholastics) to justify the use of force against the peoples of the Americas.

The man rules over the woman, the adult over the child, the father over his children. That is to say, the most powerful and most perfect rule over the weakest and most imperfect. This same relationship exists among men, there being some who by nature are masters and others who by nature are slaves. Those who surpass the rest in prudence and intelligence, although not in physical strength, are by nature the masters. On the other hand those who are dim-witted and mentally lazy, although they may be physically strong enough to fulfil all the necessary tasks, are by nature slaves. It is just and useful that it is this way. We even see it sanctioned in divine law itself, for it is written in the Book of Proverbs: 'He who is stupid will serve the wise man.' And so it is with the barbarous and inhumane people [the Indians] who have no civil life and peaceful customs. It will always be just and in conformity with natural law that such people submit to the rule of more cultured and humane princes and nations. Thanks to the virtues and the practical wisdom of their laws, the latter can destroy barbarism and educate these [inferior] people to a more humane and virtuous life. And if the latter reject such rule, it can be imposed upon them by force of arms. Such a war will be just according to natural law. . . . One may believe as certain and undeniable, since it is affirmed by the wisest authors, that it is just and natural that prudent, upright, and humane men should rule over those who are not. On this basis the Romans established their legitimate and just rule over many nations, according to St Augustine in several passages of his work, *The City of God,* which St Thomas [Aquinas] collected and cited in his work, *De regimine principum.* Such being the case, you can well understand . . . if you know the customs and nature of the two peoples, that with perfect right the Spaniards rule over these barbarians of the New World and the adjacent islands, who in wisdom, intelligence, virtue, and *humanitas* are as inferior to the Spaniards as infants to adults and women to men. There is as much difference between them as there is between cruel, wild peoples and the most merciful of peoples, between the most monstrously intemperate peoples and those who are temperate and moderate in their pleasures, that is to say, between apes and men.

From "Democrates Alter de Justi Belli Causis apud Ludos," by Juan Ginés de Sepúlveda, in *Tratado,* edited by Marcelino Menendez y Pelaya (Mexico City, 1979). Translated by Benjamin Sax.

You do not expect me to make a lengthy commemoration of the judgement and talent of the Spaniards. . . . And who can ignore the other virtues of our people, their fortitude, their humanity, their love of justice and religion? I speak only of our princes and those who by their energy and industriousness have shown that they are worthy of administering the commonwealth. I refer in general terms only to those Spaniards who have received a liberal education. If some of them are wicked and unjust, that is no reason to denigrate the glory of their race, which should be judged by the actions of its cultivated and noble men and by its customs and public institutions, rather than by the actions of depraved persons who are similar to slaves. . . .

Now compare these natural qualities of judgement, talent, magnanimity, temperance, humanity, and religion with those of these pitiful men [the Indians], in whom you will scarcely find any vestiges of humanness. These people possess neither science nor even an alphabet, nor do they preserve any monuments of their history except for some obscure and vague reminiscences depicted in certain paintings, nor do they have written laws, but barbarous institutions and customs. In regard to their virtues, how much restraint or gentleness are you to expect of men who are devoted to all kinds of intemperate acts and abominable lewdness, including the eating of human flesh?

SELECTION 5:

Do Indians Have Souls?

The Dominican missionary and bishop in the Americas, Bartolomé de las Casas (1475–1566), an Erasmian idealist, was the most severe critic of Spanish imperial policy. This policy of enslavement and general mistreatment of the Indians was based on the claim that they did not possess souls and therefore could not be converted to Christianity. Las Casas argued for an active promotion of conversion. In the following treatise, he sets forth thirty propositions for this practice of conversion, six of which appear below.

Proposition I. The Roman Pontiff, canonically chosen vicar of Jesus Christ and successor of St Peter, has the authority and the power of Christ himself, the Son of God, over all men in the world, believers or infidels, insofar as it is necessary to guide and direct men to the end of the eternal life and to remove any impediments to this goal. Although the Pontiff uses and ought to

From "Aquise Contienen Treinta Proposiciones Mayjuridicas," by Bartolomé de las Casas, in *Tratados de Fray Bartolomé de las Casas*, edited by Giménez Fernández (Mexico City: Fondo de Cultura Económica, 1965). Translated by Benjamin Sax.

use such power in a special fashion with the infidels, who have never entered into holy baptism of the holy Church, especially those who never heard tidings of Christ nor of His faith, he uses another kind of authority with Christians and those who at one time were Christian. . . .

Proposition IV. For the conversion of the infidels the Christian kings are very necessary for the Church; with their secular power, armed forces, and temporal wealth, they may help, protect, preserve, and defend the ecclesiastical and spiritual ministers. . . .

Proposition X. Among the infidels who have

distant kingdoms that have never heard the tidings of Christ or received the faith, there are true kings and princes. Their sovereignty, dignity, and royal pre-eminence derive from natural law and the law of nations. . . . Therefore, with the coming of Jesus Christ to such domains, their honors, royal pre-eminence, and so on, do not disappear either in fact or in right.

Proposition XI. The opinion contrary to that of the preceding proposition is erroneous and most pernicious. He who persistently defends it will fall into formal heresy. It is likewise most impious and iniquitous and has been the cause of innumerable thefts, violent disturbances, tyrannies, massacres, larcenies, irreparable damages, the gravest sins, infamy, stench, and hatred against the name of Christ and the Christian religion. . . .

Proposition XVI. The Roman Pontiff, vicar of Jesus Christ, whose divine authority extends over all the kingdoms of heaven and earth, could justly invest the kings of Castile and Leon with the supreme and sovereign empire and dominion over the entire realm of the Indies, making them emperors over many kings. . . . If the vicar of Christ were to see that this was not advantageous for the spiritual well-being of Christianity, he could without doubt, by the same divine authority, annul or abolish the office of emperor of the Indies, or he could transfer it to another prince, as one Pope did when he transferred the imperial crown from the Greeks to the Germans [at the coronation of Charlemagne in A.D. 800]. With the same authority, the Apostolic See could prohibit, under penalty of excommunication, all other Christian kings from going to the Indies without the permission and authorization of the kings of Castile. If they do the contrary, they sin mortally and incur excommunication. . . .

Proposition XXVIII. The Devil could invent no worse pestilence to destroy all that world and to kill all the people there . . . than the *repartimiento* [the distribution of the Indians among the Spanish colonists] and *encomienda,* the institution used to distribute and entrust Indians to the Spaniards [and who were allowed to collect a yearly tribute from these Indians]. This was like entrusting the Indians to a gang of devils or delivering herds of cattle to hungry wolves. The encomienda or repartimiento was the most cruel sort of tyranny that can be imagined, and it is most worthy of infernal damnation. The Indians were prevented from receiving the Christian faith and religion. The wretched and tyrannical Spanish encomenderos worked the Indians night and day in the mines and in other personal services. They collected unbelievable tributes. The encomenderos forced the Indians to carry burdens on their backs for a hundred and two hundred leagues, as if they were less than beasts. They persecuted and expelled from the Indian villages the preachers of the faith. . . . And I solemnly affirm, as God is my witness, that so long as these encomiendas remain, all the authority of the kings, even if they were resident in the Indies, will not be enough to prevent all the Indians from perishing.

After reading this selection and the previous one, consider these questions:

1. What were the actual relations between European and the native populations in the Americas?
2. How did Europeans justify the enslavement of the native populations of the Americas?
3. What were the main arguments against slavery?

SELECTION 6:

The Noble Savage

In the sixteenth and seventeenth centuries, observations of the nature and customs of the New World only rarely resulted in reflection on the nature and customs of the Old World. Yet in some remarkable individuals, such as Michel de Montaigne (1533–1592), the French humanist lawyer and mayor of Bordeaux, these encounters with the people of the Americas— even with the cannibals of South America—lead to a number of interesting comparisons. At the time when Montaigne wrote, France had just ended prolonged religious wars.

I think there is nothing barbarous and savage in that nation [the Americas], from what I have been told, except that each man calls barbarism whatever is not his own practice; for indeed it seems we have no other test of truth and reason than the example and pattern of the opinions and customs of the country we live in. *There* is always the perfect religion, the perfect government, the perfect and accomplished manners in all things. Those people are wild, just as we call wild the fruits that Nature has produced by herself and in her normal course; whereas really it is those that we have changed artificially and led astray from the common order, that we should rather call wild. The former retain alive and vigorous their genuine, their most useful and natural, virtues and properties, which we have debased in the latter in adapting them to gratify our corrupted taste. And yet for all that, the savor and delicacy of some uncultivated fruits of those countries is quite as excellent, even to our taste, as that of our own. It is not reasonable that art should win the place of honor over our great and powerful mother Nature. We have so overloaded the beauty and richness of her works by our inventions that we have quite smothered her. Yet wherever her purity

From *The Complete Essays of Montaigne*, translated by Donald M. Frame. Copyright © 1958 by the Board of Trustees of the Leland Stanford Junior University. Reprinted with the permission of the publishers, Stanford University Press.

shines forth, she wonderfully puts to shame our vain and frivolous attempts:

> Ivy comes readier without our care;
> In lonely caves the arbutus grows more fair;
> No art with artless bird song can compare.
>
> PROPERTIUS

All our efforts cannot even succeed in reproducing the nest of the tiniest little bird, its contexture, its beauty and convenience; or even the web of the puny spider. All things, says Plato, are produced by nature, by fortune, or by art; the greatest and most beautiful by one or the other of the first two, the least and most imperfect by the last.

These nations, then, seem to me barbarous in this sense, that they have been fashioned very little by the human mind, and are still very close to their original naturalness. The laws of nature still rule them, very little corrupted by ours; and they are in such a state of purity that I am sometimes vexed that they were unknown earlier, in the days when there were men able to judge them better than we. I am sorry that [the Athenian orator] Lycurgus and Plato did not know of them; for it seems to me that what we actually see in these nations surpasses not only all the pictures in which poets have idealized the golden age and all their inventions in imagining a happy state of man, but also the conceptions and the very desire of philosophy. They could not imagine a naturalness so pure and simple as we see by experience; nor could they believe that our society could be maintained with so little artifice and human solder. This is a nation, I should say to Plato, in which there is no sort of traffic, no knowledge of letters, no science of numbers, no name for a magistrate or for political superiority, no custom of servitude, no riches or poverty, no contracts, no successions, no partitions, no occupations but leisure ones, no care for any but common kinship, no clothes, no agriculture, no metal, no use of wine or wheat. The very words that signify lying, treachery, dissimulation, avarice, envy, belittling, pardon—unheard of. How far from this perfection would he find the republic that he imagined: *Men fresh sprung from the gods* [Seneca].

These manners nature first ordained.

VIRGIL

. . . They have their wars with the nations beyond the mountains, further inland, to which they go quite naked, with no other arms than bows or wooden swords ending in a sharp point, in the manner of the tongues of our boar spears. It is astonishing what firmness they show in their combats, which never end but in slaughter and bloodshed; for as to routs and terror, they know nothing of either.

Each man brings back as his trophy the head of the enemy he has killed, and sets it up at the entrance to his dwelling. After they have treated their prisoners well for a long time with all the hospitality they can think of, each man who has a prisoner calls a great assembly of his acquaintances. He ties a rope to one of the prisoner's arms, by the end of which he holds him, a few steps away, for fear of being hurt, and gives his dearest friend the other arm to hold in the same way: and these two, in the presence of the whole assembly, kill him with their swords. This done, they roast him and eat him in common and send some pieces to their absent friends. This is not, as people think, for nourishment, as of old the Scythians used to do; it is to betoken an extreme revenge. And the proof of this came when they saw the Portuguese, who had joined forces with their adversaries, inflict a different kind of death on them when they took them prisoner, which was to bury them up to the waist, shoot the rest of their body full of arrows, and afterward hang them. They thought that these people from the other world, being men who had sown the knowledge of many vices among their neighbors and were much greater masters than themselves in every sort of wickedness, did not adopt this sort of vengeance without some reason, and that it must be more painful than their own; so they began to give up their old method and to follow this one.

I am not sorry that we notice the barbarous horror of such acts, but I am heartily sorry that, judging their faults rightly, we should be so blind to our own. I think there is more barbarity in eating a man alive than in eating him dead; and in tearing by tortures and the rack a body still full of feeling, in roasting a man bit by bit, in having him bitten and mangled by dogs and swine (as we have not only read but seen within fresh memory, not among ancient enemies, but among neighbors and fellow citizens, and what is worse, on the pretext of piety and religion), than in roasting and eating him after he is dead. . . .

So we may well call these people barbarians, in respect to the rules of reason, but not in respect to ourselves, who surpass them in every kind of barbarity.

Their warfare is wholly noble and generous, and as excusable and beautiful as this human disease can be; its only basis among them is their rivalry in valor. They are not fighting for the conquest of new lands, for they still enjoy that natural abundance that provides them without toil and trouble with all necessary things in such profusion that they have no wish to enlarge their boundaries. They are still in that happy state of desiring only as much as their natural needs demand; anything beyond that is superfluous to them.

They generally call those of the same age, brothers; those who are younger, children; and the old men are fathers to all the others. These leave to their heirs in common the full possession of their property, without division or any other title at all than just the one that Nature gives to her creatures in bringing them into the world.

If their neighbors cross the mountains to attack them and win a victory, the gain of the victor is glory, and the advantage of having proved the master in valor and virtue; for apart from this they have no use for the goods of the vanquished, and they return to their own country, where they lack neither anything necessary nor that great thing, the knowledge of how to enjoy their condition happily and be content with it. These men of ours do the same in their turn. They demand of their prisoners no other ransom than that they confess and acknowledge their defeat. But there is not one in a whole century who does not choose to die rather than to relax a single bit, by word or look, from the grandeur of an invincible courage; not one who would not rather be killed and eaten than so much as ask not to be. They treat them very freely, so that life may be all the dearer to them, and usually entertain them with threats of their corning death, of the torments they will have to suffer, the preparations that are being made for that purpose, the cutting up of their limbs, and the feast that will be made at their expense. All this is done for the sole purpose of extorting from their lips some weak or base word, or making them want to flee, so as to gain the advantage of having terrified them and broken down their firmness. For indeed, if you take it the right way, it is in this point alone that true victory lies:

It is no victory
Unless the vanquished foe admits your
    mastery.

CLAUDIAN

. . .We win enough advantages over our enemies that are borrowed advantages, not really our own. It is the quality of a porter, not of valor, to have sturdier arms and legs; agility is a dead and corporeal quality; it is a stroke of luck to make our enemy stumble, or dazzle his eyes by the sunlight; it is a trick of art and technique, which may be found in a worthless coward, to be an able fencer. The worth and value of a man is in his heart and his will; there lies his real honor. Valor is the strength, not of legs and arms, but of heart and soul; it consists not in the worth of our horse or our weapons, but in our own. He who falls obstinate in his courage, *if he has fallen, he fights on his knees* [Seneca]. He who relaxes none of his assurance, no matter how great the danger of imminent death; who, giving up his soul, still looks firmly and scornfully at his enemy—he is beaten not by us, but by fortune; he is killed, not conquered.

After reading this selection, consider these questions:
1. How did Montaigne describe the cannibals in the Americas?
2. How did the author compare the values of the cannibals to those of the Europeans?
3. What do you think was Montaigne's purpose in making this comparison?

CHAPTER 15
The Protestant Reformation and the Catholic Counter Reformation

The Protestant Reformation permanently severed sections of northern Europe—most notably Scotland, England, the Netherlands, northern Germany, and Scandinavia—from the Catholic Church. This brought to a close the long period stretching from late antiquity to the sixteenth century in which the Catholic Church had both given ecclesiastical unity and provided a common set of values for all of Europe west of Russia and the Balkans. Ever since the Reformation, Europe has been permanently divided between Catholics and a variety of Protestant sects—mainly Lutherans, Calvinists, and Anglicans. Each of these forms of Protestantism established its own church and its own notions of the relation of the church to the secular government. The Reformation's significance lay not just in its breaking of the religious and ecclesiastical unity of Europe. Over the course of the sixteenth century a wide range of interpretations about the foundations of the Christian faith developed. The position and meaning of the Bible and the traditions of the church; the number and significance of the sacraments for individual salvation; the role of ministers or priests in relation to the truths of Christianity, on the one hand, and to the faithful, on the other, and various questions of church governance—all were issues hotly debated throughout the century.

Yet behind all these debates lay a basic division concerning the nature of God and his relation to the world. Should (or even could) individuals attempt to find their own way to God, guided only by Scriptures and their spiritual adviser, or should they be directed through the mediating role of the priest, of the system of sacraments, and of the church as the spiritual guide of Christian society? Were the highest forms of a Christian life to be found in monastic withdrawal from the world and in ascetic activities, or could men and women outside monasteries and nunneries—in their occupations, family life, and everyday activities—live fully Christian lives? Protestantism found radically new ways of understanding Christianity—ways that greatly contrasted the ones that had developed from antiquity into the Middle Ages. By turning to and sanctifying activities in this world, the Reformation grew out of and spoke to the needs of a late medieval lay society. In the late Middle Ages, many

Christians seemed to be seeking more individual forms of religion as well as more personal understandings of faith. In this sense, the Reformation was not only a response to various failures within the traditional forms of the Catholic Church but also a response to the growing and changing needs of a larger and more deeply religious community, which itself was the result of the church's success in establishing and spreading a Christian civilization.

Many individuals, both within the church hierarchy and outside of it, saw the need for change within the church in the late fifteenth and early sixteenth centuries. Not only did church government and the role of both the regular and secular clergy need reform but also a wide range of practices from those openly sanctioned by the church (for instance, the veneration of relics) to those merely tolerated by it (for instance, the open sale of indulgences for lessening time in purgatory) needed clarification. That monetary fines could be substituted for religious acts of penance, such as prayers or pilgrimages, indicated to many that the church was more concerned with making money than with saving souls. When Martin Luther (1483–1546) began arguing and then preaching openly for such reforms in 1517 (the traditional date of the beginning of the Reformation), his activities were initially seen as part of this more general call for change within the church. Luther, however, was also concerned with other matters. As he came to understand his own position in the 1510s and 1520s, Luther found the source of his challenge in doctrinal matters, in the basic set of beliefs propounded by the church. But even these questions of doctrine stemmed from Luther's personal search for faith, which he experienced from the time he became a friar and entered the Augustinian monastery at Erfurt in 1506.

Christian righteousness was both a binding of the individual to the dictates of faith and a means of liberation for the individual. In one of his three great treatises of 1520, *The Freedom of a Christian* (the others being, *An Appeal to the German Nobility* and *The Babylonian Captivity of the Church*), Luther defines his new position. In his *Freedom of a Christian*, Luther finds freedom in obedience, which probably reflects his own experience of faith. Luther further argues that only faith, and not the church's "good works," can lead to salvation. Basing his position on the theology of St. Paul and St. Augustine, Luther claimed that Christ's suffering on the cross had freed humanity from the guilt of sin. Faith alone in the divinity in Christ was essential—a faith founded on strong scriptural evidence and not on the rules and regulations of the church. To "by faith alone" and "by Scripture alone," Luther added the notion of "the priesthood of all believers." Scripture itself, and not the church or the mediation of priests, was sufficient for Christian life in this world and preparation for the next.

Responding to calls for reform from within the church and demands that the church reunite Christendom, a general council eventually convened. Meeting in 1545 in the northern Italian city of Trent (Latin Trentinum), this council was to meet in three major sessions—1545–1547, 1550–1552, 1562–1563. The council ended the clergy's overinvolvement with the political and economic powers of the world. It also addressed the generally low moral conduct of many priests and monks by establishing new standards for clerical education and for the pastoral care of the faithful. These reforms were not limited only to church governance and the clergy but also to the definition of doctrine. Certain sacraments, such as the Eucharist, had to be clarified in the light of various Protestant criticisms. Also, a number of popular beliefs and common practices needed to be reviewed. Some of these practices had been inherited from a pre-Christian Europe, as Christianity was spread throughout Europe in late antiquity and the early Middle Ages; but others represented the proliferation of new religious forms in the towns and cities of Europe in the high and late medieval periods. In the midst of these various incrustations and new growths, the Counter Reformation church declared which were true forms of faith and which were not.

The Counter Reformation of the Catholic Church represented more than just a reaction and countering of the Reformation doctrines of Luther, Calvin, and others who broke from Rome. More importantly, the Counter Reformation also marked a period in the history of Western Christianity in which the Roman Catholic Church transformed itself in a number of fundamental ways. The term *Counter Reformation* indicates this complex redefinition of the Catholic Church and Catholic Christianity and denotes that historical period in which these reforms were undertaken, stretching roughly from the sixteenth through the seventeenth centuries. But in a wider sense, the Counter Reformation marked the transformation from the church of the Middle Ages to the Catholic Church of the modern world.

SELECTION 1:

Luther's Crisis of Faith

Although the Reformation would eventually take several forms and would depend on the religious experiences and interpretations of a number of leading theologians, such as John Calvin in France and Ulrich Zwingli in Switzerland, Luther and his search for faith laid the foundations of all that was to follow. One of the leading historians of the Reformation, Heiko A. Oberman, emphasizes the importance of Luther's search for personal salvation and of his repeated failure to find certainty in this matter within the prescribed means of medieval Christianity. Luther was not alone in finding the sacrament of penance less than satisfactory in calming his consciousness of sin. Performing so-called good works did not still his inner uncertainty about personal salvation. Instead of relieving his anxiety, such acts of penance only heightened the fear that he had failed and that he would always be unable to confess his sins. This sense of utter sinfulness, and the inadequacies of the given methods of dealing with it reached new levels of intensity when Luther became a professor of biblical theology. As with many other biographers of Luther and historians of the Reformation, Oberman sees in Luther's growing understanding of the notion of "the righteousness of God" a clue to how Luther eventually found an answer to this unbearable situation.

Eighteen months after his return from Rome the master of arts and monk became a doctor of theology and professor in Wittenberg. From the critical perspective of his time Luther now joined the ranks of those stupid monks who endlessly argue about anything and nothing, who set themselves up as guardians of piety and proper doctrine, yet are unable to count their own toes. Learned theologians in his own country and ecclesiastical authorities in Rome at first dismissed the questions Luther raised as typical monkish bickering. There was as yet no way to predict that a man had appeared on the scene who was seeking the truth in the mazelike roads to salvation offered at the time.

It is crucial to realize that Luther became a reformer who was widely heard and understood by transforming the abstract question of a just God into an *existential quest* that concerned the *whole* human being, encompassing thought and action, soul and body, love and suffering. The search for salvation was not reserved for the intellect alone. Nor did Luther liberate himself from scholastic theology by retreating into his private self; it was not the battle of heart against head that drove him to raise his voice and take a more critical view of medieval theologians whom his own teachers still regarded as authorities. It was not that he found them too scholarly for the delicate business of faith, but rather that he did not find them

scholarly enough. For Luther careful heed to the Scriptures was the only scholarly basis for theology and thus the reliable standard of truth. . . .

At the end of the road to becoming a reformer stood the discovery that the Scriptures confirmed what he had sensed, sought, and seen with increasing accuracy by living with the God of the Scriptures. With the intellectual and emotional inquisitiveness that was always to characterize him, he analyzed the Scriptures to determine the truth of what [his mentor, vicar general] Johannes von Staupitz had taught him. The only obstacle still in his way—as he put it in his 1545 *Rückblick,* an autobiographical fragment referring to 1518 and 1519—was the central text in St. Paul's Epistle to the Romans: "For therein [in the Gospel] is the righteousness of God revealed" (Rom. 1.17).

A series of discoveries that proved only retrospectively to be steps in the same direction freed him from the fundamental notion common to all medieval schools of thought: the righteousness of God is the eternal law according to which He who is unattainably holy will judge all men on doomsday. Then justice will be done, and punishment or reward meted out.

But did the Middle Ages know nothing about the righteousness that Christ grants as a gift? Had no one read the apostle Paul before? Was not Luther's answer that the faithful participated in Christ's righteousness identical with the answer that St. Augustine had given in *Spirit and Letter*? Thus twentieth-century critics have tried to dismiss Luther as "superficial" and an "ignoramus." At best, they would, in their ecumenical generosi-

From *Luther: Man Between God and the Devil*, by Heiko A. Oberman, translated by Eileen Walliser-Schwarzbart. Copyright 1989 by Yale University. Reprinted by permission of Yale University Press.

ty, grant that he had discovered "for himself" what had always been plain to every good Catholic.

These critics are right in that St. Paul was generally regarded as "the" apostle in the Middle Ages and that St. Augustine had been thoroughly assimilated in biblical commentaries. But both of them were always understood to say that the Church distributes Christ's righteousness like the talents that can be increased by hard work and good investment. Christ's justice does not make a man righteous before God; it puts him in the position to become righteous. At the Last Judgment the righteous God will decide if the faithful have used and truly done justice to Christ's gift. What is completely new about Luther's discovery is that he sees God's righteousness as inseparably united and merged with the righteousness of Christ: already *now* it is received through faith. That is the reason all the faithful will be able to stand the test: "That is the long and the short of it: He who believes in the man called Jesus Christ, God's only Son, has eternal life—as He himself says (John 3.16): 'For God so loved the world, that he gave his only begotten Son, that whosoever believeth in him should not perish, but have everlasting life.'"

Why did Luther become more than an original thinker and a fascinating witness to a vanished world? He was able to become the Reformer of the Church because he was prepared to test his discovery against the Scriptures and ultimately to anchor it there. Only thus could it achieve lasting value for him and lay claim to validity for the whole Church. The "Gates of Paradise" were opened to him and a flood of knowledge swept over him once he had succeeded in grasping the passage (Rom. 1.17) in which St. Paul quotes the prophet Habakkuk: "The just shall live by faith" (Habakkuk 2.4).

"I am not good and righteous, but Christ is."

. . . Luther's autobiography, which appeared in 1545 as the preface to the first edition of his Latin works, has been the subject of exhaustive scholarly research. Nonetheless, Luther is not yet heard out, and his urgent admonition and warning has been missed: "Reader, be commended to God, and pray for the increase of preaching against Satan. For he is powerful and wicked, today more

dangerous than ever before because he knows that he has only a short time left to rage."

"Today" means that Luther not only discovered the Gospel but also roused the Devil, who is now raging terribly and gaining an unprecedented power of absolutely new satanic proportions.

This is no longer the Devil who, in a triple alliance with "sin" and "world," seduces the voluptuous flesh of man against his better "self." The medieval poltergeist is virtually harmless in comparison with this adversary, who, armed with fire and sword, spiritual temptations and clever arguments, has now risen up against God to prevent the preaching of the Gospel. As long as the righteous God reigns far away in Heaven, waiting for the end of the world, the Devil, too, will remain at the edge of world history. But the closer the Righteous One comes to us on earth through our belief in Christ, the closer the Devil draws, feeling challenged to take historically effective countermeasures. The Reformation symbol of Christ's presence is not the halo of the saint, but the hatred of the Devil.

Transforming Luther into a forerunner of enlightenment means dismissing this warning of the Devil's growing superiority as a remnant of the Dark Ages. But that would be to deprive Luther's life of the experience of the Devil's power, which affected him as intensely as Christ's. Take away the Devil and we are left with the Protestant citadel, the "better self," the conscience, which thus becomes the site of the Last Judgment, where the believer, confronted with the laws of God, acknowledges that he is a sinner and declares himself at the same time to be righteous by virtue of Christ's sacrifice.

It is precisely this conventional, conscience-oriented morality that man's innermost self struggles to fulfill, and that Luther, to the horror of all well-meaning, decent Christians, undermined. The issue is not morality or immorality, it is God and the Devil. This patent encroachment on conscience desecrates the very thing that elevates man above the beasts—his knowledge of the difference between good and evil. The two great turning points of the Reformation age, the Lutheran and the Copernican, seem to have brought mankind nothing but humiliation. First man is robbed of his power over himself, and then he is pushed to the periphery of creation.

"The Spiritus Sanctus [Holy Spirit] gave me this realization in the cloaca." If this is the site of the Reformation discovery, man's powerlessness is joined by ignominy. Must the trail of the Reformation be followed this far? There is a dignified way out: by cloaca Luther did not mean the toilet, but the study up in the tower above it. That, however, would be to miss the point of Luther's provocative statement. The cloaca is not just a privy, it is the most degrading place for man and the Devil's favorite habitat. Medieval monks already knew this, but the Reformer knows even more now: it is right here that we have Christ, the mighty helper, on our side. No spot is unholy for the Holy Ghost; this is the very place to express contempt for the adversary through trust in Christ crucified.

Christ in the privy helping one to resist the Devil is certainly anything but genteel. In their propriety later centuries recount only how Luther hurled his inkwell across the room at Wartburg Castle. If the Devil must be mentioned, then at least with decorum. There is no truth in that polite legend, and it masks the actual situation. . . . Luther attests to the birth of Christ in the filth of this world. The Son of God was truly born into the flesh, into the blood and sweat of man. He understood men because He experienced—to the bitter end—what it meant to be human.

As powerful as the Devil is, he cannot become flesh and blood; he can only sire specters and wallow in his own filth. The manger and the altar confront the Devil with the unattainable. Both the demonic, intangible adversary of God and the Son of God are present in the world, but only Christ the Son is corporeally present. Anyone who goes further, making the Devil into a living being, is superstitious. The cloaca is a revealing place. It unmasks the Devil's powerlessness as well as man's. Although far removed from propriety, it is also a place of faith, the Christian's place in life.

Thus the final sentence in Luther's *Rückblick* cannot be ignored without suppressing a facet of his belief. Wherever the Gospel is preached and bears fruit, the Devil is there to get in the way— that is his nature, "today" more than ever! Fear of the Devil does not fit in with our modern era, for belief in the Devil has been exorcized by attractive ideologies. But in the process our grasp of the unity of man has been lost: living with the real Christ in one's faith means being a whole person as opposed to an intellect that subscribes to a mere idea of Christ.

The Devil will readily help theologians to "elevate" the zealous, fighting, wrathful, loving God of Israel into the philosophical concept of an "Omnipotent Being."

For Luther the disembodiment of God into an impressive idea is one of the Devil's decisive misdeeds. Satan may be no doctor of theology, but he is very well trained in philosophy and has had nearly six thousand years to practice his craft. All the encouraging victories of God which occur prior to the Last Judgment melt under the Devil's glare. Arguments are of no help against the Devil; only Christ can come to our aid. Satan's wisdom is thwarted by the statement "the just shall live by faith"—faith not in an idea but in a God who, under the banner of the cross, is fighting for a world the Devil, too, is trying to win. Satan's power is not unlimited; he must stay within specified bounds, but until doomsday they encompass the whole world.

After reading this selection, consider these questions:

1. What was involved in Luther's crisis of belief?
2. How does Oberman interpret Luther's understanding of faith?
3. What was the significance of Luther's notion of the devil?

SELECTION 2:

Luther's Attack on the Catholic Church

The implications of reestablishing Christian faith upon individual experience were tremendous. Not only were the church and its clergy largely irrelevant to Martin Luther's faith, they were definite obstacles. Likewise, neither the intervention of priests, the veneration of relics, nor the saving powers of "good works" could no longer be considered the core of Christian life. Through his interpretation of Scriptures, Luther found a close relationship between God and the world. Following Luther, one had to find Christ within one's own life, guided by Scripture and the preaching of the word of Scripture. Preaching, in fact, became the centerpiece of Christian worship for Luther as for all other Protestant reformers. In the following sermon, delivered in Erfurt in 1521, Luther makes clear the distinctions between what he considers his true form of faith and that of the church of his day.

Dear friends, I shall pass over the story of St. Thomas this time and leave it for another occasion, and instead consider the brief words uttered by Christ: "Peace be with you" [John 20:19] and "Behold my hands and my side" [John 20:27], and "as the Father has sent me, even so I send you" [John 20:21]. Now, it is clear and manifest that every person likes to think that he will be saved and attain to eternal salvation. This is what I propose to discuss now.

You also know that all philosophers, doctors and writers have studiously endeavored to teach and write what attitude man should take to piety. They have gone to great trouble, but, as is evident, to little avail. Now genuine and true piety consists of two kinds of works: those done for others, which are the right kind, and those done for ourselves, which are unimportant. In order to find a foundation, one man builds churches; another goes on a pilgrimage to St. James' or St.

Peter's [cathedrals]; a third fasts or prays, wears a cowl, goes barefoot, or does something else of the kind. Such works are nothing whatever and must be completely destroyed. Mark these words: none of our works have any power whatsoever. For God has chosen a man, the Lord Christ Jesus, to crush death, destroy sin, and shatter hell, since there was no one before he came who did not inevitably belong to the devil. The devil therefore thought he would get a hold upon the Lord when he hung between two thieves and was suffering the most contemptible and disgraceful of deaths, which was cursed both by God and by men [cf. Deut. 21:23; Gal. 3:13]. But the Godhead was so strong that death, sin, and even hell were destroyed.

Therefore you should note well the words which Paul writes to the Romans [Rom. 5:12–21]. Our sins have their source in Adam, and because Adam ate the apple, we have inherited sin from him. But Christ has shattered death for our sake, in order that we might be saved by his works, which are alien to us, and not by our works.

But the papal dominion treats us altogether differently. It makes rules about fasting, praying,

From *Luther's Works*, vol. 51, edited and translated by John W. Doberstein (Philadelphia: Muhlenberg Press, 1959).

and butter-eating, so that whoever keeps the commandments of the pope will be saved and whoever does not keep them belongs to the devil. It thus seduces the people with the delusion that goodness and salvation lies in their own works. But I say that none of the saints, no matter how holy they were, attained salvation by their works. Even the holy mother of God did not become good, was not saved, by her virginity or her motherhood, but rather by the will of faith and the works of God, and not by her purity, or her own works. Therefore, mark me well: this is the reason why salvation does not lie in our own works, no matter what they are; it cannot and will not be effected without faith.

Now, someone may say: Look, my friend, you are saying a lot about faith, and claiming that our salvation depends solely upon it; now, I ask you, how does one come to faith? I will tell you. Our Lord Christ said, "Peace be with you. Behold my hands, etc." [John 20:26–27]. [In other words, he is saying:] Look, man, I am the only one who has taken away your sins and redeemed you, etc.; now be at peace. Just as you inherited sin from Adam—not that you committed it, for I did not eat the apple, any more than you did, and yet this is how we came to be in sin—so we have not suffered [as Christ did], and therefore we were made free from death and sin by God's work, not by our works. Therefore God says: Behold, man, I am your redemption [cf. Isa. 43:3]; just as Paul said to the Corinthians: Christ is our justification, redemption, etc. [I Cor.1:30]. Christ is our justification and redemption, as Paul says in this passage. And here our [Roman] masters say: Yes, *Redemptor,* Redeemer; this is true, but it is not enough.

Therefore, I say again: Alien works, these make us good! Our Lord Christ says: I am your justification. I have destroyed the sins you have upon you. Therefore only believe in me; believe that I am he who has done this; then you will be justified. For it is written, *Justicia est fides,* righteousness is identical with faith and comes through faith. Therefore, if we want to have faith, we should believe the gospel, Paul, etc., and not the papal breves [letters of authority], or the decretals [decrees on matters of doctrine],

but rather guard ourselves against them as against fire. For everything that comes from the pope cries out: Give, give; and if you refuse, you are of the devil. It would be a small matter if they were only exploiting the people. But, unfortunately, it is the greatest evil in the world to lead the people to believe that outward works can save or make a man good.

At this time the world is so full of wickedness that it is overflowing, and is therefore now under a terrible judgment and punishment, which God has inflicted, so that the people are perverting and deceiving themselves in their own minds. For to build churches, and to fast and pray and so on has the appearance of good works, but in our heads we are deluding ourselves. We should not give way to greed, desire for temporal honor, and other vices and rather be helpful to our poor neighbor. Then God will arise in us and we in him, and this means a new birth. What does it matter if we commit a fresh sin? If we do not immediately despair, but rather say within ourselves, "O God, thou livest still! Christ my Lord is the destroyer of sin," then at once the sin is gone. And also the wise man says: *"Septies in die cadit iustus et resurgit."* "A righteous man falls seven times, and rises again [Prov. 24:16].

The reason why the world is so utterly perverted and in error is that for a long time there have been no genuine preachers. There are perhaps three thousand priests, among whom one cannot find four good ones—God have mercy on us in this crying shame! And when you do get a good preacher, he runs through the gospel superficially and then follows it up with a fable . . . or he mixes in something of the pagan teachers, Aristotle, Plato, Socrates, and others, who are all quite contrary to the gospel, and also contrary to God, for they did not have the knowledge of the light which we possess. Aye, if you come to me and say: The Philosopher says: Do many good works, then you will acquire the habit, and finally you will become godly; then I say to you: Do not perform good works in order to become godly; but if you are already godly, then do good works, though without affectation and with faith. There you see how contrary these two points of view are.

After reading this selection, consider these questions:

1. What was Luther's criticism of the Catholic Church?
2. What, according to Luther, was the Catholic view of "works"?
3. Why did Luther place so much emphasis on preaching?

SELECTION 3:

Why Did the Reformation Begin in Germany?

Luther would not have been successful in redefining Christian faith or in eventually breaking with Rome and establishing his own church had he not attracted the support, on the one hand, of individual clergy and powerful princes and, on the other hand, of larger segments of the population in the countryside and especially in the towns of Germany. Renowned historian Gerhard Ritter explores the reasons why the Reformation occurred in Germany—as opposed to all other countries of Europe. According to Ritter, although sixteenth-century Germany was critical of the church, it was not expressing an anti-Christian attitude; rather, there had developed in Germany a deep sense of lay piety that needed new forms of definition and direction.

At the end of the Middle Ages, the moral prestige of the old papal church was severely shaken in all the countries of Europe. Open criticism of its moral shortcomings and its organizational defects had been going on for centuries. To the diverse splinter-movements of heretical sects (which were never wholly suppressed) had been recently added the great reform movements of the Wyclifites and the Hussites [derived from the religious reformers John Wycliffe and Jan Hus]. But even they had brought about no lasting and widespread upheaval. Ultimately the old hierarchy had always prevailed. Why then did the Germans, a people slow to be aroused, fond of order, and faithful to the church, take it upon themselves to carry out the most prodigious revolution in the church? And why did only their revolt against the papal church have such vast and enduring consequences? . . .

It is true that this decisively new impetus to reform was entirely the personal deed of an individual of genius, without example or precedent: the deed of Martin Luther. But how did it happen that in Germany it was not immediately branded as heresy and stamped out, but met with a loud response, which did not even abate when it became universally evident that the attack shook the dogmatic foundations of the old priestly church? Could this response perhaps become intelligible in the light of the special nature of German Christian piety?

A person coming at this time across the Alps from Italy would sense immediately the vastly greater intensity of ecclesiastical and religious

From "Why the Reformation Occurred in Germany," by Gerhard Ritter, translated by G.H. Nadel, *Church History*, vol. 27, no. 2, (June 1958).

life among the Germans. The secularization of existence, the fading of the Christian ascetic ideals of the Middle Ages, encountered at the Renaissance courts of the South are not yet felt. All life is still consummated in the shadow of the mighty cathedrals, which dominate the panorama of the German city. With unbroken force the Christian teaching of the world to come still determines all forms of life; its influence, indeed, seems to wax continuously. Pious foundations become alarmingly numerous. Hundreds of clerical benefices, many dozens of altars, accumulate in the great churches: in Cologne, a good third of built-up ground was said to have been church property, and in some other places every tenth inhabitant was said to have belonged to the clergy. The sumptuous furnishings even of small village churches and the daily influx of churchgoers never cease to astound foreign travelers. The ecclesiastical organization of the masses pushes rapidly ahead. All kinds of lay brotherhoods, for the care of the poor and the sick, for the erection of homes, for common devotions, increase in number and magnitude with extraordinary speed. Every mendicant order attracts such associations; but still others spring up like weeds, and their spiritual control and supervision cause the church authorities no little concern. These groups teach their members unselfish service of their neighbors, but at the same time an outward sanctimoniousness which is shrewdly calculated to secure for itself certain salvation in the next world by multiplying prayers and oblations. Church devotions have become popular, the most sacred has become commonplace: very often, religious excitation is combined with a rank mania for sensation and miracle. The system of pilgrimages and relics, with its thousand frauds, the spread of the belief in witches, the alarming frequency of religious epidemics, of eschatological states of excitement in the masses—all these are repellent enough. But who could on their account overlook the numerous testimonies of profound and genuine piety, the deep poetic touches of the cult of Mary with its reflections in poetry and the plastic arts and the moral effects of spreading the church's teachings among the people?

Now what is peculiar is how closely this very vigorous popular piety is combined with severe, even embittered, criticism of the church and of her clergy; this attitude contrasts very noticeably with the blind devotion of the Spanish masses to the church. This criticism, voiced with equal severity among all classes of the German people, is itself a testimony, not perhaps of diminishing, but rather of live and increasing interest in religion and the church. There is, indeed, nothing which excites public opinion more than the church and its preaching. Among the masses, and in particular among the peasants, the preaching of the radical mendicant friars of the ideal of the propertyless church, in contrast to the prelates grown rich and unscrupulous, is most effective in the agitation carried on by nameless hole-and-corner preachers, this ideal is not infrequently combined with communistic ideas in the style of the Hussites and with apocalyptic expectations of the imminent end of the world. Among the urban middle classes there is primarily the sound common-sense criticism of excessive church privileges and of the contradiction between the claims of the clergy to spiritual authority and its scandalous manner of life; finally, there is also the misuse of mass devotion by the sellers of relics and indulgences, whose fraudulent practices do not deceive the burgher's sober business sense. The lazy dronelike existence of monastics and of so many recipients of church benefices arouses the ire of the diligent artisan; the democratic consciousness of the new age offers resistance to the aristocratic, dignified, and contemplative mode of life of the higher clergy. The burgher is also apt to be critical of the overly artful scholastic sermon whose content is often overloaded with theological subtleties, of the involved casuistry of canon law and its procedures of penance; he desires an unsophisticated form of Christian teaching accessible to all, a straight-forward handling, intelligible to the layman, of the church's authority to punish. The noble too has his bitter complaints against papal administration of benefices and financial practices. And finally, among men of letters—that is to say, above all among the members of universities, academic graduates, the more studious clerics, and certain of the urban patriciate—the Humanists' criticism of church tradition gradually gains ground.

For in Germany too the reverence of the Italian Humanists for classical greatness of soul, for the beauty of classical forms of life, art, and poetry, found enthusiastic followers. At princely courts here and there, in the patrician houses of the great south-German imperial cities, and at most of the universities, the imitation of Italian patronage of arts and letters, of Italian 'academies' and literary circles was begun; letters and poems were exchanged in artful and laboriously turned Latin; old authors, ancient coins, and all sorts of antiquities were unearthed and collected. . . .

Time and again a buried antagonism comes to light, a contest between the spirit of Latin churchdom, with its outward legalism, and German piety, with its strong temperamental needs and intense seriousness of conscience. Throughout the Middle Ages, the Roman church developed more markedly into a legal institution, whose rigid juridical-theological apparatus bound the religious procedure of salvation increasingly to the execution of outward sacred acts and the fulfillment of external sacred norms. But this very development serves to conceal even further the genuine, pristine essence of religion as the direct personal experience of God. The conscience of the deepest and purest German spirits had already revolted against this in the Middle Ages. Outward exhibition of religious experience in glowing ecstasies and visions, in new and striking forms of monastic asceticism, had always been rarer in Germany than the tendency to the most intimate submersion in the divine secrets. None of the founders of the great medieval orders was a German. There was, however, a German mysticism of great historical significance, which can be traced throughout the entire late Middle Ages.

The lay piety of upper Germany and the Netherlands (in which Erasmus too was nurtured), now turning towards more mystic edification, now towards more practical and efficacious piety, shows a common trend in its most varied forms: to relegate the church's sacramental apparatus of grace to lesser importance than the personal assurance of salvation which is sought and experienced by the individual believer in direct intercourse with his God. This, of course, need by no means lead to an attitude of opposition to the church. But the more emphatically the church stressed the indispensability of priestly mediation and juridically extended the concept of the power of the keys, the closer lay the danger that the pious soul would feel this intervention as a disturbing impediment, as an interference of alien power in the innermost secrets of the heart. The boundary between mysticism and heresy was never clearly drawn and was easily transgressed, indeed Germany in the fifteenth century was almost overflowing with mystical heretical sects. And even among the great mass of church people, where heretical inclinations were lacking, the priestly performance of the sacraments could be regarded more or less indifferently and pushed aside. The more easily this was done, the lower the moral prestige of the priesthood sank, and the misuse of the power of the keys for secular purposes became manifest. Finally, there was no lack of opposition-minded reformers who were able to justify on theological grounds such a rejection or at least devaluation of priestly mediation in salvation. In the writings of the so-called 'early reformers', especially of the Dutchman Wessel Gansfort, one can already discover a revolutionary bent which resembles the Lutheran conception of the process of salvation. Also outside the mystic tradition, Wyclifite ideas, which proposed to set a new community of saints in place of the hierarchically conceived priestly church, continually excited and engaged German theologians. The conviction that all reform in theology must begin with a return to the oldest and most original truths of Christianity, intelligible to the layman, was disseminated in the widest circles; it too was among the basic teachings of Erasmus and through the instrumentality of his writings it took hold of a very broad stratum of scholars, theological as well as lay. On the eve of the Reformation there were throughout Germany pious men and women to whom, from the point of their personal faith, the church with its splendid hierarchy appeared as a place of downright sale and corruption. They lived in a religion of quiet inwardness, in uncertain groping and seeking, of which hardly anything was expressed publicly. But because here was undoubtedly the greatest religious vitality, they too constituted a dangerous threat to the dominance of the old church. It was only a matter of combining the new religious vitality of the 'devout in the land' with the already mentioned loud criticism and political opposition, which filled the whole age, against the outward aspects of the church. Once this combination had been accomplished the revolutionary momentum could no longer be arrested.

In retrospect we see both currents of church opposition at work simultaneously though at first independently. The one struggles against manifest abuses and insists on reforms, but in practice does not go beyond a patchwork improvement of institutions. Though it does not reach down into spiritual depths, it is nevertheless most impassioned, impelling, and popular. The other current is less concerned with the outward appearance of the church, but instead touches on the substance of religion and the spiritual roots of church life. Those in power long underestimate its significance because at first it lacks any prospect of practical effect. But at the same time, it has the advantage that practical power can do nothing against it. In the figure of Martin Luther the two currents combine for the first time. He is a man of the people,

an agitator in grandest style, and the most popular speaker and writer that Germany has ever produced: possessed of unprecedented hitting power and coarseness of language, of boundless anger and fighting zeal, he sways the masses most forcefully. He shares the moral indignation of his contemporaries over the outward corruption of the church: he uses all the slogans of anticlerical and antipapal opposition of the preceding hundred years and still outdoes them—but at the same time he is the most brilliant and profound theological thinker, the most powerful and strong-willed prophet-figure of his people, and a religious genius whose experience of faith is of unprecedented inwardness and intimacy.

After reading this selection, consider these questions:

1. According to Ritter, why did the Reformation begin in Germany?
2. What were the main features of late medieval Christianity in Germany?
3. What role did Luther play within the intellectual and religious currents in sixteenth-century Germany?

SELECTION 4:

The Origins of Calvinism

Luther's impact was immediately felt in widening circles throughout the rest of Europe, from Switzerland and northern Italy to France and Austria, and from Spain to Bohemia and Hungary. In all of these areas the success of Protestantism initially depended on local clergymen and even those outside the clergy picking up and spreading the new faith. In several cases, most notably those of Zwingli and Calvin, Luther's teachings encouraged further development and refinement. The French lawyer John Calvin (1509–1564) broke with the Catholic Church in 1533 and began a series of commentaries on Luther's theology that would culminate in The Institutes of the Christian Religion (first edition 1536). This work was a remarkable intellectual achievement. No reformer prior to Calvin had expounded on the doctrines, organization, history, and practices of Chris-

tianity in such a systematic, logical, and coherent fashion. Going through a number of revisions and major additions, Calvin came to define an alternative form of Protestantism than Luther's, one that was accepted by almost all non-Lutheran forms of Protestantism.

Although the doctrine of individual predestination lay behind Luther's experience of faith and his interpretation of the righteousness of God (finding his inspiration in St. Augustine as well as in St. Paul), Calvin found it necessary to work out the implications of this doctrine. In the various editions of The Institutes, *the sections dealing with predestination were the ones that grew in length and complexity. Calvin's understanding of predestination—that God destines some humans for eternal life and others for eternal damnation—became a central tenet of Calvinism.*

Having seen that the dominion of sin, ever since the first man was brought under it, not only extends to the whole race, but has complete possession of every soul, it now remains to consider more closely, whether, from the period of being thus enslaved, we have been deprived of all liberty; and if any portion still remains, how far its power extends. In order to facilitate the answer to this question, it may be proper in passing to point out the course which our inquiry ought to take. The best method of avoiding error is to consider the dangers which beset us on either side. Man being devoid of all uprightness, immediately takes occasion from the fact to indulge in sloth, and having no ability in himself for the study of righteousness, treats the whole subject as if he had no concern in it. On the other hand, man cannot arrogate anything, however minute, to himself, without robbing God of his honour, and through rash confidence subjecting himself to a fall. To keep free of both these rocks, our proper course will be, first, to show that man has no remaining good in himself, and is beset on every side by the most miserable destitution; and then teach him to aspire to the goodness of which he is devoid, and the liberty of which he has been deprived: thus giving him a stronger stimulus to exertion than he could have if he imagined himself possessed of the highest virtue. How necessary the latter point is, everybody sees. As to the for-

mer, several seem to entertain more doubt than they ought. For it being admitted as incontrovertible that man is not to be denied anything that is truly his own, it ought also to be admitted, that he is to be deprived of everything like false boasting. If man had no title to glory in himself, when, by the kindness of his Maker, he was distinguished by the noblest ornaments, how much ought he to be humbled now, when his ingratitude has thrust him down from the highest glory to extreme ignominy? At the time when he was raised to the highest pinnacle of honour, all which Scripture attributes to him is, that he was created in the image of God, thereby intimating that the blessings in which his happiness consisted were not his own, but derived by divine communication. What remains, therefore, now that man is stript of all his glory, than to acknowledge the God for whose kindness he failed to be grateful, when he was loaded with the riches of his grace? Not having glorified him by the acknowledgment of his blessings, now, at least, he ought to glorify him by the confession of his poverty. In truth, it is no less useful for us to renounce all the praise of wisdom and virtue, than to aim at the glory of God. Those who invest us with more than we possess only add sacrilege to our ruin. For when we are taught to contend in our own strength, what more is done than to lift us up, and then leave us to lean on a reed which immediately gives way? Indeed, our strength is exaggerated when it is compared to a reed. All that foolish men invent and prattle on this subject is mere smoke. Wherefore, it is not without reason that Augustine so often repeats the well-known saying, that free will is more de-

From *Institutes of the Christian Religion*, by John Calvin, translated by Henry Beveridge (Grand Rapids, MI: Eerdmans, 1964).

294 WESTERN CIVILIZATION, VOLUME I

stroyed than established by its defenders. . . .

It was necessary to premise this much for the sake of some who, when they hear that human virtue is totally overthrown, in order that the power of God in man may be exalted, conceive an utter dislike to the whole subject, as if it were perilous, not to say superfluous, whereas it is manifestly both most necessary and most useful. . . .

Moreover, when I say that the will, deprived of liberty, is led or dragged by necessity to evil, it is strange that any should deem the expression harsh, seeing there is no absurdity in it, and it is not at variance with pious use. It does, however, offend those who know not how to distinguish between necessity and compulsion. Were any one to ask them, Is not God necessarily good, is not the devil necessarily wicked, what answer would they give? The goodness of God is so connected with his Godhead, that it is not more necessary to be God than to be good; whereas, the devil, by his fall, was so estranged from goodness, that he can do nothing but evil. Should any one give utterance to the profane jeer . . . that little praise is due to God for a goodness to which he is forced, is it not obvious to every man to reply, It is owing not to violent impulse, but to his boundless goodness, that he cannot do evil? Therefore, if the free will of God in doing good is not impeded, because he necessarily must do good; if the devil, who can do nothing but evil, nevertheless sins voluntarily; can it be said that man sins less voluntarily because he is under a necessity of sinning? . . .

The covenant of life is not preached equally to all, and among those to whom it is preached, does not always meet with the same reception. This diversity displays the unsearchable depth of the divine judgment, and is without doubt subordinate to God's purpose of eternal election. But if it is plainly owing to the mere pleasure of God that salvation is spontaneously offered to some, while others have no access to it, great and difficult questions immediately arise, questions which are inexplicable, when just views are not entertained concerning election and predestination. To many this seems a perplexing subject, because they deem it most incongruous that of the great body of mankind some should be predestinated to salvation, and others to destruction. How causelessly

they entangle themselves will appear as we proceed. We may add, that in the very obscurity which deters them, we may see not only the utility of this doctrine, but also its most pleasant fruits. We shall never feel persuaded as we ought that our salvation flows from the free mercy of God as its fountain, until we are made acquainted with his eternal election, the grace of God being illustrated by the contrast—viz. that he does not adopt promiscuously to the hope of salvation, but gives to some what he denies to others. It is plain how greatly ignorance of this principle detracts from the glory of God, and impairs true humility. But though thus necessary to be known, Paul declares that it cannot be known unless God, throwing works entirely out of view, elect those whom he has predestined. His words are, "Even so then at this present time also, there is a remnant according to the election of grace. And if by grace, then it is no more of works: otherwise grace is no more. But if it be of works, then it is no more grace: otherwise work is no more work" (Rom. xi.6). If to make it appear that our salvation flows entirely from the good mercy of God, we must be carried back to the origin of election, then those who would extinguish it, wickedly do as much as in them lies to obscure what they ought most loudly to extol, and pluck up humility by the very roots. Paul clearly declares that it is only when the Salvation of a remnant is ascribed to gratuitous election, we arrive at the knowledge that God saves whom he wills of his mere good pleasure, and does not pay a debt, a debt which never can be due. Those who preclude access, and would not have any one to obtain a taste of this doctrine, are equally unjust to God and men, there being no other means of humbling us, as we ought, or making us feel how much we are bound to him. Nor, indeed, have we elsewhere any sure ground of confidence. This we say on the authority of Christ, who, to deliver us from all fear, and render us invincible amid our many dangers, snares, and mortal conflicts, promises safety to all that the Father hath taken under his protection (John x.26). From this we infer, that all who know not that they are the peculiar people of God, must be wretched from perpetual trepidation, and that those, therefore, who, by overlooking the three advantages which we have noted, would destroy the very foundation of our safety, consult ill for themselves and for all the faithful. What? Do we not here find the very origin of the Church, which, as Bernard [St. Bernard of Clairvaux] rightly teaches . . . could not be found or recognised among the creatures, because it lies hid (in both cases wondrously) within the lap of blessed predestination, and the mass of wretched condemnation?

But before I enter on the subject, I have some remarks to address to two classes of men. The subject of predestination, which in itself is attended with considerable difficulty, is rendered very perplexed, and hence perilous by human curiosity, which cannot be restrained from wandering into forbidden paths, and climbing to the clouds, determined if it can that none of the secret things of God shall remain unexplored. When we see many, some of them in other respects not bad men, everywhere rushing into this audacity and wickedness it is necessary to remind them of the course of duty in this matter. First, then, when they inquire into predestination, let them remember that they are penetrating into the recesses of the divine wisdom, where he who rushes forward securely and confidently instead of satisfying his curiosity will enter an inextricable labyrinth. For it is not right that man should with impunity pry into things which the Lord has been pleased to conceal within himself, and scan that sublime eternal wisdom which it is his pleasure that we should not apprehend but adore, that therein also his perfections may appear. Those secrets of his will, which he has seen it meet to manifest, are revealed in his word—revealed in so far as he knew to be conducive to our interest and welfare. . . .

The predestination by which God adopts some to the hope of life, and adjudges others to eternal death, no man who would be thought pious ventures simply to deny; but it is greatly cavilled at, especially by those who make prescience its cause. We, indeed, ascribe both prescience and predestination to God; but we say that it is absurd to make the latter subordinate to the former. . . . When we attribute prescience to God, we mean that all things always were, and ever continue, under his eye; that to his knowledge there is no past or future, but all things are present, and indeed so present, that it is not merely the idea of them that is before him (as those objects are which we retain in our memory), but that he truly sees and contemplates them as actually under his immediate inspection. This prescience extends to the whole circuit of the world, and to all creatures. By predestination we mean the eternal decree of God, by which he determined with himself whatever he wished to happen with regard to every man. All are not created on equal terms, but some are preordained to eternal life, others to eternal damnation; and, accordingly, as each has been created for one or other of these ends, we say that he has been predestinated to life or to death.

After reading this selection, consider these questions:

1. According to Calvin, what is predestination?
2. On what religious authority does Calvin base his doctrine of predestination?
3. What was the relationship between individual liberty and predestination?

Selection 5:

The Reformation in England

In addition to the activities of individual reformers (Martin Bucer in Strasbourg and John Knox in Scotland, for instance), Protestantism was spread in the middle decades of the sixteenth century by the conversions of European monarchs. The various Scandinavian kingdoms were converted to Lutheranism in this manner. The most dramatic, and ultimately the most violent, conversion of an entire country took place in England. Breaking from the Roman Catholic Church because of questions concerning his divorce, King Henry VIII eventually established his own church in England. Through various acts of Parliament between 1529 and 1536, Henry severed ties between the English church and Roman by making the monarch the head of the Church of England; thus, the monarch, in this case Henry VIII, was free to dispense with all Catholic properties within the realm. Although later altered, Henry's Six Articles *were the doctrinal basis for the future Anglican Church.*

First, that in the most blessed Sacrament of the altar, by the strength and efficacy of Christ's mighty word (it being spoken by the priest), is present really, under the form of bread and wine, the natural body and blood of our Saviour Jesus Christ, conceived of the Virgin Mary; and that after the consecration there remaineth no substance of bread or wine, nor any other substance, but the substance of Christ, God and man.

Secondly, that communion in both kinds is not necessary *ad salutem,* by the law of God, to all persons; and that it is to be believed, and not doubted of, but that in the flesh, under the form of bread, is the very blood; and with the blood, under the form of wine, is the very flesh; as well apart, as though they were both together.

Thirdly, that priests after the order of priesthood received, as afore, may not marry, by the law of God.

Fourthly, that vows of chastity or widowhood, by man or woman made to God advisedly, ought to be observed by the law of God; and that it exempts them from other liberties of Christian people, which without that they might enjoy.

Fifthly, that it is meet and necessary that private masses be continued and admitted in this the king's English Church and congregation, as whereby good Christian people, ordering themselves accordingly, do receive both godly and goodly consolations and benefits; and it is agreeable also to God's law.

Sixthly, that auricular confession is expedient and necessary to be retained and continued, used and frequented in the Church of God.

After reading this selection, consider these questions:

1. What were the *Six Articles*?
2. What were the central tenets of the *Six Articles*?
3. How did they differ from the positions of Luther? Of Calvin?

From *Documents of the Christian Church*, edited by Henry Bettenson (Oxford: Oxford University Press, 1947).

SELECTION 6:

The Council of Trent

The reform of the Catholic Church began with the Council of Trent (1545–1563). In the thirteenth session of the Council of Trent, the sacrament of the Eucharist, which the Protestant reforms had challenged and defined in their own various ways, was clearly defined.

Decree Concerning the Most Holy Sacrament of the Eucharist

The sacred and holy, oecumenical and general Synod of Trent,—lawfully assembled in the Holy Ghost, the same Legate, and nuncios of the Apostolic See presiding therein, although the end for which It assembled, not without the special guidance and governance of the Holy Ghost, was, that It might set forth the true and ancient doctrine touching faith and the sacraments, and might apply a remedy to all the heresies, and the other most grievous troubles with which the Church of God is now miserably agitated, and rent into many and various parts; yet, even from the outset, this especially has been the object of Its desires, that It might pluck up by the roots those tares of execrable errors and schisms, with which the enemy hath, in these our calamitous times, oversown the doctrine of the faith, in the use and worship of the sacred and holy Eucharist, which our Saviour, notwithstanding, left in His Church as a symbol of that unity and charity, with which He would fain have all Christians be mentally joined and united together. Wherefore, this sacred and holy Synod delivering here, on this venerable and divine sacrament of the Eucharist, that sound and genuine doctrine, which the Catholic Church,— instructed by our Lord Jesus Christ Himself, and by His apostles, and taught by the Holy Ghost, who day by day brings to her mind all truth, has

always retained, and will preserve even to the end of the world, forbids all the faithful of Christ, to presume to believe, teach, or preach henceforth concerning the holy Eucharist, otherwise than as is explained and defined in this present decree.

Chapter I

On the real presence of our Lord Jesus Christ in the most holy sacrament of the Eucharist.

In the first place, the holy Synod teaches, and openly and simply professes, that, in the august sacrament of the holy Eucharist, after the consecration of the bread and wine, our Lord Jesus Christ, true God and man, is truly, really, and substantially contained under the species of those sensible things. For neither are these things mutually repugnant,—that our Saviour Himself always sitteth at the right hand of the Father in heaven, according to the natural mode of existing, and that, nevertheless, He be, in many other places, sacramentally present to us in his own substance, by a manner of existing, which, though we can scarcely express it in words, yet can we, by the understanding illuminated by faith, conceive, and we ought most firmly to believe, to be possible unto God: for thus all our forefathers, as many as were in the true Church of Christ, who have treated of this most holy Sacrament, have most openly professed, that our Redeemer instituted this so admirable a sacrament at the last supper, when, after the blessing of the bread and wine, He testified, in express and clear words, that He gave them His own very Body, and His own Blood; words which,—recorded by the holy Evangelists, and afterwards repeated by Saint Paul, whereas they carry with them that prop-

From *Decree Concerning the Most Holy Sacrament of the Eucharist* promulgated by the Council of Trent, October 11, 1551, edited and translated by J. Waterworth (Chicago, 1848).

er and most manifest meaning in which they were understood by the Fathers,—it is indeed a crime the most unworthy that they should be wrested, by certain contentions and wicked men, to fictitious and imaginary tropes, whereby the verity of the flesh and blood of Christ is denied, contrary to the universal sense of the Church, which, as the pillar and ground of truth, has detested, as satanical, these inventions devised by impious men; she recognising, with a mind ever grateful and unforgetting, this most excellent benefit of Christ.

Chapter II

On the reason of the Institution of this most holy Sacrament.

Wherefore, our Saviour, when about to depart out of this world to the Father, instituted this Sacrament, in which He poured forth as it were the riches of His divine love towards man, making a remembrance of his wonderful works; and He commanded us, in the participation thereof, to venerate His memory, and to show forth His death until He come to judge the world. And He would also that this Sacrament should be re-

ceived as the spiritual food of souls, whereby may be fed and strengthened those who live with His life who said, He that eateth me, the same also shall live by me; and as an antidote, whereby we may be freed from daily faults, and be preserved from mortal sins. He would, furthermore, have it be a pledge of our glory to come, and everlasting happiness, and thus be a symbol of that one body whereof He is the head, and to which He would fain have us as members be united by the closest bond of faith, hope, and charity, that we might all speak the same things, and there might be no schisms amongst us.

After reading this selection and the previous ones, consider these questions:

1. What were the main points of contention at the Council of Trent?
2. In the Trentine Creed, what specific Catholic beliefs are reaffirmed against various Protestant challenges to their authenticity?
3. How was the Eucharist defined by the Council of Trent?

SELECTION 7:

The Origins of the Jesuits

The new understanding of Christianity associated with Tridentine Catholicism emphasized a new sense of individual faith and devotion. One of the strongest and most lasting of these new forms of devotion crystallized around the personal experiences of St. Ignatius of Loyola (1491–1556). A former soldier, Loyola directed his sense of military mission to the understanding and promulgation of the faith. He founded the Society of Jesus (popularly known as the Jesuits), which became a leading force in the Counter Reformation. It was confirmed by a papal bull in 1540. In his Spiritual Exercises, *St. Ignatius defines the type of devotion for his new order.*

From *The Spiritual Exercises of St. Ignatius of Loyola,* translated by Elder Mullen (New York: Kennedy & Sons, 1914).

To have the true sentiment which we ought to have in the church militant

Let the following Rules be observed.

First Rule. The first: All judgment laid aside, we ought to have our mind ready and prompt to obey, in all, the true Spouse of Christ our Lord, which is our holy Mother the Church Hierarchical.

Second Rule. The second: To praise confession to a Priest, and the reception of the most Holy Sacrament of the Altar once in the year, and much more each month, and much better from week to week, with the conditions required and due.

Third Rule. The third: To praise the hearing of Mass often, likewise hymns, psalms, and long prayers, in the church and out of it; likewise the hours set at the time fixed for each Divine Office and for all prayer and all Canonical Hours.

Fourth Rule. The fourth: To praise much Religious Orders, virginity and continence, and not so much marriage as any of these.

Fifth Rule. The fifth: To praise vows of Religion, of obedience, of poverty, of chastity and of other perfections of supererogation. And it is to be noted that as the vow is about the things which approach to Evangelical perfection, a vow ought not to be made in the things which withdraw from it, such as to be a merchant, or to be married, etc.

Sixth Rule. To praise relics of the Saints, giving veneration to them and praying to the Saints; and to praise Stations, pilgrimages, Indulgences, pardons, Cruzadas, and candles lighted in the churches.

Seventh Rule. To praise Constitutions about fasts and abstinence, as of Lent, Ember Days, Vigils, Friday and Saturday; likewise penances, not only interior, but also exterior.

Eighth Rule. To praise the ornaments and the buildings of churches; likewise images, and to venerate them according to what they represent.

Ninth Rule. Finally, to praise all precepts of the Church, keeping the mind prompt to find reasons in their defence and in no manner against them.

Tenth Rule. We ought to be more prompt to find good and praise as well the Constitutions and recommendations as the ways of our Superiors. Because, although some are not or have not been such, to speak against them, whether preaching in public or discoursing before the common people, would rather give rise to fault-finding and scandal than profit; and so the people would be incensed against their Superiors, whether temporal or spiritual. So that, as it does harm to speak evil to the common people of Superiors in their absence, so it can make profit to speak of the evil ways to the persons themselves who can remedy them.

Eleventh Rule. To praise positive and scholastic learning. Because, as it is more proper to the Positive Doctors, as St. Jerome, St. Augustine and St. Gregory, etc., to move the heart to love and serve God our Lord in everything; so it is more proper to the Scholastics, as St. Thomas, St. Bonaventure, and to the Master of the Sentences, etc., to define or explain for our times the things necessary for eternal salvation; and to combat and explain better all errors and all fallacies. For the Scholastic Doctors, as they are more modern, not only help themselves with the true understanding of the Sacred Scripture and of the Positive and holy Doctors, but also, they being enlightened and clarified by the Divine virtue, help themselves by the Councils, Canons and Constitutions of our holy Mother the Church.

Twelfth Rule. We ought to be on our guard in making comparison of those of us who are alive to the blessed passed away, because error is committed not a little in this; that is to say, in saying, this one knows more than St. Augustine; he is another, or greater than, St. Francis; he is another St. Paul in goodness, holiness, etc.

Thirteenth Rule. To be right in everything, we ought always to hold that the white which I see, is black, if the Hierarchical Church so decides it, believing that between Christ our Lord, the Bridegroom, and the Church, His Bride, there is the same Spirit which governs and directs us for the salvation of our souls. Because by the same Spirit and our Lord Who gave the ten Commandments, our holy Mother the Church is directed and governed.

Fourteenth Rule. Although there is much truth in the assertion that no one can save himself without being predestined and without having faith and grace; we must be very cautious in the manner of speaking and communicating with others about all these things.

Fifteenth Rule. We ought not, by way of custom, to speak much of predestination; but if in some way and at some times one speaks, let him so speak that the common people may not come into any error, as sometimes happens, saying:

Whether I have to be saved or condemned is already determined, and no other thing can now be, through my doing well or ill; and with this, growing lazy, they become negligent in the works which lead to the salvation and the spiritual profit of their souls.

Sixteenth Rule. In the same way, we must be on our guard that by talking much and with much insistence of faith, without any distinction and explanation, occasion be not given to the people to be lazy and slothful in works, whether before faith is formed in charity or after.

Seventeenth Rule. Likewise, we ought not to speak so much with insistence on grace that the poison of discarding liberty be engendered. So that of faith and grace one can speak as much as is possible with the Divine help for the greater praise of His Divine Majesty, but not in such way, nor in such manners, especially in our so dangerous times, that works and free will receive any harm, or be held for nothing.

Eighteenth Rule. Although serving God our Lord much out of pure love is to be esteemed above all; we ought to praise much the fear of His Divine Majesty, because not only filial fear is a thing pious and most holy, but even servile fear—when the man reaches nothing else better or more useful—helps much to get out of mortal sin. And when he is out, he easily comes to filial fear, which is all acceptable and grateful to God our Lord: as being at one with the Divine Love.

After reading this selection, consider these questions:

1. What was the purpose of Loyola's *Spiritual Exercises*?
2. What role did predestination play in Loyola's understanding of faith?
3. What were the central values of the *Spiritual Exercises*?

INDEX